**"WE HAVE A VC COMPANY IN CONTACT,"
THE FORWARD AIR CONTROLLER TOLD US.**

"All right," the FAC said in that articulate but tight combat voice I recognized by now, "I want you on a west-east heading. The friendlies will be fifty meters south of my smoke. You can be damned sure you'll be receiving ground fire," he added, and rolled in to mark.

I found my hand going to the throat of my flying suit, pulling up the zipper. The first moment when we rolled in, barreling down in a long flat dive, I found myself ducking down in the seat, but curiosity overcame me. We tore in, lower than I remembered ever having attacked a target. Across the pilot's shoulders I saw the village lifting into my face, hurtling toward us, surrounding us, rocking around as if attached to the plane. Sandy roads I could step out on, houses, palm trees level with my head, little vegetable gardens in which I could see the hoed rows. Our guns erupted, the plane vibrated, silver sparkles scattered across the back yards and houses, our shells kicking up plumes of dust and debris. We slammed out in a tight turn and came in for a second pass, and a third.

THE WAR
OF THE
INNOCENTS

CHARLES BRACELEN FLOOD

BANTAM BOOKS

NEW YORK · TORONTO · LONDON · SYDNEY · AUCKLAND

This edition contains the complete text
of the original hardcover edition.
NOT ONE WORD HAS BEEN OMITTED.

THE WAR OF THE INNOCENTS

A Bantam Falcon Book / published by arrangement with McGraw Hill

PRINTING HISTORY
McGraw Hill edition published 1970
Bantam edition / April 1991

This book is dedicated to the memory of

Colonel James Jabara,
UNITED STATES AIR FORCE

Lieutenant Colonel Glen Belnap,
UNITED STATES ARMY

Major Don Usry,
UNITED STATES AIR FORCE

Specialist Fourth Class John Collins,
UNITED STATES ARMY

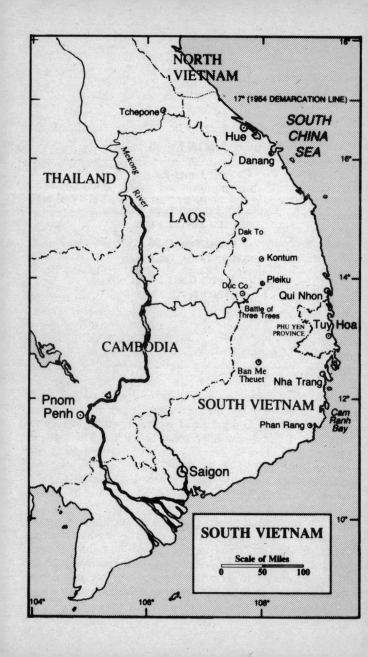

ONE

On an October day of 1966, I sat cramped in a one-man yellow life raft on the surface of Chesapeake Bay. In my lap was a survival kit filled with items ranging from a water-purification filter to a package of shark repellent, and I spent the morning in a bemused run-through of all the equipment I had been taught to use in the preceding days at the Air Force Sea Survival School.

When any kind of plane came overhead, from each of forty rafts like my own, dotted across the cold blue swells, there came the twinkling of signal mirrors. At other times I fished with the line, sinker, and hook provided, and some bait I had acquired ashore. I set up my water-purification filter and found that after an hour, true to the instructor's words, the salt water with which I had filled the plastic bag had become fresh water—not good, but no longer salty. I ate a cereal bar and a honey bar, and occasionally gripped in my mouth the non-issue cigar I had not been skillful enough to keep dry. When I saw after some hours that I was to be rescued, I sprinkled out my package of green dye marker, and watched it become a huge yellow-green stain on the sea. Finally I threw away my shark repellent and clambered up the ladder of the gray landing barge that returned me to shore.

Waiting for me on the pier was Senior Master Sergeant Jim Roth, an old friend from the days when I had lived in Japan. It was Jim who was the Svengali of this scheme, which was to give an American civilian novelist and journalist an opportunity to enter the Vietnam War not as a correspondent but as an attached member of a fighter-bomber wing.

1

To this end I had already spent two weeks at Langley Field, Virginia, doing things as varied as going through high-altitude tests in an oxygen chamber and firing a .38 revolver and an M–16 rifle.

"How'd it go?" Jim asked, a big smile on his big face. While I was physically preparing for the adventure, he was subtly pushing the paperwork authorizing it through ever-higher Information officers and Air Force commanders.

"You know, Jim," I said, stripping off my soaking orange-rubber survival suit, "I really didn't know what I was getting into on this deal."

A few days after this, no longer accompanied by Roth, I was standing on the flight line at Shaw Air Force Base, South Carolina, with a young major just returned from a tour flying reconnaissance missions over North Vietnam. He had taken me in hand for a quick run-through of the art of reconnaissance, spending two days showing me cameras, planes, and the remarkably detailed photographs which could be obtained even from high altitudes.

"I understand you're going over there with a fighter outfit," he said, looking at me with a combination of interest and concern. "Have you ever lived with a fighter squadron before?"

"No."

"Well." He grinned. "Just hold your hat."

II

There was one other interesting moment before my orientation ceased being a general one and became very specific. At Eglin Field, in northern Florida, I was taken through the Special Air Warfare Center. A more peaceful scene cannot be imagined. Palm trees lined the walks and lawns. Crimson bougainvillea climbed the green wooden sides of the one-story buildings housing the offices concerned with various weapons development programs. Neat little signs indicated the projects by their code names; DANCING SPARROW was up this walk, and FALCON SHOOT up the next.

Soon I was seated at a table in a room with screened windows through which the Florida sunshine fell. Flowers waved in a pleasant afternoon breeze, and then before me was the cutaway side of an antipersonnel bomblet. The lieutenant colonel across the table from me was pointing out the perforations in the bomblet which, upon impact, would turn the metal casing into steel balls flying in every direction with the speed and cutting force of bullets.

It was the first time in my month with the Air Force that I had been confronted with the final product, which is of course death and destruction, delivered from the air. The lieutenant colonel had warmed to his subject and was explaining the way in which these lethal pellets were superior to the configuration in an earlier model.

"Any questions?"

"No," I said, for in fact it seemed to me that I had received an answer. In that pleasant sunlit room the uncompromising nature of warfare sat as surely as if it had been a corpse or a bloody ax. Coffee was served.

.38 Cal. Revolver

TWO

A legendary figure was waiting for me in blinding sunlight when the Tactical Air Command courier plane delivered me at Homestead Air Force Base, just south of Miami. The door of a glossy blue Air Force sedan opened and a short, swarthy colonel in trim suntans slipped from behind the wheel. He came toward me with the loose-kneed gait of a cowboy, a vivid green cigar centered in his white teeth. This was Colonel James Jabara, the world's leading living jet ace, and from the moment I shook his hand I had no trouble believing that this was the man who had shot down fifteen MIGs in the Korean War. Most heroes are disappointingly ordinary in manner and appearance, but Colonel Jabara combined a singular vitality with an athletic ease; the effect was of a Lebanese gunslinger who leads well because it has never occurred to him that others will not follow.

"Welcome to the Thirty-first," he said, gesturing toward the rows of camouflaged fighter-bombers that were his command. Other people were bustling about, grabbing my one suitcase and portable typewriter, and I found myself in the colonel's car. We rolled off the flight line and past two low green concrete buildings.

Two young men in light gray flying suits were walking toward our oncoming sedan. There were bright blue scarves at their throats, and blue overseas caps on their heads. Simultaneously they saluted the colonel, cutting their hands away from their temples in a motion that was both respectful and jaunty.

"Are those the pilots?" I was looking back at their swaggering gait.

4

"Yes," Colonel Jabara said warmly.

I watched the two pilots stride into one of the low buildings. Who the hell, I thought, do those guys think they are?

The two small buildings turned out to be the headquarters of the 306th and 309th Tactical Fighter Squadrons. The Wing's 307th Squadron was on detached duty in Spain, and we were scheduled to catch up to the 308th in Vietnam, at an undisclosed but near date.

I had been attached to the 309th, which meant that a bearlike sergeant named Roger Bezio had to keep shuttling me to various supply rooms around Homestead to get me fitted with flying suits, gray leather gloves, black leather boots, and assorted items of flying gear. His own domain in the 309th squadron building looked like the equipment room of a professional football team. Big white plastic jet-pilot helmets stood in neat rows, each helmet atop an individual pilot's rack. Beneath the helmet there hung equipment including a parachute, inflatable emergency lifebelt, and the zip-on tight canvas chaps, known as a G suit, which automatically inflate to keep the blood from rushing out of the top half of the pilot's body when he pulls out of a dive.

I had a chance to wear all the equipment soon enough. Three days after arriving at the Thirty-first Tactical Fighter Wing, I climbed a yellow ladder that had been hooked over the edge of the cockpit of one of the 309th's camouflaged F-100 Supersabre jet fighter-bombers. Most of these supersonic dive bombers were one-seater D models, but this was an F, with an extra seat behind the pilot.

My pilot, a young first lieutenant named Chuck Fulton, spent ten minutes seeing that I was strapped into the back seat to his satisfaction. I could not have imagined the contortions and discomfort necessary simply to go flying. I carried my helmet and parachute up the ladder, carefully lowering the parachute into the tiny seat, which appeared wedged in as an afterthought among banks of instrument panels. Once in the seat, having tripped over the control stick, I buckled into the parachute and clipped it into the survival kit-cum-seat cushion I had studied at Langley. Then I plugged the G suit into a hose

F-100 Super Saber

that would supply the automatically regulated air to inflate it. Next I turned my attention to my upper half, twisting oxygen hoses into valves and plugging in the intercom system.

Finally, sweating, there I was, buckled in with safety harness, helmet on, and oxygen mask ready to slip over my nose. I glanced down nervously at the yellow handles on either side of my seat. These were what I would have to grab to blow myself out of the plane if we had to leave it in midair. If I could find the right handles, a charge would blast off the Plexiglass canopy, and a rocket behind my seat would shoot me up and away from the plane.

Chuck Fulton's gray eyes stared through the tinted protective visor I had lowered before my face.

"All set?"

"I guess so."

We taxied for some distance, one plane in our flight ahead of us and two in single file spaced behind us. The canopy that would enclose the two of us was at present partway up, like a gigantic transparent upper jaw hinging just behind me. All I could see of Chuck was a glimpse of the turned-up collar of his flying suit and the back of his balloonlike white helmet. The plane moved forward with the whine of our six-thousand-horsepower engine engulfing us even through the earphones inside our rubber-padded helmets.

We slid to a stop in an area just short of the runway.

"Put your hands up on the sides of the cockpit," Chuck's voice said, and I put my gray-gloved hands on the narrow metal ledge on either side of me, as if sitting in a tiny bathtub.

"Just out of curiosity," I asked after a moment, "what's happening now?" I had noticed some enlisted men in green fatigues coming up on either side of the narrow fuselage.

"They're taking the safety pins out of the guns," Chuck said. "As long as our hands are out of the way, we can't fire them by mistake."

I digested this information. I knew that we were going on a gunnery training mission, but I had assumed we simply went through the motions and did not do anything as lethal as firing our 20-millimeter cannon.

There was a plane being similarly readied on either side of us, and I had time to study them. Our Supersabres sat slightly inclined on three wheels, one under the nose, and one under each swept-back wing. The planes' undersides were camouflaged a fish-belly gray, and the remainder of the sturdy, streamlined body was painted in broad, undulating bands and splotches of merging olive and brown. The effect was that of a high-spined thrusting prehistoric bird, with the tiny helmeted head of a man placed just where its eyes and brain would be, on the down-sloping forward beak. It even had an open mouth to feed air to the whining turbines within.

We were pivoting, continuing our march onto the runway.

"Canopy clear?" Chuck asked, and I drew my hands swiftly from the sides of the bathtub.

"Canopy clear."

"Canopy coming down." There was a whirring sound, a *chunk* as the big plastic jaw closed over us, and a *clonk* as it slid forward and locked. We were lining up in echelon, with the first plane to take off just ahead of us and to the left, and the other two spaced back from us to my right.

There was a sudden roar that shook me and caused a cloud of vapor to rush from behind my head.

"Good power," Chuck said through my earphones. Just then the plane ahead and to the left exploded an orange flame through the great hole in its tail. The flaming plane began to move, and in that moment I realized that we were about to move ourselves, and that I did not want to go. I was sitting on top of six tons of fuel and gunpowder, and now it seemed we were setting the whole thing on fire.

It was far too late. We gave a roar of thunder and started rolling. Shot from a cannon, I thought. What the hell had I thought this was, anyway? Supersonic jet fighter pilots were what they used for astronauts—we were still right out there at the edge of Man's little games with his environment.

A marker on the edge of the runway moved past, and it seemed to me to be going too slowly. We'll never get off, I thought; something's wrong, we'll never get sixteen tons of plane and fuel and gunpowder off at this speed, never.

We kept roaring and rolling. I was hunched back in the seat in what I had been shown was the correct position to eject from the plane, knees tucked up so they would not be sheared off by the bottom of the forward instrument panel.

We were off. I looked over the side and gasped. The scrubby Florida grass and white sand was falling away beneath us as if the earth had stumbled. We went into a right-hand turn and I was looking straight down into the green of the tropical Atlantic. I was certain that we were about to drop sideways straight into it. Then we were level again, and there was a terrific lurch and loss of speed. God, I thought, hunching myself even further into the seat, the engine's flamed out. My gloved hands were ready to pull the ejection seat handles when I heard Chuck's voice say something over the intercom. His voice sounded hopelessly fuzzy; my imagination provided the words, "get ready to eject."

"What?" I asked in a tiny voice, hunching back into the seat as if dissociating myself from the proceedings.

"Blurbledy poo gefritz," his voice said, and I realized there *was* something wrong with the intercom. This restored me to reality, and since we seemed to be still moving horizontally, I looked around, only to duck my head and throw an arm over my face. A plane was coming up to my right so fast that I was certain we were all dead. It skidded into place just behind our right wingtip, and another plane slid in right behind his wingtip, and there we were, the four of us screaming through the diamond-blue tropical sky a few feet apart like an Air Force poster.

"Mister Flood," Chuck's voice said over the still-strangling intercom, "can you hear me?"

"Sometimes." In what seemed a matter of seconds we were over the bombing range at Avon Park, a hundred and thirty miles north of where we had started. Flashing back and forth through my earphones were all sorts of clipped remarks, given and understood, which meant nothing to me. We had spread out into a long staggered single file and started circling over the big sandy square a couple of miles below.

"There goes flight lead," Chuck's voice said calmly. I looked and saw nothing at all. I knew we had under our belly a small white tube containing miniature smoke bombs, but that was all I knew.

"Rolling in," Chuck said to me, and the world abruptly rose and stood off our left wing. "Two is in from the east," Chuck announced to all parties concerned, and the world, still standing upright, swung directly in front of our nose. Just beneath my view of this shocking panorama was the back-seat instrument panel, and on it the altimeter was unwinding at a terrific and increasing speed. The little ball behind a glass, representing us in relation to the earth, showed us diving straight into it, and our airspeed was six hundred miles an hour and going up. I raised my glance and watched in horror. The world grew endlessly on all sides of our plunging nose, the sky was all behind us, and over Chuck's shoulder I could see the steadily expanding white concentric circles centered by the white bullseye that was our target. My stomach was a couple of thousand feet above us, left there in the first downward lurch of the dive-bombing run.

"Pickle," Chuck's voice said, the plane instantly leveled, started up, and I was crushed helplessly back in my seat, my head weighing five hundred pounds and my chin digging into my chest, my arms paralyzed, and the instrument panel disappearing in a gray gathering curtain before my eyes. My stomach had been returned to me and was trying to leave my body via my legs. The sensations receded; we were skimming back up to the sun.

"There goes Four," Chuck said as we resumed our place in the merry-go-round.

"Where?"

"Right under you." He flipped the plane upside down. I raised my helmeted head from where I hung, and, as we rolled back to upright, caught a glimpse of a tiny wedge, far below, swooping across the white rings. A small puff of smoke blossomed between the bullseye and the first ring.

"Just fair," Chuck's voice said. We were back level, and I caught sight of two specks whipping through the sky at an angle to our left.

"What are those?"

"That's number One and Three," Chuck answered. I shook my head, grasping that one could not see how fast they were going until they were on a different course from ours.

Three times more we fell over onto the ready-to-consume-us earth; three times more I felt the great sandy expanse below like a magnet, flicking us to it. And with it all, the sound of Chuck's breathing in my ears, the sensation of the hot oxygen mask over the nose I longed to scratch but could not, sweat in my eyes, and a mixed sense of fascination, resignation, and unreality. For a thirty-six-year-old civilian who spent most of his days at a typewriter, it was a startling change of pace.

"Now for the guns," Chuck announced, and we were making low, swift dive to strafe canvas bull's-eyes that stood at the edge of a field. We whirled in, shifting our heading to the last moment, and there was a shuddering *URRURRUR* of the cannon, silver sparkles about and behind the target, geysers of sand, and we were miles beyond, turning, going back again.

The second time through I looked at the altimeter instead of the target, fascinated to know how low we were actually howling in. The needle was at five hundred feet, four, three, two, and then abruptly swung through zero.

"Right," I thought. "We're dead." I braced for the shock and darkness; none came, we were high in the clean sky. No one had told me that at a certain point the altimeter cannot stand it any longer and overstates the case.

II

The next morning, feeling conspicuous in a flying suit devoid of any name, rank, affiliation, I attended the seven-thirty daily meeting in the Wind command post. Known as a "stand-up briefing" for the good reason that no one sat, it began with the arrival of the commanders of the 306th and the 309th squadrons, the units which contained the pilots, planes, and flight-line crews in constant attendance upon the planes. Next came the commanders of the maintenance units, also called squadrons: Armaments and Electronics, Munitions Maintenance, Field Maintenance. Other officers appeared, representing such concerns as Flying Safety, Personnel, and Supply. They stood, talking in subdued voices, behind a plate-glass wall looking into the dimmed amphitheater which was the Command Post proper. Against the far wall were tall blackboards listing each plane and pilot, the available status of each, and the training missions flown the day before, as well as those scheduled for today. I found my name scheduled to fly again with Chuck Fulton in three hours and fought an impulse to laugh hysterically.

The prevailing mood of the officers as they studied the blackboards was one of intense concern. In the deployment to Vietnam which would take place within the next three weeks, forty-four F–100s would fly all the way, with air-to-air refueling from tanker planes and with only two overnight stops en route. Preceding them, paralleling them, and following them, nine hundred other men and a million pounds of equipment would make the same transcontinental, trans-Pacific flight in transport planes.

"Command Post—Attention!" Everyone, lieutenant colonels, majors, the officers and the sergeants at the telephones inside the amphitheater, snapped to a rigid, almost breathless posture. Colonel Jabara, his bright green cigar luminous in the dimmed amphitheater, strode in, followed by Colonel Frank Buzze, the black-haired, red-faced Deputy Commander for Operations.

"At ease," Colonel Jabara said, and the briefing began. First came the Weather Officer, with the day's forecast of flying conditions; then a young officer reported on the training missions flown the day before, mechanical difficulties experienced, and missions scheduled today. Next, the representative from Maintenance explained what corrective action had been taken on yesterday's mechanical failures.

"Rotten," Colonel Jabara growled, removing his cigar

from its usual bowsprit position. "Rotten. Not enough planes flying." His scowl included everyone, even the Weather man, as if he too might be responsible.

Next to speak was a pretty WAF captain, who I learned to my regret was not coming with us. She was in charge of personnel, and reported on the steadily increasing number of enlisted specialists who were beefing up the Wing and would deploy with it. She reminded the Colonel that two hundred of the recent arrivals would be in a nearby auditorium directly after this meeting.

Colonel Jabara asked an officer some quick questions about equipment that had not yet arrived, and then to my surprise turned and said, "I think most of you have met him, but I'd like to introduce Mister Flood. He'll be with us all the way. As far as I'm concerned, Mister Flood is a member of the Wing. Charlie, welcome to the Thirty-first." I nodded, and Colonel Jabara said "Let's go to work." Everyone came to attention, and I followed him over to the auditorium where the new men were.

I slipped in and took a seat. There was an air of anticipation. They were waiting to see not only the leading jet ace in the Air Force but the man who was going to lead them to the war and for a year over there. Coming as they did from a score of bases, from working on other types of aircraft, having little time to make friends, the personality of the commander would to an unusual extent determine what they thought of the Wing and the forthcoming tour.

They were not disappointed. Colonel Jabara moved restlessly across the stage in his gunslinger's shuffle, first telling them something of the history of the Thirty-first, how its squadrons had originally been formed from cadres of the First Pursuit Group of World War I, Eddie Rickenbacker's outfit. As the Thirty-first Fighter Group, its pilots had been sent to England so soon after Pearl Harbor that they flew in borrowed Mark V Spitfires until their own planes could be sent to them by sea. Switching to P–51s along the way, they became the most destructive fighter outfit in the Mediterranean Theater, shooting down five hundred and seventy enemy airplanes in a march that took them through Tunisia, Algeria, Sicily, Anzio, France, and, from Italian bases, as bomber escorts to targets in Rumania and Poland.

The Colonel had come right to the edge of the stage. The silence was complete.

"The only reason we have for being here is those airplanes out there. Don't forget what you're here for." There was an almost audible assent in the room. He was giving it to them straight, and from the thirty-year man to whom war was a trade to the four-year enlisted man who had his doubts about the involvement in Vietnam, they liked him, they trusted him, they knew if he started in this way he was going to be straight. "I expect my NCO supervisors to do the job for which they're being paid—I don't think that's asking too much." The Oklahoma-Kansas twang kept going. "An outfit is only as good as its NCOs. NCOs make or break an outfit. That's something I learned twenty-three years ago, and I learn it more every day."

It was during the question period that I saw something. An airman in the back of the room had been sticking up his hand all through Colonel Jabara's answer to another question. When the Colonel finished, he turned and said, in a combination of amusement and testiness, "All right, Morales, what's *your* question?" He was reading the new man's name from the name tape above the right breast pocket of his fatigues, and the man was seventy feet away. Much later I described the distance and the size of the lettering to an eye doctor, who said it was impossible. So is shooting down fifteen MIGs.

On the way home in an open **V** formation, after a terrifying repetition of yesterday's bombing and strafing, Chuck Fulton asked if I would like to take the stick and steer the plane through the skies.

I was as surprised as if someone had said "Now you climb up on Man o' War and take him for a little canter." I had no idea of what would happen, and I knew the plane was a delicate piece of equipment costing one and a quarter million dollars, with twenty-five miles of wiring inside it.

"Okay."

"You've got it."

My gloved hands closed gingerly around the top of the stick which stood straight up from the floor between my feet, ending a foot ahead of my navel. I had an idea that it would be like the tiller of a sailboat, and found it far more sensitive.

The other planes abruptly were moving about forty-five degrees to our left.

"Why did they change course?" I asked.

"They didn't." Chuck's voice was polite but amused. "Let's try to get back somewhere near them."

I tried. I got nearer, but it seemed to me as if, just when I was getting back into the **V**, just about catching up, just about level, the other three would rise as one plane, pivot as one plane, and leave me soaring off by myself.

"Let's break off for a while," Chuck said. He spoke to flight lead and received permission for us to leave the formation and land later.

With those other planes gone my confidence increased, and soon we were flashing over the beautiful oxidized-brass-green reefs and submerged beaches of the Florida Keys.

"Want to try a roll?"

Yes, I did. I really did. Chuck showed me how. Stick back a little, and then, a gentle, firm pressure to the left. The sunlit world obligingly rolled past my left elbow, over my head, and then back down my right arm. I did it. I did it again.

"Faster," Chuck said. "Faster."

III

The next afternoon I walked into the Base Information Office to attend to some minor matter, and ran into a sergeant I had been speaking to a few hours before.

"You're with the Thirty-first, aren't you?" he asked, his face far less composed than his neat suntan uniform. "Two of your planes have just gone in, over there."

I knew just enough of the new language to realize that *gone in* meant *crashed*.

I banged through the doors of the 309th, fearful that it had been two of the young pilots who had been so pleasant and cooperative in recent days, and discovered that it had been two pilots from the 306th, whom I did not know. For the moment, the flight line and the runway were closed to everyone except the Air Police and the Safety people investigating the accident. The two dead pilots had been removed. When it became clear that the people from the Wing's

information office would be allowed to go to the crash scene,
I hesitated about accompanying them. One of my shortcomings as a writer is that when I see people wearing bandages, I
feel no desire to discover what is under them. I look away
when driving past traffic accidents. Why not airplanes?

Answer: These things have been scaring me to death,
riding in them. I might as well see what it is that I have been
fearing.

A Supersabre, landing, had somehow struck one preparing to take off. One of the planes had come to rest a quarter of
a mile from the collision, and the other was flung yet three
hundred yards beyond. Air traffic had ceased, and in the
engineless silence I walked up to the first of the wrecks. It lay
twisted in brush off the runway, motionless as the piles of
brown clouds on the ocean horizon. The air was heavy.

The empty cockpit had every shard of glass blown from
it. The effect was of a huge dead bird thrown to earth, a weird
flame-blackened metal monument rather than a craft that
lanced through clouds. I walked around it once, then over to
the other silent hulk, and walked off. I realized that I had
been worrying about being maimed, and now it was clear that
I could forget it. In this business, one was either alive or
dead.

IV

Two mornings later I was staring at another wreck. An
F-104 of the Air Defense Command had crashed half a mile
short of the runway. A farmer said that suddenly he saw a
parachute blooming behind the plane, starting to suspend the
pilot, but the parachute had collapsed and the pilot had
plummeted the last hundred feet.

An ambulance's red roof-light sparked where they were
picking up the body. The plane was not recognizable as
anything that might ever have flown. The single largest
remnant was a hunched pile of ribbed metal in a plowed field;
the engine.

I walked back to the Information Office car that had
brought me out. The ambulance moved off without sounding
its siren; there was no hurry. Photographers from Flying

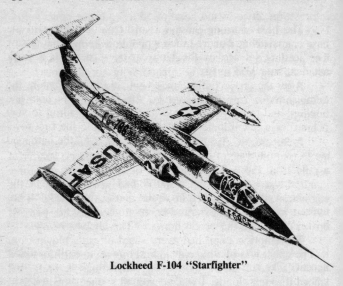

Lockheed F-104 "Starfighter"

Safety were moving across the field, taking pictures of scattered squares and triangles of seared aluminum. No voices were raised. The sky hung empty.

I am living, I decided, in a highly organized lunatic asylum.

Two nights after this I was making a gibson in my quarters, just opening the jar of pickled cocktail onions. The velvet Florida night outside the screen carried the sounds of an under-floodlights touch football game.

The telephone rang. I answered it with the open jar of onions in my hand.

"Charlie?" It was the voice of one of the airmen who worked in Wing Information. "I thought you ought to know. Colonel Jabara was killed tonight."

"Where was the crash?"

"It wasn't in an airplane. He was taking his family north by car to resettle them for while he was gone."

I sat down for a time. Then I put in my notes: *Undoubtedly the single worst thing that could have happened to this outfit at this point.*

*   *   *

The next morning there was a memorial service in the base chapel. Nine hundred men who didn't know what to say. The leading jet ace of the United States, dead in a freak accident in a Volkswagen.

After the service, Lieutenant Colonel Freddie Poston, the commander of the 309th, asked the forty pilots and one hundred and thirty-five enlisted men of the Squadron to stay behind for a few minutes. We shuffled down to the first rows of the auditorium. Around me I could hear even the hardened sergeants muttering. "Three in a row, it always comes three accidents in a row."

Freddie Poston is not a tall man. He wears his graying light brown hair short, and he has hazel eyes, a cheerful, appraising expression, and the air of a man who knows what he is doing. He'd been close to Colonel Jabara and admired him greatly.

"At a time like this," he told his men in a soft Southern accent, "there's talk that we're snakebit. But we're not snakebit. This kind of thing sometimes happens. It happens all over the Air Force. This squadron has had fine achievements in the past year. We've got a job to do, to get the planes ready and take them across the Pacific. That's what Colonel Jabara wanted, and that's what he wants you do do." He paused, while I took in the fact that he was still referring to his commanding officer in the present tense.

We were so close to leaving that the new commanding officer did not interrupt the schedule for any get-acquainted talks with the men. The first time some of us saw him was when the officers were brought to the auditorium for a final day of briefings about what to expect in Vietnam.

He looked like a fencer. He was slender, of medium height, with a high forehead, receding gray-flecked hair, and an appearance ten years younger than his forty-seven. He advanced gracefully to the same lectern from which Colonel Jabara had spoken only a few days before.

My God, I thought, talk about a tough act to follow.

"My name is Warren Lewis. My home is in Iowa. I've been in the fighter business since nineteen forty-two in New Guinea." The voice had an attractive high-pitched resonance;

it could have said "Oh, shucks" at any time. "I knew Colonel Jabara, and I regret the circumstances under which I am taking over the Wing, but I'm proud to have this assignment. I'm proud of fighter pilots. They're a different breed of cat. They have to make decisions, alone in the airplane. In recent years they have been trained to be the most professional pilots there are." I turned and looked at how it was going down. The new colonel's manner was bland, but there was the trace of an approving smile on almost every face. It was as if he had said "Listen fellas, I'm going to be me, that's the only way I know."

For the first time his eyes moved from one to another of the men sitting before him. "I assume most of you young officers are career officers. For you young men, this is about the greatest thing that can happen to you, for your careers—to go to a combat zone."

A minute later: "You can read about it, but you have to experience it. No matter what we say over here, some things turn out a little different over there. For example, an outfit leaves something lying around loose, they shouldn't be surprised if someone picks it up. And I mean something as big as a truck."

V

I took another two flights in the back seat, bought some short-sleeved sports shirts and foot powder, and felt that I was ready to go.

And we were going, right before my eyes. One evening a big transport sat on the brightly lit ramp near the squadron buildings, waiting to fly some of the Advanced Party. I happened to be having dinner in the Officers' Club. Normally the green fatigue shirt and pants were not allowed in the club, but this night a husky young officer sat at a table, wearing fatigues. Next to him sat his wife, wearing a good black dress and pearls, and, across from him, his two little daughters. It was clear that he was going to finish the meal, get up, get onto that transport plane, and fly to Vietnam. His wife smiled throughout the meal, half-heartedly telling the children to sit up straight. Then as he rose and they began walking out of the dining room, tears started running down her cheeks. She walked erect, and the only way you could tell she was crying was that there were tears pouring down her cheeks.

Then the F–100s. Twenty-two of them on a sunlit morning with the 306th pilots checking them over, walking around them, peering into wheel wells and shoving at stabilizers, and the first pair of them taxiing out and off they boomed, racing down the runway and into the sky, two and then two, the second pair joining up on the first and then they were little specks heading for Honolulu.

Jim Roth had come down from Langley in a courier plane to say good-bye, and he helped me carry an olive-drab wooden footlocker into the concrete building next to the flight line. I was in a gray flying suit; Sergeant Bezio had made me name tapes that said FLOOD where the officers' said U.S. AIR FORCE, and PRESS CORRESPONDENT on the right breast. I showed my innoculation records to one man, made out a next-of-kin form at another desk, and signed a release saying that I was voluntarily flying in Air Force planes and that no one would sue them if anything happened to me. Then Jim and I were walking across the sunlit concrete to a huge four-engine jet, a C–141 transport.

There was not much to say. Airmen in their fatigues brushed past us, walking up the ramp that had been lowered like a drawbridge from beneath the tail. No bands, no ceremony.

"Good luck."

"So long."

We shook hands and I walked into the huge cargo-stacked interior. It was the hold of a gigantic freighter of the skies, complete with portholes through which the Florida sun threw dusty rays. I found a space on the red canvas and aluminum-tubing seats against the wall and fastened a seat belt. I took off my rankless green fatigue cap and leaned back against the weave of red canvas straps. The engines started with a whine and a *phut!*, the ramp came halfway up, and as we pivoted, the squadron buildings, the auditorium, the command post, all swung past, bright pastel concrete in the sunshine, and were gone. We taxied, pivoted again, the ramp came full closed, the engines rumbled, we were rolling, rolling, and we were off.

A young airman across the way had a guitar. After a few minutes he and three of his buddies got out a pack of cards, turned the guitar over, and began playing cards on the flat polished surface of its back.

VI

The 306th had already passed through Hawaii when I arrived, and the 309th was not yet due. Since I was to fly in the back seat of an F from the 309th from Hickam Air Force Base to Guam, I had several days to spend. They came and went pleasantly, if a bit restlessly. Several times I passed through the glass-and-metal doors of Pacific Air Force Headquarters, glancing up at the Japanese bullet holes that shattered the stucco walls on December 7, 1941, and have deliberately never been plastered over. On one of these occasions I found myself talking to a colonel.

"It's too bad you're going over there so late," he said.

"How's that, Colonel?"

"Well, all significant armed resistance will be over within the next six months."

"Colonel," I said, "you want to bet?"

THREE

If anyone had told me, a few weeks before, that I would find myself missing a group of maniacs who might easily get me killed, I would have doubted it. Now I stood on the concrete of the airplane parking ramp at Hickam, gazing like a proud father as the first four planes of the 309th swept low over the field, in perfect wing-tip spacing at the end of a fourteen-hour, six-thousand-mile flight. Minutes later the planes were rolling to a halt in the parking area. yellow ladders were being hooked over the edge of the cockpits, and, stiff, needing shaves, but smiling, the pilots were coming down the ladder. The enlisted crew chiefs handed them the traditional cold can of beer at the end of a flight of this length and hovered about like anxious parents, asking if anything had gone wrong in the planes for which they had the maintenance responsibility.

The next morning I was once again in my flight suit. We gathered at dawn in a windowless briefing room near the runway, and I was struck by the difference between the fighter pilots of the 309th, who sat on one side of the aisle, and the crews of the KC–135 tanker planes who were to lead and refuel us on our way to Guam. It was as if a professional football team, rugged, trim, confident but keyed up, were next to a group of competent bankers who happened to be in uniform. It was not a question of age—the 309th had its full share of men in their late thirties and low forties—but of everything else.

By now I had learned that it was not a good sign when there were many maintenance specialists gathered about a plane shortly before it was scheduled to fly. When I stepped off the back of a blue panel truck, there was a convention of men in green fatigues around 951–F, in which I was to ride to Guam. The sergeant crew chief was deep in conversation with the pilot, Captain Don Usry, who had played end on the West Point football team of 1960.

"Charlie." Don turned his broad-shouldered bulk my way. "We've got all kinds of hydraulics problems."

I stared at the coils and switches and sprockets, revealed when panels of the camouflaged metal skin of the plane were unscrewed and removed. A month before, I would have supposed that inside that fuselage was lots of empty space, and some ribs—now I knew that no matter which panel one removed, it would reveal something that looked like a massive Swiss watch.

Another plane was sent on the first flight in our place, and two hours later, certain that today was the day we would plunge to a watery grave, I said "Canopy clear" and heard the *chunk . . . clonk* that meant we were on our way.

Standing off to one side of the plane's nose, the crew chief came to attention and saluted, something he had not done in the States. We rolled onto the runway.

It was shortly before the first time we refueled that I began to understand just how tricky these deployments were. Here we were, a single-engine plane built for relatively short, high-speed missions, and we were crossing the Pacific. A transport plane had additional engines to fall back on if anything went wrong, plus a co-pilot and any number of sophisticated navigational aids. Most important, it had enough fuel within itself to take it to its destination.

Not 951–F. Our best navigational aids were aboard the tanker we were trailing. If anything should happen to the tanker, or if we should lose it in a sudden storm, we were in trouble.

Now it was our turn to take on fuel. We maneuvered up behind the flashing silver giant until it all but obscured the electric turquoise of the Pacific stratosphere above us, looking like a huge club that could swat us from the sky. From its tail a pipelike hose began to extend toward us through the intervening yards; we inched up on it, flying just behind and slightly lower than the tanker's tail. To my right, protruding from our swept-back wing, was a metal pipe which would take on our fuel. In order to get the fuel, Don Usry would have to maneuver our plane so that our pipe slid into the basketlike end of the tanker's pipe. Once up into that basket, the tanker's supply would pour into our pipe. It was like threading a needle at five hundred miles an hour, and the necessity for doing it right was absolute. If we failed three times in a row to get linked up and hold the relative positions long enough to take on our quota, we would be at a point of no return. Every ninety seconds we consumed the equivalent of an automobile's full tank of gas, so there was no time to waste if we were unable to connect with the tanker. After three tries we would have to head, by ourselves, for the nearest Pacific island that had a runway long enough to handle jets. At certain points, this would mean a flight of close to a thousand miles.

The basket hung eerily in the brilliant air, three feet above our fuel intake pipe, and six feet ahead. Imperceptibly Don raised us, and then pushed ahead a few inches every second. The tip of our pipe, looking like a giant version of the closed spout of a small oil can, touched the edge of the basket, which flapped. We pushed further into the basket—there was a sudden stream of vapor and fuel, and we were solidly in, drinking our survival from the huge plane filling the Plexiglass cover above us.

Going into Guam I learned once and for all why fighter planes practice flying wing-tip-to-wing-tip. A terrific tropical storm was flinging us all over the place. The sky was brown, the sky was dark blue, the sky was black. We closed on the wing of the next plane and stayed in that position as we penetrated rain, clouds, and lightning, angling down out of the sky. At times we saw the other plane's fuselage only as a shadow, but the wing-tip was clear. Our four planes were so close that they were tossed by the same thing at the same time. Knowing where we were, we would not collide with each other. Like fingers on a hand, we thrust down through the storm.

FOUR

Regulations required that I enter Vietnam on a commercial flight from Guam to Saigon by myself and catch up with the Wing when they sent for me. I awoke in my hotel room in Saigon at six in the morning feeling what is, for me, a most unaccustomed sensation. I felt filled with energy, eager to jump out of bed, to be up and about and accomplishing things.

I sallied forth, not even stopping for breakfast, and walked down Tu Do, one of the principal shopping streets, toward the river. It was a Sunday, but even before the sun was truly up, the cranes of cargo ships were swinging pallets of crates to the docks. Huge United States Army trucks huffed monstrously along the waterfront, white stars on the doors of their olive-painted cabs. A few yards off, but an entire culture away, the Vietnamese squatted on the sidewalk, rice bowl in one hand and chopsticks in the other, eating their breakfast of slices of fish and pickles, filling the air with the cheerful rising and falling notes of their tongue. Bicycles slid past, and brown-burnt men with knotty legs hunched over the handlebars of their pedicabs, rickshas propelled by a bicycle rig behind the passenger.

The sun may not come up like thunder, but it breaks above the tan clouds and smoke over the river, soars triumphantly above the white and pastel plaster walls, and begins baking the corrugated iron roofs. Green wooden shutters are closed against it; plastic gray sun helmets and faded conical coolie hats are set in place.

In a small park by the river I beamed as I saw an old

man doing the ancient Chinese boxing exercises in the last cool remnant of dawn. Rhythmically, ritually, he made the graceful movements of arms and legs, and serenely left the park to the pretty children who came, older sisters holding babies, to watch men fishing from the concrete piers.

The noise of various Asian cities differs little—the theme is of *putt*ing motorbikes and high-pitched conversations, with an occasional slap of water thrown into an alley—but, for the connoisseur, each has its own smell. For me, Saigon's smell was the triangulation of two quite different phases of my life. The most recent was my years of residence in Tokyo, with frequent trips throughout the rest of Asia—from this I could instantly breathe in the hot steam of cooking rice, the smell of *nuoc mam*, the fermented fish sauce which acts as salt, catsup, and mustard to Vietnamese food, the smell of earth and herbs in the sun, the odors of human feces and smoldering charcoal and warming tea. But beneath this were the smells I had first learned in France on a summer college vacation—the unforgettably different smell of French cigarettes, still woven into the very walls despite the overwhelming quantity of American cigarettes loose in the black market; the smell of French coffee, the smell of cold stone hallways. In all this, not a single American smell, except for the contribution our trucks made to the bluish clouds that hung above the curbs.

At ten-thirty I went to Mass in the Cathedral, a Gothic red-brick creation, a several-spired North European pile which attained some measure of grace only in its gray-stone interior columns and flagstones.

The priest was a tired old Frenchman, who preached a tired-sounding sermon in French. After Mass, a good many young Vietnamese stood exchanging greetings in the sunshine before the church. They had the look of the privileged and secure, and they moved with grace. Some of the girls wore simple Western blouses and knee-length skirts. Others had on the *ao dai*, the ground-length tunic that is split on both sides and worn above flowing satin trousers. With perfect timing, these girl in *ao dai* would settle, sidesaddle, onto the back seat of their swains' motor-scooters. Without looking back, the young Vietnamese would know that she was seated behind him, balanced, perched sideways, her high-heeled slippers just inches off the ground, and off they would go in a snarl of machinery.

I watched one rich-looking boy and girl get into a red sports car and drive off. If there was a war going on, it was certainly not all sandbags and blood.

Wandering back down Tu Do, I decided to reestablish my acquaintance with my friends of the Associated Press, whom I had met on my one brief earlier trip to Vietnam, an AP assignment at the end of 1964, when it was a much smaller war.

I found them beginning a splendid lunch in the dim and dingy Royale Restaurant, near their office and the Saigon City Hall. They were the only ones in the room.

It was a scene in which I was to join a number of times during the year, and the type-casting would, as usual, make Hollywood seem unimaginative. No one could dominate the scene at a table of such high-spirited and articulate enthusiasts, all in their early thirties, but it was physically dominated, at least, by the bulk of Horst Faas. A black-haired German with a satyr's beaked nose and pouched blue-hazel eyes, he rumbled in French with the *propriétaire*, an old Frenchman who was a study in white—white hair, white shirt, white linen trousers, and a sagging cheesy skin that surely had not seen the tropical sun for two decades.

Having ordered blood sausage to begin and a veal ragout thereafter, with a bottle of Muscadet, Horst shifted his girth in the chair, looking about with the air of a man who is always amused and seldom dismayed. Growing up as a boy in Nazi Germany and experiencing American air raids, conquest, and occupation, he had evidently developed either a taste for danger or a considerable immunity to it, for he had sought out almost every battlefield since. His own association with the problems of Indo-China dated back to being a young photographer at the Geneva Conference in 1954, but his assignments had taken him to Algeria, the Congo, and finally to Vietnam, where he sensed that he had found a war with stamina. Arriving in 1962, he had covered all of it since—the original American advisory group of a thousand men, the build-up of the Special Forces camps, the fall of Diem in

1963, the eighteen succeeding months of *coup* and counter-*coup,* the emergence of Nguyen Cao Ky, still in power on this hot pre-Christmas day in 1966, and the American involvement to the tune of 425,000 men, with thousands more arriving each week. His photography had won him a Pulitzer Prize.

A new voice: "They told us Long Huu was completely pacified, but every time I went out the back of the house where the District Chief brought us, I got sniped at." Another Pulitzer Prize winner, reporter Peter Arnett, a close friend of Horst's and another of the tiny handful who had made it all the way through from 1962. Shiny black hair slipping down one side of his forehead, thick eyebrows bouncing, brown eyes rolling and boxing-flattened nose wiggling as he spoke, Peter's sallies in his murderous New Zealand accent kept everyone laughing. I had met Peter when he was covering the 1964 Olympics in Tokyo, and on my previous trip to Vietnam, and I had seen him and his Vietnamese wife Nina when they had been in New York on vacation ten months before. Then it had been business suits and lunch atop a skyscraper, but, wherever he was, Peter had the ability, with his shambling boxer's gait and exuberant, confident air, to make people turn and think "Now there's *somebody*."

Rounding out the party was John Wheeler, six foot one, broad-shouldered, with a black crew cut just turning gray and a face tanned from constant living with troops in the field. At a distance, one might have thought that John was a major whom Horst and Peter were pumping for information, but John was as professional a reporter as any in Saigon. A part of the matchless AP team since 1964, John had carried a wounded United States Marine officer eight hundred yards under constant fire in a retreat of Vietnamese and American Marines in a battle near Danang in 1965. Having finally gotten the officer to safety and having seen that his wounds were being tended, John decided to stroll down the reverse slope of a hill, away from the action, to catch his breath and have a cigarette.

Halfway down the hill he became aware that he was being followed. He was, indeed; a company of Vietnamese Marines, seeing a helmeted American walking away from the battle, decided that they would not be the last to leave the field. John looked at them, pointed at his cameras—which made no impression—and finally shrugged his shoulders and went back up the hill with the Vietnamese company following him back to battle. The Marines recommended John for the Silver Star, but due to a regulation which prohibited the awarding of the medal to civilians, he received only the Navy Department's Distinguished Public Service Award, sometimes given to actresses for tours entertaining the troops.

Having finished some delicious Vietnamese shrimp, I asked "Which are the best troops in the country?," wondering whether I would hear the Marines, the One-Seventy-Third Airborne, the Australians, the Green Berets of Special Forces, or what.

Horst's fork stopped just short of his lips.

"The VC," he said, and popped veal into his mouth.

After our coffee we strolled back up the sun-blinded street, threading through Vietnamese squatting about little sidewalk coal braziers. Others were sleeping, curled in the shade behind wooden display booths selling wallets, watchbands, shoelaces, and the inevitable black market cigarettes. As we were saying good-bye outside a barnlike office building, I felt a hand on my shoulder. Turning, my head pleasantly filled with sunshine and wine, I found myself staring into the businesslike face of an Air Force lieutenant colonel who had been processing my papers in the press liaison office.

"You're all set," he said. "There'll be a car and driver at your hotel at four-thirty tomorrow morning. That'll get you to a plane that stops at Tuy Hoa."

"Uh—good." I could feel that damned F–100 closing in around me, right on the sunlit sidewalk in Saigon.

FIVE

The first thing I saw at Tuy Hoa Air Base was a clump of cactus growing beside the perforated metal matting of the airplane parking area. Two hundred and forty miles northeast of Saigon, the sun was gone in December, and the salty sky was gray and cold. This coastal base, operative but still under construction, was isolated on a freak strip of beach stretching inland for two miles from the South China Sea. The beach lay at the open end of a great **V**-shaped valley; inland were bright green rice paddies and knots of farmhouses, and these halted at a steep wall of hills, some gray and boulder-studded, others green and forested, where the Viet Cong units hid.

Down the center of the valley, north to the base, ran the Da Rang River, which I had seen, shallow and broad, from the plane bringing me in. On its far shore was the town of Tuy Hoa, stretching the last flat mile down to a beach less arid than ours. One hundred and thirty miles to the west, through hills progressively higher than the massive ones in sight, lay the Cambodian border. We had positive control only of the sandy plain where we stood, and we did not always have even that.

I put my bag and typewriter into a jeep and we bumped off across the metal matting. There was a whining sound as three F–100s came taxiing past in single file. Big brown-and-yellow bombs, which I had never seen in Florida, hung beneath their wings, beside long silver tubes of napalm. The white-helmeted pilots' faces were impassive. I was swept by the sensation I had felt that sunlit afternoon at Eglin when I had been shown the antipersonnel bomblet. This was what it

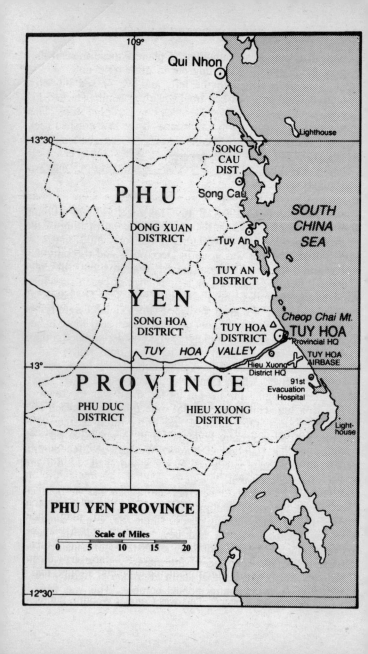

was all about; these camouflaged planes, these men in their gray flying suits, were going out to do it right now.

The jeep turned to the left, and we passed big olive tents, passed long flat-bed trucks hauling bombs stacked like cordwood, passed small yellow vehicles and blue jeeps. Then we were bumping down an unfinished road of crushed rock, past smaller tents that were the airmen's living quarters, and a few silver boxlike trailers. Finally we were at the ocean itself, and I was walking into a green wooden building that was Wing Headquarters.

"Charlie! Welcome to Tuy Hoa!" It was Colonel Frank Buzze, the Deputy for Operations, his red face cheerful; he wore a flying suit, a pistol was on a black belt around his waist and a sheaf of papers in his hand. He took me into the bare plyboard office of the Wing Commander; Colonel Lewis shook my hand and asked me how much trouble I had been able to get into in Saigon.

I smiled distractedly. I knew that if I was ever going to get up the nerve to get into that damned F–100 again, I had better start right in.

"I'd like to go on a mission tomorrow," I heard my voice tell them.

Both colonels nodded approvingly.

"We'll fix you up," Colonel Lewis said.

An hour later I was all smiles, with no thought of the morrow. The reason was the quarters. Having arrived with roach powder and DDT, prepared for tents, sleeping bags and mosquito nets, I found myself in one of the silver trailers I had glimpsed on arriving. It had a bedroom on either end, paneled in the same wood I had seen in so many briefing rooms in the United States that I had come to think of it as Air Force Oak. It was about eight feet by ten, had a linoleum floor, two big screened windows, and air conditioning. There was a closet, a bureau, an Army cot with brown blankets stamped US in black letters, and a wooden desk and a metal chair. Between the two bedrooms was a bathroom with not one but two sinks, mirrored medicine cabinets, a toilet, and a hot shower.

"How about a beer?" This was Colonel Woodfin Sullivan,

who had the other bedroom and who had been over here for a month with the advanced party.

"Great."

He went to the refrigerator to which he was entitled as Assistant Deputy for Operations. Sully had a punched-in nose and the air of an incorrigibly naughty boy who nonetheless does well in his studies. The shortest officer in the Wing, Sully was big-shouldered, erect, and walked with the best fighter-pilot swagger of them all. The impression was of a virile elfin, his Southern voice and conspiratorial smile promising that there was fun to be had, fun in the air, fun on the ground, fun even on this beach in Indo-China.

One beer led to another, and I was in Sully's jeep and we were cruising down the beachside road toward the officers' club. Sheets of mist were cast from seas that smashed the steep tan sands. The planes were down for the night. Darkness falls swiftly in Indo-China, and the lights of a jeep coming the other way served to heighten the feeling of isolation and adventure in this desert-beach. I felt penned in by the sea on one side, the rice paddies and hostile hills on the other, and pressed down by rushing black cloud ranks.

Considering what was going on inside, the club's exterior was remarkably silent. The humming of a sandbag-surrounded generator glanced off a low-roofed building of pale green boards. We made our way to its door via a wooden-slatted walk that divided two ranks of the Honda motorcycles that the pilots were using to get from their nearby tents down to the flight line.

I walked through the door and a bell clanged; a huge derisive cheer went up. I had entered without removing my rankless green fatigue cap, and this meant that I had the pleasure of buying every officer in there, about forty at the moment, a drink. After working this out with the sergeant bartender and discovering that at twenty, twenty-five, and thirty cents a drink the damage was not as bad as I had thought, I had a chance to look at the social center of my new home. It had a concrete floor; on the unpainted wood-plank walls were the insignia of the 306th and 309th Squadrons, along with that of the 308th, who had moved here from several months at Bien Hoa, near Saigon. Behind the home-made bar there was a huge refrigerator loaded with beer;

above it a tape deck played the jouncing tones of the Tijuana Brass. Dead center behind the bar was an oil painting of a nude blonde, reclining on a bed, the calf of one golden leg poised daintily atop a rosy knee, smiling confidently and invitingly at her all-male audience.

Then there were the members, or drinkers, or officers. At a table in the far corner a handful played at poker, some dressed in gray flying suits, some in the green fatigues of the ground officers, some in short-sleeved sports shirts and Madras shorts and sneakers.

The center of action was at the bar. There was an Old West atmosphere about the men in flying suits and fatigues, their feet in boots, pistols on wide black leather belts, leaning with their backs to the bar, while others clustered around jolting dice cups. The laughter and profanity were loud. A sudden snarl and hammering of machinery, and a young pilot drove his Honda motorcycle through one door, scattering the men in the area between the card table and the bar, and out the open back door into the sandy night. No one knew why.

Pilots of the 309th came up and shook hands, welcoming me, telling me that most were just beginning their missions; many had not flown yet. Even as I talked with them, I kept staring at a group at the far end of the bar. Their flying suits were faded almost white; their young faces were yellowish and drawn. These were the pilots of the 308th, just moved up from the base at Bien Hoa, most of them with a hundred or more missions, and six months of the twelve-month tour behind them. They had seen planes shot down. They had lost friends. As they stood there, the impression was of an indissoluble team, with no room for quarrels or differences. Gazing about the bar, I had the sudden feeling that it was, in its way, one of the most exclusive clubs on earth.

II

The next morning, tired and bewildered before the day began, I was at the seven-thirty stand-up briefing. It was a far cry from the glossy paneling at Homestead; the Weather officer put up his charts on a small easel in a tent lit by naked light bulbs hanging from the tent poles, while a high wind flicked sand under the flapping sides. Weather was followed by an Intelligence officer, who had not been part of the program at Homestead. This captain began talking about the totals of "structures destroyed" and KBA—Killed By Air—as reconstructed from the debriefings of the pilots who had flown yesterday's missions. As he spoke, my attention went to the blackboard listing the missions scheduled for today. There was my name.

The Intelligence officer took me in hand after the briefing. We walked down an alley between tents and entered a dimly lit interior of maps and wooden tables and bookshelves stacked with mimeographed forms. He sat me down and gave me twenty minutes of advice on what to do if I came floating down by parachute. Then we worked on my Authenticator—a set of questions and answers that a rescue helicopter could ask me over my survival-kit radio if they thought that my radio had fallen into the hands of the VC and the VC were luring them in to shoot them down, as had often happened. The rescue team would have, for example, my sister's nickname, and ask me what it was—something no impostor could know.

Having completed this, the captain said, "You have a little time before you brief. You might want to read the Dieter Dengler stuff." I sat down with the lengthy account by the German-born Navy pilot who was shot down over Laos, was captured, tortured, escaped, and after four months finally made it to a place where he was picked up, ending weeks of hiding in jungles and eating lizards and snakes. Having digested his recommendations, the principal one being not to get shot down in the first place, I made my way to the Personal Equipment tent of the 309th. Here were the helmets, the parachutes, lined up as they had been in Florida, but without the air conditioning, the linoleum floors, the soundproofed cement-and-plate-glass building. With Sergeant Bezio, who had come right along with the equipment, I looked over some items that had not been part of the flying gear back in Florida. On my upper half would be a survival vest, complete with small emergency radio, compass, pocket knife, emergency dressings, fishline and fish hooks, and a dozen other items. I had bought two pistols at a gun shop in Miami, and today I would carry these as well. Over it all—G suit, inflatable water wings, flying suit—would buckle the parachute, complete with a second radio, which automatically sent out beep signals if one ejected.

"Just like the fighter jocks," Sergeant Bezio said approvingly. I left my equipment on a wooden counter and went into the next tent, where the members of my flight were assembling. I was to be in the back seat behind Captain Pete Kehoe, whose red hair, red eyelashes, red eyebrows, and freckled square face were now being joined by the beginning of a mustache that was emerging in bristles of red, black, and white. It was his first combat mission. Next at the table was a Navy pilot, Skip Staub, whose former flying had been on aircraft carriers with Navy planes, and who was making this tour as part of a pilot exchange program.

"I've been in the service since April Fool's Day, Nineteen Fifty-Four, and this is the first time I'll fire a shot in anger," he said, grinning not at all angrily as he bent his bald head over a card giving him data on take-off time, load, and speed.

Our flight leader was one of the most beat-up looking members of the 308th, Captain Edd Fowler, a stooped, wiry, graying Kentuckian who had started his service career in Navy submarines and later switched to flying thirty thousand feet above ground with the Air Force. He briefed us with a thoroughness that stemmed from his own past year, which had started off with his flying two hundred missions in fighter planes. Then he had been assigned as a Forward Air Controller, directing fighter strikes in a tiny light plane, without a parachute. One day a fighter, coming off the target, had collided with him. Miraculously he and his spotter plane had come to earth leaving him still alive, but with a broken back. Now, one Distinguished Flying Cross and any number of Air Medals later, he was back on the bombing end, and he intended to see to it that we did not collide with anything.

After this meticulous talk-through of every detail of the coming flight, we got in a blue panel truck and drove to the club for lunch. The eating facilities were in a long silver trailer near the now-deserted bar. It was like entering a stripped-down Pullman diner that had come to rest on the sand in Indo-China. We filed past the serving counter and picked up a bowl of soup and a sandwich. Very little was said. We ate at a plastic-topped table, then drove back to the

9 mm Browning

Personal Equipment tent. With Sergeant Bezio playing squire to me as an unlikely knight, I was soon fitted out. I had a big survival knife like a hunting knife in a pocket on my G suit, another knife in my survival vest, my 9-millimeter Browning pistol in the shoulder holster of my survival vest, and my little .25-calibre Colt in a zippered pocket in the G suit. With two guns, extra clips, two knives, two radios, and a pack of hand flares, there I stood—the perfect noncombatant.

A sergeant drove us out to the flight line in one of the bread-delivery trucks that the Air Force has bought and painted blue.

"One Three Three." The driver announced the tail number of the first plane as he stopped, and Edd Fowler, a quick smile on his craggy face, said, "See you on the ground." He scooped up his parachute and the bag containing his helmet, and stepped out the back door and walked heavily toward the single-seater in which he would lead the flight. A moment later we stopped for Two Five Five, and Skip Staub, his Navy suntan overseas cap jauntily worn as the one non-Air Force piece of equipment, dropped off the back.

"Four Five Two." I swung down with my equipment and walked toward the big camouflaged plane. Under each wing it had a seven-hundred-and-fifty-pound bomb, green-brown with a yellow ring painted around it just behind its nose and another yellow ring just forward of its tail fins. Next to the seven-fifty hung a long bomb-shaped aluminum tube containing several hundred pounds of napalm. I climbed up the yellow ladder, tossed my parachute into place on the seat, and went to work strapping myself into the bathtub.

"If anything goes wrong," Pete Kehoe's Boston accent said through both my metal ears as we rolled into place at the end of the three-plane echelon for the take-off, "I'll try to give you a couple of seconds to eject yourself. If I have to go right off, my seat triggers yours anyway."

"I'm in the ejection position right now," I said into the itchy gray rubber mask over my nose. There was the oven-roar of the first plane starting to roll, and then the second one moved after it. I sat there, thinking of the added color that napalm and fifteen hundred pounds of high explosive bombs would add to the 20-millimeter shells and six tons of fuel we were carrying, should my fear of crashing on take-off materialize. The idea that there might be enemy bullets waiting for us out in the hills seemed a legitimate risk; it was getting this thing off the ground that frightened me.

We were rolling, rolling past helmeted Air Policemen in jeeps with machine guns mounted on them as they cruised the sands, and then we were up and the sands behind us and we were banking steeply over the electric green of the rice paddies, even this first turn jamming my buttocks into the seat as I turned my head to the right and stared straight down into the landscape. A flashing glimpse of small houses with red-tiled roofs, palm trees, hedges, dirt roads, and we were up into the wet clouds, droplets of water on the outside of the Plexiglass canopy, nothing but white mist. God we were lost, God we would crash right into the others.

We were up through the mist and there were the two others, alone above an endless carpet of gray clouds. We slid in beside them and I lurched again in the seat as Pete took us out of afterburner and reduced to cruising speed. There we were, nowhere over Asia and going like hell, a level of clouds beneath us and the sky above us domeless white.

Flight lead was talking to someone on the radio. Pete explained on the intercom that we were not just whistling along aimlessly looking for the rest of Vietnam. Radio beacons emanated from certain installations throughout the country, and by combining these, our compasses, and our distance-measuring equipment, we knew where we were. More important, we could fly a mathematically perfect line to rendezvous with our assigned Forward Air Controller in his little spotter plane.

So it proved. Twenty minutes and many miles later we drove down wing-tip-to-wing-tip through the clouds and broke out over a wild mountainous area of dark forest valleys and brilliant-green upland slopes. A river twisted inland, and hilltops and peaks rose and became a horizon as we slid down thousands of feet through random balloons of clouds. We were in a deliberately ragged single file now, moving through silver wisps, through rain that seemed certain to crystallize into blinding fog.

The flight lead was talking to the Forward Air Controller.

"Come on up the river," the FAC's metallic voice told him. "I'm holding just over the fork up here." I strained my eyes. From this altitude there was not the sign of a human being down there, and, in this part of the country, not the sign of a village, a hut, a bridge, a road. The forests reached up trees that looked like green sponge rubber.

"I've got you in sight," flight lead told the FAC. There was more palaver, while I kept looking over the side to see the spotter plane. Finally I saw him, a tiny white wing circling against the green below. He stopped turning, and we went into a large orbiting circle thousands of feet above him. The spotter plane floated up a valley, disappearing at times under clouds.

"Okay," he radioed us. "I'm rolling in to mark." The little plane tipped, swooped toward the ground, and swung up. A pure white puff emerged from the jungle beneath it.

"Okay. Hit fifty meters east of my smoke."

Now it was our turn.

"Lead is in from the north." Fowler's plane was dropping like a rock on a long arc taking him down between two cloud-covered ridges. The suspected VC concentration was beneath hundred-foot trees at the inner end of a narrow horseshoe of forest cliffs. He arced down toward the white puff made by the FAC's smoke rocket. Then his plane was bouncing back up into the clouds. I watched the white puff.

There was a red flash next to it, a double blossom—a bloom of gold-red fading toward its center, and a flower of dark brown that rose and kept spreading.

"Good bomb," the FAC said. "Two, put it twenty-five meters west of that." Skip Staub was streaking in from a different angle, his plane low and flat, so low it was as if the plane was yelling *"NAVY!"* Then we fell in toward the target, our left wing-tip digging toward the earth. As we fell, we rolled over on our backs, hurtling forward and down through clouds that flashed past us. Indo-China came turning up at me, revolving one way, then the other.

I had no idea that we could drop our bombs upside down, I thought, hearing Pete's quick breathing through the intercom. Then we snapped over, there was the white smoke in the trees, surrounded by a brown dirty haze, and *thunk!* a jolt as two bombs went, and we were facing a wall of trees and my chin was on my chest and I weighed a thousand pounds and a jungle ridge swept past below us and we were shooting up through clouds.

That evening Sully and I were invited to the Taj Mahal for drinks. This structure, nicknamed for its opulence, was a huge square silver-metal trailer next to ours. It had been made for their own use by some of the American civilian contractors who were building the base and turned over to the Wing's top echelon when they arrived.

Colonel Frank Buzze, his usually cheerful red face pale from a stomach ailment, greeted us at the door, and my jaw dropped as I saw the living room. The building had been made by slapping together half a dozen trailers of the type Sully and I shared, then removing a number of the resulting inner walls. The living room was easily fifteen by twenty feet, wood-paneled and with wall-to-wall carpeting. In the bedrooms off it lived the top brass: Colonel Lewis, the Wing Commander; Colonel Ray Lee, the Vice-Commander; Colonel Frank Buzze, the Deputy for Operations; and Colonel Bill Myers, the Deputy for Materiel.

A martini in my hand, I settled into a tubular steel and imitation-leather armchair, and listened to the combination of joking and shoptalk that swirled around me. A tape machine like the one in the bar at the club played the Tijuana Brass, and on the plastic-topped coffee table in the center of our square of chairs and couches there were copies of the Asian edition of *Stars and Stripes*, plus the last two *Playboys*.

I sipped my martini, half my mind still back in the air in those swooping, body-jamming passes at the jungle, "jinking" the plane until the last moment to zigzag and throw off an enemy gunner, the lifting jolt as we dropped each pair of bombs, the lurching burp as we fired our cannon. Our mission had been uneventful; no one had shot at us, as far as we or the FAC could tell. After the bombs had been dropped and the 20-millimeter strafing runs had been completed, the FAC had circled in low over the target area. He had been able to see nothing but a couple of trees down, a few craters, a scorched patch from our napalm.

I was offered some hard-to-come-by pretzels. It seemed to me that somebody might inquire how my first mission had gone. No one did. They had all flown similar missions themselves that day; only Frank Buzze had a "divert," a call on the way to the planned target area to divert to an immediate target where friendly troops were under attack. Even then, diving at six hundred miles an hour from thousands of feet up, looking through a sight at the FAC's ball of white smoke, he had not seen a single human being, although on the ground they had been trading shots at a hundred meters.

"What do you think of our place here?" It was Colonel Bill Myers, who voluntarily flew combat missions although his responsibilities were in maintenance. His gray hair crew cut, his leather face still containing fragments of metal from two earlier wars, he was the pipe-smoking picture of a composed professional.

"Fantastic," I answered, glancing at the squadron emblems on the walls, the cooking alcove in the corner, the separate bathrooms off each bedroom.

Colonel Lewis nodded. "Sometimes I think it's too much," he said, "and then I think of two years in New Guinea under a mosquito net, and I think, what the hell."

Then they were talking of other wars. Listening, I began to realize that I was living with a group of survivors. Colonel Lewis had shot down seven Japanese planes in the South Pacific; Sully had knocked off four German planes in Europe;

Frank Buzze had four in the Pacific; Bill Myers had four in Europe, plus six destroyed on the ground and a strafing record of one hundred and twenty German locomotives blown up. Frank Buzze and Bill Myers had been among the first pilots rushed to Korea when that war started, and had flown three and four missions a day for months, covering our first desperate retreat, our advance to the Yalu, and the horrendous winter breakthrough when the Chinese smashed into the war.

"I used to have a real mad on for ack-ack," Colonel Lewis was saying in his Iowa voice as he put some laces into a new pair of jungle boots. His fingers flew at the job; it was done in seconds. "Over Hollandia, I used to take my pulse just before I rolled in to strafe those guns." A minute later he was talking about the realities of war. "There's nothing glorious about killing people. A couple of times we got the Japs retreating right off a beach into the water. I was flying a P-39 with a thirty-seven-millimeter cannon in the nose. We used to go in so low and that thing would hit them so hard I'd come back with pieces of them and blood all over my plane."

There was a fly zipping around the room, and one of the colonels reached from where he sat and destroyed it in one quick grab. I realized that he had succeeded not because he had been so swift, but because he had known how a fly flies, and how to intercept it. I smiled, looking at these trim men with their bouncy strides. At a fraction under six feet I was easily two inches taller than any of them, but I had a feeling that if any of them had been asked, he would have said, "Charlie? He's about my height."

Sully and I thanked our hosts, and made our way to the dining trailer at the officers' club. Soup and sandwiches again. Then into the bar. The 308th was having a squadron party. They had decided to wear coats and ties, so one was treated to the sight of a fighter pilot wearing only a madras jacket, a bathing suit, and sure enough, a tie hanging down his hairy chest. Periodically some of the younger 308th pilots grouped with their backs to the bar, their malaria-pilled faces solemn. In the manner and strains of a choir, they sang the filthiest lyrics imaginable, while a young mustached pilot, his back to the rest of the crowd, led them with elaborate conductor's gestures. Looking toward heaven as if butter would not melt in their mouths, they closed on a fortissimo rendition of a double word of incestuous meaning, and sang, "Amen."

I was just noting the fact that *crème de menthe,* of all things, seemed to be very much of a fighter pilot's drink, consumed in large dollops, with ice, as if it were a highball, when I felt a hand on my arm. It was Chuck Fulton, who had taken me for my first rides at Homestead.

"How'd you like your mission?"

"Great," I said.

"We've got a back seat open tomorrow. Nine o'clock brief. Want to come?"

I felt like saying, no, not really. "Sure."

The phone at the end of the bar gave its little burping buzz. A major from the 308th answered. His voice became crisp.

"Okay. Inform Colonel Lewis. Tell Maintenance Control. Get in touch with the contractor's people."

The Air Police had reported sniper fire, and one rifle grenade, hitting the perimeter of the base. As Sully and I left the club to go to our trailer, silver flares were hanging in the sky to the southwest, sinking slowly beneath their small parachutes, dripping occasional sparks beneath them like the tail of a kite. There were no sandbagged bunkers yet in our area, so I wandered among the trailers near mine, stopping to talk with officers who were also in the position of spectators.

Outside one "hooch," as all nontent, nonbunker structures were known, I heard the voice of an officer making a tape which he would send his wife instead of a written letter. With the Air Police deploying on the perimeter, flares popping, enemy rifle fire coming over our barbed wire, he was saying,

"It's all real quiet here. So far this tour is a real snap."

The enemy stopped, our flares stopped, I went to bed.

The next day we howled through the brighter skies to the southwest of our base, three armed planes in a loose **V**, with all the greens of Indo-China stretching away beneath us, checks of bright green rice paddy here, and black-green forest there.

"We've got a divert," the pilot said, and I listened to

flight lead receiving instructions for a rendezvous with a FAC other than the one we had been scheduled to meet.

"I hope it's something good," I heard myself saying. The pilot clicked a transmit button on the control stick, twice, in the fighter pilot way of agreeing without speaking.

Next I heard flight lead telling the FAC our call sign, type of aircraft, armament load, and how much fuel we had, the last so that the FAC would know how long we could stay in the target area before we had to head for home.

Then the FAC spoke. "This is kind of a ridiculous target," his metallic voice said, apologetically. "It's an ox trail by a stream. They want us to cut it."

Three fighter pilots and one civilian swore. But three million-and-a-quarter-dollar planes dropped twenty thousand dollars' worth of bombs to make an ox trail temporarily unusable.

III

That night the Taj Mahal was the scene of one of the most colorful parties I have ever attended. It was the evening of December 23, and was in a sense a Christmas party. It was also the Wing's first entertaining of the Allied power structure in our area of the war. Our base was in Phu Yen Province, one of the forty-four provinces comprising South Vietnam, as fifty states comprise the United States. Ours was a coastal province of some three hundred and ninety thousand Vietnamese. Its southern boundary ran inland from the sea fifteen miles below our base, and the northern line was up the coast some forty miles. Shaped almost square, Phu Yen encompassed two thousand square miles. The coastal plains held ninety per cent of the rice paddies and eighty per cent of the population; the hilly interior had the more primitive Vietnamese villages and farms, a few thousand *montagnard* tribesmen of different ethnic stock and language from the Vietnamese, and an estimated five thousand North Vietnamese and Viet Cong troops. Tonight was my first look at the top men on our side.

I blinked as I entered the Taj. The colonels had shed their flying suits and were turned out in crisp suntan uniforms with silver command pilot wings over the left breast pocket of their short-sleeved shirts. Three sergeants presided behind a bar and a heaping cold buffet. The tape deck was faithfully playing the Tijuana Brass.

There was a terrific racket outside, and I stepped to a window of the living room. In the dusk, a helicopter was landing. Across the sand, a small party of tall helmeted Americans, carrying M–16 rifles, made their way to our door. A moment later I was being introduced to Colonel John Austin, commander of the First Brigade of the United States Fourth Infantry Division. His command post was just outside of the province capital town of Tuy Hoa, north of the river from our base. He and his staff doffed their helmets and leaned their rifles against the wood-paneled wall. They made for the bar, keeping on their web-belt harnesses, from which hung ammunition pouches and grenades. Their green jungle fatigues had a red-dust tinge to them; it was as if the war had walked into the room, to the tune of the Tijuana Brass.

I found myself staring at one of the Army officers, a tall, blond-haired lieutenant colonel with a rugged aloof elegance. He swallowed his drink with the air of a man whose mind was out in those hills.

Pretty damned cold fish, I thought. If anyone had told me I was looking at the best friend I would make in Vietnam, I would have said it was going to be a damn thin year.

There was a flashing of red lights on the gravel area just before the door. Led by jeeps armed with machine guns, the officers of the Korean 28th Regiment were arriving from their headquarters down the beach to our south. Broad-shouldered, barrel-chested, all hearty smiles and heavy tread, they gave an impression of determination and efficiency. Without exception, their English was good. They were proud men, and, as I was to learn, ruthless. Charged with the responsibility of, among other things, providing a screening force for an American air base which would eventually be worth more than a hundred million dollars, they were hell-bent on showing that the Korean Army had come a long way from the questionable item of 1950–1953. They made it over to the bar in short order, and within minutes there was on every Korean face that telltale flush that comes to an Asian with even a single glass of beer.

The next thing that rolled up was a caravan composed of older jeeps and varicolored International Scouts, built like big jeep station wagons. From them stepped twenty Vietnamese and Americans, some in uniform and some in civilian clothes. These were the Vietnamese province officials, and the American officers and civilians assigned to them as advisors.

The Americans in this group pointedly made way for a small uniformed Vietnamese to enter first. He came through the door, and for an instant his hooded eyes opened wide at the lavish interior. This was Lieutenant Colonel Nguyen Van Ba, the Province Chief.

What would he like to drink?

"Scotch with water," he said with the resigned tones of a man who would much rather have a cup of tea. He turned and began talking vehemently to a Vietnamese major who never left his elbow. In a moment the major was introducing himself to me; Major Heung. We spoke for a few moments; in excellent English he said that he had been a professor of French Literature at the University of Hue, made it clear that he wished the war were over and he were back there, made it equally clear that he was the Number Two man to Colonel Ba, and then said, indicating the interior of the Taj with a graceful sweep of a small, pudgy hand, "Very expensive." He said it with just the trace of a question mark.

"Very expensive," I affirmed, and he nodded and turned to Colonel Ba and said that yes, it was very expensive.

The American infantry officers were making their goodbyes, putting on their helmets with the green camouflage cloth covers and their patina of red dust. A minute later their helicopter was rising, blinking red lights and whirling rotor blades, straight up, slightly forward, faster forward and then slanting away into the night.

I returned my attention to watching Colonel Ba. On the chest of his green fatigues were a number of French and Vietnamese ribbons. His face was intelligent, skeptical, and bored. When he smiled, the entire performance took less than a second. When he spoke to the other Vietnamese—the chief of the National Police in the province, resplendent in white uniform shirt with braid on black shoulder boards, the Chief Judge, a tired old man in a dark suit, white shirt, and black tie, and the rest of his entourage—there was an air of absolute agreement as to who was boss. On the little finger of his right hand he wore his fingernail an inch long, the old Mandarin symbol that here was a man whose fingernails would never be broken by manual labor.

I grinned. I had heard the term so often, but here was an Oriental war lord, and I had a year to watch him at work.

One of the American advisors, big and bearlike, came over after two more drinks and put his arm around Colonel Ba's shoulders. The Vietnamese winced.

"I'm getting short," the American said, in the term meaning that he was coming close to the end of his year's tour. "I hope you come to the United States. Come and stay with me and my family. Have another Scotch."

Colonel Ba smiled, said a general thank you, drained the Scotch as if it were cough medicine, and, as the big hairy foreign devil went off to the bar, turned to Major Heung and gave him a little general hell.

After a while the Vietnamese left. On their way out, with everyone milling around, they managed in some cases to shake the same hand three or four different times. To Asians, all Occidentals look alike.

SIX

Three days after Christmas, it occurred to me that I was in a rut. I was walking along the shoulder of one of our ankle-twisting crushed-rock roads, with a gray sky above me and a gray flying suit around me. The road stretched far ahead on the great distances of an air base; there were tents here, then half a mile of sand, then tents there, and in the background the thunder of a jet engine being put through its paces on a big concrete block called the Test Cell.

I had flown four missions. The flying was sensational. It was by no means boring to be scared to death on the take-off and to watch the dance of silver pinpoints in the jungle as a strafing pass was made, but I was seeing the war from thousands of feet up. To participate in a mission, from briefing through the debriefing afterward, took about five hours. After a mission I was so loose-headed that I could not go back to my typewriter and do anything. I needed some variety.

It arrived quickly.

"There's a back seat open in a FAC plane," someone in the command post tent said after a morning stand-up briefing. "He'll be here in about ten minutes. You want a ride?"

A blue pick-up truck deposited me at a taxiway just off the runway. I stood alone in the vast flat floor of the Tuy Hoa Valley, looking at the overcast sky. Right out of the gray came a tiny matching gray plane, slipping in like a toy of early aviation history. Built like a Piper Cub, the Cessna spotter plane bounced right up to me, pivoting so that it pointed back out to the runway. The propeller kept spinning, and the door flipped open.

Cessna "Birddog"

"Hop in." The smiling pilot, wearing a flying suit, white plastic helmet, and an olive-drab flak vest, motioned me to climb toward the low seat behind him. He had me put on a flak vest and watched over his shoulder as I strapped into a seat belt and shoulder harness. I noticed that he had an M–16 rifle with him. There were no parachutes.

"Put on that headset."

I did, slipping the earphones over my soft fatigue cap.

"Set?" he asked over the intercom.

I pressed the button that activated the mouthpiece. "All set."

We putt-putted back out to the runway. He called the tower for clearance, revved the engine, and we shot ahead. The engine, with far less horsepower than an American car, pulled the light frame into the sky within seconds. I smiled. It was the first take-off I had enjoyed. We banked, heading inland, passing low over our barbed-wire perimeter with its sandbagged watchposts, and cruised along a few hundred feet in the air, the eggbeater engine reassuring me more than all the resistless roar of a jet. It was delightful to see the beautiful rice paddies and neat thatched roofs slide past so slowly. We crossed Route One, the nominally two-lane coastal road which was the main, and in many places the only, north-south road in Vietnam. Down there were all the gradations of Vietnamese travel; peasants walking, others on bicycles, motorbikes, and scooters, while larger groups were crammed into three-wheeled minibuses in which an open-sided body had been built around a motorscooter engine. Bigger red-green-and-yellow buses took their packed-on riders for longer distances, honking little donkey carts off the road. Heavy loads passed by in light-blue vans, which gave way only for the olive-drab military vehicles. In a jet, all this had whisked by so quickly that I had never seen the highway, let alone the details of the traffic.

We headed southwest. The farms thinned and vanished, and we climbed over the escarpment that wedged in the valley.

"This out here is what we call a free-strike zone," the FAC told me. "Nobody's supposed to be out here." We were passing over a series of forested ridges. "If they're out here, they're Charlies," he said, using the generic term for the VC, Victor-Charlie in our radio alphabet. His head poked out the window. "There's four of them right now," he said in a surprised voice, and banked so that our left wing was pointing at the ground.

"Where?"

"That trail. In the saddle there." I looked just in time to see a man in gray loping down the trail with a black sack banging on his shoulder. He plunged into the woods.

"I'll try to get some gunships," the FAC said, reaching over his head and turning a switch on his radio panel. He started talking to someone called Mildew Throne.

"This is Mildew Throne. Negative gunships available at this time."

With no attack helicopters available, my companion called the U.S. Army artillery belonging to the helmeted Fourth Division men I had met at the Taj Mahal party.

"Ready to copy," an eager voice replied. The FAC spread a map on his lap, alternating between studying it and looking out the window as we kept whizzing above the area where we had seen the men. He read off letters and numbers from the map, and then drove back through the sky several hundred yards in the direction from which we had come.

"Holding to the east," he said to the artillery that was miles north.

"You want us to mark with Willie Peter?" The artillery was asking if they should first send in a round of white phosphorus so we could see if they had the range.

"No, go right to high explosive," the FAC snapped with the urgency of a hunter on top of his quarry. "These guys may not wait around."

"Roger, understand." A few moments passed. "On the way."

I watched the place where I had seen the man disappear. A pair of flashes lit in the woods near the trail, then another pair. A moment later came the sound—*KRUMPP! KRUMPP!*

"Move it fifty meters west."

"Roger." Brown smoke and dust hung over the woods. "On the way." More seconds, then the flashes, then the sound.

"Drop it twenty-five."

"Understand drop twenty-five."

"Affirmative."

More shells, dirt flying up, branches falling in, more smoke. It kept up for ten minutes as the FAC moved the shells through the area in which the men might be hiding or fleeing.

"All right," the FAC finally said, looking at the blue-brown haze that hung over the target area. "Turn it off. Thank you much. I'll let you know if I see anything."

"Roger. Let us know if you need more."

"Thank you. Out."

We drove back in at treetop level and circled all through the haze. Some craters were visible down through the trees, some bushes were thrown aside, and that was all.

"Did you just hear something?" the FAC asked as he made the plane leap out of there.

"No."

"When you get shot at, it sounds just like a little click from up here. I thought I heard it just then."

I digested this. "Are you going to hit 'em back with something?"

"Not now. They could be anywhere by now. I might sneak up on this area tomorrow before sunrise. Cut the engine and glide in and see if I can spot their cooking fires or some activity."

I was about to ask him where he'd be if his engine failed to come on again, and thought better of it. We motored north, crossing over the rice paddies of the valley at its narrow inland end.

"This is sort of interesting," he observed. "The VC control the dam up here at the top of the valley. They could cut all the water off, but they want the rice to grow, too, because they get a lot of it, one way and another."

To my right, the town of Tuy Hoa slid past, and, just north of it, a huge woman's breast of a hill, three thousand feet high, called Cheop Chai. It stood quite apart from the V of hills that formed the valley, inside the V and near the sea. The alternating green grass and gray rocks of Cheop Chai slid past, and we were back over hilly jungle.

"What's that?" I inquired. The top of a green hill to our left had a crown of red dust.

"That's a battalion base. Want to take a look?" He turned the plane inland and we crossed the hilltop. There were tents, a few large and many tiny, a perimeter of foxholes, and several cannon hunched within sandbagged circles. Their arms looking orange as they protruded from green jungle jackets, American troops moved singly or in small knots. There were no roads, or even visible trails, leading to the hilltop.

"How do they get those cannon in there?"

"All done by helicopter. Everything—food, ammo, mail. For the artillery they sling the guns under the big ones, the Chinooks. They call 'em Hooks."

We flew on, and passed over American infantrymen, working out at a distance of a mile from the fire base. They were moving along a trail, carrying packs. From the air they looked like small living toys, the same color as the jungle but for their orange arms and upturned faces as they looked at us.

I stared from them to the blanket of green jungled hills that stretched forever. There was another battalion hilltop base in the distance to the north, but these bases looked lost in this sea of green. It was clear to me that this jungle could

Chinook

sop up battalions as a room-sized sponge could consume glasses of water.

We bounced to a landing on a grass field in paradise. To our right was a glittering bay, complete with a white sand beach and palm trees. To our left, Route One wandered past grass-roofed mud houses surrounded by tropical flowers. This was Song Cau, the northernmost coastal town in the province. In the French era, it had been the provincial capital, rather than Tuy Hoa, which showed that the French knew a good thing when they saw it. The French finale at Song Cau had consisted of their naval vessels lying off shore and flattening the town and its strong Viet Minh population, an act which had not proved helpful to the American advisory team when they appeared here a decade later.

A jeep and driver were waiting for us. The FAC wanted to check some suspected Viet Cong positions with the intelligence maps of the advisory team here, so we headed south to the center of town. The pedestrians and vehicles I had seen from the air now became life-size, Vietnamese life-size; tiny farm women in white coolie hats and black pajamas with baskets hanging fore and aft from a wooden pole over the shoulder, moving in a fast stiff-legged gait like that of a distance-walking athlete; little rubber-tired donkey carts heaped with men, women, and children. Vietnamese Regional Force and Popular Force soldiers, the equivalent of the National Guard and a local militia, wandered down the road in green fatigues with World War II American weapons balanced on their shoulders. Big olive trucks filled with stocky helmeted Koreans thundered past the tiny-waisted erect Vietnamese soldiers. Children in shorts, faded checked shirts, and floppy canvas hats rushed to the edge of the road, shouting "Okay!" with brilliant smiles as we passed, some holding out their palms in hopes of a handout conducted at fifteen miles per hour.

We turned off Route One and slid to a stop in a complex of buildings and tents. The stablelike structures were the headquarters of the Vietnamese Army captain who was Chief of Song Cau District, one of the six districts comprising the province, as six counties might comprise an American state. The American district advisory team had its double-decker bunks, weapons, radios, kitchen, and dining area in a screen-sided wooden bungalow. The palm-surrounded tents belonged to the Americans who were advisors to a battalion of the 47th Regiment of the Army of the Republic of Vietnam, commonly known as ARVN, which was for the moment quartered here.

We had just finished a cup of coffee and a long comparison of maps when there was a stir among the fatigue-clad Vietnamese outside the tent. There had been a skirmish on the outskirts of town; a wounded VC was being brought to the District Dispensary. We piled into the jeep and rolled into a straw-littered yard before a white concrete building, scattering chickens as we came to a stop. We passed up the steps, under the corrugated iron roof of the porch, and into a cool room through which blew the salty, sunlit breezes of Song Cau.

On a table lay a boy of fifteen, wearing thin black cotton trousers. He was barefoot, and lying on his stomach. His left arm was extended off the table, his hand gripped by a toothless old woman in black trousers, a dingy blouse, and a faded flowered bandana around her frizzly gray hair. The nearest thing to a doctor possessed by this district of forty-five thousand, a handsome man in khaki shirt and trousers, was probing with a shiny forceps in one of several holes in the boy's back. The Viet Cong, under his shock of black hair, had a young face that happened to be much like the doctor's, except that it was frightened, in pain, and yet motionless.

There was a crowd of Vietnamese of all ages in the room, with more arriving at every moment, staring silently at the red holes in the boy's back. In shock, his skin was more gray than yellow. Several Vietnamese in fatigues, holding their rifles at end-of-hunting-trip angles, stood near the table with a proprietary air. They explained that the boy had run out of the side of a house during the firefight, holding a grenade with one hand and fumbling at its pin with the other. Before he could arm it and throw it, someone had thrown a grenade at him which went off behind him and put him out of business.

I asked who the old woman was.

"Mother," I was told.

"You mean grandmother."

"No," one of the advisors said. "These farm women get old mighty fast."

An hour later the FAC and I were having a hamburger and a milkshake in the Base Exchange cafeteria at Qui Nhon. We had reconnoitered the coast at the very northern end of the province, north of Song Cau, and then slipped over into Binh Dinh Province to refuel and eat at the big base there. Before eating, I had made a goggle-eyed tour of the Base Exchange, which had everything we at Tuy Hoa did not. You could be measured for a suit from Hong Kong, buy the latest American record albums, or invest in a small refrigerator or a television set. But what interested me, after thirty straight soup-and-sandwich meals at Tuy Hoa, was a shelf holding such things as tinned anchovies, pickled cocktail onions, sardines, and peanuts. Beneath my chair as I wolfed down my hamburger was a paper bag filled with all these gustatory changes of pace, plus two jars of caviar and a bottle of champagne for the upcoming New Year's Eve. It was just noon, and I felt as if I had lived a lifetime.

The strangest moments were to come. After lunch the FAC said that we would fly over the headquarters of the 95th North Vietnamese Regiment. We headed southwest, back into Phu Yen, moving well inland and flying low over beautiful wild land. The hills became steep forested ridges three and four thousand feet high. We had left the sunlight at the coast, and the mists gave the trees a bright green luminosity. Where a Chinese or Japanese scroll might show a slope slipping into mist, a rocky spur emerging from a clouded valley floor, here was the whole mass from which the vignettes came. Feathery waterfalls wavered in the winds that swept through these green mountain clefts. The plane bucked as we worked our way through the higher passes.

"They're all through this area," the FAC's voice remarked in my earphones.

"Here?" The streams threading down blue rock beds looked as if no man had ever knelt beside them to drink.

"We know they've got a regimental command post, a hospital, warehouses in caves—about a thousand NVA," he said, using the term for North Vietnamese Army, "and whatever the VC move in and out of here to support them. They come down out of here and do their stuff and slip back up here again."

I stared down at this scene, crystal gorges as on the day of creation. "Why don't we bomb them?"

"Oh, we do," he said, "we do. But we don't have enough manpower to come back in here and see if it does any good."

We turned out over a small river heading down toward the plains and the distant band of sunlight that was the coast. The radio cut in from Sector Headquarters, the military side of the American advisory effort at Province Headquarters in the town of Tuy Hoa.

"Quebec Alpha Two has something going at the following coordinates," the voice said. "Ready to copy?"

"Go," the FAC replied. With a red crayon he copied the numbers on the window of the plane's door. "Roger. We'll be over there in approximately one zero. Out." He hit the intercom button. "Okay. Get settled in back there. They've got some kind of ground action going just south of Tuy An."

I tightened the seat belt and shoulder harness, and found my hand working at the zippered front of my flying suit to close it right up to my Adam's apple. I smiled at myself; some cloth was not going to make any difference, putting it between my neck and whatever else might be around. We

putted on toward Tuy An, the one sizable town between Tuy
Hoa and the paradise at Song Cau. The river beneath us had
become enormously wide and flat. Its bed consisted of an
infinite number of round ivory-shaded stones, with the river
flowing in a score of different channels through these stones
and small strips of saw-bladed grass. Islands lay in the river,
great fertile patches with farmers working on them.

"This is Quebec Alpha Two," a voice over the radio
said from the ridge to our left. "We're in contact with an
estimated VC platoon, but they're falling back to the east
pretty fast. I'd like you to see if you can find some of them
and bring something in on top of them. Be advised there's
ground fire all through the area." My hand went back to the
zipper at my throat.

"Roger, understand," the FAC replied. "Pop some smoke
and let me see your location."

"Popping smoke."

We hummed in low toward the ridge. A stream of red
smoke came up through shiny purple leaves.

"I identify red smoke," the FAC said, checking, since
the VC often listened to our transmissions and popped captured smoke grenades, hoping to lure us in and shoot us
down.

"That's affirmative," the voice beneath us said. I saw
helmeted Vietnamese troops moving along a hedged road
among farmhouses, their rifles hunter-fashion under their
arms. Two Americans were standing in the center of the road,
one with a radio pack and an aerial on his back, both looking
up at us. "The leading friendlies are about one hundred
meters due east of my location," the ground voice told us.
"The Charlies are pulling back southeast."

"We'll start looking," the FAC said quickly. We zipped
out over the fields beyond the farmhouses, with me looking
out the opened left window in back, the wind tearing at the
bill of my fatigue cap, and the FAC looking out his right
window. It had become misty.

"There's some people digging something," I said.

He whirled and looked out. "They're digging a grave,"
he observed, banking in above them. The little L of human
beings kept digging as we snarled down on them. "What a
time to be digging a grave," the FAC added. He turned and

we kept pushing over toward the southeast, hunting something more. We shot over the edge of the slope that dropped toward the river, angling across it at an altitude of fifty feet.

Eight startled faces looked up at me. They were under coolie hats, and most were wearing brown ponchos. They were huddled under bushes beside a trail.

"There they are!" I cried. "Directly behind you!"

He turned the plane inside out and we were sailing back in.

"I see 'em," he said tersely, but by the time we were over the spot, they were gone. We climbed sharply to the right, and he was on the radio, requesting Vietnamese authorization for an immediate air strike at these coordinates. We whirled back again. The ground didn't look the same to me. I wet my lips. The radio said the air strike was approved and requested; fighters would be on the way.

Do we know the right place? I thought. *Were* they the VC? They certainly had been where we had been told to look for them. And what was I doing, anyway? You got involved awfully fast in a situation like this. You were just trying to be helpful and the next thing you knew eight men had fighters coming to kill them. The bottle of champagne and jars of caviar rattled behind my seat in the paper bag from my lunchtime shopping at Qui Nhon.

We heard from the fighters long before we saw them. The call sign meant they were a flight from the 308th at Tuy Hoa.

"I have you in sight," the FAC told them. About two minutes later I saw them too. It was raining; the gray sky spread from ocean horizon to mountain horizon. Against the gray, three F–100s were circling well above us, deadly short black darts.

"I want you to make your passes on a west-east heading," the FAC said. "The nearest friendlies will be three hundred meters to the northwest of my smoke. I'll be holding to the south. Rolling in to mark."

On the last words, our nose flipped down and we went toward the trail on the slope like a roller coaster. There was a strange silence in the plane. Then *BAAM!*, with a ringing whack the first of our white phosphorus rockets was gone from the rack under the wing. As we swooped back up the roller coaster, straining to the right, I saw the smoke explode beside the trail.

"Hit twenty-five meters east of the smoke," the FAC said, looking up at the fighters as he gave us full throttle to get us out of there.

"Lead is in from the west," a cool voice stated. We flew out over the river bed and turned, flying abreast of the ridge, now a quarter of a mile off. Black against the silver sky, the F-100 came tearing down from inland, maneuvering with evasive lateral rocks. Then he was just above the farmhouses atop the ridge, his green-brown camouflage coming into focus, his dive very shallow, flat. A bomb slipped from beneath him, flying along beneath him, gradually, reluctantly arcing down, moving faster but still reaching forward like an arrow, the plane away, lofting, and flash, silver-gold-red flash, dirt everywhere, the closest I'd been to one of our bombs, and then *KRUUMP!* The next plane was already in. He let go one of the silver napalm canisters. It hit; there was a large gold-orange splash, quickly to red, not much smoke, and an area of bushes at a corner of a field was black and smoking, some branches glowing red.

Beneath us a farmer in one of the island fields went on plowing behind a water buffalo. We edged back in closer to the bombing. I started to shrink down in my seat. Then I looked at the almost paper-thinness of the aluminum side of the plane. There was no use hiding behind that. I straightened up.

After a while the last dance of 20-millimeter strafing flashes flicked out in the bushes. We cruised back over the ridge, turning sharply, sweeping, looking under the trees just beneath our wheels. No bodies. Some craters, some burnt patches. Otherwise, nothing.

The little tins of goodies I bought at Qui Nhon made such a hit with Sully and at the Taj Mahal that I decided to take any opportunity of getting to more lavish Base Exchanges than ours. I was in a sense the guest of the Wing; there was little I could do for them, but if they liked an occasional snack of sardines or anchovies to supplement the daily sandwiches and soup, I would try to help.

So it was that I found myself hitching a ride to Saigon

aboard a C-47 two-engined transport on the morning of New Year's Eve. The plane was delivering a few of our pilots for a party to be given by the then-premier, Nguyen Cao Ky. Having spent his adult life as a career Vietnamese Air Force officer before emerging from the political welter as chief of state, Ky wanted representatives of every flying unit in Vietnam to attend a New Year's Eve party, all guests to come in flying suits.

I sat in a shaped-metal bucket seat, facing a row of similar seats across the aisle in the narrow tubular interior. These planes, which had flown under the commercial name of DC–3s and were known as Gooney Birds, first went into the air in 1936 and had proved to be one of the most durable and efficient aircraft in aviation history. They had been the workhorses flying The Hump in Burma during the Second World War and had played a large part in the Berlin Airlift. In Vietnam they were proving invaluable as transport planes with a capability of landing on a short runway, and a number had been adapted with batteries of special machine guns used to thwart night attacks on Allied positions.

This one was unarmed. It belonged to the Wing and was used to pick up and deliver, all over Vietnam, small groups of the Wing's personnel or special consignments of supplies. I happened to be sitting next to the crew chief, a bony, freckle-faced young man, Sergeant Tommy Poindexter of Oil City, Louisiana. I asked him a few questions about this particular plane's history, and a tale emerged. The young sergeant had been working at Tan Son Nhut Air Base in Saigon when he had noticed this plane in the grass off the runway, missing one engine and a number of parts, including a tail wheel. It was being cannibalized, gradually being eaten up to provide parts for other Gooney Birds, but Tommy thought this one might have some life left in it. After work, on his own time, he began begging and bartering for various parts. After a few weeks he had a complete airplane. The authorities rubbed their eyes, assigned it to Tuy Hoa, and sent Sergeant Poindexter along with it.

"You gave the Air Force back an airplane," I observed.

"No, Sir," he said, shocked. "The Air Force had it all along. It just wasn't running, that's all."

* * *

We landed in noon sunlight at Tan Son Nhut, and the crew began shutting down the plane and locking it up. Since I had been planning only a brief stroll over to the Base Exchange, I asked them what time that afternoon they were going back.

"Didn't you get the word?" They stared at me. "We're not going back until tomorrow. No point running back up there this afternoon and coming right back down here to get these fighter jocks tomorrow."

So there I stood in hazy heat, wearing flying coveralls which it was illegal to wear in downtown Saigon, and with nothing so lavish as a razor or toothbrush to face the twenty-four hours ahead. I thought of the New Year's Eve parties I had been invited to at Tuy Hoa, and the one to which I was not invited at Premier Ky's. Things did not look good.

An hour later I slipped into the Associated Press office in downtown Saigon, delighted that no Air Police had asked me to explain my rankless, illegal-downtown, funny-name-tape flying suit.

Peter Arnett hooted. "Well, I've seen correspondents in every other sort of costume; we might as well have this."

"I need some logistical support," I said, and explained the situation. Ten minutes later I was presenting a note from the AP to the desk at the Continental-Palace Hotel, a marvelous old white plaster barn complete with black-and-white checked marble floors and ancient overhead fans going *chunk-chunk-chunk*. A bellboy in white tunic let me into a French open elevator, which creaked up to Room 22, the AP quarters for some of its reporters who spent most of their time in the field, serving also as a guest room for friends of the family passing through town.

After I had taken a shower and followed the AP's advice to change into the first near-to-fitting slacks and sports shirt I could find in the big wooden armoire, I took a good look at Room 22. Under the *chunk-chunk*ing fan in the high white ceiling, there was a big square inner room containing twin beds against one wall, and another bed beside the huge armoire. Twin arches opened into the outer room, where blinds kept the sunlight at bay as it beat at tall French windows.

What made it, of course, were the effects of the occupants. What had been designed as a ladies' low dressing table, complete with unused three-way mirror, was strewn with military maps and pistol clips. Atop the armoire were a field pack, a poncho, two helmets, and a web-belt harness faded to tired muddy pink. In one corner stood a pair of crutches. In other corners were easily six pairs of jungle boots, their green canvas tops faded dirty gray. In the armoire hung white-faded green jungle fatigues, a few unexplained girls' dresses, and some unused men's tropical suits. A long chest of drawers had many half-empty bottles, *U.S. Camera Annual* for every year the war had been going, and paperbacks ranging from detective stories to the reminiscences of General MacArthur and Robert Murphy's *Diplomat among Warriors*. In the white-tiled bathroom, the bidet was filled with bottles of malaria pills and cans of foot powder.

That evening, after lunching in the usual gargantuan style with Peter and Horst at the Royale, I arrived at an apartment building just up Tu Do street from my hotel. Peter had told me there would be a New Year's Eve party at a certain-numbered apartment. I made my way up musty gray stone steps with their ineradicable smell of French coffee and cigarettes.

Saigon is not a place of wall-to-wall carpeting, or overly much furniture. This sparse tropical tendency, heightened by wartime, was taken to its extreme in the high-ceilinged set of rooms I entered, for they were owned by two American civilians whose time was spent mostly in a province west of Saigon. There was, however, a dining-room table heaped with bottles of liquor, soda, tonic, soft drinks, and trays of simple canapés such as cheese and crackers or rye bread and Spam. One of the tape decks found everywhere in American installations in Vietnam was playing, to my delight, something other than the Tijuana Brass. Most of the AP people were there, in sports shirts and slacks; it made me feel properly dressed in my attire, from an unknown lender, except for the jungle boots which I had retained on my feet from my flying gear. A few Western wives were in evidence, most notably Horst's wife Ursula, a tall blonde beauty with a charming German pronunciation of English. Seeing such beauty under such circumstances reminded me of a long-remembered line in a long-forgotten book: "It was a face worth going through a lot to see."

On the one couch in the next room, Peter Arnett was surrounded by what seemed to be a Vietnamese harem. This proved to consist of his wife Nina, and Nina's two sisters. One of them, Miriam, was wearing a stunning powder-blue *ao dai* over white-silk flowing trousers. For a country boy from Tuy Hoa, I felt, things were looking up.

It was a New Year's Eve not likely to be confused with others. An American Army officer, in sports shirt and slacks, a red-headed, tipsy Red Cross girl on his arm, wandered about the room, half-seriously raising his non-female-holding arm and asking people to take the Oath of Allegiance. At one point Hugh Mulligan, the Associated Press feature writer, led everyone in singing a version of the "Twelve Days of Christmas" which began:

> *The first day of Christmas,*
> *The VC gave to me*
> *—A* plastique *in a Dauphine....*

This reference to a plastic explosive destroying one of the little Renault cars was followed by other verses passing through similar disasters, lost patrols, and the like. Miriam and I stood on the terrace outside the French windows, catching the cool evening air and the racket of motorbikes below. She asked me where I had been the New Year's before, and I replied that I had been in Times Square, with a Chinese girl I had met in earlier years in the Far East, whom I had taken to see the non-Chinese welcome to the non-Chinese New Year.

"You must come to my house for dinner at Tet," Miriam said, referring to the Vietnamese celebration of the New Year, coming in early February.

"You don't have to say that twice," I replied with a smile. Then I was dancing with Miriam, and it was midnight and we stood in a circle, holding hands and singing "Auld Lang Syne"—a New Zealander, his Vietnamese wife, her sisters, a German and his German wife—all in an apartment still smelling of France.

Lost, I thought, lost we are and going nowhere. These men, most of them, had seen it from the beginning, but the inescapable fact was that we were just observers, just living on the surface of it, mere tourists in history.

Then I was dancing with Miriam again, trying to lift my jungle boots lightly.

SEVEN

With January the rains came. And stayed. I had seen rain in Africa, the Caribbean, the Fiji Islands, but I had never seen anything like these winter monsoon rains and winds.

Flying stopped. Big and sturdy as the F–100s were, they had to be lashed down on the flight line.

The pilots went stir-crazy. In their rain-blasted leaking tents on the beach, there was nowhere to go but the dining trailer for soup and a sandwich, or the bar. Fewer and fewer sandwiches were eaten; more and more drinks were consumed. The gray sky pressed down; the gray ocean boiled and thundered, night and day.

"I haven't thrown my pink body at the ground for a week now," a tall 308th pilot complained to me. It was hard for me to get, at first, but gradually it sank in; these men were part bird. They gladly took the risks of being shot at, in return for the joy of flying their planes. Every day they did not fly was a day they were sure of living, but to them it was a day lost, a poor bargain.

Everyone walked tilted into the storm. The contractor's bulldozers kept going, their bearded American civilian drivers wearing Sou'wester hats and yellow rain suits. The Vietnamese laborers huddled miserably under their white coolie hats and a wild assortment of rain gear. The Vietnamese women workers blossomed in Western-length raincoats acquired somewhere, in colors of lavender and plum and peach that made them tiny bright spots on our dismal soggy plain.

I, too, was tired of staring at the walls of my hooch, or the painting of the nude blonde behind the bar. I decided to go looking for someone who had to be outdoors in all this, someone who was *really* miserable.

Thus I found myself, on the worst day yet, in an open-sided jeep riding beside Captain Leonard Mittelman of the Air Police. In the States, the Air Police are those starched creatures who stand at the gates of air bases, wearing white gloves and fancy scarves, waving traffic through and saluting officers' cars. In Vietnam they became the men who crouched in foxholes behind a narrow apron of barbed wire, the last and sometimes the only thing between the enemy and barracks of unarmed airmen whose job was to fix engines, not to cope with infiltration or mass attacks.

"Captain," I asked, "what's the worst single post out here?"

He smiled at me from beneath the dripping rim of his helmet.

"I guess the one where the southern end of the perimeter hits the beach."

"Could I spend some time out there?"

Under his poncho he shrugged his shoulders. "Be my guest."

With the jeep in four-wheel drive, we moved through the sandy cactus dunes on a set of tracks so rough that it knocked an inlay out of the right side of my mouth. Finally we arrived at a small sandbag bunker set twenty meters north of the point where the barbed wire sloped down to the pounding surf. The sands had pushed up in drifts around the tiny one-man fort.

I struggled out of the jeep, trying to keep my oilskin brief case dry beneath successive layers of a poncho, an Air Force blue raincoat, and a field jacket I had almost decided not to bring because Vietnam was going to be so hot.

"Neidecker!" Captain Mittelman's stocky body bent toward a wet pink face that appeared behind the muzzle of an M–16 through an opening in the sandbags. "This is Mister Flood! He's going to put you in his book! Tell him anything he wants to know!" The Captain was shouting in the howling rain. "And don't forget to tell him how much you like it out here on this post!"

The boy laughed, the M–16 disappeared, and he waved me to come on in. I crawled in as the jeep took off. The

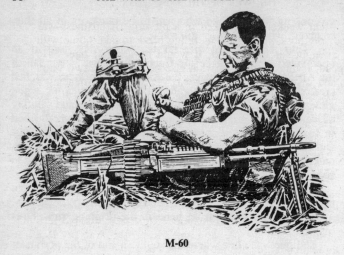

M-60

shallow bunker had a sandbag roof, but one could not really call it an enclosed space. Only the north wall, behind us, was solid. To my right was the aperture through which I had crawled. To my left was an open log-framed window looking out to sea. In front of me, facing southward to the barbed wire and the cactus field beyond, almost the entire side of the bunker was open, with an M–60 machine gun on its bipod pointing toward a fishing village a quarter of a mile off in the rain. We were being rained on horizontally, along with ocean spray, but not vertically.

"Like something to eat?" the young airman inquired politely. He pointed toward a tan paper case filled with smaller brown paper cartons of C-ration cans.

"No thanks."

After a while we began talking. He was Airman Second Class Ronald Neidecker, of Lakewood, California, nineteen and a 1965 graduate of David Starr Jordan High School in Long Beach. His father was a foreman with the Union Pacific Railroad, and his stepmother soldered electric parts in a Douglas Aircraft plant.

What kind of a student had he been in high school?

The blue eyes were amused. "Just barely average."

What else had he done before the Air Force?

"On weekends I worked in a pizzeria. If business was good, my boss would give me a big pizza to take home with me at night—if it was bad, it would be a small one." He stopped, trying to think of what else he had done, two years ago and seven thousand miles away. "I liked to go dancing a lot. Used to swim in some of the pools. Sometimes I'd go fishing with my father."

He had joined the Air Force nineteen months before, for the usual four-year Air Force enlistment. He smiled. "This may sound funny, but I didn't join the Army or the Marines because I was afraid they'd send me to Vietnam."

Then he was talking about living conditions for an airman second class at Tuy Hoa. When he was not in this bunker, he shared a tent with five other air policemen. "We're in C Flight. That's the good Flight. Everybody keeps trying to transfer in there with us." He had been at Tuy Hoa for three months, one of the first units to arrive. "We haven't had any hot water since we got here. We have outhouse-type latrines, cold showers—mirrors on the walls—we shave cold out of basins."

We chatted a while longer, and he pulled out a wallet and showed me a picture of his girl, Linda Henderson, from Colorado Springs, where he had been stationed before Vietnam. "She's going to Fay Ross Beauty College in Greeley, Colorado."

The wind was blasting through chinks in the lower sandbags. I asked him what he thought about, sitting out here.

"I think about home. Past memories. The good times. The bad—everything." He paused. "I think about what we're doing here."

"How do you feel about it?"

He nodded, with an expression of "Okay, you asked for it."

"I was talking to a guy the other day, he was saying he didn't know what we were doing over here, fighting for people who would trick you or steal from you every other minute. I think I'm over here fighting for something I've got back in the United States, and that other people should have, too—freedom and the right to do as they please, within limits." It kept on coming, without a pause. "In America, we

have the right to do as we please, and to vote—if these people
want those things, and they *do* want those things, then I think
we should help them get them. I don't know that much about
Communism, but I know *I* wouldn't like to live under it."

He shook his head ruefully then, and told me that the
only three Vietnamese he'd really had anything to do with
were three Vietnamese soldiers he arrested who were stealing
Christmas packages bound for Americans. But that hadn't
changed his mind about anything.

"I think the draft-card burners at Berkeley ought to be
shot. I think that if they believe in the same things I do, then
they ought to be willing to come over here, too." He stopped,
his reddish face and blue eyes looking out through the sheets
of whipping rain. "But I guess the answer is that they don't
believe in the same things I do. I believe it's every able-
bodied American's duty to fight for his country when he gets
the chance. I think it's an honor to fight for your country and
die for your country." He patted the machine gun. "VC give
a hundred-dollar bounty per stripe to anybody who can prove
they killed an Air Policeman."

Then we were talking about what Christmas had been
like for him.

"Christmas," he said, attaching considerable importance to it, "we didn't have any C rations. Another flight
relieved us out here so we could go into the chow hall and
have the Christmas dinner."

He crawled out of the bunker and looked around to make
sure that no one was sneaking up behind us. Soaking, he
came back in, and sat thoughtfully behind the machine gun.

"I haven't done too many important things in my life,
but I think this is the most important thing I'll ever do." He
looked down at the sand. "Helping people to help themselves."

After a while he opened the field pack he had pushed
into the driest corner. He pulled out a harmonica and smiled
at it. Then he played "Home, Sweet Home."

II

The weather lifted; we were flying again. I found people
coming up to me in the bar, telling me that they had a back
seat open—"Nine o'clock brief, okay?"

"Okay." And there I was, carrying my parachute up that yellow ladder, fumbling with the oxygen hose, strapping in, pulling down the tinted plastic face shield in my big white helmet, hoping that no one would know that I was every bit as frightened of the take-offs as I had been at Homestead two and a half months before.

We flew north, and sometimes a flight that had been scheduled to strike a point just south of the Demilitarized Zone was diverted to a target across the border into North Vietnam. We flew south, we flew west, we bombed hills and valleys and trails. Certain missions on cloudy days were known as Skyspots. On these we flew at high altitude, guided by radar to a point where the bombs were released above an unsuspecting Victor Charlie who could not hear us from the many, many thousands of feet up at which we flew. The first he would know about it was when the bombs landed on his camp in the jungle. It was fantastic, but it worked. Of all the incidents in Vietnám of bombs landing in the wrong place, never one was a Skyspot.

Being fighter pilots, my colleagues hated these stratospheric milkruns. It was bad enough that they were not flying deep into North Vietnam where the MIGs were, although all but the slowest MIGs could have outmaneuvered the F–100. Denied the dogfighting, denied the flak-filled skies that the F–4s and F–105s regularly encountered over the Hanoi–Haiphong area, the least they wanted was to divebomb. Skyspot became Combat Proof in our language.

But there were other days. One afternoon I climbed into the back seat behind my hoochmate Woodfin Sullivan. Sully's cock-of-the-walk stride, conspiratorial smile, and common sense were translated into the way he led a flight. He got us into the air with a minimum of time and words. Our target was in a stand of trees within a few hundred meters of the Cambodian border. The FAC marked with white smoke; as flight lead we screamed in and dropped the first bomb. Twisting up out of the target area, our nose pointed to the sun, I saw right on top of us, so big that it seemed to be growing out of Sully's shoulder, a lumbering camouflaged Gooney Bird.

We are dead. It was my only thought.

Sully wrenched us left, the Gooney Bird flashed across

F-105

my right shoulder, and we were a thousand feet above it and still climbing.

The FAC came on the air. "Be advised there is a Gooney Bird in the area."

"We have him in sight," Sully answered in the understatement of the year.

We completed our bombing and headed back to Tuy Hoa. The rains had let up for the day, but the winds were still with us, creating unpredictable brief sandstorms over the base.

In a tight echelon we approached the base, our plane leading and two young pilots from the 308th in their planes angled off behind us to our right. We flipped to the left, pitching out, and circled around to approach the runway from up the valley, the other two planes following in single file. Descending, we started our final turn. Everything on the base was visible, all the way over to the yellow earth-moving trucks creeping along the road by the beach. Without warning, the entire base disappeared in a brown cloud of sand. Sully pulled back on the throttle and advised the rest of the flight, and the base tower, that we were coming around to give it another try. As we zoomed out over the beach and the

sea, the sand subsided as if a fan had been turned off. Every
hooch, every tent, was clear. We swung left over the river,
over a corner of Tuy Hoa town, up the valley, and then made
our final turn and approach. I was studying our fuel gauges.
If we took too many tries to get in here and could not make
it, we would not have enough fuel to head for another base
and try for a landing there.

We were sliding in, the runway broadening before us,
when everything turned to a boiling brown whirlpool of sand.
The runway disappeared, yanked beneath a brown fluffy rug
fifty feet high.

Sully pulled up our nose and added power. "We're
going to Phan Rang," he said, and got on his radio. The
three of us headed down the coast in a **V**. Phan Rang advised
that weather there was perfect, and we relaxed. Sully let me
take the stick, and I tried the first roll I had done since Chuck
Fulton showed me how, over the brilliant turquoise waters off
Miami.

"Hell," Sully said, "you do better rolls than I do. Go
ahead and do another."

As I did the next one, I happened to glance in the
rear-view mirror affixed to the canopy above my control
panel. The two high-spirited young 308th pilots were taking
formation flying to its acrobatic ultimate. As if it were not
enough to fly close behind an amateur who was wavering all
over the sky, now they were rolling their planes upside down
in perfect unison with my hesitant, jerky motions.

We climbed down at Phan Rang and the four of us
crowded into a jeep. For the second time in two weeks, I was
at an airport, facing a night ahead, without a toothbrush or a
razor.

The jeep dropped us off in front of the command post of
the fighter unit flying out of Phan Rang. The door opened,
and in the hallway were no fewer than eighteen pilots from
Tuy Hoa, all forced in here the same way during the course of
the late afternoon.

Colonel Lewis, slender, debonair, pistol on his hip and a
fatigue cap tilted over his high forehead, looked at me.

"You, too!" He threw his cap on the floor in mock
disgust. "Isn't *anybody* left up at that base?"

*   *   *

For a boy from the slums of Tuy Hoa, the Phan Rang officers' club was hard to believe. Set atop a mountain overlooking the base, the hills to the north, and the South China Sea, this was no soup-and-sandwich operation. Our Base Exchange having been out of cigars for a while, I spotted stacks of cigar boxes behind the bar of this Shangri-la, and diffidently asked how many cigars were allowed to a customer.

"As many as you like, Sir," the sergeant bartender replied, a bit offended at the implication that there might be less than a lot of everything. He began to get the picture when I bought a hundred cigars, and ducked into a back room when he saw the rest of the Tuy Hoa gang advancing on his end of the bar.

I passed down a long gleaming steam table, thrusting out my plastic tray again and again, trying not to drool on the mashed potatoes and pot roast with gravy, the little salads, the apple pie à la mode. Twenty-one pilots and one civilian from Tuy Hoa went through the line without a single one taking soup. Not wanting to miss the violet sunset, I made my way through the screen doors and out to one of the tables on a terrace overlooking the base and the ocean. I was joined there by a pilot whom I shall call Special Stud, for a number of reasons. His job was different from that of the other pilots; he flew alone. His sex life was a little different from that of the other pilots; after three children and a divorce, he had himself sterilized, a point which he mentioned almost immediately to any young lady he wished to add to his staggering life-total of bedmates.

Special Stud and I had just begun our pot roast and mashed potatoes when the shooting started. We put down our forks and watched the tracer bullets flying, three quarters of a mile away. The Air Police on the northern perimeter had seen men moving on the rocky slope just north of the base, and were opening up with their M–60 machine guns. Viewed from behind, or nearly behind, tracers appear simply to sail out toward their target, more like a baseball line drive than a bullet.

We resumed eating, perfectly aware of the irony; here in the same lavender sunset some men were drinking Scotch and lighting cigars, while others were breathing hard, moving fast, and dying young.

After dinner a movie projector was set up, and we all moved our chairs in front of a good-sized white screen. Under the tropical stars, Hollywood sent us a dreadful Technicolor film involving Indians, the United States Cavalry, General Custer, and a cavalry officer who was sympathetic to the Indians. At one point in the movie two Indians, miles away from the nearest paleface, obligingly spoke English to each other, with heavy accents. At another moment the actor who played the cavalry officer sympathetic to the Indians refused to obey an order; the reaction of the real officers on the Phan Rang terrace was one of chilly silent disapproval. I sat there, thinking of the ethnic relationship of Asians and American Indians, and of how, in that context, we had been fighting Indians almost steadily for three hundred and fifty years.

Things were not going at all well for the Seventh Cavalry. They went at Little Bighorn and the situation was deteriorating. They were in fact surrounded. Here came a particularly numerous band of shrieking Indians.

An Air Force major turned to the one enlisted man on the terrace, the sergeant who was running the projector. Pointing at the oncoming Indians, he said, "All right, Sergeant, you take over."

The sergeant laughed.

After the movie I sat in the bar, enjoying my newly bought cigars and chatting with three young pilots of the 308th. Irreverent to the end, they were discussing the twanging Vietnamese music that kept coming onto our radio frequencies at unexpected times during missions; the 308th called it "Music To Strafe By." Two of the three pilots sitting with me were the ones who had been in my flight that afternoon. One was describing how a squadron mate had taken a remarkable hit from a VC .50-caliber bullet the day before. The bullet had been coming at an exact right angle to the plane, and the plane had run into it as it crossed two feet in front of the pilot's face. The bullet cut a crease in the Plexiglass panel at the front of the canopy and went on its way, leaving a spiderweb of fissures on this front window, but no hole. The pilot was planning to have the panel made into the top of a coffee table. The four of us laughed at that, and drank, and made plans for who was to wake who for the next morning's take-off for Tuy Hoa. Four of us; five months later half of us were dead.

EIGHT

The FACs had an idea. If I really wanted to see them work, why not move up to the headquarters of the Fourth Division's First Brigade, north of Tuy Hoa town, and spend a few days with them?

Why not, I thought, and arrived one January evening on a sandy knoll outside the town. These FACs were Air Force pilots assigned with their little spotter planes to this Army brigade of five thousand men, and I was abruptly dropped into the Army standard of living. It was foggy and raining; I shivered as I took an outdoor shower, the unheated water pouring down from a perforated empty napalm canister that the FACs had ingeniously rigged beside their tent. Clean but frozen, I slipped under two blankets on a cot and fell asleep.

An explosion brought me bolt upright. Looking about me wildly, wondering whether to dive for the floor, I saw a figure calmly dressing in the predawn light.

"What the hell was that?"

"Six A.M.," the FAC said. "We start the day around here by firing a cannon at Charlie out in the hills."

I went FACing day after day, hours on end. There were exciting moments—circling tightly above American soldiers who were running, firing, advancing on an enemy we could not see—but my main reaction was frustration. Here were dedicated pilots, often going down to treetop level in slow-moving planes, and we saw so little sign of the enemy. It seemed impossible that there were five thousand armed men in these hills and valleys.

74

. I asked Colonel Austin, the brigade commander, where they were.

"It's this jungle," he said with a smile. "I ran off one operation where I had two of my companies going in from different sides. I was over them in a chopper. They went into the woods, and that's the last I saw of anybody for four hours—and I *knew* where my people were." He invited me to a briefing to be held the following morning, in a big tent. Although the Vietnamese were represented only by a liaison officer, the charts and reports proved useful as a clarification of the set-up of the forces in Phu Yen Province. On the Vietnamese side, there was a fixed set of administrative positions; Colonel Ba, as Province Chief, was the top man in the Province; below him were the various chiefs of services for the Province, many of whom I had met at the Taj Mahal; the Judge, Police Chief, Chief of the Medical Service, and so on. Directly under the Province Chief's command were the Regional Force companies, equivalent to our National Guard and used only within the Province, and the Popular Force platoons, a village militia rarely required to move out of their respective Districts within the Province. Operating within the Province and coordinating with the Province Chief was the 47th Regiment of the ARVN, the Regular Army of the Republic. The nation was divided into four Corps areas, the First or I (pronounced "eye") Corps being the top of the nation, our own area comprising the provinces in II Corps, and so on down the long, scimitarlike land.

Paralleling this structure was the American team of military and civilian advisors. An American captain in the advisory team in Phu Yen Province would not have an American company under his command; he would be an advisor to a Vietnamese officer and his troops. The American civilian who was advisor to the Refugee Service would not have refugee camps directly under his control; he would work with the Vietnamese who ran them.

This was the extent of the regularly present Allied structure in the Province, but had this been all, the Viet Cong flag would long since have flown over Tuy Hoa. Just as the 47th ARVN was in effect on loan to the Province, so for the time being was Colonel Austin's First Brigade. The Korean forces in the Province were in a similar status.

The briefing in the big tent was thorough, and not without its surprising moments. The American chief dental officer reported that 10 per cent of the draftees in the Brigade needed false teeth. The S-1, or administrative officer, gave an amazing rundown of where the men of the Brigade actually were. Some were in other Corps areas, observing techniques or attending special schools. Some were on their R-and-R—the Rest-and-Recuperation week-long leaves which came up once in their year-long tour and were spent in such places as Bangkok, Singapore, Taiwan, and Japan. Others were on emergency leave in the United States because of deaths in their families.

Colonel Austin shook his head. "We've got men defecating in Brooklyn and fornicating in Hong Kong."

The American civilians present had something to say. A red-headed young man in a sports shirt, the Refugee Advisor, rose to say that because of Korean secretiveness about their operations, he had not known about an offensive that had been mounted in the north of the Province. This had sent fifteen thousand newly generated refugees fleeing south.

"That's fifteen thousand more for dinner," he said. "We would have appreciated," he added in stunning understatement, "a little advance notice so we could take care of these people."

A few minutes later an introduction was performed that made me blink. "This is Mister So-and-So of the Embassy. He has all sorts of good things like assassination teams that you battalion commanders might be interested in." This was the first time that I had heard this euphemism Embassy, which it was understood meant CIA. As I mused on the singular inappropriateness of choosing as a cover name the one American office in the country which was not meant to engage in other than formal relations between sovereign states, the talk turned to the Rules of Engagement. The tall blond officer who had struck me at the Taj Mahal party as being tough, frosty, yet somehow elegant, was on his feet and giving everyone hell.

"We need some clarification of the Rules of Engagement," this lieutenant colonel was complaining. "We need some Standard Operating Procedure on Vietnamese moving after dark." He was told that the Province Chief had not yet, six years after the start of the shooting in this American phase of Vietnam's bloody twenty-year postwar history, set any curfew to restrict movement in the countryside after dark.

I emerged from the tent, slipping my clipboard of notes into my oilskin brief case.

"Charlie." It was Colonel Austin.

"Yes, Sir." As a former private in the United States Army, I found it easy to say "Sir" to Army colonels.

"I'm going around to see some people in my chopper. Want to come?"

"Yes, Sir."

The day had turned drizzly. We walked down a sandy slope past olive tents and a few old Vietnamese plaster buildings with corrugated iron roofs, and I approached my first helicopter ride. The craft sat on perforated metal matting, a brown dragonfly with bulging joined plastic eyes, tubular steel runners supporting it, and a tapering tail. A pilot and co-pilot were in place. Behind them was the area that could carry passengers and cargo. From the runner on the ground to the floor of the helicopter was a step up of three feet, but I managed to haul myself in. A bench of red cloth ran along the rear wall, and I sat down along it and strapped on a seat belt. Just behind this area, recessed into the fuselage on either side, was the place where a machine gunner sat, facing out at whatever might appear off the side.

We were in, and the engine hammered into life behind the wall against which I sat. The driveshaft ran upward to power the big horizontal rotor blades which would move us forward, lift us, or hover, depending on the angle at which the pilot's controls commanded the blades to cut the air. At the end of our tail was a small rotor blade which whirled vertically, fore and aft, stabilizing us as we flew.

Grass tumbled away from our craft as the engine revved up; the sound was a heavy eggbeater hammering. Then we were off, rising just a yard or two at first; our nose dipped lightly, we swept ahead, rose, turned, and we were on our way. Sitting next to me, wearing a brown rainjacket that bore his radio call sign WHIPCRACK in black letters over his right breast, Colonel Austin doffed his helmet and slipped an earphone-speaker combination on his head. Cheop Chai slid past to our right, massive, imposing, and isolated. We headed west, following the river up the valley, and then crossed the hills forming the valley's north wall.

We came down in what can only be called a mud-field. Whipcrack took off his headset, put on his helmet, picked up an M–16, and jumped out of the chopper. Standing fifteen yards off was a young helmeted captain who was trying to ignore the gobbets of gray mud that the wind from our slowing chopper blades was flicking at him. I jumped out behind Colonel Austin, noticing that he seemed to walk across the gray mud without getting his jungle boots wet, while mine were gray to the ankles in three strides.

The young officer advanced and saluted; we were introduced. This was a composite artillery battery, made up of the two heaviest cannon we had in Vietnam. There were two 175-millimeter self-propelled cannon with long, graceful barrels, and two heavy-set howitzers, eight inches across the muzzle, which, like the others, were mounted on a body like that of a tank.

This was the first time I had seen an artillery unit. Offhand, I could not imagine a more miserable occupation than standing long hours in mud beside these cannon with rain pouring down one's neck, but there was an air of pride and enthusiasm in this mudhole. As we approached each cannon a sergeant came forward through the mud as if on a parade ground, drew himself up before the gun, saluted, and reported in a clear, quiet voice which gun in which section it was, and that the crew were all present and accounted for. In other words, they were ready to go, and in fact the big muscular boys behind the sergeants stared hopefully at Whipcrack, as if he had brought them news of something to shoot at. The sergeants looked lean and weather-burned and capable, and the captain in charge of them looked like a college graduate from a softer stratum who had sense enough to let them do their stuff.

Whipcrack, followed at this point by the captain, the battery's first sergeant, and me, turned to the sergeant on one of the guns.

"Is there anything you need, other than women?"

"Men, Sir," the sergeant replied. Whipcrack smiled and began a catechism that drew in the captain, the top sergeant, and the sergeant who had made the answer.

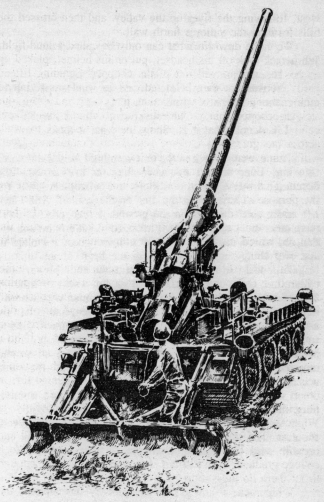

Self Propelled 175

"How many men are you authorized?"

"Two hundred and eleven, Sir."

"How many men do you have?"

"One hundred and sixty-five, Sir."

"How many do you really need?"

"Twenty-five more, Sir."

"If I got them from the One-oh-fives, could they do the job here?"

"Yes, Sir."

"You've got them." He moved on, and stopped by a sick cannon. "What's wrong with it?"

A new sergeant. "The rocker arm cylinder, Sir."

"Show me what it is. Show me what it looks like."

That evening, back in the tent with the FACs, I did some thinking. Everything I had seen thus far in Vietnam—the bombing, the FACing, the artillery, the helicopters—was for the purpose of supporting the man on the ground. And I had not really seen the war on the ground. I realized that there were other sides to the effort, I intended to get around and see that red-haired man who worked with refugees, I wanted to see everything, but now I was in the heart of an Infantry brigade, and I had not yet gotten out to the end, the very end of the line. Once upon a time I had sixteen weeks of Infantry Basic Training at Fort Dix, New Jersey; the men with whom I had trained, the squad whose leader I had been, had gotten on a train and gone to fight in Korea, and I had been assigned to further duty at Fort Dix. Now it was as if, years later, those boys in 1953 had come to life again. They were all around me, the same black faces, the same white faces, the same accents.

I went to Whipcrack. When he found out what I wanted, he grinned.

"We'll send you up to Tom Lynch's battalion tomorrow for a couple of days. Tell the Sergeant Major I said to fix you up with what you need."

II

The man who saw me off the next morning was a FAC, Captain Estan Rodriguez, known as Rod. In a jeep on his way to a spotter plane, he saw me stumbling along, trying to adjust a black-market ARVN pack I had acquired in Saigon, while balancing the M–16 the Sergeant Major had given me. I asked him for a lift to the olive communications vans that controlled the flow of supplies to the battalions on their temporary jungle hilltop bases.

"You must be going to see how the other half lives," he said, helping me keep my equipment from sliding out of the jeep as he drove. His narrow swarthy face sported a handlebar mustache that put to shame those I had seen in England and Kenya, and I knew from flying with him that he had an extraordinary pair of eyes and a powerful hunting instinct.

"I'll be back in a couple of days," I told him. He wished me luck and let me off in front of an olive van that had a big sign beside it: DRAGOONS—WE TRY HARDER. The men working around the communications van were all wearing the Avis Rent-a-Car orange buttons bearing the same legend, in black: *We Try Harder*.

A tall first lieutenant appeared at the top of the metal steps leading into the steel box.

"I guess you're Mister Flood," he said, looking down at this helmeted civilian who kept dropping and picking up ponchos and rain jackets. "We heard you were coming. I'm just trying to get through to Battalion now."

I wrestled my possessions up the ladder. My shoulders and back were too broad for the Vietnamese pack, so I could only carry it by looping one of its straps over one of my shoulders, and this set the stage for my inability to control the other equipment the Sergeant Major had heaped on me.

The lieutenant was back on his radio. "Be advised you are about to receive a gentleman from the Poppa Romeo Easy Sierra Sierra. Whipcrack is fully aware of this. Shall I put him on the next load, over?"

"This is Charger," a crackling voice said, landing hard on its *r*s. "Send him along. Out."

A jeep drove up. In the back, under guard, were two bareheaded Viet Cong prisoners dressed incongruously in U.S. jungle fatigues with the Fourth Division patch on their shoulders. I was told that they had said they would try to lead our troops to what had been their headquarters. In contrast to the teenaged VC I had seen at Song Cau, these men were in their forties, slight by our standards but stocky for Vietnamese. They gave the impression of being very tough, and unintelligent.

The chopper lowered itself near the van, causing the

usual sandstorm, and the prisoners and their guards were put aboard first. Then came a pile of C-ration cases, some orange bags filled with mail from the States, and me. I sat atop some cases of C rations, and as we went off past Cheop Chai, my M–16 balanced on my knees, I worried alternately about falling out of the chopper from my perch and whether the two VC would make a suicidal break for it and try to take us with them out the door. Staring at them suspiciously, I realized that they were petrified at being in the sky.

We slid in over the crest of a hilltop circled with foxholes and barbed wire, landing in a field of prime gray Phu Yen mud. I slid and splashed my way across what had been a rice paddy, finally picking up a trail of stones that had been the dike separating this paddy from the next. I completed my way to higher ground in a balancing act, my ARVN pack banging my back every lurching step of the way. I passed through a hedge. Before me, on a green slope, were two olive tents that had been rigged so that they made one fair-sized canvas room. A low wall of sandbags surrounded it. A blue metal sign, driven into the earth next to the pulled-back flaps, said DRAGOONS CP, the initials standing for Command Post. Striding out of the gloom with his hand extended toward me was that tall, cold fish of a lieutenant colonel I had seen at the Taj Mahal and Whipcrack's briefing.

Tilt, I thought. This guy and I are just not going to get along.

His handshake was strong. An amused smile played on his thin lips, and he said "Come on over to my tent and we'll get rid of that crazy pack." He ducked back inside the command post tent, re-emerging with a helmet on his head and an M–16 in his hand. With his other hand he took my pack. I followed him across the muddy grass. "Around here," he said in his sharp voice, landing on the *r*s, "you keep your helmet on and your rifle with you when you're outside of a tent. If anything starts, night or day, just get behind the nearest sandbags or into the nearest hole. Particularly at night, if something starts, get in a hole and don't move. Anything that moves around here when something's going on, we shoot at it."

We had arrived at a small olive tent that bore a resemblance to the single-peaked tents of King Arthur, with one pole at its center, the canvas falling from it in six distinct panels, forming a hexagonal base. Outside it was another small metal sign with a background of Infantry light blue and, in white, CHARGER, the call sign of my host, Lieutenant Colonel Thomas Patrick Lynch. He pulled back the tent flap, revealing the center pole, the mud-and-grass floor, and two wood-and-canvas field cots. There was a five-gallon can of water and, at the far end, between the heads of the two beds, a small dark-green table that had on it a few C-ration cans of the same shade, a bottle of Tabasco sauce, and a portable radio captured from the VC.

"You'll be in here with me," Tom Lynch said. He dumped my pack on the empty cot, and I followed him back to the command post tent. Within, men in jungle fatigues and jungle boots sat on gray metal chairs before tables that had radios on them. There was a steady hissing sound from the radios; occasionally someone would speak to a radio or be spoken at by one.

Tom produced a cup of coffee in a plastic cup and settled us down on two metal folding chairs before a map that stood on an easel.

"Shall I start from the beginning?" he asked with a smile.

"Please." There was an explosion; I spilled half my coffee on my fatigues.

"Boy, you'd better get used to that around here," he said with another smile. Another of the cannon I had not seen, sixty yards away, went off, and then another. The sound was a terrific *WHAAM*, shaking the earth and moving the sides of the tent.

Pointing frequently at the map, he educated me. I was now in the TOC, Tactical Operations Center, of the Third Battalion, Eighth United States Infantry Regiment. Once they had been Dragoons, mounted infantry; hence the informal name. The Eighth Infantry Regiment no longer existed as an operating entity, but each of the three infantry battalions in this brigade kept alive the name of one of the battalions of the regiments that had formerly comprised the Fourth Division. The Division had its headquarters well to the northwest of us, at Pleiku; two of its brigades were operating there, and this brigade, the First, was here in Phu Yen. The other two

ground-fighting battalions of this brigade were similar to this
one; their supplies and personnel replacements came forward
from the beach area. Paperwork, most medical attention, and
the Brigade's headquarters were back there; this was a fighting base, known as a Fire Support Base. On this hilltop were
the attached artillery pieces, and the mortars integral to the
battalion, plus varying numbers of infantrymen, the foot
soldiers.

The three rifle companies, of approximately one hundred
and forty foot soldiers apiece, were out in the hills around us.
They were what the Battalion structure existed to support.
These companies were totally mobile; a company would
come in here for a day or two of comparative rest, then it
would move out, totally self-sufficient, the men carrying on
their web harness and in their packs all the food, water, and
ammunition they would need for several days, plus their
entrenching shovels and everything needed to put up their pup
tents and sleep under them. They could be resupplied by
coming back here to the fire base, or they could be resupplied
by finding, or chopping down, an area big enough to let in a
helicopter.

As Tom Lynch spoke, I kept staring at the map before
me. I had heard this referred to as "The Three Hundred and
Sixty Degree War"; now I saw that it was so. In past wars a
battalion such as this would have been on line, a battalion to
its left and one to its right, all facing forward and trying to
move ahead. Behind it would have been roads, a constant
open supply line through territory controlled by our side. In
those past wars, victory was achieved by driving ahead,
battalions side by side, and seizing territory and cities. When
the enemy ran out of territory and cities, the war was over,
and fighting ceased.

By those past standards, we had won this war. The flag
of the Republic of Vietnam fluttered over the capitals of all
forty-four provinces; Allied vehicles and men moved through
their streets. We had in effect secured the conventional
victory, and were in the occupation phase, but the fighting
went on. The old standards of physical possession equaling
victory were not applicable. The enemy was everywhere, in
the jungles or wearing civilian clothes on the streets of
Saigon. He had no intention of massing his guerrillas in

large, visible units and holding trenches or marching down roads. Thus, in the countryside, it was meaningless to drive across a river or capture a crossroads, trying to push back the enemy's front line. He had no front line. Today this battalion might fight northeast of this hill, and tomorrow it might fight to the southwest.

This new kind of warfare had a new kind of scorecard, to which my eyes now shifted. It was a sheet of white cardboard taped to the bottom of the map of this hilly part of Phu Yen. In parallel columns, it listed enemy dead and our dead; our wounded; enemy captured; suspicious persons taken into custody; enemy weapons captured, enemy rice caches discovered. It was for these statistics that we sat on a hilltop, with no road leading out of here, with water, food, and ammunition delivered by helicopters from the coast. With our helicopters, there was no need to keep a road open behind us; with the enemy we were fighting, the only reason to move from one hill to another was to get into a better position from which to hunt men. The whole hilltop base was a gigantic hunting camp. The artillery acted as an umbrella of shells over the company-sized hunting parties that sallied forth into the jungle for days on end.

"If you were operating on flat land," I said, gazing at the infinite number of steep hilltops shown by geodetic rings, coloring, and numbers on the map before us, "how many vehicles would you have at your disposal?"

"I have a hundred and twelve vehicles sitting back at the beach right now," Tom said wistfully. "Right now, not even one jeep would be useful up here."

It was nearing noon. A helicopter hammered in and soldiers pulled off big olive thermal containers holding food that had been cooked back at the coast a few minutes before. I joined the quickly forming chow line, my M–16 slung self-consciously on my shoulder, copying the troops as they kept a five-yard distance between them so that if something came whistling in only a limited number would be hurt. I looked in vain for the metal mess kits and canteen cups of Korean days. At the start of the chow line one picked up a paper plate, a paper cup, and a plastic knife, fork, and spoon.

My plate full, I turned back toward the TOC tent, scarcely noticing the gray mud as I stared at the food. There

was fried chicken in gravy, mashed potatoes, corn, and
stewed tomatoes. A separate compartment of the paper plate
had some corn bread and a dab of butter, and yet another
compartment held ice cream. Someone had shoved an apple
into the breast pocket of my fatigues. My paper cup was
filled with lemonade. I shook my head, thinking of the soup
and sandwiches at the air base. Up here, men slept on the
ground, but when the Army could, it gave you fried chicken
and ice cream.

Back in the TOC, the leisurely atmosphere was gone.
Men move swiftly past the tent flaps; sergeants were appearing.
Tom was on the radio to Brigade. Helicopter gunships had
reported killing ten VC near Cheop Chai; now we were
readying troops to follow up and see what more was in there.

I sat down on the sandbags and started eating quickly. A
sergeant was moving along the holes and pup tents just inside
the barbed-wire perimeter, and boys who were digging, stripped
to the waist, put their shovels down and slipped into their
dirty green jackets. They buckled on their web harnesses that
had ammunition pouches, canteens, and bayonet on the belt,
with two over-the-shoulder straps to distribute the load. Grabbing the rifles and helmets they kept near them while digging,
they were ready to go, and I was not even through my corn
bread, let alone the ice cream. Men came to the map, placed
pencils on it, copied down coordinates, and went back to their
radios. Nobody's voice was raised; it was just that everyone
was on his radio at once.

"You want to come along?" Tom was slipping into his
harness as a man puts on a vest.

"Sure." I wolfed down my corn bread.

"You understand what it is?"

"You're going to put some troops in somewhere."

Tom gave me an oh-what-the-hell look, smiled, and
said, "Come on."

I took one regretful look at the untouched ice cream and
tagged along behind him as he strode through the gray mud to
where the helicopters would come in. For the first time I
glanced at the hand grenades that were fixed on the harness
the Brigade Sergeant Major had signed out to me. I had every
intention of leaving those grenades alone; I just wanted to
make sure that they were not going to catch on something,

pull a pin, and blow me up. I felt silly, but there was something about Tom Lynch's long strides and straight back, as that tall helmeted figure preceded me, that suggested there was one man around here who knew exactly what he was doing.

Three figures were waiting for us in the mud. In front was Captain Paul Titus, the small, slender artillery liaison officer who was the link to whatever heavy firepower the Battalion needed. Behind him, holding between them a crate with a set of radios in it, were the Battalion Sergeant Major and the Pfc. who had been chosen as this week's outstanding soldier. Sergeant Major Hannon was a stooped, wiry man of forty-three with a long, alert, sad face; his protruding jaw was constantly in motion as he chewed a cud of something, and his fatigues, worn almost white, retained an unnatural crispness even in the jungle. The soldier of the week was Raymond Alvarado, a draftee from Los Angeles who had been put in for the Bronze Star as a result of a recent action. Stocky, his masklike Mexican Indian face lit by brilliant teeth and kindly brown eyes, his reward for excellence was to spend a week at the fire base rather than hacking through the jungle with his company.

The chopper whirled us out of there as soon as we had the radio aerials affixed to the side of the craft, and we zipped toward Cheop Chai, passing en route a small fleet of helicopters coming to pick up our infantrymen who were to make the landing.

For me, what ensued was like watching a stunning panoramic film without a sound track. Tom, Paul Titus, and the Sergeant Major all doffed their helmets and put on headsets; Alvarado and I were left to guess what was happening. A combat assault, sometimes called an eagle flight, is the aerial equivalent of sending a landing barge at a hostile beach. As in an amphibious landing, the area to be attacked is frequently softened up by combinations of artillery, fighter strikes, and helicopter gunships before the troop-carrying helicopters arrive. The object is to deposit as many troops as possible in the shortest time, cutting to a minimum the seconds that the choppers and their human cargo are hovering vulnerably above the landing zone.

We did an aerial slalom down a narrow valley that gave

onto the broad paddy-land near the river above the air base. Two helicopter gunships, like ours but with rockets mounted on their landing runners, were circling a knot of farmhouses that had red tile roofs. Baskets and hoes had been thrown aside in the yards; no one was in sight. A gunship darted in like an angry hornet and let go two rockets; I saw a spurt of smoke behind the chopper, and then in the palm trees behind a farmhouse there were twin red flashes and brown smoke.

We circled the area, looping low over trails, trees, the grass slopes on either side of the valley. We swung low over the valley, where a helicopter was sitting with its runners across an earthen dike between two rice paddies. Its rotors were still beating swiftly, and one of the green-uniformed crew was standing a few yards away, calf-deep in mud and water. As we banked, I saw that with one hand he was holding up out of the paddy the limp corpse of a Vietnamese wearing gray-smeared black pajamas; with his other hand he was searching the body. As I watched, the American let the body slide back into the paddy and splashed toward his chopper. The Vietnamese lay face down, his arms and neck as gray as the mud of the paddy, sinking into the water.

One of our pilots was watching Tom while the other flew. With his hands Tom could give signals even faster than by verbal description, and now he motioned to go straight ahead, to a meadow on the far side of the farmhouses. Tom was talking on his headset, Paul Titus was talking to the artillery, the Sergeant Major was talking to someone, and Alvarado was leaning out the door on his side, his rifle ready, his helmet swiveling back and forth as he studied the ground.

Then I saw our helicopters. Violet smoke was beckoning from the far end of the meadow, and four of the troop-carrying choppers, in a diamond formation, whipped in low, slid to a simultaneous sloping stop in the air, and hovered a yard or so above the ground. From their doors green figures began jumping into the grass, some stumbling, others landing smoothly, all running from the choppers toward the outer edges of the field. The effect was of a gradually expanding circle of green-clad men racing away from each craft, as the choppers lifted off, moving forward and away. From my vantage point two hundred feet up it looked mechanical, like animated toy soldiers and pilotless little craft on strings.

Another four choppers slid in right where the first had landed and repeated the performance. The first wave of men was lying behind hedges surrounding the meadow, many of them already invisible. We headed up the valley, spinning around a steep bright shoulder of a hill, and then into another, smaller valley, this one without cultivated fields.

Tom pointed at the slope we were passing, its ridge well above us, and shouted at me "Spider holes!"

I nodded, looking but seeing nothing except a grassy hill. I knew that "spider holes" were the camouflaged holes into which the Viet Cong sometimes dug themselves, but as far as I could see this was just a sunlit upland slope.

Tom was looking out the left side of the craft. He bent over, staring down intently, his head way out over the side as we moved perhaps fifteen feet above the bright grass, and straightened up swiftly. With his right hand he urged the pilot to move us up, out, away. We wheeled again, I losing all sense of direction, and plunged back at the shoulder of the hill as if we were a dive bomber. Tom was yelling at the door gunner who sat just behind him, facing outward and pointing at something. The gunner bent over his machine gun and let go a high-pitched rattle of bullets, the tracers flicking into a big bush which revolved beneath us as we spiraled up. Then we were down the bigger valley, over the paddies again, the farmhouses, and I could see our men moving through the dirt yards and on into the palm trees behind.

We landed back at the hilltop fire base at the same time that some of the infantrymen were being deposited after their sweep through the valley. The sky was dark gray; for an instant, gazing at the sweaty-faced muddy boys relaxing, talking as they headed for their pup tents on the perimeter, I felt the atmosphere of a cold New England dusk, the players coming off the football field, stiff, numb.

Then I saw the Viet Cong. At first I thought he was dead. He was lying on a stretcher beside one of the helicopters that was getting ready to go back to the coast. His skin was as gray as the mud on his shredded black jacket and trousers. He was tall and good-looking. A fresh roll of bandage was around his left thigh, and there were streaks of just-dried blood on his legs, his forearms, and his face. His eyes were barely open.

A GI, his helmet in one hand and his rifle hung loose in the other, looked down at him.

"You're in a world of hurt, aren't you, fella?"

I walked slowly and alone toward Tom's tent. Several of the gunship pilots were standing in front of it, talking animatedly to Tom, who had taken off his helmet and web belt. One was gesturing, his hands showing how he had come in on a pass, where the rockets had hit, what had happened, what he had done next. Tom brought out a bottle of whiskey and plastic cups. Men kept coming over from the TOC. The final score was twelve killed by gunships and ten killed by the infantrymen we had put in, plus some prisoners. One American had broken an ankle.

"Drink?" Tom offered a cup to one of the young warrant officer gunship pilots.

"No thank you, Sir, I don't drink." The pilots kept standing there in the sunset, pink-cheeked and excited.

In the growing dark I sat on the low sandbag wall outside the TOC tent and had my first C-ration meal since a bivouac at Fort Dix in 1953. With all the things that might have been in my head, I was thinking about how much the Army food, both hot and canned, had improved since then. Comparing this can with its Korean War ancestors, which had in 1953 been aging since 1945 or earlier, I hardly noticed when Tom sat down beside me in the dusk.

"You remember when I was leaning way out of the chopper?" he asked. Paul Titus had temporarily shut off his cannon, and he came out of the tent and stood beside us in the gloom.

"Yes," I said, remembering Tom straightening up and gesticulating to the pilot.

Tom turned toward Paul's crew cut and slight body.

"I don't know if I should tell Mister Flood this or not. I kept looking out, seeing something bobbing along in the grass underneath us. Then some dirt flew up, and I realized an automatic weapon was tracking us. That's when I got us the hell out of there."

I looked at Tom, as if he were talking about something that had happened long ago.

"You mean we were getting shot at."

Paul chuckled. "That's affirmative."

III

The next day I landed with Tom in a handkerchief of grass near the top of one of the highest mountains in the area. Our troops were spread through all these thick trees and bushes, many of the green-clad men visible only when they moved.

When the rotor blades stopped, two figures detached themselves from the nearest bushes and moved smartly toward us. This was B Company, on the move, and the swarthy man in the lead was Captain Toby Colburn, its commander. He was from Hawaii—at West Point he had been called "The Royal Pineapple"—and the races in his veins had produced a strikingly handsome lean face, neither Asian nor Caucasian. He moved like a cougar and saluted like a West Pointer.

"Got something I'd like you to see," he said in his husky voice. Behind him, the same height but thicker, was his first sergeant, Gengoro Higa, a Nisei, also from Hawaii. Toby turned and we followed him up an enemy-made trail, across rocks, under low trees that turned noon into evening, over fallen trunks, into an area of interlocking chambers and caves. The top of this mountain was formed by a gigantic pile of huge boulders, each so big and many-angled that they formed crooked vertical and horizontal passages running hundreds of feet in dozens of directions.

As I climbed and slid and climbed again, never seeing the sky because of the vine-hung trees growing up and around and through everything, I thought of the FACs and the fighter planes. The enemy could have been down in this rabbit warren by the hundreds and we would never have seen them from fifty feet, twenty feet, above the trees. And if we had, and had bombed them, the boulders on top, the right-angled stone passages, would have absorbed the blast and the shrapnel. Even napalm would not have splashed very far, nor, with all this cross-ventilation, have pulled the air out and suffocated the enemy. Struggling past the thirtieth of many hundreds of room-sized boulders, I saw that the only way to get the enemy out of here was to come in as B Company had come in, and dig him out.

We emerged in a fern-filled space, a circle within tall trees that felt like a chapel. There were rocks shaped like a Druid throne. Sitting there, looking sick and unhappy, was a Vietnamese in his forties. His face was that of an intellectual who has been outdoors for a while; his hands were not those of a farmer.

Toby pointed at him. "He had a Chieu Hoi pass," he said, referring to the propaganda safe-conduct passes that our psychological warfare planes showered on the jungle. If one came in voluntarily with a pass, one was treated more leniently than if captured. Toby smiled. "He says he was up here looking for someplace to give up."

At that we all smiled, except the Vietnamese.

"It's too late," Tom said. We took the prisoner and made our way back to the chopper. When we got back to our hilltop base the prisoner was placed inside a small circle of barbed wire. His companions in the prisoner-of-war cage were two Vietnamese detainees, sunburned men with calloused hands. They had been without weapons when they were picked up, but they had been far from where any farming could be done.

At dusk when the chopper came in with hot food, on my way to the chow line I detoured to have a look at our prisoners. The Vietnamese from the mountain was squatting before the other two, speaking earnestly.

That evening I told Tom that I had found the last couple of days extremely valuable, and that if it was all right with him I would like to stay a little longer, rather than go back to Brigade and the air base tomorrow, as had been planned.

We were sitting on our cots, which was the only place to sit.

"We're glad to have you," he said in a tone I had not heard before. He pulled out a bottle of Scotch and we began talking. He had entered the Army in 1945, at the age of seventeen; now it was 1967, he was thirty-nine, and a lieutenant colonel.

"I was an enlisted man for six years," he said. Then, for the first and only time that I heard him display overt pride in speaking of himself, "For five of those years I made a stripe a year." When the Korean War was under way, he was commissioned, and fought in Korea.

We spoke of many years and many things, but one memory fascinated me. After World War II he had been assigned for some months in Schenectady, New York, one of a number of soldiers who were staying in the service and who were given the job of returning to families in the area the bodies of their sons who had died in the war. At any time a coffin was in public sight, even changing trains, the American flag had to be draped over it. Sometimes bystanders would try to grab the flag, or spit on it, or hurl insults at the escorting soldier.

"We had an allowance of three dollars and fifty cents a day," Tom told me. "With that we were supposed to get three meals and a bed."

I went to sleep on the hard canvas cot that night, listening to our cannon blasting out at the jungle, thinking about those days and the nation feverishly demobilizing, and the handful of men who had stayed in. Although I had been fifteen when the war ended, and could remember the war perfectly, it was still a shock to me to find that men who had been under arms at the time were real figures, like Whipcrack and Tom Lynch, and not lost in our collective national memory. It all seemed so long ago, P–39s and the young Air Corps cadets with their crushed brown caps and white scarves, and yet that was exactly what Colonel Lewis and Colonel Bill Myers and Frank Buzze and Sully had been. And here they still were, not relics of the past but the flying leaders of a Wing of supersonic jets, climbing into the cockpit for a combat mission every day.

IV

Two afternoons later I went on a Civic Action patrol. The purpose was to hold a rudimentary sick call at the one tiny hamlet in our immediate area, but there was always the possibility of ambush, and we took more bullets than pills. We moved out in a single file of fifteen that included a medic and the Vietnamese interpreter attached to the battalion. We slipped downhill through some bushes, picked up a dry stony stream bed, abandoned it before we came to the turn in it that made a perfect ambush site and crossed a series of abandoned small fields, some of us staying on each side of their hedges. It was my first time out on the ground away from a strongpoint, and I took it seriously, freezing each time the point man raised his hand to stop our strung-out file.

At one point I had yet another demonstration of why we did not see more from the air. One by one the men in front of me stepped through a hedge, turned left, and disappeared. When my turn came I found myself on a double-width path reminiscent of the abandoned roads one finds sometimes in Connecticut, with a waist-high wall of loose stones on each side, and trees and bushes growing from outside the walls to form a tunnel overhead. I could not see the sky; looking to my left, I could not see the men of our patrol, only a few yards off, who had yet to enter the tunnel. The tunnel ran for a quarter of a mile, indistinguishable from the woods through which it passed.

We thrashed through one side of this leafy tube before its end, and crossed another field. The patrol leader pushed some men out to our left, and posted another pair on a small knoll to our right. In an advancing line abreast, the rest of us moved the final hundred meters in to the village.

There were black-clad men and women working in the fields, and some children running about the village. A man spied us and straightened up. As we came on, several men of our patrol moved around the edge of the village and took up positions on its far side, spread out and lying or crouching behind hedges.

Dragoon patrols had been to this hamlet before, and everyone seemed to know what to do. In a minute the population, less than a hundred, were formed under shade trees in the threshing yard of one of the bigger houses, standing and sitting in several rows facing us, as if for a group picture. The setting was an Eden; sparkling meadows, a few palms, eucalyptus trees, a crystal brook, forested slopes, and a quiveringly clear blue sky.

The people were something else. They were ethnic Vietnamese, not *montagnards,* but this isolated mountain pocket paradise had trapped them. There had been too much intermarriage; why the New England parallels struck me in this corner of Phu Yen I do not know, but their faces reminded me of those I used to see in the movie theater on an island in Penobscot Bay, the results of intermarrying generations on the island, and not enough new blood from the mainland. Here, even the faces that appeared normal were atop stunted bodies.

A few of the soldiers were searching the houses as the medic began unpacking a load of soap, pills, and food. I went with the searchers, and what I saw confirmed this sense of a timelessness that was not benevolent, no dream of Shangri-la, but oppressive. There was nothing in the thatch-roofed mud houses that might not have been there in 1400 A.D. The battalion Civic Action officer, who was walking beside me as we moved from house to house, pointed at some C-ration cans in a rubbish hole, distributed there on an earlier patrol.

"See how they opened them?"

I bent down. The small olive cans had been hacked open by something like a machete.

"Didn't you leave them any openers?"

"Of course we did. We showed them how a dozen times. They can't get the hang of it."

I straightened up, perplexed. If that was true, if they really could not or would not use can openers, we really were back a while in time. I stared again at the houses, the mud walls built around a framework of woven reeds, the hard-packed part of the farmyard where threshing was done. Hand-woven baskets, hand-made sickles. There was no road leading out of this village.

Back in the center of the hamlet, the Vietnamese interpreter attached to the Dragoons was engaging in a soft dialogue with the black-clad head man of the village. The interpreter was telling them that this area might become unsafe for them. If they came to a refugee camp along the coast, they would be safer.

The village chief, certainly the most competent-looking of the middle-aged men, asked if they could bring their cattle and their goats and chickens.

Not the cattle and probably not the goats. There would not be room on the kind of helicopters that would take them out.

In that case, the head man said, they would stay.

Listening, I had not the faintest idea of whether the cattle were really the decisive factor or simply a polite way of telling the interpreter that they had no desire to leave.

The Civic Action officer, the medic, and a soldier helping the medic had laid out their wares. There were bandages, pills, and salves for the treatments about to take place, soap to be given to the mothers for their babies, and the final gifts of cigarettes, chewing gum, candy, and C rations, complete with more C-ration openers.

The head man said something more. The interpreter nodded and turned to the Civic Action officer.

"He says thank you for these things."

"Tell him that's okay."

Everyone lined up. In this village, if one did it, all did it. Some of the healthiest came up and pointed perfunctorily at their throats or foreheads. They were given two aspirins, and returned to squat in the main group, satisfied. Others went through glorious pantomines, brilliant finger-motions at the temples expressing flashes and bands of pain, clutches at the stomach indicating conditions that I had no doubt were true.

I turned to the Civic Action officer.

"These are the most run-down people I think I've ever seen anywhere."

He was hurt. "You should have seen them when we started," he said. "We've been building them up with vitamins. They've come a long way since then."

A moment later I blinked. A beautiful woman was coming forward in the shuffling line. Her body was sturdy, her feet were bare, she was in the peasant dress of black cotton trousers and jacket. Beneath her faded straw coolie hat was a face of surpassing beauty, neither intelligent nor stupid, neither thoughtful nor thoughtless. Just sheer sparkling animal beauty.

I stared at her, incapable of turning my head away.

She smiled. As her mouth opened I saw nothing but dark reddish-brown teeth and gums, totally dyed from chewing betel nut.

She laughed at me, a pleasant, inoffensive laugh. After all, I was a funny-looking foreigner.

*   *   *

On our return to the fire base, sweaty and well exercised, most of the patrol settled into pup tents surrounding one that had a pole in front of it. Atop the pole was a human skull, and just beneath it was a miniature red-and-white guidon of the type one sees in Western movies, riding in front of the Cavalry. It was then that I discovered that the alert, silent-moving men in my patrol were of the Reconnaissance platoon, and that they were under the command of the hard-bodied man, stripped to the waist, who was washing out his socks in an upended helmet.

When one says *lieutenant*, an image rises of a youth, glowing with health, perhaps a bit self-conscious and officious, erect in posture and filled with enthusiasm.

First Lieutenant Jack Crumley was close to thirty. He had spent so much time in the dust of three continents on his nation's service that the dirt seemed literally to have mixed with his skin. His hair was brown, his skin was gray-beige. He sat before his pup tent, beneath the guidon with its skull, like a special satyr found somewhere in the pantheon of the gods of war. With his serene manner, his wisecracks, his muscled forearms moving as he washed his socks in his helmet, it was impossible that Jack had not been sitting on this slope in Asia since the beginning of time.

He started telling me stories. He had been in and out of the Army since he was eighteen. He would make it up to sergeant and say to hell with it and get out and drive a caterpillar tractor in Alaska and the next time he saw a recruiting sergeant it was like a bar for an alcoholic and there he would be, back in again. He had come out here as a helicopter gunner in 1962, when it was the small, unpublicized, advisors' war. One day his troop-laden helicopter had been shot down deep in the jungle, killing or wounding everyone but him. The nearest helicopter, already laden with troops, dropped in and had just room to take out the wounded, leaving Jack alone with some corpses. He shrugged his shoulders and disappeared into the jungle. In a few hours he was captured by four Viet Cong, who kept him with them as they moved many miles a day. During one afternoon siesta he saw that the Viet Cong nearest him was industriously making *punji* stakes, the foot-impaling wooden spikes made to be hidden in leaf-covered holes on the trails. Jack rolled over from his sleeping position, grabbed a *punji* stake, stabbed the Viet Cong through the stomach, darted beyond him to a tree against which a carbine was leaning, shot another Viet Cong, and disappeared.

"They didn't follow me," he said, not looking up from his rhythmic washing of the green-slime-encrusted socks. After a week of wandering through the jungle, eating two snakes en route, he emerged in a clearing outside a Vietnamese government outpost. He waved at the sentries behind their barbed wire; they waved their arms in return. As he dazedly made his way across the grass toward the camp, he noticed that there seemed to be more and more arm-waving and shouting, and he waved back appreciatively, glad that they were so pleased to see him. When he got inside the camp, he discovered he had walked through a live minefield.

When that tour in Vietnam ended, he decided to be a little more serious about the Army. He went to Infantry Officer Candidate School at Fort Benning, and emerged number one in a class of one hundred and sixty-four starters.

Thus Jack Crumley, and the air of confidence in himself and his ability to command. From his lips there came a torrent of praise for his men. The Fourth Division, he pointed out, was an outfit without glamour, straight-leg Infantry, eighty per cent draftee. The other outfits—paratroopers, Marines, the crack First Infantry and First Cavalry Divisions—all had arrived with fanfare and Public Information Officers working overtime. The Fourth Division just came ashore and went to work in the nasty bush-whacking aspect of the war, and the high school dropouts, the poor boys of all races who had not wanted to be here, were fighting as well as the outfits laden with volunteers.

"This battalion came over here with one hundred and fifty men and six hundred and fifty boys," he said. "Now we have eight hundred men." Jack put away the socks and started chipping the dried mud from his boots. The impression, he said, was that the American juggernaut was just tearing Vietnam apart, rolling around the country recklessly and at will. I could see for myself that nothing was going to roll through these jungles. Often it came down to hand-to-hand. His platoon was Reconnaissance, its job to scout rather than fight, but sometimes you stumbled on something and there you were. One day he had found himself in an idiotic position; he was holding onto the foot of a Viet Cong who was trying to escape through the bushes. "All I could see was the foot." Another day one of his men had thrown a body-block on him from the side, knocking him down and bayonet-ing a VC who had just been raising a rifle at him from a hole in the deep brush. One of his friends, Lieutenant O'Brien, had been at the head of a platoon when one shot had been fired at O'Brien from an old Mauser rifle. The bullet went into O'Brien's left breast, tunneling through the flesh between his skin and his ribs, and came out under his shoulder blade, flying on to break the arm of the next man in the file.

"That was the entire engagement," Crumley said, shaking his head. "One bullet. We never saw the VC. We never caught up to him."

Talking without emotion, he told of how men's attitudes had hardened. One night a man in another battalion had heard a friend of his, who had been captured near the base of Cheop Chai in a dusk ambush, pleading for mercy.

"Please don't kill me!" the boy had cried.

They had killed him, and left the body for dawn.

"The story got around," Jack said. Now one of the companies in this battalion carried a supply of Fourth Division shoulder patches. When they killed a Viet Cong they left him prominently displayed, with a Fourth Division patch in his mouth as a calling card. One day they had killed two young men near the edge of a village, taken their weapons, and left them there with patches in their mouths. The following morning they had come back through the village. A woman had been kneeling beside the two bodies, moaning, chanting, wailing. When the American file walked past she screamed at them, she waved her fists. Every man went past silently, until the last young American in the line. He looked at her and said, "Shut up, bitch, or I'll kill you too." She became silent and he walked on.

"One of my men got upset when one of his buddies was wounded and evacuated back to the States," Crumley told me as he put on his faded jungle shirt. "He said the next VC he got a hold of, he was going to put a bayonet up his ass. A couple of days after that we got into something and this kid didn't use his rifle. He sneaked way around behind the VC and came up behind one who was shooting at us. He didn't get the bayonet up his ass, but he got him through both kidneys.''

I asked Jack if his men sometimes fought among themselves.

"Not inside the platoon," he answered, and then, his face softer, he told me what had happened Christmas Eve, while I had been having highballs in the Taj Mahal. The battalion had been back in base camp along the beach, brought in from the field after fifty-seven straight days in the jungle.

"They had steaks for dinner in the mess tent, and my men were in no mood to be hurried. Some of the guys from one of the line companies came in, there were a lot of them, and they pushed my people out before they were ready to go.'' Jack shook his head. "So my guys got some smoke grenades and went back to the mess tent and tossed them in. When the other guys came staggering out, my guys were waiting by the tent flap, and they knocked them silly, one by one." He grinned. "I wasn't there, but I heard about it pretty quick. Nobody got really hurt.''

That evening Tom Lynch and his Soldier of the Week were talking outside his tent, standing under the stars. Alvarado wanted two things, to ride in a FAC plane, and an emergency leave to go home to Los Angeles and see his wife, who was expecting a baby. Tom had promised him the ride in the FAC plane, and now they were discussing the leave.

"I'll let you have it when the baby comes," Tom said quietly. "If I let you go now, your leave might be up and the baby still might not have come." He put his hand on Alvarado's shoulder. "Babies come when they come. I've been through it five times. When she needs you is when the baby is there. And this way you get to see the baby.''

Tom went back into his tent, and I talked with Alvarado in the clear night. He told me what it was like, being point man as the platoon moved through the jungle.

"When it happens, it's all over in a few seconds. These guys are so quick—if you don't get them right then, you'll never get them. They say we should chase them and catch them—you can't catch them.''

We talked about home, and he spoke of his wife.

"She was always my girl," he said. The stars were bright.

V

The water was freezing, but it felt good. It was my last afternoon on this hilltop with the Dragoons, and despite washing as best I could in Tom's green plastic wash basin, I still felt dirty. Sergeant Major Hannon had told me there was a shower off at one end of the hilltop, and so there was. A spring came out of some rocks, and someone had split a big bamboo, knocked out its inner sections, and made an elevated pipe that poured a constant trickle from a point five feet in the air. It felt marvelous.

As I stood under it, soaping myself, a company came in from the jungle for their turn at the fire base. I had hefted the packs these men were carrying, so I knew what I was seeing. A fully loaded Dragoon had his poncho and poncho liner, which was what he used to make his bed on the ground, and the shelter half which, with another man's, was used to make a pup tent overhead. He carried extra socks, but what loaded him down was food and ammunition. Because no one knew when conditions, combat or weather, would make it impossible to resupply him by helicopter, he was supposed to carry nine C-ration meals. This involved twenty-seven small cans of food, and he carried at least two hundred rounds of spare ammunition, which could be burned up in a few minutes in a severe firefight. Additionally he would carry a few pounds of C–4, the blasting material used to fell trees. Every infantryman carried at least three canteens filled with water, and there were the personal items, such as Bibles, writing paper, and a bottle of Tabasco sauce to liven up the C rations. Complete with his first-aid kit, entrenching shovel, the standard pouches of ammunition and the grenades on his web harness, his load weighed seventy pounds, in addition to which he was carrying a rifle and moving along under a helmet.

The boys coming in looked dead-tired and glad to be in the relative comfort and safety of this hilltop. Few of them wore shorts under their fatigue pants, and the thorny underbrush of Phu Yen had slashed their trousers to ribbons. Some slogged past in trousers that had been reduced to ragged shorts, their bare legs a mass of scratches, welts, and jungle sores. The abbreviated trousers of others were ripped vertically as well, right up to their belts. Despite what I was seeing, it was still hard for me to believe that a citizen of the world's richest nation would be reduced to a state in which he was walking along in such rags that his genitals were exposed, but the young troopers were oblivious of how they looked, wanting only a hot meal, possibly a couple of cans of beer, and sleep.

On my way back to Tom's tent, my fatigues still dirty but my skin clean, I stopped by some lean-tos that were off by themselves on the slope above the TOC tent. This was the home of the LURP, the Long Range Reconnaissance Patrol, who were different from and a smaller unit than Crumley's Reconnaissance Platoon. They were moving about, packing their special small knapsacks with great care, and I asked them what they were doing.

"Goin' out for a few days," said a tall, blond boy who was wearing a camouflage cap with a floppy brim. He had an old German Iron Cross fixed to his cap, a relic of the days when he had been a surfer at Malibu and read *Mein Kampf* on the beach. I looked around. The Lurps were strictly a volunteer squad, and their dress and equipment was highly individual. One wore a black beret; another carried a machete. None wore helmets. Their lives depended on stealth. Slipping through the jungle, their mission was to give periodic whispered radio reports on what they had and had not found. If they got into trouble, a hurried "emergency extraction" by helicopter would be called for. They were to use their weapons only as a last resort, if trapped.

I asked one stocky boy with the look of an American Indian why he had volunteered for the Lurps.

He looked embarrassed and amused.

"Well, to tell you the truth, Sir, I got so tired of walking around under that helmet——"

The sun went down behind one of the steep forested hills west of the fire base. In the shadows, the Lurp leader gathered his men around him in a small, intent circle and briefed them a final time. Talking in a Kentucky hills voice, he told them that for tonight they would just slip out a couple of thousand meters and lie low until dawn.

"Any questions?"

No questions. Without a word they rose and started single file, a few meters apart, down a trail that led through the barbed wire, along a hedge by a meadow, and into the darkening forest. Going over the edge of the slope, one of them gave me a friendly wave.

VI

Two days later I was at the air base, looking at a glossy photograph of a road in Laos. The bombing mission I was going on was after a suspected truck park in the forest beside this dirt road, part of what was known as the Ho Chi Minh Trail. Until now my missions had been only within Vietnam; for these we used maps, and sometimes a relief map of the target area. But these photographs were marvelous, conveying to the pilots a far better idea of what the target area would look like when they saw it. For an instant I remembered my orientation tour of Shaw Air Force Base in South Carolina, staring at all sorts of photographs taken from many thousands of feet up. At the time I had grasped what a good technical feat this was, but it had taken some firsthand staring at the sameness of the jungle when approached at five hundred miles an hour to show me the advantages of anything that could familiarize one with how a certain patch of jungle was going to look.

After the weather briefing, the Intelligence officer had a few words to say, but his map of Laos was more eloquent than he. In the Intelligence portion of briefings for missions within South Vietnam we were always advised that there was a Special Forces Camp thirty miles southwest of the target area, or a District Headquarters twelve miles east, or some friendly force toward which we should head if we were shot down.

The map of Laos was not so equipped. The best the Intelligence officer could do was to suggest that some places were less filled with North Vietnamese and Pathet Lao than other places. Our target was in the vicinity of Tchepone, where the North Vietnamese had 37-millimeter and 57-millimeter automatic antiaircraft guns. The first two planes in the flight were carrying the bombs that would try to hit the truck park; the plane in which I was riding, an old 951F in which I had

North Vietnamese 37 mm AA

flown from Hawaii to Guam, was carrying dispensers containing hundreds of the little bomblets I had first seen that sunny, peaceful day in Florida. If the rapid-firing cannon opened up on our flight, my pilot's job was to zip in low and level and drop these bomblets all over the antiaircraft guns and gunners.

We took off, joined up, and headed northwest. The mountains rose, a new station I had never heard before came on the air with instructions for us, and we were on our way out of Vietnam.

I am one of those people who is surprised, when flying from one country to another, to find that there is not a big red stripe on the ground marking the border. There was no big red stripe, but Laos *did* look different. Coming toward the border we had been flying over steadily steeper green mountains, but inside Laos it was high plateau country, much of it brown with trees in clumps, curving strands scattered thickly across it. There were several well-defined roads, but there was a strange mist on the ground.

We spotted the FAC flying around near the bend in a river, and I found myself fondly shaking my head as I looked down at the little toylike plane. Here he was in the presence of known automatic-firing antiaircraft cannon, gliding around as low as his colleagues inside South Vietnam. His voice came on the air, cheerful and excited. He had just seen a truck down there, under the trees. What ordnance did we have?

Flight lead told him that Numbers One and Two were

carrying four seven-hundred-and-fifty-pound bombs apiece and that Three would hold with canisters of bomblets, if needed.

"Beautiful!" the FAC exclaimed on hearing what we had brought for him. He told us the antiaircraft guns were about two thousand meters away, on the other side of a ridge, so they would have only a limited shot at us, and we could cut down even that by the headings on which we bombed and turned.

We went at it. The FAC darted down over the main road, across a tiny sandy road branching off it, and the white smoke from his aiming rocket rose from trees that seemed to hold nothing more than the acres of woods all around. Number One plummeted in, let go two seven-fifties, and pulled off. Two flashes in the trees; otherwise nothing. I kept staring down from where we were making a wide turn high above the target area.

Number Two went down the chute, twitching back and forth, then straightening out, bombs off, Number Two just past the target, up into the sky. His bombs flashed and then came a huge boiling up of smoke, a spurting column of lead-gray. It rose, it rose, it went two thousand feet in the air.

The FAC was ecstatic. "There was a truck there thirty seconds ago and it's not there now—I'll give you one truck right now!"

Number One was back in, into the smoke, through the smoke, dropping his bombs.

Just then I saw something new to me. Feathery white streaks were ripping past me, off and above the right wing.

"Say," I said to the pilot, "you see anything off to the right just then?"

"No."

I shrugged my shoulders. Number Two was in and out. It was over.

"I think it was a fuel truck or an ammunition truck," the FAC said as he putted through the smoke to take a closer look. The column was diffusing, a ghostly gray pillar. He became more formal, gave us time on target, time off, hundred-per-cent target coverage, hundred-per-cent target destruction, and then added gaily, referring to the antiaircraft, "Sorry I couldn't wake that Thirty-Seven up for you."

I was not so sure that the Thirty-Seven had been asleep.

NINE

"One may be starving on one's father's birthday," a Vietnamese adage says, "but one is always full during Tet."

Saigon was happy. There was a truce, and in contrast to some other years, both sides were keeping it. The Vietnamese people could get on with the celebration of their one towering national holiday.

I checked into the Continental-Palace, Room 22, and rapidly encountered my first manifestation of the lunar New Year festivities; no laundry service. Buying some soap powder at the nearby Exchange, I laundered a drip-dry shirt, a pair of shorts, a T shirt, and some socks, and hung them to dry on the crutches in the corner.

For the foreigner looking for religious processions or public events, Tet is a disappointment. It is essentially a family matter, celebrated in the home. It is as if Thanksgiving, Christmas, our New Year, and Easter were combined, with every member of the family making extraordinary efforts to be home for the few days of reunion.

On the first day of the New Year, the family, in new and handsome clothes, prostrate themselves before their Buddhist family altar to welcome the spirits of their ancestors, who they believe have returned to be with them for Tet. Then, as in Chinese tradition, the children kowtow before their parents, wishing them health and prosperity in the coming year. Gifts are exchanged.

Then comes the first visitor of the day. Since the health, wealth, and prestige of the first visitor to set foot in the house on New Year's morning are believed to attach to the house through the year, the identity of the first caller is not left to

106

chance. Many a well-regarded Vietnamese spends his entire New Year's morning being the first visitor in one house after another. It is only after noon that every house is open to all the family's friends, and a great round of visiting begins. Traditionally the visiting and giving of presents goes on for two days, but the general air of gaiety and the wearing of one's best clothes continues for a week. No one works, not even the housewife in her kitchen, for she has done her cooking before Tet, so that she will not chance breaking a dish and bringing a year's ill-fortune upon her family.

I first caught up with Tet on Le Loi Street, a wide boulevard in the French style running from the City Hall to the river. The dozen or so flower stalls permanently there had been supplemented by two hundred temporary ones. The boulevard was closed to vehicles. For five blocks it was an outdoor display of flowers, most of them potted plants in bloom. Crowds of Vietnamese women in their best *ao dai*, colors of the flowing skirts vying with the flowers, their men in uniform beside them, promenaded the aisles between flower stalls, admiring the fantastic orchids and violets of their tropical land. Wandering through the panorama of bloom, I found that even cactus were on display, with the Chinese character for longevity carved through them. Everyone bought some kind of plant to beautify their freshly painted houses for the imminent New Year.

I strolled the block back to the Continental-Palace and had dinner with some AP friends and a three-man crew from BBC Television, just out from London to do a series of short features on Vietnam. After dinner we sat drinking on the terrace overlooking the square. Now that the wartime firing had stopped in this truce, a rattle of New Year's firecrackers was heard through the city. Urchins stuck dirty arms over the whitewashed low sill of the terrace, holding out enormous firecrackers and asking us to buy.

Someone told a story that there had been an investigation of why a Vietnamese artillery battery had fired so many short rounds, dropping them on their own men far short of the target, and it had been discovered that the commander had been cutting down on the powder charges and selling the powder to be made into firecrackers for Tet.

"Charles," one of the Englishmen said, his voice

marvelously sane amid the firecrackers and the Vietnamese children's piaster-begging cries of "You give me five P!", "we *do* want to do something on the Air Force. Do you think your place—uh, Tuy Hoa—might be suitable?"

"Hell, yes," I said, all enthusiasm for my place, my outfit, my friends, thereby releasing a chain of funny and less-funny incidents that would occur some weeks later on.

Late the afternoon of the day I was to go to the house of Peter Arnett's sister-in-law Miriam for a celebration of Tet, I decided to spend the empty hour before me by going to the Five O'Clock Follies. This institution, not always held at five, was the daily briefing for the correspondents of all nations.

I went into the big concrete Joint United States Public Affairs Office and entered a handsome air-conditioned auditorium, sitting in a movie-theater seat just off the aisle sloping down to the stage.

The correspondents came wandering in. Most were young, many very young. Some wore sports shirts and slacks, as I did. A few affected a tailored set of beige slacks and matching safari shirt. Half a dozen were in fatigues and boots, including a couple of girls in their twenties who looked as if they might be promising material for psychiatric study.

From the wings appeared a portly American, wearing a tie and lightweight sports coat, who stepped to the lectern. His job was to talk about American civilian activities in such fields as disease prevention and refugee work. He was clearly the curtain-raiser and was listened to in good-natured boredom. In the meantime, the back of the theater was filling with officers of the various services, who I later learned were Information officers there to see to it that their branches of service were not maligned, misrepresented, or under-represented.

The sacrificial lamb appeared; he happened to be a Marine Corps lieutenant colonel. On a map of Vietnam thrown on a screen by a projector, he pointed to places where the truce had been violated by the Viet Cong in the past twenty-four hours, describing the incidents. He was interrupted constantly for amplification of his remarks.

After a few minutes I began feeling sorry for him, sorry for the correspondents, and sorry for the world. It was from this room and this daily meeting that the world's headlines and radio reports and television newscasts were formed. Considering the gravity of the Vietnam situation, one would have expected the armed services to have a top-flight man representing their activities. One would certainly have expected the Saigon press corps to be outstanding.

It was clear that neither was true. The briefing officer was a pleasant person, patient, obviously disliking this job and wanting to command a battalion rather than do this. Most of the time his attitude seemed to be "I've told you everything that *I*'ve been told"; it had evidently not occurred to him to check back on anything for amplification or clarification; he was handed something and told to go out there and brief it, and that's what he did, like taking a hill, like taking an order.

I found the correspondents' questions as inadequate as the officer's briefing. Half of them either had hearing trouble or a real inability to concentrate; there were constant amateurish requests for him to repeat what he had said slowly at almost parade-ground volume. There was a bearded show-off who asked a question so that he could demonstrate that he had recently been to a certain place himself. I had no doubt that the bigger organizations were not sending their best men to cover this, but the fact remained that this was where everybody's wrap-up story of the day was coming from. The general attitude among the reporters was one of superiority to the briefing officer, and I had the feeling that it was an attitude of superiority to the military as a whole. Most of the faces in the audience looked pleased with themselves; they were young, it was an adventure, they had been shot at and not run away, and it was the best consistent news story in the world. From my truly veteran AP friends, I knew that virtually none of them spoke Vietnamese.

They finally let the Marine retreat, and an Air Force officer took the stage. Fortunately for him, his job was shorter, since it was Tet and no bombing missions were being flown, north or south. He told us that from the reports of reconnaissance planes it had been determined that the North Vietnamese had their trucks lined up bumper to bumper on the eve of the Tet truce, ready to pour them south in the bomb-free days to resupply their forces in Laos and South

Vietnam. On the basis of photographs taken of trucks and sampans, it was estimated that now, halfway through the truce, they were in the process of moving thirty-five thousand tons of supplies.

I found this fascinating, in view of the world-wide speculation that this truce might be continued indefinitely. It did not sound like an enemy who was planning to pause for even a moment, or to reduce his efforts. I waited for questions on this central piece of real news, from all these correspondents who had been so eager to pin down the Marine officer as to whether it had been a truck or a bus that had hit the VC land mine outside Danang. No questions came. None. The Follies were over for another day.

We arrived in the driveway of the handsome white house of Peter Arnett's in-laws—Peter, Hugh Mulligan, the AP feature writer whom I had last seen leading satirical songs on New Year's Eve, a publisher from Pennsylvania, and I. We crossed the pretty yellow-tiled terrace and entered a large white living room. In the tropical and Asian way, its glossy floor was without rugs, and the furniture was handsome but sparse.

Peter introduced me to his father-in-law, a tiny white-haired gentleman with beautiful Mandarin hands who was wearing a gray silk suit that was the best piece of tailoring I had seen in Vietnam. He had been born in North Vietnam, and brought his family south after the Viet Minh victory in 1954. Sensitive, scholarly, affluent, and apolitical, he bore no resemblance to the Vietnam I had been seeing.

Two more guests arrived; a young German who was the first mate of the German hospital ship *Heligoland,* which was moored in the river not far from the flower market, and a Vietnamese Army captain in civilian clothes.

The girls entered, Peter's wife Nina first, her two unmarried sisters behind. They were wearing *ao dai,* looked ravishing, and knew it. Some Westerners say that Asian women giggle; it may be, but to my ears it is like the chirp of a bird having an awfully good time. In any event, giggling or chirping, they gave us each a small red envelope with Chinese characters printed on it in gold and a small sum of Vietnamese money within.

We sat at a teak table to play a card game on the order of Blackjack. Like Western cards, the backs of the cards are identical. The suit is determined by a Chinese character on the face of the card, and there is an arabic numeral in one corner, with the cards of each suit going from one to ten.

One was dealt a card, which he picked up without showing to others. The idea was to come as close to ten as possible without going over. Thus, if dealt a seven, there was an interesting decision to make. Even if one gambled on a second card and drew a three, if someone else had a ten total in which more of the points were in cards of a higher suit, he could still lose.

Since none of us Westerners could keep track of the Chinese characters for the suits, we all played to get as close to ten as possible, and then, when no one wanted any more cards, I would show mine to Miriam, Peter would show his to Nina, each American would consult with a Vietnamese, and we would be told who had won. The winner cries "Bop!" and the cards are shuffled and dealt again. We played for twenty piasters a hand, worth about seven cents at the black-market rate or six at the official. After twenty minutes the publisher from Pennsylvania said in a mock-suspicious voice: "Has a non-Vietnamese won yet?"

No non-Vietnamese had, and amid laughter we went ahead for a few more hands.

Then food was served. There were glutinous brown-tinted rice balls with a sticky center of bean-curd paste, and after that watermelon. In deference to our Western tastes, the next things to appear were bottles of Scotch. Two drinks, more pleasant chatter, and we were in the driveway under a velvet night. Hanging from the branch of a tree was a long string of firecrackers, every tenth one bigger than its neighbors. Someone lit the string and we stood smiling as the New Year's popping and banging went on for the better part of a minute.

"It sounds just like a firefight," Peter observed. "The lighter ones for the small arms, the bigger ones for the grenades."

I shook hands with Miriam and got into Peter's car. Nina leaned in the window and started giving Peter very explicit directions on how to drive us back to the center of town. At first I thought it was some sort of security measure, but then I realized this was a matter of astrology—we were to go in such a way that, except for a moment turning one traffic circle, at no point would we be headed west.

"It's like sailing a boat," Peter quipped, and off we drove into Vietnam's New Year.

TEN

Tet and its truce ended on a Saturday night, and combat missions resumed at Tuy Hoa. I was scheduled to fly on Sunday afternoon in the back seat behind a captain I shall call Jones, the briefing to be at one-fifteen.

Each of the three squadrons was now housed in big new buildings that looked like corrugated iron barns. At one-fifteen I opened the green metal door of the 306th and walked down a corridor between plywood partitions to a small briefing room where I was supposed to begin the routine I had now been through on ten missions.

The major in charge of the flight was already talking to the other two pilots, neither of whom was Jones. They looked up to see what I wanted.

"Where's Captain Jones?"

"He's not here," one of the pilots said in an odd tone; they turned away and the briefing went on. I backed into the hall and went to the room containing the squadron operations blackboard, which told the story. Jones had been switched to fly earlier in the day. The last that had been seen of him was as a big tumbling ball of fire over the target area, complete with one wing coming off. He was dead and I was alive.

I walked the half-mile back to my hooch. This was the first pilot we had lost at Tuy Hoa, a tall fair-haired man, courteous and soft-spoken. I knew him less well than a number of others, but for some reason I knew he had a wife and two children.

As I walked, it was just another gray afternoon at Tuy Hoa. Yellow earth-moving machinery roared past, the bearded American civilian workers halfway to the sky on small

113

vibrating seats; from the sky, the whistle-whoosh of a flight coming back from a mission. The base, flat; Cheop Chai massive in the distance.

The news of this death was hitting me not as it would an observer but as a member of the Wing. The reaction was on a nonreasoning plane, and it continued as I deliberately busied myself about the hooch. It was a physical depression, as if I had been struck in health and pride and dignity. It was a sickness, not nausea, but a diminution of the ability to concentrate—a loss of energy.

The club was quiet that night, with only a few men playing cards. No one spoke of what had happened. By the next day, when I did go on a mission, every trace of that pilot had been removed—his name scrubbed from the squadron board, his mailbox empty and nameless, his possessions packed and on the way home.

For some reason, I understood. In the strange impersonality of aerial warfare, where a man slept between sheets, took a shower, had scrambled eggs for breakfast, then took off and never came back—the place to leave his memory was out there, where it had happened. It was the only way to go on.

Two days after our first loss, I was in a panel truck with Special Stud, going out to see a remarkable sight. One of the 309th pilots had taken a hit through his engine coming off the target on a mission to the south of us. Flanked by the other two members of his flight, he had nursed the plane back up the coast. He was just over the base when the engine froze. Aiming the plane for the least-populated corner of the base, he steered it down to the lowest altitude at which he could still eject, punched out of the plane, and landed by parachute just on the friendly side of the barbed wire.

When we got out to this sandy area by the perimeter there were all sorts of people swarming about in official and unofficial capacities. The pilot had been taken to the dispensary to make sure he had broken nothing. In its last seconds of flight, the Supersabre had just cleared the tents of an Army detachment that ran a ration-storage point; the Army boys were standing around, staring at the wreck, gripping their limbs to make sure they were still alive. The young pilot, professional right to the end, had shut off everything in the plane that could ignite the little fuel he had not consumed or jettisoned, so the wreck was free of the sickening black stains I had seen at Homestead.

"You know," Special Stud said quietly as we walked back to the panel truck, "this is what we get for having a truce last week and letting the enemy load up their guns." I nodded, and we drove on around the runway and went to the post office. As the wreck receded our spirits brightened, and Stud reverted to his favorite topic: women. One way and another, the Wing was managing to get its pilots a few days off once every six weeks, and he had just hitched a ride up to Taiwan for a few days. Where other men might hire a girl for a week or try a different girl every night, using the bars and hotels of Peitou, the hot-spring resort outside Taipei, Stud had worked it out differently. He had made friends with four hostesses in a bar who shared an apartment and moved right in with them. As we drove along, he handed me excellent color snapshots showing them all horsing around during the daytime, off for a picnic, sightseeing. In others they were all sitting around the pleasantly furnished apartment. The girls looked young, pretty, and easily amused. In the evenings the girls went off to their bar to flatter men into buying them as many drinks as possible, but who was waiting up for them when they got home? Uncle Stud.

I smiled. He was a dedicated man. The pilots had been moved out of tents and into a new shipment of trailers like my own. In his, which he shared with a pilot who could scarcely believe it, he had a zebra skin on the wall, black silk sheets and pillow slip under the regulation US-marked brown blanket on his bed, and a splendid collection of sex books—some clinical, some pornographic.

We went to our respective boxes at the post office. He found a slip telling him to pick up a package at the window. It was a book from one of the several book clubs, some conventional and some offbeat, to which he belonged.

When we got back into the cab of the truck he ripped open the wrapping of this month's selection from a book club which occasionally had sent him something right up his alley.

Out came a volume: *The Infinite Varieties of Music*.

"Oh, *shit!*" he said, and we drove on. He dropped me

off in front of the club, and I walked in. I was barely inside
the door when there was a terrific clang of the bell by the bar.
I put my hand to my head, not believing that I could have
walked in again with my cap on.

It had nothing to do with me. Behind me had entered
young First Lieutenant Wilson Heppler, of High Point, North
Carolina, whose crashed plane I had just seen. He was out of
the dispensary. Short, black crew-cut, grinning from ear to
ear, glad to be alive, he rang the bell as everyone smiled and
cheered.

"Just keep setting 'em up," he said to the bartender,
"as long as anybody's left standing." Men crowded around
him, shaking his hand and patting his back.

The following day I came out of the railroad-car dining
hall, so anesthetized to soup and sandwiches that I could not
have told, if my life depended on it, what sort of soup and
sandwich I had just swallowed.

Chuck Fulton was sitting behind the wheel of a panel
truck. On its side was the cheerful 309th squadron insignia,
one of Walt Disney's designs for combat units. This was an
avenging Donald Duck, a bolt of lightning in one hand and a
board with a nail through it in the other, zipping splay-footed
through the sky.

"You want to hear something that'll get your attention?"
Chuck beckoned me toward the truck, his hazel eyes glinting
with excitement and concern. "Colonel Buzze just punched
out over Laos."

I had been heading toward my hooch, to catch up on my
notes of Tet in Saigon and the one man and two planes we
had lost in the past four days. Instead I climbed into the front
seat and drove down to the flight line with Chuck.

The Wing Command Post had moved from its sand-
blasted tent to a large room in the back of the 309th squadron
building. As at Homestead, there were big boards along the
wall. In front of these lists of pilots and planes there ran a
long desk at which sat the duty officers and sergeants,
manning telephones and radios that could reach everything,
from our own planes in the air to the Saigon headquarters of
Seventh Air Force, which ran the air war in Southeast Asia.

The only indication of something extraordinary was that

all my colonel friends were sitting at a table a few yards from
the desk, all except red-faced, black-haired Frank Buzze, who
was down with his parachute in the mountainous jungle of
Laos. Colonel Lewis sat there in gray flying suit, his green
fatigue cap pulled down over his eyes, his slim legs crossed,
leaning back so that the two front legs of his chair were off
the floor. His face was composed but stricken. Next to him
was Colonel Bill Myers, who always made me think of
substituting "grizzled air dog" for "grizzled sea dog," his
close-cropped hair gray, a pipe in his hand, engineer boots
protruding beneath the legs of his flying suit. Sully had risen
and was standing by one of the men working the telephones,
his short frame erect and braced, as if *willing* Frank to be
alive, not captured, and somehow, somehow to be returned to
us.

Intelligence had spread on the table the aerial photographs of the target area. A 37-millimeter had opened up on
Frank after he had finished dropping his bombs, and he had
whirled his plane around and driven back in, shooting it out
with the bigger gun, using his four 20-millimeter cannon. No
one knew if it was the cannon he was dueling or another, but
something had torn into his plane, it had caught fire, and then
he had just seconds to get out. His parachute had disappeared
in a jungle that erupted with cannon and small-arms fire
aimed at the FAC and the other two planes in the flight. That
had happened an hour ago, and there was no further word
available through any of our telephones. Rescue attempts by
helicopter were under way; that was all we knew.

I poured myself a cup of coffee. As the word got around,
more officers were appearing in the command post. It was
hard to believe that Frank Buzze had been shot down. Like
Colonel Lewis, like Sully, there had been about him an aura
of success, experience, skill, and luck. When Frank walked
into the bar and shouted "Is there a fighter pilot in the
house!" and was answered with a chorus of cheers and
affirmative yells, it was because they knew he was the real
thing, four Zeros knocked down in the big war and all kinds
of hits taken in the Korean War. As Deputy for Operations,
Frank was not only involved in scheduling and tactics and
every aspect of flying; he was the Dean of Men. It placed him
in a special relationship to the pilots. It was up to him to spot

the man who might be labeled qualified but was not, up to him to spot the glory-grabber or the infrequent shirker; up to him to "hire and fire," as he said he would, and had.

We were in a high-ceilinged room in Vietnam, but I remembered Frank at a good-bye party one night at Homestead, Frank and his red-headed wife Wylene dancing one of the latest dances, Frank in a wild, handsome jacket with a big blue Paisley design. In the Taj Mahal he had played me some tapes, sent instead of letters, from their one son, Buzz, who was graduating from the Citadel this coming June. He would receive his commission in the Air Force and had been accepted for pilot training.

"Another fighter pilot," Frank had said with quiet satisfaction.

I stood beside Sully for a minute. As Frank's deputy in operations, and as an old friend, Sully had been very close to him. It was the first time that I had seen Sully under stress; all the stability and poise promised by those broad shoulders, cocky walk, and friendly smile were now being delivered. He was overseeing the rest of our missions, paying as much attention to weather and landing conditions as two hours before, and still directing our telephone search for news of Frank.

At times Colonel Lewis would walk over, take one of the telephones, and call Danang, one hundred and forty miles north of us, to find out if they had any news through their channels. They said no, but they were working on it.

"Sure appreciate it." Colonel Lewis hung up, his face a mixture of hope, grief, and determination. "I can't understand what's taking so long," he said, sitting down again and pulling the bill of his fatigue cap over his eyes.

After two hours there was some news. A rescue helicopter from the outfit known as the Jolly Green Giants, sent in to try to get Frank out, had been driven off with its pilot killed and copilot wounded. Damaged badly, they had limped back to base. They reported that the beeper device on the radio in Frank's parachute appeared to be coming from one point on the ground.

At that moment I felt that Frank was probably dead. If he could possibly do it, an experienced pilot would disconnect the automatically beeping radio on his parachute and talk to rescue aircraft via the walkie-talkie type of radio carried in his survival vest. It sounded to me as if he were lying there dead, never having gotten out of his parachute.

The sweep-second hands on the wall clocks kept moving. We occasionally spoke of things different from the overwhelming anxiety that filled the command post. It was like talking to each other from under boulders. At one point Colonel Lewis was telling me that mink coats were a bargain in Hong Kong, and that if I wanted to buy a mink coat, a good place would be the Siberian Fur Company in Hong Kong. As a non-mink-coat-giving bachelor it was not vital information to me, but I kept expressing interest; anything to keep the conversation going a few more seconds. The coffee urn ran out; an airman filled it up and started it perking.

There was a call for Colonel Lewis.

"Yes, Sir," he said, and eyebrows lifted. For him to answer the telephone with a "Yes, Sir" it had to be a superior—a general officer. It was Lieutenant General William Momeyer, the commander of Seventh Air Force. From Saigon he was now on every net involved with the rescue, throwing everything into it, giving Seventh Air Force a blank check to get Frank out.

We settled back around the table. A few minutes later Danang passed a message. The second Jolly Green Giant, sent in from some distance away when the first was hit, had also been driven off by gunfire and was limping home. Further efforts were under way.

Gradually I realized that a full-scale air war was being fought up there at this moment in those mountains, fighter-bombers attacking the enemy ground guns while helicopters tried to slip in and find Frank or what was left of him.

Colonel Lewis was discussing something with Sully. Three hours had passed; the regulation was that a telegram notifying the next of kin must be sent, when possible, four hours after a pilot was killed or missing. I sipped the fresh coffee and thought of Wylene and Frank dancing that night just before we left.

Colonel Lewis sat down again. They had decided to wait, and to telephone Wylene in a couple of hours and explain the situation to her.

Four hours passed; new sergeants came on duty to replace the men on the telephones, but the men who were relieved never left the room, just standing there, looking at the clock, stiffening every time there was a call that might have news.

At six o'clock I stepped out the back end of the squadron building for the first time since I had walked in. The sun was low over the mountains to the west. It was windless and clear. Cheop Chai stood silent to the north. A returning flight whistled high above the runway in tight echelon, the three planes circling back over the silent valley in single file to land.

I walked back into the command post and sat down at the table. The ashtrays were piled with cigarette butts, and there were paper cups of coffee everywhere.

The telephone rang, Danang asking for Colonel Lewis. Sully handed him the phone. He listened carefully. Then he let out his breath, took it in again, and turned, his face like a child's on Christmas morning.

"They've got him out! He's okay!"

Men swallowed, there were a few relieved cheers, some compulsive pats on backs and grabbing of arms above the elbow. Everyone was talking at once.

General Momeyer on the telephone. "Yes, Sir. We just heard. Yes, Sir."

Frank was returned to us late the next morning from one of our bases in Thailand, where he had been taken after his rescue. An uncamouflaged silver Gooney Bird with markings unfamiliar to us taxied in and stopped before a crowd of a hundred men, ten of whom were supposed to be there; the others had slipped away from their jobs and walked over here because they liked Colonel Frank Buzze.

The plane's silver door opened, and there stood Frank. He was bareheaded, wearing only his gray flying suit. There were scratches and scabs all over his face. He looked very young and defenseless. Even as the ladder was slid down and men rushed toward him, he delayed another moment in the doorway, his face expressionless. It was as if he were for one more moment in a special state of purity, looking like a young squire in the clothes worn under armor. Then he was coming stiffly down the ladder. There was handshaking, and he climbed into a jeep and was driven off to the Taj Mahal.

That evening there was a special meeting of all the pilots in the Wing, held in a big briefing room. Reports had been filtering in all day indicating that it had been the biggest rescue effort of the war. Forty-three aircraft, of ten different types, had been involved in the battle. Now what we wanted to know was what had happened on the ground to the man for whom it was fought.

Frank stepped behind the lectern, looked at us with a smile, and said, "Okay, gents, I want to tell you about a long afternoon."

He started with the moment his parachute opened. Looking up, he saw that two panels in it had been torn by the opening shock of leaving a plane at such high speed and were missing; fortunately there was one good panel between the two wedges of sky.

Then the enemy started firing at him as he floated down. Bullets cut the two shroud lines that were holding in place the one good triangle between the two missing ones, so that an entire section of the parachute above him was no longer there.

"This increased my rate of descent appreciably," Frank told a flying-suit-clad audience that was leaning forward in its seats.

He landed in a bamboo thicket, hearing "many voices shouting what appeared to be commands in an unknown tongue." In his haste to get away from the voices, he slipped out of his parachute and got going without bothering to disconnect the beeper on the radio in the parachute. Thus, while the beeper had indicated to us that Frank was lying in one place, he had actually been moving up the slope from where he landed, getting out of the bamboo thicket and under some trees. He slipped into another bamboo thicket that had a view of the sky, hearing searchers moving about him in every direction, and flashed his signal mirror at one of the Skyraider fighter-bombers, slower and better able to hover than our Supersabres, that had arrived to try to help him. Once the Skyraider knew where Frank was, this plane and its companions proceeded to blast the areas where he was not, to disrupt the men who were hunting him.

After an hour the first rescue helicopter appeared and started in toward Frank, who signaled them with a hand-fired flare. Two 50-caliber machine guns on the ground near Frank, which he had not known of until now, opened up on the rescue helicopter, and he saw his chance for safety lurch away through the air in such condition that at first he thought it had been shot down.

The enemy now had an approximate idea of where Frank was, and bullets began snapping through the thicket in which he was hiding. He moved on up the slope, and suddenly heard someone coming his way in the stillness when the bullets stopped.

"Flyer," an accented voice called, "Flyer, me Pathet Lao," apparently on the assumption that Frank might be more willing to surrender to the Laotian Communists than to the North Vietnamese.

"A second voice called out below me," Frank told us. "The man responded and moved downslope from me."

Another hour passed. More fighter-bombers arrived. They kept bombing behind where they had last seen Frank, and he took advantage of the noise. Each time a plane came howling in, he moved a few yards to a new place.

"I was really just working my way uphill between guns," he said. Passing between two 50-caliber machine guns, he reached the ridgeline. Up here he found a good place to signal with his mirror again, and the second Jolly Green Giant came in to try to take him out. The machine guns raked this one, too, and it staggered away through the air.

"At this point," Frank said, "rescue from the air seemed impossible. It appeared senseless to expose any further rescue crews to the terrible onslaught of gunfire. I planned to find good concealment about halfway down the mountain and hole up until two hours after dark. I had decided I was going to walk out of Laos."

As Frank lay hidden, losing all sense of time, he became aware of his physical condition. He had no water with him, and there was none nearby. He had become so dehydrated that skin peeled from *the roof of his mouth*.

More air strikes. At this point both the enemy and our Air Force had an idea of where Frank was, within three

.50 Cal. M.G. (V.C.)

hundred yards. The difference was that this was enough knowledge to enable the fighter-bombers to go on disrupting the enemy without hurting Frank, while it was not enough to enable the enemy to find the human needle in the jungle haystack. At one point, working his way down a dry streambed, he heard something rustling through the bushes. He hid, taking out his pistol for the first time. Speaking of a strange surge of confidence, he said, "I felt that I was the meanest mother in the valley." The source of noise, whether animal or human, crashed on downhill.

More strikes were being made ahead of Frank, and he decided to move toward them, on the theory that other people would be avoiding that area and that it might be a good place to hide until darkness. He arrived at a point that had been burned out by napalm, and found one of the enemy's own foxholes. From here he signaled again to a Skyraider, who waggled his wings and promptly started a series of strafing runs that silenced two 50-caliber guns.

"Much to my surprise," Frank said, "a third chopper came overhead." Covered by the noise from the chopper, Frank had his first chance to shout into his survival-vest radio without being overheard. "You just overshot my position!" he yelled. The helicopter swung around, spotted Frank, and lowered a jungle penetrator seat on a cable. Frank struggled toward it through thick burned vines, got onto the anchorlike device, and was snatched out of the jungle with enemy bullets suddenly crackling around him.

In his formal written report, Frank took it from there:

> Before I knew it, I was at the door and whisked inside, safe, happy, relieved, but most of all, humble over the self-sacrifice, raw courage, outstanding airmanship and determination demonstrated by all the participants involved in my rescue. My total ground time was four hours and twenty minutes. So ended a long, long afternoon.

ELEVEN

"Tomorrow I give you baby." I was the startled person to whom this remark was addressed, and the speaker was Ngo Thi Hoa, the Vietnamese maid who took care of our hooch and one other like it. What she meant was that she was going to give me one of those Vietnamese dolls made in the shape of a pretty girl wearing a coolie hat and an *ao dai,* and the next day she brought from Tuy Hoa town a doll for me and one for Sully.

Ngo Thi was five feet and three-eighths inches tall, according to the laminated ID card she carried, and weighed eighty-eight pounds. She had large, burning brown eyes, dark skin, and a marvelous long cloud of black hair.

Her husband had left her to work full-time for the Viet Cong, and the last word she had was that he was in Saigon. She spoke of him with a shrug of her graceful shoulders, but her face lit when she pulled out a snapshot of her four-year-old son. She had a daughter, too, but there was no snapshot of her. At twenty-three, Ngo Thi was a frustrated woman, lacking a man to live with, lacking an education, lacking money. She had energy far beyond the simple demands of mopping our linoleum floor, making our beds and doing our laundry. Wearing a pink blouse and black trousers, she paced around my room like a smoldering whirlwind, looking for things to do. She shined our boots, dusted and redusted my typewriter, and sneaked away at noon to spend an hour working for eight sergeants who shared a wood-and-screen hooch a quarter of a mile away. I never doubted that in that hour she made eight beds, shined eight pairs of boots, washed

125

eight sets of fatigues, and swept and mopped a considerable floor space.

We communicated in English of purest pidgin.

"How you too-die?" she would inquire breathlessly as she burst into the trailer at 6:45 A.M., catching me with shaving lather on my face and less on the rest of me. She spoke her few words of English as if her Vietnamese singsong had been combined with an Australian dockworker's accent.

"How're you, Mama-san?" Single girls were *baby-san*, married ones *mama-san*.

"Fine thank you," she would say, nearing the end of her English vocabulary. She would stare at me as I finished dressing. She could never believe that Americans were as big as they were, but she rather liked these ungainly technicolored hairy creatures, with their big noses and skinny eyelids. Occasionally she would sidle up to me when I was working at my desk, caress me with her eyes, and say "You *beaucoup* Number One."

So there we were, using "Mama-san" from the slang of the American Occupation of Japan, in which the woman running a bar was called that; "Number One," which originated in China with "Number One Boy," meaning the major domo of the servants in a Westerner's household, connoting excellence; and the French contribution *beaucoup*. It was a strange confrontation, Mama-san and I smiling at each other inside a metal trailer on a beach in Indo-China. The air conditioner would hum, sunlight would pour through the window, and Cheop Chai stood eternal in the distance. I would smile at her once more and turn back to my work, and she would look at me for a few more seconds, shrug her shoulders, mutter something in Vietnamese, and then find a towel to wash or a wastepaper basket to empty.

Just why I did not make a good solid pass at Mama-san is a mystery to me. There were many days when I was in the hooch, working on notes or correspondence, while all the colonels were off at their desks or in their planes. On those days I would keep running into Mama-san, brushing past her, chatting with her, asking her to sew on a button, and the desire was there. She was a sinuous sexy little brown cat, hard and soft at the same time. I suppose I had some silly notion that you shouldn't fool around with the help.

What was happening to me was symptomatic of the

Wing's sexual condition. We had been out of the States for three months. I was one of the few who had not spent every day of it on the sand of Tuy Hoa Air Base. Tuy Hoa town was on limits only in the afternoon, and the time spent getting there and back meant that it could only be done on one's once-a-week day off. In any case one was not allowed to go further into any building than to stand at the counter in an open-front store. The MP-enforced rules were violated by some, there were prostitutes and they were visited, but most men pinned their sexual hopes on the R and R leaves to major cities in Asia.

Having lived in Asia before, it was fascinating to me to watch American men making their discovery of Asian women. Many returned from Bangkok, from Taipei, from Tokyo in a bemused state. I flew one mission with a pilot just back from Hong King who literally purred all the way to the target. Some men were looking only for sexual relief, and they found it. Others were looking for that and for some companionship, some laughs; they found that and often more.

"I fell in love," a young captain said to me, speaking of an airline stewardess, a Japanese. He looked scared.

Quite enough has been written concerning the psychological ambushes that the American man and the Asian women have set for each other—both feel, quite rightly, that they have never been treated so considerately before.

Not as much has been written about the physical aspect of the matter. The absence of the Western cultural emphasis on romantic love and on sex makes the Asian woman a less self-conscious lover. In the Asian Garden of Eden, free from the notion that sex is terribly important, one encounters a charming spontaneity and lack of inhibition. The Asian virgin is not thinking about sin. She will either do it or not do it, but she has an altogether wholesome view of what it is that she is considering. She is not a tease, she is not neurotic, and she will either go for broke or stay behind her fan.

Their bodies are lovely. Their skin is warm gold satin. They are agile. The same well-stretched ligaments and muscular control that enable a Japanese girl to sit in a kneeling position, buttocks resting on her heels for an hour at a time, are not wasted in bed. Asian young women make their American counterparts look as if they have arthritis.

They are habit-forming, and marvelously feminine. A friend of mine who returned from living in the Far East remarked of American women, once he had taken up with them again, "They're like men with holes in them."

Thus womanless Tuy Hoa. While all the men waited their turns to go to Singapore or Penang or Manila, Special Stud solved the problem in his predictably unique manner. He picked out a girl who worked in our dining trailer. The next thing, she was working as his maid and he was riding her on the back of his Honda.

The authorities, seeing this, murmured. They told him she could not ride on the back of his Honda because she did not have a plastic crash helmet. He bought her a plastic crash helmet. The authorities mumbled again. He was an officer, a pilot. It did not look good for a pilot in flight suit to be whizzing around the base with a Vietnamese girl hanging onto him from behind with her arms around his waist, both of them laughing and shouting over the motorcycle's din.

Special Stud paid no heed. He was never disciplined, but I suspect it influenced his Efficiency Report. I found the official attitude hypocritical. Here he was achieving what most of the Wing, married or not, wished they had—a good, steady female companion, *on base*—and they were telling him it was a bad example. Staring after them as they shot around a corner, Stud waving at me and the girl smiling and leaning forward and saying something in his ear, I thought they looked very nice together.

II

Returning one day from a mission, I saw a column of Army vehicles being loaded aboard C–130 transports through the big ramp doors that swung down beneath their tails. Standing beside a jeep that had radios mounted on it was Tom Lynch, surrounded by a knot of officers and sergeants of the Dragoons.

"Where are you going?" I asked him as we shook hands.

"Up to the Cambodian border."

I was suitably impressed. The rest of the Fourth Division was based at Pleiku, eighty miles to the northwest of us, and they were having vicious bushwhacking battles with the fresh North Vietnamese units that came across the border from Cambodia after moving down through Laos on the Ho Chi Minh Trail. Now the Dragoons were headed for Polei Djereng, an advanced base near that border.

"Could I come with you?"

"If you can get here before the plane leaves. You've got about twenty minutes."

I raced back to the hooch, got out of my flying suit, and put on my jungle fatigues. Eighteen minutes later I was sitting inside a C–130, helmet on my head, web belt with pistol and canteen around my waist, and my pack on the shiny floor between my legs.

We took off, our four propellers lumbering into the sky at what seemed the pace of a dray horse after the jet mission from which I had just returned. I stared at the combination of land and air mobility about me. Near the tail, pointed toward the ramp and ready to roll out first, was Tom's jeep, with a two-wheeled carrying trailer behind it that contained his tent and all that went in it. In front of me was a big truck holding the TOC tent, its radios, maps, wooden tables, folding metal chairs, and the coffeepot. Tactical Airlift was what the Air Force called this capability of moving Army men, Army trucks, Army cannon, but one really had to see it this way to understand that an Army motorized column could actually turn off a road, roll up to airplanes, and be flown quickly and safely across jungles and mountains, past ambush sites, high above mined roads.

We landed on a runway of perforated metal matting. The ramp came down with a hydraulic wheeze and whine, and a thick cloud of sunlit red dust poured into the plane. I walked down the ramp, blinking and coughing. Tom's jeep had already been freed from the cables and chocks that secured it, and was being driven down the ramp. Several officers, their fatigues, helmets, hands, and faces coated in terra cotta, were greeting Tom and talking quietly and earnestly. Beside the runway a tank rattled past on a red road, stringing a sinister red dust pennant behind itself. Cannon blasted toward the low bushy horizon under a baked blue sky. In the cloudless distance, a pillar of smoke rose straight as a tree.

I had never seen the Dragoons set up shop. We jolted down a road in Tom's jeep, turned into a cleared area the size of a supermarket parking lot, and slid to a halt. As Tom stood talking into one of the radios on his jeep, men converged on the truck that had been with us on the airplane and started setting up the TOC tent. Within fifteen minutes it was the same Tactical Operations Center I remembered from the hilltop, each radio on its wooden table and a sergeant in place on a chair in front of it. Other men were filling sandbags with red earth and building a wall around the tent. Tom switched off the radios on his jeep and went into the TOC, now that the same frequencies were being received on the radios in there. A minute more, and his King Arthur living tent was in place.

More planes were arriving and more trucks came down the road, red clouds boiling behind them. A mess tent appeared, with oddly reassuring bags of sugar, crates of oranges and apples, and stacks of white paper plates. We were inside a perimeter being guarded by other units. Our job was to get ready to receive our own riflemen, and they were not long in arriving. A businesslike column of trucks rolled in from the airstrip. Their canvas roofs and sides had been rolled off so that the troops sitting in them could look out, shoot out, and leap out if necessary. One man in the back of each truck had set up a light machine gun on the top of the cab. Entering this new and more hazardous fighting zone, the boys looked poised, worried, and intensely curious. They were sweating, and already dusty.

The truck stopped; the troops swung down, seventy-pound packs right with them. This was C Company, commanded by Captain James Powers, a big, red-faced West Pointer I had met in the hills of Phu Yen. His first sergeant moved through the milling troops like a referee at a football game striding off the yards of a penalty, moving the ball back, and suddenly there was C Company, lined up in formation. Captain Powers and the first sergeant came to attention in front of them, facing toward Tom, who was heading their way, his boots striking puffs of red smoke with every step.

When Tom was forty yards off, the first sergeant pivoted and faced the troops. His rifle slung on his shoulder, he raised his hands in marvelous imitation of a tail-coated orchestra conductor, and the troops began to sing, to the tune of "Here Comes the Bride":

> We like it here,
> We like it here,
> Weeeeee liike it here.

"Charlie Company all present or accounted for, Sir," Captain Powers said with a straight face, saluting Tom as the troops roared through a second chorus.

Tom had the troops stand at ease and take off their packs. He told them that it was going to be tougher here, but if they went on being alert as they had been down on the coast, if they stayed on their toes, if they used their heads, they would be all right. They would have to work harder. They would have to dig more overhead shelters, fill more sandbags, build more bunkers. This enemy, regular North Vietnamese, were just as well armed on the company level as we were. The Viet Cong had occasionally given us a break, either through the amateurism of some of them or the foolhardy bravery of some who would charge an American squad single-handed.

"This guy will only try to take you when he thinks he has you outnumbered," Tom told his men. He said that they should expect to go out into the field from here almost immediately. The mail might be a couple of days catching up to them. Hot chow would be when the kitchens were set up; they could see that they were being worked on right now. There was a shower point here, and we needed it in this dust. Once they had dug in, they could take turns going down to the showers.

The troops nodded. They were being given it absolutely straight, and they could live with it.

"Carry on," Tom said to Captain Powers. The troops came to attention, and the first sergeant turned to them again, lifting one hand and dropping it. A hundred and forty voices shouted *"FIGHT FIERCELY, SIR!"*

This time Tom had a really hard time keeping a straight face. No one knew who in the battalion had started this "fight fiercely" business, but it was a family joke cum battle cry, varied for the occasion to "eat fiercely," "dig fiercely," "wash fiercely," with a particularly alliterative version for a man just going on R and R.

Looking at them all, standing at attention, Tom's face working to keep from laughing and the troops grinning as they watched him not laughing, I felt an invisible net tying them together here in the hot red dust of a strange land. As he finally saluted them and strode away, I studied these boys as the formation broke up. They were all races, all sizes, every kind of face. Even in the dusty sameness of their faded green fatigues, one had a tattoo on his arm, another sported a mustache, and another had a rosary of wooden beads the size of olives around his neck. One boy had LINDA inked on his camouflaged helmet cover, another had MAKE LOVE, NOT WAR, and a third had only UTAH.

Many of them wore the blue Combat Infantryman's Badge with its silver flintrock musket. A few had it in its proper place, above the left breast pocket of their fatigues. Quite a number had it on the inside of the flap of their breast pockets, with only the two small metal clips on the back side of the badge visible, as if it was really nobody else's business if they had won it or not, least of all that of a sniper who might be attracted by its twinkle. The interesting thing to me was that they would keep this badge with them, through swamps and monsoon rains, though they were not required to wear it in the field. It meant they were proud of it.

There they stood, Infantry, hot, young, and dirty, with an occasional thirty-year-old sergeant in their midst. Lighting up cigarettes, laughing, heading in their respective squads to take up positions on the perimeter, they are the ones who go and do it after everyone else finishes talking about it.

The next day was a Sunday. Captain Powers' C Company and the Royal Pineapple's B Company had been joined by A Company, under the command of First Lieutenant Chris Dorny, a lanky West Pointer who was the youngest company commander in Vietnam. With all the troops in one place before sending them into the lethal jungle hills just beyond this scrubby plain, Tom asked for something a little special in the way of church services. I went to the Catholic Mass, which was held in a trampled-down grassy spot near the perimeter.

"All right, boys," the chaplain said, standing before his improvised altar of ammunition crates. "If anything starts, just jump in the bushes." His vestments were made from a camouflaged parachute. This was a memorial Mass for the dead of the battalion, and he had borrowed helmets from the congregation to make two neat rows on the grass beside the altar, each helmet representing a dead Dragoon.

Up to this point I had heard nothing but bad sermons in Vietnam; a Catholic chaplain giving some airmen hell for celebrating Christmas with too much whiskey; another Catholic chaplain wasting everyone's time with a long explanation of how to explain to non-Catholics that it was not against the Catholic Church's regulations to gamble; and a couple of odious sermons on the theme "You'd better repent now, because you might be dead tomorrow."

This sermon was on the meaning of suffering, the lesson to be learned from sharing under hard circumstances. Christ's suffering had not been a solo performance; it was an offering, a sharing. This, the wiry chaplain said, is the meaning of the Cross.

"This sharing with your fellow man learned here is not to be forgotten when you get home and are riding around again in a big car."

The troops nodded as they sat on their up-ended helmets, their weapons beside them. This was another guy who was giving it to them straight. We rose and went up to Communion, shuffling in a double file, Tom Lynch the last man in the line.

At the close of the Mass the priest mentioned the names of the boys who had died—"Al . . . Frankie . . . Ramon . . ." and sprinkled holy water on the helmets. Everything seemed to come together in this morning light: the drops of holy water sprinkling the camouflaged helmets, the grass beneath them, the raw wood of the ammunition-crate altar, bread and wine in the sacrament, sweat on men's faces, the sky above us, the dirt on our hands.

As he was taking off his vestments and putting back on his fatigue jacket and helmet, I introduced myself to the chaplain.

"Oh," he said. "When you came up to Communion, I was asking myself 'I wonder who this old sergeant is?' "

We chatted for a while. He was Father Conall Murphy, originally from Arlington, Massachusetts, and more recently of the Franciscans at Thirty-first Street in New York City. He had worked in the civil rights movement, had gone to Selma, had been opposed to the Vietnam War. Then when he saw that hundreds of thousands of Americans were going to Vietnam anyway, and heard that there was a shortage of Catholic chaplains, he had volunteered, and here he was. He stood in the red haze under the climbing hot sun, neat, soldierly, joking with the troops, and it was hard to believe that he had come to this type of ministry only in his mid-thirties.

I wandered around the Brigade Headquarters area that afternoon, discovering a tiny tent PX, a medical clearing station, and the outside of a tent that was the morgue. Walking wounded from another battalion were coming in as a result of a fight earlier in the day, hobbling, still holding their weapons, a study in red; red-dusted faces with white rivulets of sweat, fatigues more red than green, new white bandages turning red from dust, with black-red stains surfacing from the wounds beneath.

Back at Tom's tent I found him sitting on his cot with a yellow-leather brief case, doing the few minutes of paperwork he had each day. Fifteen yards away a bulldozer was pushing aside great mounds of earth, creating what looked like an excavation for a building as a score of men, wearing helmets and stripped to the waist, watched in sidewalk-superintendent fashion.

"What's that bulldozer doing?" I asked.

Tom shook his head as he signed the papers his administrative officer had brought him. "I don't know. I don't ask. I have enough to worry about. I assume they know what they're doing."

Big goggles were being issued to the troops who had to drive vehicles in this dust. The Battalion Executive Officer, Major McGinley, had a pair of these on his helmet, and the troops thought it made him look like the German general Rommel, the Desert Fox.

"Sir," one boy said as he lugged two five-gallon cans of water past us, "you're the Jungle Fox."

The next morning I went for another of my walks around what had become my reporter's, or observer's, beat. Outside the medical clearing station I found Father Murphy, who was waiting for the results of a nightmare that had been happening even as we had been kidding about bulldozers and goggles. A company of another battalion had been attacked in the jungle the afternoon before, hit while they were on the move through what is known as triple-canopy jungle—three levels of trees, the highest in this part of the country being one hundred and twenty feet high. Five of the company were killed outright and sixty-one wounded.

The worst of that company's ordeal was still to come. Down to half their strength and still under attack, they had tried to cut some kind of hole in the jungle to let helicopters in to evacuate the worst wounded. One big Chinook helicopter had tried lowering a litter on a hundred-foot cable, but the Chinook could not go beneath treetop level and the litter had spun aimlessly twenty feet above the men for whom it might mean the difference between life and death. Darkness had fallen before anything more could be done, and the company and all its wounded had spent the night out there. Only this morning had enough power saws and blasting powder been lowered in to solve the problem, and the most seriously wounded were on their way here right now. The big Chinook bringing them would be met at the air strip and ambulances would carry the wounded to the spot where we were standing.

At the moment, it was silent and peaceful. This sense of now-you-see-it, now-you-don't was beginning to strike me as the principal feature of the war. In other wars there had been a front. When you got to it, that was where the fighting was, and the bleeding, and the dying. Here you could be the point man on a patrol a few hundred meters from the Cambodian border, and hear nothing all day except the footsteps of the man behind you, while at the same time a truck driver on the coast might be fighting for his life in an ambush created by a dozen men.

Two ambulances came down the road and stopped before Father Murphy and me. The door was opened and a boy was carried out on a stretcher. I had been prepared for blood, or writhing in pain, but not for what I saw. The boy was immobile and ashen, eyes closed, one arm lying beside him and the other across his chest. His stomach and chest were wrapped in bright white tape.

They carried him past me and into the tent, and another boy was lifted out of the ambulance on his stretcher, bandaged just as the first, also unconscious. Father Murphy followed the stretchers into the tent. Other stretchers passed me, with bandaged legs in stiff pyramids, each boy out cold. The last stretcher supported a big black soldier, stripped to the waist, one arm bandaged from wrist to shoulder and tape on the side of his chest. He was the only one conscious. With his remaining good arm he motioned laterally, slowly, in an "I'm okay" gesture like a benediction.

Four men came out of the tent carrying the first boy who had been brought in. From the direction they were moving, it was clear that they were taking him to the morgue.

They passed a yard away. The boy's face was neither tortured nor serene—simply unconscious. He had a lengthening dark crew cut, and his body looked as if it had grown to its full height, but would fill out more in the chest and shoulders.

TWELVE

No sooner had I walked into the club on my return from Polei Djereng than I ran into the three-man BBC television crew I had met in Saigon at Tet. They had remembered what I had told them about the hospitality and cooperativeness of the Thirty-first, and here they were.

"Er, Charles, do you think I could get on a mission?" asked the cameraman, a stocky Englishman named Graham Veale who sported a fine mustache started in his own past days in the RAF.

"Believe me, Graham," I said as I motioned the bartender toward us, "you stand around here and you'll have your choice of squadrons to fly with."

So it was that the next afternoon I presented Graham to my bearlike friend Sergeant Bezio, who took one look at the cameraman's ample waist and began letting out the adjusting strings in the back of a survival vest. Half an hour later I was standing on the yellow ladder beside old 951F, helping Graham get strapped in while the pilot walked around the plane making his preflight checks.

Graham shook his head as he looked at the control panels hemming him in from three sides. "What these kids have to bloody learn!" he said with a shake of his white-helmeted head. I handed him his heavy movie camera; he placed it on his lap, smoothed down his mustache, and clamped the oxygen mask over his face.

I came out to the plane when they taxied in and shut down the engine after the mission. Graham handed me out his camera. He was all smiles, as was the pilot, and when they climbed down they told me why.

"We came diving in," Graham said, looking twenty years younger, "and here was this little bloody winking circle of lights."

The pilot laughed. "He asked me, 'We're strafing now, are we?' and I had to tell him, 'Negative. *They're* shooting at us.'"

At this point Graham had muttered a restrained British "Really," and kept on whirring away with his camera as they fired back and swept on through.

That evening Sully and I entertained the three fatigue-clad Englishmen in our hooch, going through a number of cans of beer. Sully had somewhere acquired a marvelous air pistol, and we borrowed a couple of sandbags from a nearby bunker, set them against the bathroom door, and pinned to the sandbags a target made by drawing concentric circles on a sheet of my typing paper. We had been banging away at this with gusto for ten minutes when the BBC sound man, Eddy Mills, started laughing helplessly.

"What's so funny?" Sully inquired.

Eddy, gasping: "Here we are in the middle of a war, playing with an air pistol."

The next afternoon things took a different turn. The third man on the BBC team was a young Oxford graduate who decided what vignettes of the war they should report, wrote the script, and narrated it while Graham Veale's camera whirred and Eddy Mills adjusted the sound. Without saying just what he was after, he expressed interest in doing a story on our bomb dump and was given full cooperation. The commander of the Munitions Maintenance Squadron, which supervised the many acres of bombs and 20-millimeter shells, was Lieutenant Colonel Larry Sparks, who had started his military career by joining the Navy on his seventeenth birth-day in 1945. ("With a name like Sparks," he had said to me one day, "they took one look at me and made me a radio operator.")

Acceding to all of BBC's requests, Larry found himself standing in front of a rack of napalm bombs. The camera began whirring, and the Oxford accent asked him what he thought about dropping napalm in Vietnam, and his part in it.

Larry looked at the camera and said that what happened from napalm was no better or worse than what happened when one was hit by a large piece of jagged metal moving at a speed upwards of one thousand miles an hour.

"Human beings instinctively fear fire," Larry added, as the Oxford man began to realize that he had picked the wrong person for his purposes. "Uncontrolled fire elicits a response of animal fear. That is why napalm has such a bad reputation." Larry went on to say that if a person was genuinely opposed to killing under all circumstances, or specifically opposed to killing in Vietnam, then one had no more business being a uniformed clerk than in being the man who delivered the bombs to the planes, or the pilots who dropped the bombs.

BBC never used the piece.

II

It was Easter Sunday morning, and I was in the back seat. We flew sixty miles northwest, and it appeared to be just another splinter mission. We dropped our bombs into trees, producing not only the splinters but also the condition we called "smoliage," a contraction of the FAC's frequently used formula—"further bomb damage assessment impossible due to smoke and foliage."

We were circling above the target area, our bombs expended, waiting to see if the FAC would want us to go in and strafe with the 20-millimeter cannon. Suddenly the FAC told us to head east at top speed and rendezvous with another spotter plane who *really* had something.

We went screaming toward the coast, and sighted the new FAC circling low just west of a river that wound through a valley. Across the river from him was a village.

"We have a VC company in contact," the FAC told us. The enemy company was in the village, and the friendly forces were just fifty meters to the south of the village, trying to get into it.

"All right," the FAC said in that articulate but tight combat voice I recognized by now, "I want you on a west-east heading. The friendlies will be fifty meters south of my smoke." This meant that he intended to dive right at the enemy-held edge of the village. "You can be damned sure you'll be receiving ground fire," he added, and rolled in to mark.

I found my hand going to the throat of my flying suit, pulling up the zipper. The first moment when we rolled in, barreling down in a long flat dive, I found myself ducking down in the seat, but curiosity overcame me. We tore in, lower than I remembered ever having attacked a target. Across the pilot's shoulders I saw the village lifting into my face, hurtling toward us, surrounding us, rocking around as if attached to the plane. Sandy roads I could step out on, houses, palm trees level with my head, little vegetable gardens in which I could see the hoed rows. Our guns erupted, the plane vibrated, silver sparkles scattered across the back yards and houses, our shells kicking up plumes of dust and debris. We slammed out in a tight turn and came in for a second pass, and a third.

"I've got another flight coming in," the FAC said, indicating there was no time for verbal formalities or an assessment of what we might have accomplished. "Thank you much."

We flew home and landed. At lunch I ate fried chicken, my appetite good and my feelings cheerful. There had been an excitement and pleasure about this mission different from anything I had felt before. There was a sense of accomplishment, and a sense of survival; there *had* been something there; it had been shooting at our troops. I was glad I had been along, and I was damned glad I was back.

That evening Sully and I had a beer in the hooch. I told him I had finally seen something, anyway, besides the jungle spinning around beneath the nose of the diving plane. Then I said that it was a funny way to spend Easter.

He had flown today, too, and it was the first time he had considered that it *was* a funny way to spend Easter. Then he was telling me about his Easter Sunday, 1944. He was with the 354th Fighter Group in England, flying the first P–51s to enter combat. That morning he took off with extra fuel in drop tanks and escorted some B–17s across Germany, getting shot at, across Denmark, and down into Poland. They dropped their bombs on a target in Poland that shot back, and came on back, being shot at on the way.

B-17

"When I got back," Sully said, "there was a letter from my aunt waiting for me, saying that she hoped I'd have a nice, peaceful Easter Sunday."

We talked some more, about this war. Sully was no man to give a lecture, but he knew I was interested and a sometime participant.

There was such a thing, he said, as aerial doctrine, and it had yet to be proved wrong. The great new dimension that the airplane had brought to warfare was the capacity to hit the enemy right at his heart—hundreds, even thousands of miles behind the mailed fist he chose to bring to the battlefield. Hitting him at his heart was the most effective use of airpower.

All of which brought us to the North Vietnamese port of Haiphong. We were allowing ships to sail in there and unload their cargoes. We had reconnaissance photographs showing entire square blocks of war materiel piled high.

So what did we do? We let them load it onto trucks, and then we chased it, truck by truck, down jungled-over roads all through Southeast Asia. I had been on a mission that had gotten a truck, he said, I had seen how hard it was to get just one truck in this war and that one had been standing still. I had seen that bombs did not always hit where they were aimed, I had seen that the targets down here were often obscured or minimal in importance. The place to put bombs was where there was something to hit.

Sully went over to the club, and I stayed in the hooch at the end of my Easter Sunday. I was torn, and not for the first time since I had come to Vietnam. I did not often stop to think of my friends in the United States, but I had no doubt about what many of them—publishers, writers, professors— thought of this war. They were opposed to it. They wanted the entire effort liquidated, but to this desire they added a corollary that I was not at all sure was logical. If they could not have it cease altogether, they wanted it limited, held to a minimum of provocative activity.

I thought of the face of that dead boy when they carried him past at Polei Djereng. What were we supposed to say to him? Sorry, son, that weapon that killed you might have been destroyed six hundred miles north of here, but there were policy considerations? The policy considerations, the untested notion that bombing a port in North Vietnam would substantially widen the war, was not going to do that boy any good—he was as dead as he was ever going to be, and we went on letting his brother draftees be attacked from a sanctuary in Cambodia that outflanked South Vietnam in a way that the Korean peninsula had never been outflanked.

I sat back at the end of my long Easter Sunday, wishing that the eloquent American protesters would do what I was doing—spend a good long time with the reality of what they were protesting. They might not change their minds, they might be reinforced in what they thought and felt, but I would have liked to see them over here, gathering their own data and using them, rather than anything else, to form their conclusions.

THIRTEEN

One morning I had a run-in about vehicles with an officer whom I had privately given the name of Misfitte Glare.

Misfitte may well have been right in telling me I could no longer have the use of the panel truck I sometimes borrowed from an understanding officer on base, but what made me and others angry was the man himself. He was one of those men who can bid you good morning so that it will make your blood boil. In the normal run of a peacetime military base, where officers live with their families and the pressures of duty are not excessive, the abrasive qualities of a man like Misfitte may never be felt by any but those working closest to him. Here, however, it was a different matter. He was the only officer on base who seemed to me to be acting a part, and he acted it constantly. Rather than being the officer he was, he seemed to have an image of the officer he ought to be, and he threw himself into the role.

At the dawn stand-up briefing we were subdued, slouching a bit, sipping coffee from paper cups, perhaps a trifle hung over.

Not Misfitte. He came striding in, having done his half-hour of sit-ups immediately on arising, and handled his paper cup of coffee as if it were a field marshal's baton. When the Weather officer said for the seventeenth day in a row that the condition west of Pleiku was variable cloudiness with scattered thundershowers at ten thousand feet, Misfitte cocked his head, face intent as if he were listening to bulletins of incalculable significance. When we were told that there were thirteen repairable afterburners on hand, he would

143

mutter "hmm," as if the figures were not one of the more standard and seldom-varying statistics. With the demeanor of a schoolboy who is determined that if he cannot get *A*s he will at least impress the teacher with his desire to learn, Misfitte would occasionally turn in the midst of the recitation of the most mundane repetitive statistics and nod knowingly at some other officer, whose response would be anything from a stunned double-take to a quickly suppressed snort.

Although Misfitte could and did worry about everything, it was the Vietnamese hooch maids and women dining-hall workers who roused him to particularly self-righteous heights. To sit opposite Misfitte in the dining trailer was to be exposed to a running harangue on how greasy the plates were and to have invisible specks of dust pointed out on every knife, fork and spoon.

"Dysentery," he would say. "We'll have a full-scale epidemic here if these people can't be brought to understand even the simplest elements of hygiene."

His living quarters were never right. The mirror had not been polished, the sink was a disgrace. Pointing at his bed as one points out a mess to a puppy, he asked the bemused hooch maid, who knew only the standard ten words or so of English, was that her idea of a hospital corner? Well, was it?

At this point Frank Buzze said to him, "You know, if you've lived all your life in a hut with a dirt floor, it may take just a little while to learn how to use a waxer."

In any case, my run-in with Misfitte made me suddenly quite homesick for Tom Lynch and the Dragoons. Up there where they had nothing, a young soldier would open a can containing four crackers and offer you two of them. Suddenly I didn't want any more arguing whether I could make better use of a vehicle than did some of the paunchy clerical sergeants who used them to roll from their barracks to the office, from the office to the mess hall, back to the office, and finally to the NCO club for cocktail hour. Misfitte could take his truck and shove it.

I found the Dragoons dug in on a hilltop west of Polei Djereng, three miles from the Cambodian border. It was only my third trip to them, but there was a heartwarming quality about their welcome. Tall, bald "Pappy" Green, the forty-year-old supply sergeant who looked like the cowboy he had once been, offered me a cup of the excellent coffee he always had brewing, and asked me if I could use an air mattress. In the TOC, which was housed in a deep underground sandbagged bunker, the young radio men shook hands. They started telling me not about the enemy but the fire base from which they had just moved. It had been in a valley with trees two hundred feet high, and at night there had been elephants trumpeting around them.

Tom appeared and shook my hand. The dust that was constantly blowing on this hilltop had infected his left eye, and he had a gauze bandage over it. He sat me down in front of his map on its easel, explaining that we were sitting astride one of the main infiltration routes from Cambodia. No big contacts, but the Dragoons were picking off a North Vietnamese here and a North Vietnamese there, and this was all right with him. If a big fight came up the Dragoons could handle it, but the way it was going he was losing no men at all, and each North Vietnamese they got out there was a *bona fide* enemy, complete with uniform and weapon.

He smiled as he spoke of his A Company, under the command of Chris Dorny, the youngest company commander in Vietnam. Chris was from Brooklyn, and most of his boys were by chance from New York City.

"These kids have never seen a tree before," Tom said, "and they're setting the best ambushes along the whole damn border."

It was too late in the afternoon to do much in the way of getting out to see the companies who were beating the bushes in this treacherous terrain, so I spent the time looking over translated excerpts from the diary of a North Vietnamese who had been killed here. The entries began after the soldier had reached Laos, walking down the Ho Chi Minh trail.

> Laotians come trading food for things we are carrying. It is forbidden to do, but many of the men do it anyway. Today I was caught trading some clothes for rice and was reprimanded. Then I discovered that the sack I had traded my last extra pair of pants for was a sack of dirt with just a layer of rice on top.

A few days later:

> Southern Laos. This place is miserable. The
> green jungle is full of birds twittering. Flies sting
> and sting and the holes don't stop bleeding.
> Five men have died of malaria. I didn't think
> people died of malaria.

Among the Laotian *montagnards:*

> Mountain people here are very superstitious.
> They killed pigs and buffalo when we arrived, not
> for us, but as sacrifice to the gods in case we defile
> the earth, which they hold sacred.

In South Vietnam:

> Stopped at Station Nineteen. This is said to be
> the safest place on the trail. The station easily took
> care of 2000 people in it.

I had another cup of Sergeant Green's excellent coffee
and thought that one over. Here we were, pushing companies
through the underbrush and tirelessly flying over every square
yard with helicopters and FAC planes, and they had a place,
still undiscovered by us, where they could hide two thousand
men at a time. I suspected it would be a series of caves, with
camouflaged entrances concealed beneath the triple-canopy
jungle.

> Damn the Americans. They force us to sleep in
> the jungle with only rice and, if we are lucky, salt to
> eat. I am determined to fight and save my people
> until my last breath.

The next two entries indicated that they had arrived at a
rest camp in the Central Highlands and had received a supply
of rice from Cambodia. "We now will have a month to
recuperate from our ordeal." This and subsequent passages,
on the eve of this man's entering active combat, indicate that

he was a demolition expert, a specialist in the laying of antitank and antipersonnel mines and bobby traps.

Then, after he had been in combat for some time, a poem. The first half tells about how he misses his home, and his native North. Then:

I look about and ask
What here needs "Liberation"?
The market crowded with people in a festive mood?
The rice field green with burgeoning crop?
The curve-roofed pagoda and its worship bell?
The classrooms,
Full of happy children singing in joyous chorus?
The garden
With tiny butterflies busy on the yellow cabbage
    flowers?
Peace and happiness reigned all throughout this
    quiet land.
Why did they order me to burn these quiet villages,
Destroy the rustic bridges,
And sow the explosive seeds of sudden death
Among the people?
How my hand trembled when I set a mine—
And then, I watched it do its work—
Blasting human flesh and spattering a rain of
    blood—
Whose blood, my mother?
The blood of people like ourselves—
My people's blood, mother—
That night my eyes filled with bitter tears,
And my sleep was filled with guilty nightmares.

Two more prose entries:

We are not greeted as liberators in the villages. When we enter the people come and ask us to leave, saying that if we do not the enemy planes will come and strafe the villages. I feel like a leper.

A number of cadre and soldiers said that the Americans are strong, brave and determined to remain in their positions.

The last entry before he was killed is this poem.

I WILL LAMENT FOR TEN THOUSAND GRAVES
When the war is over and the road is open again,
The same stars will course through the heavens.
Then will I weep for the white bones
   Heaped together in desolate graves
Of those who sought military honors for their
   leaders.

Night falls swiftly in Vietnam, and a handful of us gathered at the sandbagged entrance to the TOC, watching the sunset. The sun was dropping through the haze over the steep forested hills that lay between us and the narrow river that marked the Cambodian border. A misty violet-pink light covered us, and, looking at the lavender hills, I was struck with a sense of the newness of that which is oldest. Like so many parts of Vietnam, this landscape looked as if a dinosaur might lumber into sight, or a sabre-toothed tiger. A pterodactyl circling above would have been more in place than a helicopter. It was nightfall and the world was timeless, the jungles well off without Man.

In the hush, two helicopters rose from a position in the middle distance to our north. They had been at that hilltop fire base for the day and were flying back to their nighttime revetments at Polei Djereng. They hammered past and all was silent again, young faces thoughtful as we looked at the violet mists, the lengthening shadows, the light being pulled back across the Cambodian hills like a filmy scarf.

There was a boom. Another boom, and then *boom boom boom*. Our radio came on with a tight controlled voice from the hilltop the helicopters had just left.

"Be advised that we are receiving mortar rounds at this time."

We looked at each other, rousing from the sunset, stunned by the cleverness of the enemy, who had waited until the helicopters were gone so that they could fire their mortars without anything above them in the air to observe the muzzle flashes. Their timing was perfect; there was still just enough light so that they could see exactly where their rounds were landing on their hilltop target, and correct their fire.

There was with us a young artillery lieutenant. He had a shy, ill-at-ease manner, fair freckled skin, eyelashes longer than any girl's. I never saw him again, but in that moment he responded like a sprinter while the rest of us were gawking. He leaped down the sandbagged steps of the TOC, grabbed the artillery radio, and in less than a minute he had our cannon blasting away at predesignated possible enemy mortar positions he had plotted hours before. It may have been coincidence, but the enemy mortars fell silent. The young lieutenant reappeared at the sandbagged doorway, his face as if nothing had happened, as if he had not been the master of the moment, as ill-at-ease as ever. The sun was down.

The next afternoon Tom left me for a couple of hours in the jungle with B Company, while he flew on to check his other two companies that were on the move. The last time I had seen B Company in the field they were searching that mountaintop network of caves back in Phu Yen, flushing out that Vietnamese who, in the remotest spot imaginable, claimed he was trying to find a place to turn himself in as a defector.

This afternoon the hundred and forty men under the command of "The Royal Pineapple" were spread out in bamboo thickets surrounding the small helicopter landing zone they had cut with the machetes carried by one in every several men. They were being resupplied in the field from cartons and crates that were coming in by helicopter. Certain items were being issued on a one-for-one basis. The stocky Nisei first sergeant, Gengoro Higa, stood watching as one squad after another came out of the jungle and stripped off their torn and muddy fatigue shirts and trousers, tossing them into a big cardboard box and rummaging in the cartons of fresh fatigues to find the sizes closest to what they needed.

A young trooper would show Higa his faded, torn jungle boots, and Higa would say, "Hell yes, these are shot," directing the boy to one of the clumps of new boots that were set out by sizes. The atmosphere was of a cheery market place where everything is free. One young soldier presided over the distribution of small plastic bottles of insect repellent, while another handed out green cloth bandoliers whose stitched pockets were filled with clips of M–16 ammunition. While the company was thus at rest, every effort was made to bring in to the landing zone the things that soldiers wanted. A helicopter tossed off several orange canvas bags filled with mail, and from everywhere soldiers came running with letters they had been writing on pads they carried in their packs. Helicopter door gunners became voluntary human mailboxes, and the chopper rose into the air with the helicopter gunners' baggy trousers pockets filled with mail that needed no stamps to travel home to the United States. A hot meal was brought out, and some brown metal thermal containers filled with cans of pop and beer packed in ice. Back at Tuy Hoa we considered ourselves lucky to get a copy of *Stars and Stripes* that was four days old; here, a few hundred meters from the Cambodian border, I saw a young soldier reading yesterday's edition, while sitting on a crate of apples from the state of Washington, with a crate of California oranges nearby.

The Royal Pineapple was huddling with his platoon leaders, all of them sitting in tramped-down high grass studying a plastic-covered map spread on the ground. Just behind him were the company's radio operators, and I had a chance to talk with them as the jungle shadows lengthened in the late afternoon. The most animated was a slender, twenty-three-year-old black soldier from Washington, D.C., who went by the name of "Mo" Thomas. In addition to his competence in handling the company commander's radio, Mo saw no reason to subsist on the forty-seven dollars a week the government was paying him. A pair of dice and a deck of cards added little weight to his staggering load of rifle, pack, ammunition, and back-pack radio, and he whiled away the jungle hours in games of chance. Thus far he had relieved B Company of twelve hundred dollars, and had given them a million dollars' worth of entertainment in the process.

"Ready to copy." This was the Jimmy Cagney-like boy next to Mo, working the radio that linked the company to the TOC back on the hilltop. He was Specialist Fourth Class James S. Tomlinson, of Pittsburgh, who had joined the Army as a Regular at seventeen and had arrived in Vietnam just after his eighteenth birthday. With as much fuzz as whiskers, a handful of moles on either cheek, and a quick, lopsided smile, Tomlinson was a junior edition of Lieutenant Jack Crumley, leader of the reconnaissance platoon; at eighteen he looked so thoroughly at home under his helmet, so clearly at home in the field, that it was hard to believe that he had not been stepping warily through somebody's forests since the beginning of time.

The last young radio man was politely but firmly curious about what I was doing there.

"You mean you could go home any time?" he asked. "Tomorrow?" This round, strong young face belonged to Specialist Fourth Class John Collins. While most of the other foot soldiers, tanned or not, had a yellow tinge from their malaria pills, Collins had the proverbial apple cheeks. There was a quality of goodness, kindness, and alertness about him that stood out even in a group where these characteristics were common. He told me about his family's small farm in the country near Vandergrift, Pennsylvania, and his mare Princess. He spoke of his job delivering newspapers on the RFD route where he lived, and he spoke about children in Vietnam.

He hated the idea that children were getting hurt in this war. Right now this company was moving through jungles that had few villages, but at other times they had moved through villages that had been attacked by one side or the other, and he hated the idea of children becoming orphans. He and Sergeant Higa had started a fund drive to help children in the II Corps area. The men of the company had given, Mo had given from his winnings, and now some of the men were writing people in their home towns, and a chaplain at Brigade was handling the money.

A chopper was coming in. I looked up at it hopefully. Things seemed quiet enough, but the sun was going down and I would just as soon spend the night behind the barbed wire and trip flares and claymore mines at the fire base.

Collins stood, shook hands with me formally, and said that it had been a pleasure to meet me and that he wished me success in what I was doing. He hoped I would come out and see them again. These things happened to me sometimes, moving around the country. In me a young soldier might see an uncle, an older American man who was not in the military but had at least some understanding of what they were doing. Occasionally, on a transport plane, riding in a truck, I found myself in the role of father confessor, being asked what I thought of the war, being told all sorts of problems in a quick confiding rush that I felt sure was not given to the other boys in the young soldier's squad. Collins had too much dignity to unburden himself in any embarrassing way, but he was clearly a thoughtful young draftee, conscientious, soldiering with the best of them, but deeply concerned as to what all this really added up to.

Cheerfully these boys waved good-bye as I walked toward the chopper. First Sergeant Higa, who was a year younger than I, put a hard hand on my shoulder and said, "You old man, you come back and see us any time."

I swung up into the chopper and buckled into the greasy red canvas seat. The helicopter rose, its blades making the tall grass bend and ripple, and the boys on the ground turned their heads away from the blast of air and the sudden flying empty packs of cigarettes, the empty C-ration cartons skittering end over end through the silky grass. Like a little family, the troops went about their business, digging in as night fell.

Back at the TOC, Tom was holding his evening meeting with his staff. In the notorious first year of Harvard Law School I had been exposed to some pretty rough public questioning on the cases we had to prepare for each day's classes, but Tom's staff meetings, where the answers could affect lives, made that former trauma look like the academic exercise it was.

Just at the moment Tom had elicited from an embarrassed officer the information that some of his men had found bloodstains in some grass as a result of our mortar firing the night before, and not mentioned it until late afternoon.

"That's right," Tom said, standing beside the map on its easel in the shadowy lights of the sandbagged cave, the gauze bandage over his eye adding to his expression of scorn. "Keep it a secret. Save it for your memoirs."

Re the radios: "A lot of you are talking, not transmitting. Be brief. You have code words for referring to north, south, east, and west. Use them. You know the NVA have men listening in on our net who can speak English as well as we can."

The sessions were not without their humor. Taking a quick count of the various units in the fire base, all of them

understrength because of a lack of replacements, one lieutenant answered, "I have thirty, but there are going to be
thirty-one."

Tom: "What—is somebody going to give birth?"

II

I was out on patrol with some of the men from Jack
Crumley's Reconnaissance Platoon. The leader was a tall
young sergeant from Kentucky, and he ran the patrol as jungle
choreography. At every moment he knew where each of his
twelve men was, even when we could not see each other in
the high grass and bushes and vines, and he sensed every
slope and gully about us. He moved us across country like a
high-stepping football team, the line moving forward and the
backfield working its way around the end. Then he would
turn us and we would be a single file, retracing our steps,
cutting across a trail, wading up a stream, moving in a loose
diamond formation across dried leaves in cathedral dimness
under tall trees. When we rested, it was in hiding, rifles
ready, overlooking a swift-rushing river at the fork where it
entered the river marking the border with Cambodia.

"Alpha," he breathed into the hand-held black plastic
speaker of the radio on his back, "this is Finite Queen. This
element is at—" and he gave the coordinates from the greasy
plastic-covered map folded in his hand.

We found things. Three hundred yards from the fire
base, on our way down to the river, I had walked right past an
old *montagnard* dugout canoe that lay upside down on four
forked sticks that kept it above ground. It had been shaped
from the trunk of a big tree, and the hull was warped and
cracked. The sergeant stopped, knelt beside it on all fours,
nodded. The grass beneath it was bent and broken; an enemy
scout had slept there the night before, under the nose of our
hilltop arsenal of artillery and machine guns.

Further into the jungle we found a place where a North
Vietnamese unit had spent a night or more. We searched their
horseshoe-shaped foxholes, the small cooking tunnels that
had hidden their fires and filtered the smoke through piles of
branches.

As I stood looking down at their ration cans, the cardboard tubes that had held their mortar rounds, the sergeant was on his knees again, poking in the ashes of their cooking fires. He radioed our position and what we observed, and we moved on in the shadows, heading down a slope into thick undergrowth. There were thickets of thorny bushes, fallen trees, and great nets and webs of vines.

The soldier in front of me tried to sidle and shake his way through a dozen leafy vines, and suddenly he was caught, standing upright with both arms pinned to his sides. Two men converged on him and worked on the vines as one works on a knotted string, finally freeing him, and our patrol moved on.

That afternoon, back on the hilltop, I sat with my fatigue jacket off and sunned myself, reading a paperback about the French Foreign Legion. There were passages about their experiences here in Indo-China that did not make good reading. The French had lost five generals in the coastal mountains just south of where we had now built Tuy Hoa Air Base. Their hold on the area in which I sat sunbathing had been weak at best.

I stared at the misty hills of Cambodia, thinking of that boy this morning, so trapped in vines that it took two men to free him. Moments like that had to be witnessed in order to understand why we were not getting more results from the efforts of our half-million men in Vietnam. And that vine-trapped man, at least, had been out where there was a possibility of finding the enemy.

I shook my head as I thought of what I had seen in these months. Anyone who thought that we had five hundred thousand men *fighting* over here was crazy. At the air base there were sergeants whose job it was to repair air conditioners. I was not disposed to argue the point that many men and machines remained efficient only because their shops, offices, quarters, and mess halls were air-conditioned, but by no stretch of the imagination could those repair men be called combatants. The seldom-stated fact was that, of our half million men, no more than forty thousand, at best, were actively seeking this elusive enemy every day.

Even if one called into question the varying theories about the ratio of superiority necessary for a conventional force to beat a guerrilla force—five to one, eight to one, ten to one—*no one* had suggested that a first-rate guerrilla force could be beaten when one's own offensive spearhead was outnumbered by them. This was our situation in Vietnam, and it remained true even when one added in the Army of the Republic of Vietnam, which on any given day had fewer of their men out looking for the enemy than we did, with many units not really trying.

A sergeant came out of the TOC, grinning and shaking his head.

"What's up?"

He shook his head again. "Charger," he said referring to Tom by his radio code name. "Charger's in there breathing smoke, as usual."

I nodded, and tried to concentrate on my book. Here at least I was with a unit that was trying, that was constantly sending out patrols, that had never once been badly ambushed, that was killing ten or more of the enemy for every man we lost. Even in a battalion like this, the simple arithmetic of the situation worked against us. The Fourth Division's area of operations was in excess of one hundred miles long, and more than forty miles wide. That was four thousand square miles of some of the densest jungle mountains on earth, and since we could hardly expect the NVA to trip over our cannon-roaring fire bases, it meant that we had to go out and find them. When all was said, when one remembered Whipcrack's "We've got men defecating in Brooklyn and fornicating in Hong Kong," it meant that at any given moment there was fewer than one soldier per square jungle mile out looking for an enemy legendary for his invisibility. One officer, speaking of how this enemy could shoot at you and never be found, had suggested that my book be called *Bullets Without Guns.*

I put down the Foreign Legion book and picked up *Concussion,* the mimeographed newspaper that was published unofficially and irregularly by the Dragoons' rear elements at the Dragon Mountain division base camp at Pleiku.

> Radio-teletype operator, Pfc. Allin, after abandoning his rig which had been inundated after a recent monsoon rain, reportedly was seen stumbling

around the battalion area muttering "GOD IS DRUNK."

When Penfield, the Battalion's only real, live surfer, received his draft notice, he was forced to put his surfboard on the market with these words: STATUS SYMBOL FOR SALE. OWNER UNFORTUNATELY CHANGING STATUS.

My favorite item:

Sir Francis Drake is the English Admiral who circumcised the world with a forty-foot cutter.

As in every army in history, a good deal of the real news moves fast, from mouth to ear. That evening as we stood on the sandbagged steps of the TOC gathering for the evening staff meeting, Major McGinley, "The Jungle Fox" with goggles, said to Tom, "Lieutenant Remington out in A Company just inherited two million dollars."

Tom: "I assume he kept on walking?"

The red dust at Polei Djereng was the same clinging ankle-deep powder I remembered. Waiting for a plane back to Tuy Hoa, I sat beside the airstrip with Sergeant Bellanca, the battalion communications chief noncommissioned officer, who was going to the Army installation near the air base for a day to reenlist for three more years. Beside us were boys who wanted nothing more than to get out of the Army and stay out of it. The sun was hot, there was no shade, we drank from brown plastic canteens. Helicopters rattled in over our heads, raising tornadoes of red dust that settled on our sweating hands and faces.

The C–130 for which we were waiting landed on the matting runway and the crowd of us along the edge of the strip got up, shouldering our packs. There was yet another wait as we stood around the plane. I got talking to a barrel-chested boy who had blue tatoos just visible under the layer of red dust on his forearms. He was from one of the Second Brigade battalions that had been catching hell up here. He had come into the country five months before. Now he was the only man in his original platoon who had not been killed or seriously wounded.

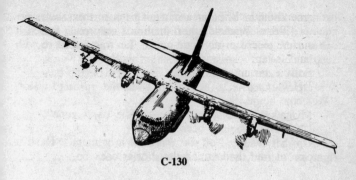

C-130

"They're all gone," he said.

We walked up the ramp of the plane to find all the canvas seats folded against the wall, and the center partitions and seats taken down to make room for a mountain of crates. We were to be packed aboard combat-loaded, which meant that we were to sit on the steel floor plates. We sat inside the baking metal hull, one man's knee bent over another's, one man leaning back against the pack on the man behind him, rifles jabbing into ribs and men keeping their helmets on because there was no place else to put them. We sat sweating and cramped in the silence as helicopters flew past the rear door and kicked more clouds of red dust over us.

A young soldier came up the ramp, his pack on his back and M–16 in his hand. He stopped for a moment, looking at the sea of muddy red faces and jackknifed knees.

"Ah, the champagne flight," he said, and sat down as the troops broke into laughter.

III

Mama-san's hand flew to her mouth as this red-dyed monster opened the door and trudged into the hooch. I said a couple of reassuring words and began to strip, dropping everything directly on the linoleum floor rather than messing up my cot or the desk top. I went into the bathroom and got under the shower for twenty minutes. When I emerged and used a white towel, it became red. I tossed the red-stained towel out from behind the door and indicated that she should hand me another. She did and I got back in the shower for another fifteen minutes. Again the towel was red. I tossed it out and she tossed in my final towel. Ten minutes more with soap and water.

Sully came into the hooch.

"Hey, Charlie," he called over the rushing water. "Welcome home."

"Thanks. You lose any planes while I was gone?"

"No. How about a beer?"

On that, I turned off the water for a moment. "Hand it right in," I said, and turned the shower back on.

FOURTEEN

So I got talking to this curly-haired guy at the bar and he turned out to be in charge of nine hundred of the Vietnamese workers on base. His name was Duane Strandquest, and although he was a civilian now, it was not too surprising to find him with the Air Force; he had started out flying B–17s with the Eighth Air Force over Germany in World War II.

Maids like Mama-san were paid by the occupants of the hooches where they worked, but Duane's responsibility was the nine hundred Vietnamese, three hundred and fifty women and five hundred and fifty men, who were hired and paid by the Air Force. A good many worked in the dining halls, but the majority were under the direction of the Civil Engineering Squadron assigned to the base. This involved the heaviest kind of work, and by Vietnamese custom the women did as much of it as the men.

"It's awfully hard for some of our sergeants to put a woman to work lifting beams or carrying rocks," Duane said. He went on to tell me that the entire temporary runway we had been using, made of big, solid metal slabs laid together like tiles, had been put in place by women shortly before I arrived.

How about the Viet Cong? I asked. Surely, among nine hundred Vietnamese—Duane nodded. The security clearances were handled by the Vietnamese. There were loopholes. Just a few weeks before, a Vietnamese worker had been found with a map of every gun position on the perimeter. Thus far, however, there had been no sabotage. No one could stop them from seeing what they could from where they worked. On the other hand, there was a shakedown point at the gate, manned by our Air Policemen, Vietnamese National Police, and some girls hired to search the women workers. Nothing suspicious had been found being smuggled onto the base, but all kinds of things, indicating the poverty outside, had been removed from workers on their way out. One woman had been found wearing two stolen T shirts under her blouse, and two pairs of GI shorts under her long black pants. Another had three stainless steel spoons nested in her vagina.

We talked about the things the Vietnamese were hired to do. Although 99 per cent of them had been farmers, they were now apprentices and journeymen in every craft needed at an air base—plumbers, masons, carpenters, welders, electricians.

If he were in my shoes, I asked Duane, how would he proceed in learning about the Vietnamese workers? He answered that there would be, in a few days, the first meeting of the Civilian Works Council, a group of sixteen Vietnamese men workers, each one elected by the workers in his section—Dining Halls, Airfield Section, Pre-Fabs, Carpentry, Soil Cement, and so on. This was the first elected representative group of its kind at any air base in the country.

"There was a lack of understanding when we first took the ballots out to them where they worked," Duane said. "There was an inclination to vote for the immediate boss in each small group, even though we told them that the point was to get the best man in the section. Then"—he smiled—"there was a great deal of wonder that I had simply not appointed some Vietnamese working in my office."

I started out of the bar, having jotted down the time of the meeting.

"You know," he added, "our employee suggestion boxes just don't go over in the Far East, because using it might be interpreted as criticism of the boss. They just won't use them."

At the appointed hour I strolled into the conference room of the Civil Engineering Squadron. Duane introduced me to his interpreter, an earnest Vietnamese in his late forties dressed in the Vietnamese bureaucratic status symbol of white shirt, necktie, and dark slacks.

In a moment there were feet on the concrete walk, and

the men of the Works Council entered. Moving with the grace and dignity natural to all Vietnamese, they seated themselves around the other three sides of the table. Half a dozen wore subdued sports shirts and slacks, and the others, including those who worked in the dirtiest and dustiest occupations, had managed to have on, for this occasion, spotless cast-off Vietnamese Army fatigues.

Speaking slowly, waiting for the interpreter after every phrase, Duane stated for the record what the function of this group was to be.

"The Council is the medium through which a mutual exchange of information can be accomplished between the civilian work force and management officials. It is not for personal problems of the council members—it is only to discuss problems of welfare, safety, morale."

Duane then said that it was time to have nominations for candidates for election to the position of Chairman of the Works Council.

Unfamiliar with the custom of one man nominating another, five of the sixteen around the table nominated themselves.

Slips of paper were distributed.

"Do not put your own name on the paper unless you wish to vote for yourself," Duane told them through the interpreter. "Put down only the name of the man you wish to vote for."

The workers nodded, each huddling over his slip of paper. On my note pad I wrote "They *like* it, I think."

The slips of paper were passed to the head of the table as all eyes watched Duane and the interpreter counting them. The atmosphere in the room was one of intense interest and good feeling.

The results: Tien Tran Phi, 7; Phong Hu, 3; Nguyen Ngoc Chuong, 3. Two others received two votes and one vote.

The new chairman stood, very businesslike. He was about thirty, with fine black hair brushed straight across a broad forehead. My notes read "Pleased but doesn't show it—sits down—smokes—takes out notebook and jots down when he is to see Duane in Duane's office."

Now it was the workers' turn. They said that the floorboards in some of the trucks that took them to and from their jobs and the base gate were rotten, broken, and unsafe. Duane told them to get the numbers of the trucks involved and give them to the new chairman, who would pass them on to him.

They said they had not received their Form 50s, which were their copies of record of employment and promotion. Duane said he knew that, and the forms would be prepared soon.

Several stated that many workers had not yet received the authorized increases in family allowances. Duane nodded, agreed that it was true, said he was sorry, and told them it would be added to their next pay.

The representative of a group laying concrete said they wanted a lunch hour in the shade, instead of on the sand by the runway. Duane said he would look into it.

One man said they should have double pay for working on Sundays. Duane answered that the Seventh Air Force pay scales for the Republic of Vietnam were copied from Vietnam's labor laws. Those laws called for time and a half for overtime, not double time, and that was what they were going to get. If they didn't want to work on Sundays they did not have to, but if they did, time and a half.

Through all this I was struck by the attitude of the interpreter. Duane's answers were given in a pleasant, calm, firm voice, but the interpreter bristled when addressing the workers, and his voice was angry. I was witnessing the problem of class that was at the root of much of Vietnam's trouble. The interpreter, an educated man, could not forget that he was talking to peasants. Peasants were supposed to keep quiet and not make trouble; under no circumstances were they supposed to fill the air with a lot of yammering about double pay on Sundays.

After this meeting, Duane took me over to a simple wood building and introduced me to Technical Sergeant Charles B. Eversgerd, of Evanston, Illinois. After Duane left, I got out my clipboard and began making notes in my most reportorial manner.

"How is your position described?"

Eversgerd said, pleasantly, "I'm the liaison man between the Eight-Twentieth Civil Engineering Squadron and the Vietnamese workers."

"Just how would you describe your duties?"

"If they got a bitch, they can come in here and we try to take care of it for them."

He took me on a tour of some areas where Vietnamese were working. We went first to a big garage, like a hangar, where the engineers pulled maintenance on their trucks. In here were the oldest sergeants I had seen in the Air Force, pot-bellied but with forearms like sacks filled with stones. One of them pointed at a tiny Vietnamese man kneeling on the fender of a truck with its hood raised, working on the engine.

"We hired these people to do things like wash vehicles and change tires. Now some of them can take an engine apart without supervision."

We passed to a smaller building that smelled pleasantly of freshly sawed lumber. In this carpentry shop the man working with the Vietnamese bore an uncanny resemblance to Spencer Tracy. He was Technical Sergeant Lewis P. Owens, of Harbinger, North Carolina, forty-three years old and a born supervisor. While I stood beside Vietnamese working buzz saws, I saw Owens confer respectfully with his foreman, then mimic a woman who was complaining, copying her so effectively that first the women in her crew, and then she, began to laugh, the complaint forgotten, and, finally, deliberately misaim a kick at a young man who was sloughing off on the job.

"Real workers," Owens said, pointing about him. "They work real hard. Language was the biggest problem when we started." One day he could not get a point across to his foreman, so he rang Sergeant Eversgerd's office and had them put an interpreter on the telephone. The foreman had never spoken over a telephone, and picked up the receiver as if it were a snake. When the call was over, he wandered back across the shop muttering, "Number One, number one."

"That man"—Owens pointed at his foreman—"turned in a VC who was working here. The VC killed somebody in his family once. He really doesn't like the VC."

Over in the electrical shop, the supervisor told me

"They've been a tremendous help. They're coming to a point where they can wire buildings without supervision." In some ways the comments sounded patronizing, but they were simply the reflection of a truth. In a nation where the great majority had never been seen by a doctor or spoken over a telephone, where there were only a few thousand passenger cars in a population of fourteen million and most people lived without electricity and running water, one could not expect a built-in familiarity with machines.

Interspersed with the observations were words of praise for the women, ranging from a Sergeant Jenkins, in prefabricated housing, saying "The women are twice as good as the men" to someone talking about a woman who had worked carrying metal slabs until the morning she gave birth to a child. A crew of fifty Vietnamese women had stacked three million board feet of lumber in a shorter time than the Americans had believed possible.

I had a beer with Sergeant Eversgerd at his hooch, watching him feed a pet mongoose, and walked back to my part of the base. In my mind were quick images from the afternoon; the Works Council voting; an eighteen-year-old Vietnamese boy with a welding mask over his face; an old woman digging a ditch. Here, at least, we were successfully working with the Vietnamese.

Sully greeted me at the door of the hooch, his gray flying suit showing the sweat marks that meant he had gotten out of his parachute and survival vest and G suit within the hour.

"We lost another one, Charlie."

"Who?"

He told me. Sully had been in the flight himself and had seen the fireball as the plane went in. The man who had been shot down was a major in the 308th, a fine man, as good a flyer as there was in the Wing. That morning I had sat across from him at breakfast. He had swarthy skin, shaggy black hair in a modified crew cut, and a pleasant slow smile. He had finished his fried eggs and ridden his motorcycle down to the flight line, and someone else had to bring the motorcycle back tonight.

The door opened and we welcomed the big, cheerful man who entered. This was Lieutenant Colonel Preston

Flanagan, known as Pres. He had arrived at Tuy Hoa later than those of us who had come in the big deployment, but he had quickly won the affection of us all. He was a pilot, but not a fighter pilot. He ran the Command Post, and flew the Wing Gooney Bird.

Apart from his pleasant smile, consideration for others, and wit, there were two things for which Pres was known. He was the best chef at Tuy Hoa Air Base, and he had been an All-American end.

At forty-nine, thirty years and thirty pounds heavier than when he played football, Pres did not look like one of its stars. One evening we started tossing around a football from the base recreation office, and with his first pass I realized that I had never understood what a football could do. This football hunted me down, it compensated for my mistakes, it sought out my hands, my arms, my chest, and insisted that I tuck it away nice and warm.

What brought Pres to our hooch this evening was some steaks that he and Sully had in the refrigerator. As always, they insisted that I join them, and as always I murmured weakly and accepted gratefully.

This particular evening, perhaps because of the loss of that pilot, perhaps because I was driving from my head the superimposed images of too many Vietnams, I drew Pres out about his past. None of us wanted to talk about the present. I opened cans of beer, and Sully set out knives and forks. We followed Pres in and out of the hooch as he took steaks, beans, garlic bread for which he had managed to find the garlic, all out to a charcoal grill which had been made from part of a retrieved and otherwise useless napalm bomb. I had never thought of brown beans as a delicacy before I became involved with the Air Force; indeed, steak and baked beans had at first seemed to me a contradiction in terms. But Pres, Pres with a touch of brandy, Pres with a whisk of sugar, Pres with a dash of Tabasco placed a culinary benediction even upon beans.

Against, through all this—Cheop Chai in hazy lavender sunset, mist over the runway, an early flare hanging over the mountains where the French had lost five generals, the lights of fishing boats on a purple sea—Pres told me of his life. He was born in a logging camp near Ogemaw, Arkansas. His mother died when he was eleven months old, and his father soon thereafter. He had no relatives.

"I was handed from one family to another," Pres said, his broad face staring into the yellow flame leaping through the black bars of the grill. He was put in an orphanage, did not like it, and determined to run away when he felt he could make a clean escape. His moment came at the age of eight. He took a bicycle and rode forty miles on it, to Eldorado, Arkansas, and got a job selling newspapers on a street corner. He lived in a trash box behind the newspaper office. Those copies of the newspaper which were ruined in the press were thrown into the box, still warm from the machinery, and this kept him warm in the winter nights.

His newsstand, made from a couple of crates, was in front of the Hollywood Café, a diner. When he was not selling newspapers he would wash dishes in the diner, and for this he received his meals free.

In September of his eighth year, Pres went up to the grammar school, waited in line with the other children and their parents, and registered himself for first grade. Thus, at eight, he had solved the problems of housing, food, spending money, and education. Eventually the owner of the Hollywood Café took Pres into his house, but he warned him that it could not go on for very long. The owner was planning to move to Longview, where the East Texas oil boom was hitting. He put Pres in another orphanage, and Pres waved good-bye to him, slipped out of the orphanage, and rode in an empty freight car to Longview.

When Pres showed up the owner shrugged his shoulders. Pres soon had his newsstand out front, his old job washing dishes in the New Hollywood Café, and registered himself in the Longview school. The café owner arranged for Pres to stay at the Roosevelt Hotel, and here Pres saw even more of life than he had before.

"It was a typical boom-town hotel," Pres said, turning the steaks and brushing them with a mixture of brandy and melted butter. At the Roosevelt he swept out halls, toilets, the lobby, and in return he had a rollaway bed which he kept in the men's room, setting it up at the end of the hall at night. The prostitutes living in the hotel mothered him.

"There were two or three deaths in Longview every night," Pres said, the fire shadows on his face and the Southern Cross above us. "I saw men literally cut each other's throats, over a woman. Once I saw a man with his head cut off in a barber's chair, because he was running around with the barber's wife."

Pres knew he was big for his age, he knew he was strong enough to do all the jobs he did, but what happened to him when he started playing sports in junior high school was a surprise. Nobody else was close to him in anything. He could run faster than anyone, jump higher, throw things farther and more accurately. No matter what he asked his body to do, it did it for him.

In the beginning he viewed sports as a diversion, a luxury too expensive in the time of a poor boy. He asked the school board to help him find a job, and they did, on bridge construction for the county. Every morning he swept the sidewalk surrounding the county court house. He had a paper route for the Fort Worth *Star-Telegram*. In those Depression days, Pres nonetheless made enough money to move from the sordid hotel to a decent boarding house. He still dropped by the New Hollywood Café, and Rudolph, the black cook, superintended his efforts as he cooked his own lunch for school.

"I had the best lunch at school," Pres said as he took our steaks off the fire. "Every day."

By the time Pres reached high school, adults were turning out to watch him practice—just practice—sports. A member of the school board gave him an attic room in his house. The owner of a grocery store gave him an easy job. The rest of the time he was free to play sports, encouraged to play sports, expected to play sports.

Pres smiled as we settled down inside our hooch, sitting on the edge of Sully's cot, the paper plates in our laps.

"I was practically a paid professional football player my first year in high school."

In the summers he worked in the oil fields as a derrick man, working up topside in the oil rigs. Out there, thrown upon his own resources, living in a shack, he perfected the cooking that Rudolph had taught him in the café. It kept him from being hungry, and concocting new and increasingly better ways of cooking beans kept him from being bored.

In the autumn of 1938, Pres entered the University of Texas, one of the nation's football powers, where Dana X. Bible was head coach. One hundred and twenty-two freshmen were invited to try out for the freshman team; every one of them had been a high school All-State player in his home state. Twenty-two were kept after the last cuts were made, and Pres was the starting left end. In his sophomore year he beat out the older players to become the varsity starting left end, and he held the position for three years in an era when players stayed in the game on both offense and defense, also doing all the team's kick-offs and field goals. There were other seasons of the year, and Pres won his varsity letters in basketball, baseball, and track.

"Wait a minute!" I said. "Didn't spring track and baseball run concurrently?"

Pres shrugged as if he were discussing someone else. "I was the catcher on the team, and between innings I'd go over and throw the javelin."

In his senior year, the autumn of 1941, the University of Texas was the number one team in the nation, and Pres was voted All-American.

"You know," I observed, "your early background. Do you think that gave you a competitive drive that some other people didn't have?"

Pres nodded. "I used to fight almost every morning for the best corner to sell newspapers at. It formed my attitude in competitive sports." He grinned. "I'm not a good loser."

Pearl Harbor swept Pres into the Air Corps within weeks of his final football game. He was trained as a transport pilot. In February 1943 he walked up to a brand-new C-47 in Miami, holding a sheaf of papers in one hand and the key to the plane in the other. He opened the door to 49572 and flew it to Brazil, then across the South Atlantic, and into a grueling two years of shuttling men and equipment throughout an area ranging from Casablanca to Kunming. Of flying the Hump from Burma to China, Pres said: "That really wasn't too good—you can't get over the escarpments—you have to go through the valleys."

One day the war was over, and Pres flew 49572 back across the Atlantic. He patted the wing of the plane he had commanded for twelve hundred hours of flying time, and walked away. A few days later and many miles away, he discovered that he still had the key to 49572 in his pocket. He decided to carry it with him as a lucky piece, and it was with him five years later when he was sent to Korea, manning an SA–16 seaplane rescuing downed pilots off the coast of Korea. It was in his pocket when he set up a task force at Mauritius Island, in the Indian Ocean, for astronaut John Glenn's ride around the world, ready to recover him if he came down in the vast area assigned to Pres and his men.

When Pres arrived at Tuy Hoa he had nine thousand one hundred hours of flying time, the equivalent of being at the controls night and day for a year and a half. He walked out to fly some men down to Nha Trang in the Wing's Gooney Bird, the plane that Sergeant Poindexter had resurrected from its cannabilized abandonment at the edge of Tan Son Nhut Air Base in Saigon. Pres looked at the tail number, blinked, and pulled out the key he had carried ever since he stepped aboard his first command in Miami twenty-four years before. 49572. It was the same plane. Pres patted its wing, climbed aboard, and settled down at the controls.

FIFTEEN

COLONEL LYNCH WOULD LIKE TO SEE YOU AT DRAGON MOUNTAIN.

This was the message from Tom, handed to me in the Wing Command Post by a young captain who had no idea of what it meant. I headed for my hooch, folding the piece of paper. Tom obviously felt that something noteworthy was about to happen. I smiled as I hurried down the road to start packing. The secondary significance of this piece of paper was that I had just entered an exclusive club, that small handful of correspondents who did not have to ask what had happened, but who were invited by commanders to be there when it did.

For the first time since they had come to Vietnam, the Dragoons had come in from the field to the relative comfort of the Fourth Division's base camp at Dragon Mountain, near Pleiku in the *montagnard* country by the Cambodian border. My ARVN pack slung over my shoulder and my helmet on my head, I wandered through drizzling darkness down a muddy street flanked by single story wooden barracks.

The troops were yelling. It was an eerie sound, repeated with only minor variations in each barracks I passed. The men were overwhelmed with such luxuries as cots to sleep on and hot showers at the end of the company street. They were singing, they were laughing, they were fighting and arguing and cheering at once. They were cleaning their rifles and rolling their packs. It was the eve of battle and pints of whiskey were passing from hand to hand; there were cases of beer everywhere, and the boys were shouting as if it were a football rally before the big game, waving their arms as they sang, howling at the moon.

In the darkness I collided with the adjutant, who led me to Tom, who was looking at maps. He shook my hand and slapped me on the back, motioned for me to throw my pack down beside a cot in the corner of this screened cabin, and told me I had just made it. The Dragoons were moving out before sunrise on an independent sweep to the south, into an area where no American unit larger than a twelve-man Special Forces team had operated before. For this operation Tom had his own miniature army, not just his own battalion but attached units of tanks, engineers, some extra helicopters, and a big supply column of trucks.

We went over to the mess hall. The cooks were going all out, serving steaks, cake, ice cream. Around the corner in the L-shaped dining hall the offices of the battalion were gathered, and they put down their glasses of whiskey and came to attention as Tom strode in.

Tomorrow's operation had already been planned to the last fuel can, flare, and bandage. This meeting was to do some drinking, a little joking, and to say good-bye to Major McGinley, "The Jungle Fox," who was being promoted to Lieutenant Colonel and whose new duties would be in Saigon.

Major Mac rose from his place in a corner of the shadowy wooden mess hall, and the young faces of the Dragoon lieutenants and captains turned fondly, respectfully, to hear him speak. He had been with the battalion for two years, ever since it had been taken out of the files at Fort Lewis, Washington, and activated for yet another war. He had seen the arrival of young recruits who had received their basic training right in the battalion, and he had worked with them through advanced maneuvers. Major Mac had helped organize them for shipment to Vietnam, and he had seen these same draftees and volunteers killed, wounded, decorated for valor.

He spoke quietly, in his Arkansas accent. He thanked them for their cooperation, told them that they knew what was necessary to keep the battalion strong. The words were simple, but without mentioning the concepts, he was speaking of loyalty, endurance, courage, comradeship. The faces of the young officers were riveted upon his: Toby Colburn, The Royal Pineapple, had tears in his flashing brown eyes. Next to Toby, nodding his head, sat the sunburned C Company commander, James Powers, whom I had seen presenting his company, singing "We Like It Here," to Tom in the red dust at Polei Djereng.

Major Mac finished, and we ate steak. Halfway through the meal Lieutenant Jack Crumley of the Reconnaissance Platoon saw his platoon sergeant frantically summoning him from the mess hall. In a while Jack was back, and the story was too good not to get around. Some of his men had decided to test the defenses of Dragon Mountain. They had slipped out through the barbed wire, crawled a quarter of a mile along the outside of the perimeter, right under the noses of guards in their watchtowers and bunkers, and then had penetrated the defenses at another point. It was when they were back inside, muddy and laughing, that some MPs had asked them what they were doing. The replies had been less than polite, and Jack had arrived just in time to prevent the MPs from calling reinforcements to try to take his boys into custody.

My pack and I were on a helicopter at six in the cold black morning, waiting for the engine to start and the operation to begin. Shadows came and went, voices spoke, matches were struck. I waited. The sky turned spongy gray. Light tore the curtain in the east. Vehicles moved slowly down the red clay road beside the landing strip.

A jeep pulled up. Tom walked toward me, the Sergeant Major behind him, slender Captain Paul Titus of the artillery last. Tom raised the index finger of his right hand in a circular "wind 'em up" motion, and the helicopter engine whacked into life. We vibrated, we were off, the sky was light and the earth was new.

I looked down and saw our task force. It was everywhere—twenty vehicles on a side road waiting to come into the main road, thirty vehicles on another side road, forty vehicles already under way, tanks and armored personnel carriers spaced out in the long column of canvas-sided trucks.

There were two hundred and forty vehicles down there, and I was excited. There was a tremendous surge of purpose and adventure. This was what we knew how to do, roll out in great force and hit with everything we had.

By evening we had not heard a shot fired. We were dug in on a meadow a few miles northeast of the *montagnard* town of Ban Me Thuot, beside Route Fourteen, the only two-lane north-south road in II Corps other than the coastal Route One. In parts this road was even paved, but traffic on it this first evening was zero.

With dawn came one of those inexplicable things. Two armed Viet Cong appeared on a grassy road that ran into the woods from the highway. They were four hundred yards from us, and they stood staring at our camp, making no motion to conceal themselves in the bushes.

Our mortar platoon commander was Lieutenant Andrew O'Brien, through whose body a bullet had passed while he was leading a rifle platoon in the hills of Phu Yen. He took one look at the two VC through his binoculars and tiptoed to the nearest mortar and whispered the interesting tidings to the section chief. The mortar was leveled, aimed, a round dropped into the tube with a *THUNK-BAAM*. Everyone watched the round soar into the sky; everyone watched the two VC. They stood staring at the camp; they were still staring when the round landed between them and killed them, throwing them apart like long gray sacks. The operation was off on its eccentric course.

An hour later Tom was making a fast helicopter trip around the area, matching up places on his map with the physical realities. Our companies were out in the rolling countryside, whacking the bushes. We flew over some elephants, the first I had seen since I had spent a few days in this area on my first quick trip to Vietnam two and a half years before. They looked like moving boulders as they glided through trees and bright grass.

We landed in a dewy green meadow where there was an ARVN artillery battery. Through the Vietnamese interpreter whom I had last seen at work when we went into that fifteenth-century time-lost village in the hills of Phu Yen, we double-checked with the ARVN so that they would not inadvertently fire into an area where one of our companies was moving.

The conference was cheerfully concluded, and, walking in the morning sunlight, we strolled back to our helicopter. We took off, heading out between two trees at the far end of the gemlike meadow, and there was broken Plexiglass all over us, the helicopter engine was choking, and we were sinking swiftly. The craft lurched in the air, corkscrewing, rotor blades still moving, gasping back in over the grass.

We landed with a shaky slam and leapt out. Wrapped many times around the vertical driveshaft that connected the engine with the blades was a cable that had no business being there. Unseen by us, unmentioned by the ARVN, one of the few telephone lines in the Central Highlands happened to be strung between two trees at the end of the meadow, and we had flown straight into it.

Tom and I looked at each other and began laughing. We were still alive, and the sun was shining.

That afternoon I spent learning one more aspect of the difference between myth and reality. A squad was detailed to go out on the highway and stop all vehicles and search them.

Stopping them was no problem. A big blue Dodge truck would come barreling over the rise, see a dozen men armed with M–16s and grenade launchers, and screech to a respectful halt. Usually there were at least three Vietnamese in the front seat in addition to the driver, and they would get out while the driver produced some papers and spoke volubly in Vietnamese. Since the battalion interpreter was somewhere else this afternoon, none of the Americans could either read the truck manifests or the passengers' Vietnamese identification cards or understand a word said to them.

Then came the searching. Starting off with a high sense of responsibility, the young soldiers swung up on the tall tailgate of the truck, only to be appalled by the difficulty of handling what they saw. Jammed into every corner, piled right to the roof, were bicycles, sewing machines, bags of grain, furniture, oil drums, crates of tinned goods. To empty just one truck and really search the contents would have taken the entire squad half an hour, and by now vehicles were already waiting on each side, half a dozen stopped on their way north and half a dozen trying to get south before the hazards of darkness.

So the vehicles were searched, and yet they were not searched, just as areas of Vietnam were secure and yet not secure. I would have been willing to swear that we did not let anything larger than a 75-millimeter cannon get through.

Walking about this fire base in succeeding days, I had a good view of the surrounding forested plains and the hills in the distance. During the day F–100s in flights of three would appear, orbiting high above this plateau, and then plunge in and drop their bombs at suspected enemy hideouts along the chains of hills surrounding us.

One evening I sought out the man who was our liaison with the fighter-bombers, the man who actually transmitted our requests. He was a twenty-four-year-old Air Force staff sergeant named John Fritchey, and I asked him how he liked being out here with just a jeep, radios, and a small tent, far from the amenities that most other Air Force men enjoyed at their bases.

"I like isolated duty," he said in a Midwestern accent, and went on to give me proof of that statement. He had spent 1961 through 1963 on a hilltop in Morocco, fifty miles from Casablanca, one of five men tending a radio relay station. In 1965 and 1966 he had been one of six men working on a special communications test at Grand Turk Island in the Bahamas on an atoll six miles wide and two miles long.

Then he had volunteered for Vietnam.

Why?

"Because I thought I'd like to be able to look back and say I'd been there, instead of I should have been there." He looked at me, and I tried to smile back at him out of a week of Vietnamese and *montagnard* faces on the road, too much sun, helicopters, cannon slamming away. "I believe in this war," he said. "I think it's for a just cause, but it's a shame people have to die fighting for freedom. I rest assured in my own mind that if this war comes to an end, we'll just have to move in somewhere else."

What did he think would happen in Vietnam?

"Eventually the Communists will have to break down, at which time we will nonchalantly bring the thing to an end."

II

There were days when it seemed that events conspired to keep me from eating. We had moved to a new fire base, the troops cursing as they emptied the dirt from the sandbags in our position by the highway and baled them up as we headed to our new spot deeper in the woods. Instead of eating, I spent an hour holding the open empty sandbags as the young radio men of the TOC shoveled dirt into them. As each bag was filled, I handed it to a man who would tie it at its top and place it on the wall we were building around the tent.

Thoroughly dirty and hungry, I had just managed to heat up some soluble C-ration coffee and a can of pork and beans when all the radios came to life. Tom's jeep was outside the TOC, and I put down my coffee and beans and ran to listen to what was coming over its radios. Tom was aloft in the command and Control helicopter, and now, out of our sight, he was directly over the place where B Company was suddenly shooting it out with a force of unknown size in thick brush at the bend of a river. I had my clipboard with me, and jotted down the tight voices as Tom, using his call sign of Charger, talked with the company commander on the ground, who was asking for a dustoff, a medical evacuation helicopter.

Charger: "Negative Dustoff at this time. If you're in contact, stay in contact. Over."

I kept writing as men were being wounded.

"Charger, this is Eight-Two Six. Over."

"This is Charger. Over."

"One of my men has a chest wound that doesn't look too good. I'd like to get him out of here. Over."

"This is Charger. Roger. Out."

A minute passed.

"This is Eight-Two Six," the ground commander said again. "The medic says this chest wound doesn't look real good. Over."

"This is Charger. We'll get him out as soon as possible. Out."

A new voice, that of a FAC who had appeared in his little plane, grabbing from the sky a flight of F–100s that had been headed somewhere else.

"Charger, this is Cider One-One. I've got four canisters of CBU." These were the maiming pellet bombs I had seen that sunny day in Florida. "I'd like to run them down the riverbank. Over."

"This is Charger. Run 'em. Over."

Twanging music closed over the American voices. The North Vietnamese were jamming the radio. After a minute the music was somehow broken, and, cool as could be, the voice of Captain James Powers of C Company came on, indicating that his troops were now making contact, too. More transmissions, more twanging Vietnamese music. Captain Paul Titus of the artillery was pacing in and out of the TOC tent, running a hand through his shaggy black crew cut. He was all set with his cannon, but the troops in the bush were now fighting at such close quarters that our shrapnel would kill as many of us as of the enemy.

Things moved fast at a good headquarters in the wake of an action, helicopters tearing in and out, and later that afternoon I was at the small landing field that belonged to a Special Forces camp nearby at Buon Blech. Lying on a stretcher at the side of the strip was a tall, fine-looking young Viet Cong who had been wounded fighting with a group of mixed Main Force Viet Cong, their full-time regulars, and North Vietnamese Army men in today's collision. An American Army doctor in fatigues was sewing up a gash that looked as if the front of his foot had been hit with an axe at ankle height.

While the doctor worked on the prisoner's foot, a Vietnamese in civilian clothes was squatting by his head, putting into Vietnamese the questions being asked of the prisoner by a dull-looking American from a Military Intelligence detachment.

I stared at the interpreter. His round face looked familiar, and then I realized that he had been the interpreter at a Special Forces Camp called Buon Mi Ga, near here, when I spent the New Year's of 1965 there on my first trip to Vietnam. He was fluent in English, the *montagnard* tongues, and spoke French as well as his native Vietnamese. I remembered a strange night when he and some of the Special Forces team and I had been invited to an on-stilts thatched long house of the Rhade tribesmen. There had been cymbals beating, totemistic freshly whittled wooden mobiles hanging in the flickering light of a charcoal fire, and rice wine in tall terra cotta jars, the sickening brew like dirty water as it entered one's mouth from a long reed sunk in the shadows of the jar. There had been no nonsense about a Rhade party, no parlor games or singing or dancing. Just beat the cymbals and get smashed.

I remembered something else about this man. His father had been killed by the Viet Cong. He had declared a personal war against them, and here he was, two and a half years later, still fighting in his own way.

The interrogation finished, the gray-faced VC was placed aboard a helicopter to be flown to the hospital at Pleiku.

I introduced myself to the Vietnamese and he remembered me, or said he did. He was now working for the CIA, and referred to it as that, rather than using the American euphemism "The Embassy." I asked him about the camp at Buon Mi Ga; his face clouded. The camp had been closed, he told me. Now Buon Mi Ga was one of the Viet Cong strongholds in the area.

There was not much more to say. We shook hands, wished each other well, and parted in the dusk, I walking with the Military Intelligence man toward a helicopter headed back to the Dragoons' fire base. I was thinking about Buon Mi Ga in those days, a strategically located camp, the base for a *montagnard* strike force of three hundred men working smoothly under the direction of Special Forces. In the big village thirty-five hundred *montagnards* had protection at night, going out to work little gardens and cut wood during the day.

They had closed the camp. Doubtless they had their reasons, but it meant that someday we would have to fight our way back into a place that had once been secured. It was the same old story, invisible except to students of the situation on the spot. Unpalatable as it might be, the fact was that, structured as our forces were, fighting this type of enemy, we did not have enough trigger-pullers to do this job and then hold our gains and make them stick.

I was in a foul mood when I walked into Tom's tent, but his mood was a far more Celtic black than mine. We had killed five enemy, and had one NVA and one VC prisoner, but five Americans had been wounded.

I told Tom that I had overheard the interrogation of the Viet Cong prisoner, and thought that the American Military Intelligence man had asked superficial questions.

"Stop putting this super-spook stuff on me," Tom snapped. "Now you're talking like a newspaperman instead of a Dragoon."

"I think that prisoner is the most important thing this operation has turned up so far," I shot back.

"All he can tell you is who's in his own squad," Tom spat out. Then he walked out of the tent and collared the Military Intelligence man, telling him to get after that prisoner wherever he was and find out more.

The next night Tom was no longer angry. He was just sick. In midafternoon two of his men at the head of a patrolling file had been killed with one burst from an enemy automatic rifle. No trace of the enemy. Tom had swooped in by helicopter and gotten the bodies out of there. Sitting on his cot as we sipped at Scotch, he told me that, coming back in the chopper, looking at the two dead boys on the floor, one of them black and one of them white, he had thought about it all, what he was doing here, about the war, about his military career.

Speaking slowly, of the war, of what we were trying to do out here, of the attempt to halt the Viet Cong–NVA takeover of South Vietnam, of his efforts to inflict the maximum damage on the enemy while keeping our own to a minimum, he said, "I just kept thinking one thing. I hope what I'm doing out here—I just hope we never have to run this thing through again."

It was obvious to me that although the two dead boys were in rubber bags now at Buon Blech, waiting to go to the morgue at Dragon Mountain, he still saw them lying right in front of him on the muddy grass between our cots. I said something about how well the black soldiers were fighting.

He nodded. "If there's one group over here that's *good*—" For the first time since I had known him his voice broke. He went outside, and after a few minutes I went through the tent flap. Tom was in the TOC, his voice calm as he gave orders, but out here in the darkness, with a bottle, was Toby, The Royal Pineapple. He had not been in the actions of the last two days because he had been told to hold himself in readiness to travel on an amazing set of orders. A request had come down from Division, a few days before, for this battalion to forward the name of a captain who had commanded an infantry company for at least six months and had the Bronze Star or higher. Toby had won the Bronze Star, and his name had been duly forwarded for what everyone had assumed would be a staff job at Dragon Mountain. Instead he had been told to hold himself in readiness to go to Tokyo and help run the Rest and Recreation leave center there for a couple of months. No one could believe it, least of all Captain Toby Colburn, The Royal Pineapple.

He and the Sergeant Major and I started working on his bottle as we sat on the low sandbag wall in the darkness. After a while Toby, for the first time, called me Charlie instead of the Mister Flood he had rigorously observed. Someone said something funny, and the Sergeant Major slapped me on the back.

I beamed. I always thought of Sergeant Major Hannon as "Sergeant Major," as if he were a piece of Army equipment that had no family name. Sergeant Major Hannon, twenty-seven years in the service, lantern-jawed, always chewing something, never smiling, always correct, had slapped me on the back.

The next day the rains came, and so did an invitation. Through the American advisors in the area, two Frenchmen who ran a big nearby plantation were inviting us to come to lunch the following day.

Tom smiled at me. "Your free ride is over. You can speak French, can't you?"

I replied that I had studied it, had been to France a number of times, was not good at it, would do my best, and would he please do himself a favor and get somebody else if he possibly could?

"You're my interpreter," Tom said, and I said, "Yes, Sir."

Back Pack Radio (PRC-25)

*   *   *

Early the next morning, hours before the time to have lunch with the Frenchmen, I stopped in by helicopter to see my friends of B Company, who were dug in and having a morning of rest and resupply in the woods. Sergeant Higa, the stocky Nisei one year younger than I who insisted on calling me ''you old man,'' greeted me and then left me in soaking grass among the young radio operators sitting beside their hissing olive back-pack radios.

We talked as light rains sprinkled us, stopped, and the highland breeze tugged at our quick-drying jungle fatigues. Young, round-faced John Collins spoke more of the progress of collecting funds for orphans than of the recent firefights they had been in. Mo Thomas had increased his gambling winnings from the rest of the company to fourteen hundred dollars, up from twelve. Tomlinson, the boy who looked like a young Jimmy Cagney, was chewing gum, making transmissions on his radio, and cleaning his M–16, all at the same time. Next to him was a big young man named Henry Green, who had been a groom at a trotting track, the Northfield Raceway, in Northfield, Ohio. I noticed a handsome panther's-head tattoo on his brawny bicep, and he told me that it had been acquired just before he sailed for Vietnam, in a tattoo parlor in Tacoma known as "Painless Brenda's."

"I got it on there," he said. "I just liked it—then I found out that the Second Brigade had a panther for a mascot, and all the guys in the Second Brigade were getting them." So, with the distinguishing mark of the Second Brigade, rather than his own First, indelibly on him, he carried his barracks bag aboard the transport.

There was a new young second lieutenant named Berg, from Seattle. Instantly he reminded me of my Tuy Hoa hoochmate Sully: small, strong, ready to laugh. His movements were quick, graceful, and effective. In a few minutes I found that there was something more to the resemblance. He too had been a pilot. Before ending up as a ground-pounder in the Infantry, he had been a bush pilot in Alaska. He had walked away from two crashes near the Arctic circle, and thus far Vietnam had been a safer place for him than Alaska.

There were four boys sitting nearby, silent, facing each other in a circle. They were not staring into each other's eyes. There were no religious objects visible. For half an hour they sat that way. I learned that they often did this, a silent communion, and no one knew anything more about it than what I had just witnessed.

Somebody was kidding Tomlinson. He was copying a radio transmission on a sheet of lined paper. It turned out that he literally could not write on a sheet of paper that was not lined. If he wanted to send a post card, he had to draw lines on it before he could write a message.

A chopper came in, the one I would have to get to be on time for lunch at the plantation. "Good-bye, old man." Sergeant Higa shook hands, the boys turned their backs against the sudden wet winds the chopper poured through the rainy tall grass, and again I saw this little American family draw in, smaller and smaller in the jungle as the chopper rose.

At the fire base Tom was chipping the dried mud out of the cleats of his jungle boots, getting ready for a civilized house. I hastily followed suit, and then one of the sergeants from the TOC came over with a piece of information that made Tom's jaw drop. The senior American advisor in the district was on his way over in the helicopter that was to take us, but now it developed that he was accompanied by two American females and a correspondent.

Tom emitted a four-letter word and summoned the Sergeant Major.

"Smadge," he said, using the contraction for Sergeant Major, "I don't know why, but there are two women dropping in here in approximately one-zero." He pointed at the immediate area, which included two GIs cheerfully chatting as they sat, shirts off and trousers around their ankles, on one of the open-air two-holer latrines made from ammunition crates, and another soldier urinating into one of the pipelike fixtures made from artillery powder tubes. "I don't want any lilies dangling. Nobody relieves himself until these women get out of here. And have them put on their shirts." Then, a mischievous expression on his face, he went into the TOC and started arranging things so that the ladies would get a taste of the war.

If events had conformed to the American experience in Vietnam—optimism followed by disappointment and frustration—what should have emerged from the helicopter would have been two nuns, or perhaps a couple of the beefier, fatigue-clad nurses from one of the field hospitals. Instead, the drizzle stopped, the sun appeared, and a perfectly lovely tall blonde stepped out with a graceful bounce, followed by a shorter girl with long black hair, a slender waist, and a gorgeous bosom displayed in a thin red blouse.

As Tom met them and led them to the TOC, the effect on the troops was summed up by the reactions of four young artillerymen near me. The four of them wordlessly sank to the grass.

I followed the group into the TOC, and blinked. Metal chairs and wooden benches were neatly lined up facing the map on its easel, there was a display of captured enemy weapons and equipment, and one of the tables had been swept clear of maps and codebooks to make way for a coffee urn, paper cups, paper napkins, and a tray of cookies.

The girls were seated directly before the map, along with the reporter. This young man had earned instant distrust by his appearance, which included a set of old-style fatigues with a shirt hanging loose instead of tucked into his trousers, no headgear, hair unnecessarily long for one who could have it cut any time in Saigon, and a pair of yellow suede boots guaranteed to attract an enemy's attention at three hundred yards.

Wearing helmet and web harness complete with grenades, Tom began his briefing of the girls and the reporter, explaining where we were and what we were doing. I was getting a different kind of briefing, whispered to me in the back of the tent by the American district advisor. The girls, he told me, were International Volunteer Service workers who taught classes in sewing, hygiene, and home economics to *montagnard* women at Ban Me Thuot. The blonde had been out here for two years and had recently survived a helicopter crash. The curvy brunette had just arrived in Vietnam.

As Tom continued his briefing, he nodded to Paul Titus, who quietly gave the signal for every cannon in the fire base to open up on targets they had been planning to shoot at anyway. We had some self-propelled 155-millimeter "Big Boys" with us on this operation, in addition to the usual six 105-millimeter guns, and they all opened up at once, their projectiles crossing our tent a split-second after leaving the cannon muzzles. The brunette leaped halfway to the ceiling, almost slipping out of her red blouse on the way back down. The blonde did not flicker an eyelash. She had been here for two years.

With not a change in tone or expression, Tom kept talking earnestly and pointing at his map. The cannon stopped, and a moment later the Air Liaison Officer brought across the fire base at treetop height three F–100s that had just finished a mission nearby. This time half of us ducked—three jet fighters in a tight **V** with their afterburners going can sound as if the end has come.

We had coffee, and then Tom scooped up two of his officers and me. Off we went in a chopper following the District Advisor's chopper, which held the girls and the reporter, the last of whom seemed to feel I was not quite a legitimate observer of the war because he had never met me in Saigon.

The plantation was a dream of quiet beauty. It lay in flat high country, the grass brilliant from the rain. The *montagnard* villages on its boundaries, their thatched houses set on stilts in mathematically straight ranks, gave way to equally arrow-straight long rows of rubber trees and coffee bushes. The cool

M 102 105 mm Howitzer

mists gave one a sense of being in a northern climate, and our two helicopters swung in over a series of hedges, gardens, and white-washed stone barns and warehouses that spoke of Normandy.

Our rotor blades stopped and we walked in post-rain silence across long wet grass toward a driveway filled with white pebbles. Beyond it was a white château with outside stairways, balconies, French windows—a clever, tasteful ad-aptation of northern European architecture to *Indo-Chine*. In the driveway stood a group of Vietnamese children and adults. Among the women, the distinction between those who worked in the fields and those who worked in the house was marked on the one side by lusterless black cotton pajamas and on the other by pastel blouses and shiny black trousers.

Waiting before the house were two Frenchmen, one in his late forties and the other in his early fifties, both wearing cotton pullovers of a different make from anything in our PXes. I moved ahead of our group, ready to start my role as interpreter by performing introductions in French, my heart sinking, feeling like a damned fool, when the first Frenchman smiled, shook my hand, and said, "It ees the fairst time a helicoptair evair comes here." A moment later both the brunette IVS girl and the correspondent were introducing themselves in solid French, and I retired gratefully to the edge of the handshaking knot in the driveway. We were motioned up the outside stairway to the second floor, and passed over the yellow-tiled covered balcony into a large white-walled room. For the first time in many months I sank into a couch made not of imitation leather and tubular steel, not of wicker, but of cloth and stuffing and springs—a couch couch.

The Frenchmen offered us excellent Scotch, and we sat drinking, in a real house, talking to Caucasians who were the second generations of their families to live on this plantation. They were brothers-in-law. They had packed up their wives and children and sent them to France two years before, and each took a long vacation to visit them each year, but this was indubitably their residence.

How much it was their residence I discovered when I made a brief excursion to a splendid bathroom, complete with a big tub, shower, bidet, and the kind of running water I had left behind at Tuy Hoa two weeks before. Emerging from the bathroom I made my way back through one of the Frenchmen's bedrooms. His bed was a big canopied four-poster, there was a marvelous stuffed tiger on a pedestal near the center of the high-ceilinged room; but what interested me was what I saw in a large open armoire. On hangers were about fifty exquisite *ao dai,* and beneath these dresses were some thirty pairs of high-heeled shoes. The Frenchman had sent his wife back to France, but one could not say that he was simply camping out in the Central Highlands.

The lady of the many *ao dai* did not appear, but no additions to the party were necessary. Aided by the Scotch, the presence of pretty American girls, the uniqueness of the occasion from each person's point of view, the conversation flowed well. Strangely, despite our helicopters, despite the weapons of our men monitoring the back-pack radios on the steps outside, it was the Frenchmen who seemed the powerful figures in the room. They were only mildly curious about what we were doing marching and countermarching through Darlac Province, and were quite informative about their own operations—up to a point. No, they had had no trouble with the Viet Cong. Yes, the war had ruined conditions for growing rubber and exporting it—now they grew coffee and sold it within Vietnam.

Last year, the older of the two told us, they had to pay the equivalent of thirty thousand American dollars in taxes to the Saigon government.

They waited for us to commiserate. We, on the other hand, felt they had a pretty good thing going here. Although we did not say it, all of us had simultaneously decided that if they could afford those taxes and find it worthwhile to continue, they would have to look elsewhere for sympathy.

One of Tom's officers caught my eye and we exchanged a quick smile. We were both thinking the same thing—I wonder how much in taxes they pay the VC?

APC M 113

Lunch was enough to make me cry, after forty-three straight C-ration meals. There was white wine and a delicious cold fish, surrounded by tiny ringlets of eel, sprinkled with *nuoc mam*, fermented fish sauce, which had somehow been melded with a French touch of oil and vinegar. Then soup. It was quite simple, but the best soup I had tasted since my last trip to Paris. Then bottles of red wine and the meat. Rabbit. Delicious. Freshly shot and cooked. I could not help it; I had a picture as if I had seen it myself. While we are hunting the Viet Cong, an enterprising VC is hunting rabbit. He brings a bag of them to the door, is paid, yes, the Americans are coming for lunch tomorrow, yes, and life goes on in *Indo-Chine*.

The correspondent got good and drunk, which suited me well, for I was not far behind him and happy to have him as the front runner.

For dessert, chocolate mousse. All of this deftly served by an old Vietnamese woman and two teen-age girls.

We left amid much handshaking, Vietnamese children all over the place, me trying to find out how I could see the tall blonde again, the blonde polite but not interested. The correspondent made his way to the chopper in a cheery stagger, tripping over the taller blades of grass, a beatific I-forgive-the-world smile on his face. *Merci, merci bien*, and the white houses spun away beneath us in dark highland mist.

The next noon I was staring at leeches. They were on the legs of a patrol that had just waded up a jungle stream to rejoin those of us who were manning a tank and four armored personnel carriers in a clearing miles from the fire base. Pulling the bottoms of their fatigue pants from the tops of their boots, they revealed these leeches that had slipped through folds of cloth and onto skin during their walk through marshes and upstream. Some had climbed a good deal higher than the men's calves. These wormlike creatures were small and pink when they painlessly attached themselves unnoticed to a man wading through a marsh, but now, filled with the men's blood, they were horrid swinging appendages the size and color of dark glistening cigars.

They met their end by the application of lighted cigarettes to their heads, which caused them to relax their jaws as they died, dropping off and leaving ugly blood-running holes on the young black and white legs of the patrol. The men shrugged, pulled up their trousers, and started opening their C rations.

On the way back to the fire base I rode on the jouncing metal deck of the tank that was in the rear. The road was bright red clay. The shades of France were still with me; the roads led past abandoned plantations with borders of plane trees as in France, and the hedgerows outside villages created the sense of an upland Normandy. At moments we looked like a World War II newsreel come to life.

The illusion was not complete. We encountered groups of Rhade, invariably walking single file through fields, carrying baskets on their heads, neatly spaced in their files with the instinctive sense of order evident in the rigid rows of stilted houses we occasionally glimpsed from the road.

A quarter of a mile from the fire base our iron monster turned a sharp corner and came to a crunching halt. We had slipped a tread. The other armored vehicles cheerfully rolled on through red dust. The crew of the tank climbed out, said that they would be here for quite a while, and I might as well walk on in. I strolled along slowly toward our barbed wire, alone under the cloudy sky, thinking of how even our own machinery occasionally defeated us.

When I came through the door of my trailer at Tuy Hoa, my first thought was that Mama-san had been stricken with a virus. Her face was white. She moved in a way that was graceful as always, but it seemed to take all her effort.

"Papa-san," she said, speaking of her husband who had left her to go with the VC in the Saigon area. *"Cec ce dao."*

She drew her hand across her throat, her dark eyes alight with pain.

Cec ce dao. Death. He was dead.

"Oh, Mama-san," I said. "I'm so sorry."

"Number Ten," she said in a choked voice, shaking her head. *"Beaucoup* Number Ten."

She had more to say.

"VC say I work for Americans, they *cec ce dao* I."

My eyes closed and I shook my head.

She was back at work the next day.

SIXTEEN

The morning after my first night-flying mission, I awoke in an earthling mind. They could keep their planes for a few days, and I would try to find the country over which they were flying.

At nine that morning I presented myself in the screen-sided office of Sergeant Eversgerd, the liaison man with the Vietnamese workers on base. He said that I had come on a good day. He and another sergeant were en route to Tuy Hoa town to have lunch with a Vietnamese friend. Before lunch, they were planning to buy a few things in the public market and also to look at an orphanage to which they were planning to donate some used clothes and scrap lumber.

Soon we were on the road, smooth asphalt on the base and broken, rutted, and bumpy once outside the perimeter. Cheop Chai grew larger. A Korean MP signaled us to make a right turn onto Route One where it ran along the river, and then we were in a long line of vehicles waiting their turn to cross the one-lane bridge into Tuy Hoa town.

I had ample time to study the composite of vehicles and people waiting in the cool sunshine by the broad stony riverbed. Huge olive American Army trucks, white stars on their doors and helmeted drivers wearing flak jackets, goggles, and faces of dust, waited along with tiny two-wheeled donkey carts filled with Vietnamese of all ages, clutching to them things as varied as baskets of bananas and bicycles. Despite the tragedy that stalked the country, there was often a festival air in Vietnam. The people were cheerful, their vehicles colorful, the women's pastel blouses and *ao dai* invariably tasteful and pretty. A boy came past with a huge pig, a rope around its neck, moving just as would a dog on a leash. Popular Forces militia ambled past, feet in rubber sandals, wearing old but clean fatigues, with headgear that looked like—and were—old Boy Scout hats.

We crept across the long bridge and soon turned into the broad main streets of Tuy Hoa. This town of sixty thousand, the capital of a province of three hundred and ninety thousand, was physically little scarred by the war. It gave the impression of having been laid out as if it had been supposed to become a much larger city. We were proceeding down a wide boulevard, and yet there was nothing more than two stories high on either side of it, with many a grassy gap between buildings. Its post office would not have served an American town of five thousand; it had one movie theater and seven small restaurants. In short, its sixty thousand people lived simple, marginal lives.

There was no one style of architecture. In the countryside one saw mud walls and thatched roofs, or plaster walls and orange tile roofs. Here the style appeared to be a mixture of slanting roofs of corrugated iron or orange tile, one-story houses back from the main streets, while the boulevards had flat-roofed two-story houses, the ground floor invariably an open-front shop with counters running back into the shadows.

We parked on a street off the boulevard and proceeded on foot. The yellow plaster market buildings indicated a national economy that was hard to measure. Here was a nation undoubtedly crippled by war, and yet by the standards of what I had seen in other and peaceful parts of Asia, and in Africa and Latin America, there was a profusion of the simpler consumer goods. They were apparently priced so they could readily be afforded by the simply dressed buyers who were making their purchases at the hundreds of small stalls in the various buildings. Metal pots and plastic basins, kerosene lanterns, rope of good quality, reed mats were all doing a brisk trade. There was a huge display of glasses and stainless steel knives, forks, and spoons that I had no doubt came straight from American mess halls. There were small suitcases made from defective stamped sheets of the metal for the sides of beer cans. To my delight, I saw that you could have a suitcase whose entire pattern was Budweiser labels, a piece of pop art so authentic as to deserve reimportation to the country that had been happy to sell the defective label sheets at any price.

I stopped beside one yellow building where there were thousands of red earthenware pots, and an entire building was given over to selling bolts of gaily colored and patterned cloth for women's *ao dai*. Across the street were crates of apples, bins of squash, and banana bunches. Under a massive corrugated iron roof was the open-sided fish market, emptying now that the sun was well up, but still with a quantity of fish and shellfish.

Waiting for the two sergeants to complete their purchases and come back to the panel truck, I found myself bewildered by this seemingly healthy bustle of economic activity. Since the entire economy was agricultural, and since there was little statistical knowledge of how much was bartered in the villages and the district market places, I decided to keep an open mind about the real state of the Vietnamese economy. It was undoubtedly experiencing convulsions and inflation on the monetary plane, but it resembled the bee, who is aerodynamically much too heavy for his wings and cannot fly, but does not know it and keeps flying anyway. The market reinforced a feeling I had had for some months; Vietnam was a Pandora's box of social evils, but no one was starving.

We presented ourselves at the orphanage, a bare yellow building up a rickety side street. Crowds of children are no rarity in Vietnam, but the group that clustered around us here had a special clannishness about them, as if each one was the only thing the others had, and things such as fights or cliques were luxuries they could not afford.

One of the five diocesan nuns who ran the orphanage appeared, smiled at us, and nodded at her ragged charges.

"Good morning!" they chorused, exhausting their English, and she asked us into a room with stools and a table to which she brought three warm Coca-Colas. In the best Asian tradition, she did not inquire what our purpose was in coming, but her halting English indicated that she had had experience with Americans before. This orphanage with its hundred and fifty children had been located inland, and all of them had been scooped up and brought here by American soldiers when the fighting in the hills had intensified the year before.

They lived, she said, as they could. There were contributions from the United States arranged by the soldiers, and Phu Yen Province gave them two hundred piastres per child per month, perhaps a dollar fifty at the rate of exchange, but worth more than that in Vietnamese buying power. The older boys in the orphanage lived in a brick and corrugated iron structure a few hundred yards away, which they shared with the pens holding the convent's herd of pigs. The boys' most important job was to care for the pigs, which could be sold for seven thousand piastres apiece, or fifty-three dollars, when grown.

She took us on a tour of the building, first out to a back area where a number of old people in black farmer's dress were eating at wooden tables. The withered old people rose when they saw us, and we quickly smiled and went on. I inquired and found that in Vietnam it was common for orphanages to take on helpless people at both ends of the spectrum of age.

We climbed to the second floor and entered what she called the "baby room." It was certainly the best room in the place, light and with cross-ventilation from big windows, but the babies were not in keeping with the brightness of the room.

For the three of us Americans, accustomed to the first-waving radiant vitality and powerful little cries of an American baby, these infants were a shock. They lay silent in row upon row of cribs. The limbs of many were wasted, loose flesh hanging on tiny arms that are balloonlike in the United States. There were rashes, there were sores, and yet there were teen-age Vietnamese girls tending them. The room was clean; their bodies were washed.

The nun explained that many of these babies came to them already suffering from malnutrition and malaria. Then, looking down at one of the healthier babies, who nonetheless gazed at us listlessly, she said: "Our babies are usually sick in their first year, because they lack the warmth of their mother."

I stayed looking down at the child as the others moved on, struck with what she had said. It seemed that I had always known it, but I had to come far from my country to understand an international truth. Despite these Vietnamese girls who occasionally picked up a baby and hugged it, there was *no* substitute for the constant loving attention of a mother. No one could care that much about whether these babies lived or died, so the baby itself did not care, since it had not been able to sense the importance of its own existence, which can first be sensed only by feeling through caresses that one is important to another human being.

I moved down the aisle between the small wooden cribs, and stopped again. Under a mosquito net lay a little girl who was half American Negro and half Vietnamese. She looked totally Negro, very pretty, healthy, and, eyes open, just as cut off from her surroundings as did the other babies.

I felt a chill. From living in Japan I knew the future that awaits the illegitimate children of black servicemen and Asian women; they are pariahs in Japan. Although the Japanese government will not admit it, efforts are made to ship all of them to the large Japanese settlements in Brazil. A Eurasian orphan in Asia, no matter what the color of the father, lives a life that proves Asians to be as racist as ourselves. Because Asians prefer light to dark shades of skin even among themselves, and because they are aware of Caucasian prejudices about Negroes, the chances for a happy life for a half-Negro orphan in Asia are zero. This little girl needed more than mother love. She needed a miracle.

We emerged on the street silent and depressed, but there was still the lunch Sergeant Eversgerd had mentioned.

The house to which we drove was that of Tuy Hoa's leading entrepreneur, Mr. Nguyen (pronounced *Win*) Khoa Lieu. His living room was in what had been an open-front store in a two-story building he had bought. Thus we simply crossed the sidewalk and were instantly among the pieces of his furniture, a sort of horrid Asian Grand Rapids of light varnished maple.

Mr. Lieu was sixty and looked forty, and lived in the Chinese-derived patriarchal merchant tradition. This was his living room, and yet there were pens and ledgers at hand. As we arrived, he ushered out two Vietnamese with the unmistakable air of a business meeting well concluded. He introduced us to a man who was apparently his secretary, and poured us bourbon and Coke. At various times there passed through the room one of a dozen children and grandchildren, two maids, and sufficient older women to indicate that, whether they were sisters or cousins or concubines, Mr. Lieu was the male center of a large and bustling amorphous family group.

He appeared genuinely fond of the two sergeants, whom he had met because he had the base laundry contract. Beneath the glass top of the hideous maple table at which we were soon to dine there were scores of photographs. Among them was one of Sergeant Eversgerd and the other sergeant, standing on either side of Mr. Lieu's son, a young noncommissioned officer in the Vietnamese Air Force.

Another guest entered, and I recognized the Vietnamese interpreter who had been unconsciously imperious at the Works Council election and meeting I had attended at the base.

Mr. Lieu began talking of business. He was negotiating with the Air Force to carry all the Vietnamese workers from Tuy Hoa town to the air base each morning and back each evening, by bus. He already had the laundry contract with the base, to do all the sheets and pillowslips.

I asked him what some of his other interests were. He owned real estate, he said, and was a building contractor and supplier. To support these activities he had a gravel quarry by the river and a brick kiln at the edge of town. He owned trucks to conduct his business, and these trucks were also for hire. He used some of them to bring the thousands of sheets from the air base back and forth from his laundry.

I smiled. Mr. Lieu may not have known the word *conglomerate*, but that's what he had.

Mr. Lieu abandoned his not-bad English and began speaking through the guest who was the interpreter at the base. Lieu's face and hands took on all the earnest expression of a man who wants to convince you how broad-minded he is before he launches into a particular prejudice. He was not against the government, he said, not at all. In fact he had once been a district chief himself, in 1936, at the age of twenty-nine, under the French. But he had to say that the Saigon government's taxes were the devil. He was paying personal income tax to Saigon via the Province offices, and a *taxe mixte* that was part personal income and part real estate tax, and licensing taxes so that he could be in business in the first place.

He sighed. There was the forestry tax, which struck him as pretty silly because with the war the forestry agents didn't get out to the forests anyway, so what was the use of supporting them? But what really infuriated him was the tax he had to pay on his laundry concession with the base. The Americans had brought their sheets to Vietnam, he said, and what was the Vietnamese government doing, charging him for the privilege of washing American sheets?

I was really enjoying it. He sounded like a conservative American businessman growling "What the hell do these ivory tower think-tank professor economists know about it? *They*'ve never had to meet a payroll."

Realizing that it might be a blunder, I asked him what he paid in taxes. The laundry tax about which he was complaining came to nine thousand piastres a year, or just short of seventy dollars. When I considered that every man at Tuy Hoa slept between two sheets every night, I found the tax less than harsh, although I sympathized with his thought that it should not exist. His licensing taxes came to another nine thousand piastres, and his personal income tax was four thousand. Those were the major ones. Thus it was safe to say that the richest merchant in Tuy Hoa paid less than three hundred and fifty dollars a year in taxes. From this I could understand why it was the United States that was paying 94 per cent of the Vietnamese government's annual budget. The Vietnamese taxpayers were coming through with only 6 per cent, and at these rates I could see why.

Mr. Lieu poured me another bourbon and Coke and asked me if I knew where he could buy an airplane.

I choked. "What kind of airplane did you have in mind, Mister Lieu?"

He gave me a perfect description of a FAC plane. I told him that the Air Force FAC planes were not for sale, but that aircraft manufacturers in the United States would be delighted to sell him one and ship it here if he could get an import license.

Mr. Lieu nodded. While he fixed the sergeants another drink, I found myself wondering what he had in mind. It would certainly be a way of escaping from Tuy Hoa in the event of the town being overrun, but he did not look like the kind of man who would leave this menage behind, and, to take them, he would need a Gooney Bird at the least. Besides, I was not sure that he would have to worry in the event of a Viet Cong takeover. He had gotten along with the French well enough to be a district chief. When the Viet Minh had grabbed this town after World War II and held it for nine years, he had been right here, a successful capitalist paying taxes to them. Now he was probably on fine terms with everyone.

Wondering when I would cross the Asian line that distinguishes legitimate dumb foreign-devil questions from rudeness, I finally asked him what he would use the plane for.

He turned, smiled, and broke into a youthful series of gestures and singsong words at which the interpreter chuckled.

"He thinks it would be fun to learn how to fly a plane."

We moved to the lunch table. The opening course was small rings of squid sitting atop bamboo sprouts, liberally soaked with *nuoc mam*, the spicy sauce that I was fortunately beginning to like, since the Vietnamese managed to slip it into everything. As we snapped away with our chopsticks, I asked these residents how the war had affected Tuy Hoa, and from this we moved into their views on the war.

They began with the proposition that if the United States had not intervened with a massive injection of foot soldiers in 1965, the Viet Cong and North Vietnamese would have wrapped up the war and there would be nothing for us to be discussing now. Then they proceeded to say, in effect, that they did not like having all these Americans around, but they much preferred it to a Viet Cong victory, and preferred it to the French rule that both men remembered well.

"I was taught French as a small child," Mr. Lee, the interpreter, told me, "but it was engraved in my mind that the French were bad. I never allowed myself to work for the French. I did not receive one P from Frenchmen."

Mr. Lieu chimed in to say that he did not like the Koreans, that they acted like a brutal occupying army instead of an ally. Then both of them started in on the ARVN, that the ARVN treated the farmers badly, and that it shook down merchants by threatening to accuse them of being Viet Cong unless they made payoffs. Mr. Lieu said that he wished there were fewer "intermediaries," as Mr. Lee translated it, involved in the flow of aid to the people. He wanted to prove to the people in the countryside that the aid was going to them and not into assorted pockets along the way.

It was Mr. Lee, the interpreter, who spoke of the difficulties facing the Saigon government, which he had just finished roasting for its corruption. The Viet Cong, he said, were dealing in promises, and committed only to producing results in areas and activities of their own choosing. By contrast, the Saigon government was forced to deal with visible problems, and was responsible for all areas and activities. Badly as they might perform, the Saigon government was responsible for maintaining roads, telegraph offices, fire engines, files of birth certificates, and so on. The Viet Cong could stand back, mine the roads, and poke fun at the bureaucracy.

I had the feeling that it was not easy for Mr. Lee to say all that he was saying to me, but he plunged on. To give South Vietnam a chance to build its own administrative ability, he said, he hoped there would remain a permanent division between North and South. He wanted to see South Vietnam become a democracy, but right now too much democracy would be fatal.

"I want a strong dictator who works for the people," he said, and then surprised me by adding that the Americans should virtually run the country for a while.

Another dish was on the table, fried rice with bits of egg and seasoning in it, and I chanced a last question of Mr. Lieu, asking him how strong the VC were in Phu Yen.

In Tuy Hoa town, he replied, 90 per cent of the people were against the VC, although not actively so. In the countryside, however, the lack of a continuous and strong government presence gave the VC their chance to propagandize and conscript, and they had a considerable majority among the farmers.

Briefly the subject of the first national elections, some months ahead in September, came up. Mr. Lee said that 50 per cent of the people didn't like the whole idea of balloting, and on that cheerless and candid note we finished lunch and went to see a house Mr. Lieu was building.

This newest enterprise in the Lieu conglomerate was half a mile away, next to what might be called an annex of his family compound. Here in a shabby plaster house lived his ne'er-do-well brother and a half a dozen females ranging in age from fourteen to seventy. The women's wealth and social status was determined by whether their black trousers were shiny black or simply black cotton peasant-pajama cloth and by how much gold they displayed in the form of earrings, necklaces, and gold inlays set for no medical reason into their front teeth.

Where the new house was going up there were half a dozen carpenters working, and I watched for some minutes. They were fitting pieces of wood together without using nails. Disdaining the use of pencil marks as a way to indicate where one should chisel or saw, they worked by eye alone, eye and hand, joining boards at right angles as tightly and permanently as nails ever did.

Mr. Lieu was pointing at the vacant acres that ran on down this side of the road.

"He will build several houses," Mr. Lee told me. I nodded. One could see that the town was growing this way, across these flat lands, away from the natural boundary of the river on one side and the political and military uncertainty in the Tuy Hoa Valley on the other side.

I asked Mr. Lieu how many big businessmen there were in Tuy Hoa.

"There are four of us," Mr. Lieu answered, staring across his acres and seeing, I am sure, the day when, no matter what flag flew, the houses he was now building would be pulled down to make way for small apartment houses and office buildings.

Back at Sergeant Eversgerd's office at the air base a new Vietnamese girl had reported for work as a typist with theoretically bilingual skills. Eversgerd took out a mimeographed page of regulations concerning employees, written in English. He asked an interpreter to have the girl read it in English and then say in Vietnamese what it said.

The girl nodded, took the page, studied it gravely for a minute and then handed it back with a quick phrase in Vietnamese.

The young interpreter, seeing nothing funny in what he said, told us: "She can read it but she cannot understand it."

Amen, I thought, amen to the whole situation.

At Tuy Hoa one had only to discuss one bombing mission to be instantly invited on another. I now found the principle applied to orphanages. I was sitting at lunch with the Catholic and Protestant chaplains attached to the base and spoke of having seen that orphanage the day before.

With a "Why didn't you tell us you were interested in orphanages?" air, they both began talking at once. They were headed downtown right now, and I dazedly bounced down the same long road to Tuy Hoa in another panel truck, headed for a different orphanage.

At the wheel was Chaplain George Crosby, a Southern Baptist who had been in the Air Force for ten years, and to the other side of me was Father Justin Maurath, a Maryknoll missionary with the same length of uniformed service. Father Maurath was a fixture at the nightly poker games in the bar of the officers' club, raking in a majority of the pots, and he gave his winnings to the orphanage toward which we were headed.

The contrast with yesterday's orphanage could scarcely have been greater. We swung off Route One into a complex of large, freshly painted buildings and a swarm of healthier and less ragged children. One of the little boys who ran alongside our truck was wearing a white T shirt with the blue lettering OAKVILLE UNITED BRETHREN. There was no Protestant orphanage in Tuy Hoa, so Chaplain Crosby gave the clothes he received from Baptists in the United States to this Catholic institution.

This orphanage, Lac Thien, meaning "Charity," had been founded nine years before by the Sisters of St. Paul de Chartres, an order which had its mother house in the French cathedral city but had eight hundred Vietnamese nuns working throughout Vietnam. The orphanage had one hundred and fifty children living there, and fifty-two old people. They raised hogs, too, but the sisters were a teaching order, and it was this that placed them on a far more advantageous plane. Next to the orphanage buildings was a large and spacious three-story concrete school building. They had six hundred and fifty children in their elementary school classes, and one hundred and fifty in high school. Only 20 per cent of the families in Tuy Hoa who sent their children here were

Catholics, but they felt that the school offered the best education in town. Thus the orphans attended tuition-free, the other students paid, and the entire operation came close to breaking even.

A slender Vietnamese nun in a white habit stepped across the sandy courtyard to greet us. She was Sister Theresa Antoine, and as she guided me around she told me something of herself. She had gone to high school in her native Hanoi, leaving the North as part of the large Catholic exodus that had taken place after the Communist victory in 1954. Her religious life had begun with three years at the mother house in Chartres and a year at Lille. Then she had spent three years at St. Paul College in Manila, where she learned English. From that time on she had been teaching French and English, first at Danang and then here.

As she showed me through the large, airy classrooms, I found myself thinking that here was a Vietnamese who surely could have escaped the trials through which her country was passing. There was about her the never-extinguished air of one who began life comfortably, with servants, protected, monied. I had no doubt that this pretty, graceful woman could be living in Paris, married to one of the thousands of Vietnamese doctors who successfully resisted the thought of returning to heal their suffering countrymen.

We were standing on the concrete terrace outside the classrooms on the third floor of the building, looking across the rice paddies of the Tuy Hoa Valley toward the misty enemy hills to the west. I mentioned that I had visited Chartres three times, and that I loved the Cathedral and had described it in a couple of my books.

For a moment she was lost in thought.

"It is lovely there," she said quietly. Then, looking out toward those hills, she said that one night two years before, Viet Cong mortars had struck this compound. Seven babies had been wounded, and two killed—one seventeen months old, and one two years old. She added that she thought the shelling had been a mistake, that the Viet Cong were trying to hit an artillery battery a quarter of a mile away. Then somehow she came back to the subject of the French.

"They were colonists," she said. "The U.S. is quite different." Again she paused. "Before, we studied French because we had to—now we study English because we like to.''

We came back downstairs. She was mentioning that in Phu Yen, 70 per cent of the children in the Province were able to go through the first six grades of school. She spoke as if this were an accomplishment. I asked her what she thought would be the outcome of the long struggle.

She was an intense person, her eyes bright under unplucked brows.

''I have no idea of what will happen in Vietnam.''

Why, I asked her, why do the Viet Cong fight so well?

''I don't know why they fight.'' Then she observed that the Viet Cong had their orphans too, many children who were just left to grow up under VC auspices. ''When they suffer,'' she said softly, ''they are told it is the fault of the other side.''

And as for herself? How long would she be here in Tuy Hoa?

''It makes no difference. I will serve where I am told to serve.''

I asked her if some of the children here were half American.

She nodded. They had three at the moment. ''The boys are a problem. The girls can stay with us all their life.''

Two big Air Force dump trucks were being loaded with sand at an excavation where a new classroom annex was going up, and as we rejoined the chaplains they told me what they had worked out. Instead of coming up from the air base empty to get at the Cheop Chai quarry the crushed rock that was needed for the air-base roads, the trucks would start with loads of sand, which was certainly in abundance at the air base. They would drop the sand off at the one Protestant church in town, which was filling in a marshy area so that it could build a school. Then the trucks would take a short run over here, and haul another load of sand, from this excavation to the Protestant church. They would continue empty to the quarry, load up with crushed rocks, and return to the base.

We're going to pull it off, I thought quite suddenly as I stood in the dust and sunlight, the trucks being loaded, the slender nun talking to the two big chaplains in their green fatigues with the crosses on their collars. We're going to fumble through somehow and this country is going to have peace, a choice of churches, justice, education, health.

"Thank you, Sister," I said, and got into the panel truck.

II

Back at the hooch there was a letter from a friend of mine, James Lowenstein. Jim was a consultant to the Senate Foreign Relations Committee, and he was coming to Vietnam with Senator Philip Hart of Michigan. Was there any chance we could get together in Saigon?

I pulled out a calendar, which I seldom looked at, since the numbers and names of days lost all significance in this environment. Jim's letter had been mailed from Washington, but the date he said he was arriving was the very next day. I decided that it might do me good to see a face from home, a friend from my past.

By a fairly remarkable coincidence, when I consider that Jim and the Senator had come halfway around the world while I had to fight the military transportation system from Tuy Hoa, I arrived to call on him at the Caravelle Hotel at exactly the moment that he and the Senator were emerging from the Embassy car that had brought them from the airport into the center of the city. Half an hour later we were having a drink in the Jerome and Juliette bar on the hotel's eighth floor—one of the highest manmade points in Vietnam.

Senator Hart proved to be the most pleasant and unassuming man I have met in public life. He had been wounded in Normandy when he was with the Fourth Division in World War II, and he had asked to visit the Fourth, at Dragon Mountain, and was on his way up there the next day. Jim was to be taken on a trip to the Delta.

The Senator asked me about the morale of the American troops. Thinking of my Dragoons, into whose territory he would be going the next day, I found myself making a political speech of my own, my constituents being those boys out there in the jungle.

"The morale is outstanding," I told the Senator, and went on to say that all the Army and Air Force colonels I knew, who had seen the recruits of three wars, were agreed that these were the best young men yet. I added that I thought the cheerful dedication and self-sacrifice of these young men was particularly remarkable in view of the fact that it was an unpopular war at home, that these boys had only wanted to be left alone and not be drafted, and that they were perfectly aware that they were not being supported by anything like the manpower and resources available to us. We spoke of other things, and then the Senator and Jim were off for a dinner at the Embassy.

I looked around the dim bar. There was a luscious blonde in the corner, and suddenly I saw that the deeply tanned crewcut man sitting with her was motioning for me to come over and join them. It was my friend John Wheeler of the Associated Press, whom I had last seen lunching with Peter Arnett and Horst Faas in the drab but excellent dining room of the Royale. He introduced the girl, who worked for an American civilian communications firm in Saigon, and then said that he had just been in a hell of a firefight with a unit I knew—the Dragoons.

I sat down and took a good look at John. Despite the healthy color, he looked shook up, and I soon found he had excellent reason to be. He had gone up to the Central Highlands with a notion of doing a feature on day-to-day life in an American infantry company. He had ended up with C Company of the Dragoons, and had slogged with them for three days through the hilly forests over by the Cambodian border.

"C Company?" I asked. "How's Captain Powers?" I smiled, thinking of the tall red-faced West Pointer who had presented his company to Tom in the red dust of Polei Djereng, saluting as his first sergeant led the men in a roaring chorus of "We Like It Here."

"Dead," John said. "I was next to him when he was killed." They had been climbing a hill on the third day, near the end of their march, ready to link up with B Company at the top of the hill. They had been taking a break, sprawled on the ground before tackling the last part of the ridge, when the enemy opened up on them with everything. Captain Powers rose to see what was happening and was killed instantly.

John told me that the fight went on for four hours. The

enemy made eight separate charges sideways across the hill, and the Americans kept driving them off and attacking uphill at still more North Vietnamese who were blocking their chance of linking up with B Company on the crest. A lieutenant I had known, Clay Johnson, was killed leading the attack uphill that began to break the enemy resistance, and was being put in for the Distinguished Service Cross. The first sergeant who had led the singing at Polei Djereng had taken over, leading the rush that broke through to join up with B Company, which was fighting its way downhill toward them. He had been wounded through both hands, and was also in for the Distinguished Service Cross.

Ten Dragoons had died, all within a few yards of John. Although Captain Powers had died with the first rounds, he had saved his company because, even resting beside a trail in sloping rain forest, he kept them spread out in a big diamond formation. When the unexpected attack came, they were ready, simply because of the way they had been placed, and were able to maneuver instead of being trapped in single file on the trail.

"I've been in some tight spots with the Marines and some Army companies," John said, "but I've never seen a rifle company as good as that." He told me of a young black soldier who should have been looking for a medic, once they linked up with B Company and the enemy fire was lessening. The man's bleeding left arm was hanging useless at his side, and he had no helmet. He still had his M–16 in his right hand, and as the Americans formed up to drive into the bushes after the North Vietnamese he walked over to John.

"Gimme your helmet," he said. "We're going to assault."

"*You*'re going to assault?" John asked, staring at the man's shattered arm.

"We're all going to assault, man," the black soldier said.

I stared at John in the cool quiet bar.

"What did you do?"

John shook his head, still seeing the boy right in front of him. "I gave him my helmet, and he assaulted."

I ate alone, and went back to Room 22 for what turned out to be a bit of comedy that I needed just at the moment.

One of the more frequent transients of the room was a free-lance photographer who was the nearest thing to a nonstop fornicator I have known. He was the sort of young man who suffers genuine discomfort and distraction if he does not have sexual intercourse daily. Of course, such a man would be better off in Pocatello with a healthy and understanding wife than in the catch-as-catch-can world of Saigon and frequent trips to the womanless marshes and jungles. But this particular man had a great deal to prove, it seems, and not only sexually. When he had been in the pre-Vietnam-era peacetime Army, he had earned his paratroop jump wings and had successfully completed the Ranger course. Although a good many correspondents in Vietnam had won these and considerably more prestigious strips of cloth during their pasts, my sometime roommate was the only one who wore these badges on his jungle fatigues. Even better, he was the only man in Vietnam who had artificially built-up jungle boots, making him two inches taller but giving him a gait that appeared as if he would pitch on his face with every step.

I opened the first of the two doors leading into Room 22 only to hear a shrill yelp of "Wait a minute!" from the bedroom within. I waited somewhat less than that and opened the door, more or less aware of what the situation would be, but damned if I was going to spend the evening walking around the block. Keeping my face set straight ahead, I walked over to the single bed against the wall some ten feet from the twin beds nearest the door.

I ventured a look over my shoulder. There, looking innocent and even angelic, were two little heads on the pillow of one of the twin beds, both staring at the ceiling as if it bore a message of intense interest. They looked truly like children, the American with reddish-brown hair, the Vietnamese girl with a wonderful cloud of long black hair framing her pretty, solemn face. The entire scene was well illuminated by a bedside lamp next to the man, which he made no effort to put out. I shrugged, slipped out of my shoes, slacks, and sports shirt, and got into my bed, which happened to be made up so that I was facing them. I likewise found myself staring at the ceiling as if tablets of wisdom were engraved there.

After a minute there was a bit of whispering and some

rustling, then silence, then some more rustling. Marvelous to say, the outside door opened again. In walked Kim Ki San, an Associated Press photographer from Korea with a great reputation for courage in the field. He was altogether faithful to the wife whose picture, along with that of their five children, sat next to his bed, the foot of which was just beyond the head of mine in the big room's outer alcove.

Kim Ki San nodded politely to me, his face betraying not the slightest acknowledgment of what was going on. He undressed beyond the alcove wall, slipped swiftly into his bed, turned on his bedside lamp, and lay there reading *Is Paris Burning?*

With the arrival of Kim Ki San, we now had four people occupying three beds. There was more whispering, and the photographer and his girl rose from their bed and went into the bathroom. I turned on my side and was almost asleep when the door opened again and in walked Lou Garcia, a photographer from the AP's Atlanta bureau. He was heading straight for the bathroom.

"Lou," I said, "there are two people in there right now."

He came to a teetering halt with his hand on the doorknob of the bathroom, and backed away. After a minute the perplexed expression faded from his face; he shrugged as I had and got into the unrumpled of the two cheek-by-jowl twin beds. He reached across the rumpled bed, turned out the light, snorted "Good night, all," and was asleep a minute later. I wanted to stay awake and catch subsequent developments, but sleep engulfed me too. By morning the rumpled bed was empty.

I was not scheduled to meet Jim Lowenstein again until midafternoon, so I had lunch with the Associated Press crowd at the Atterbe, a restaurant near their favorite Royale and used by them almost as often. Always looking for a change from the healthy but uninspiring military diet, I had pumpkin soup, stewed rabbit, and red wine.

Peter Arnett was at his raucous best. Someone asked me what Tuy Hoa Air Base was like, and Peter, who had seen the sands, the sinister background hills, our stark layout of bright corrugated iron buildings, let his eyebrows soar and chimed in with his New Zealand accent: "It looks like the first American settlement on the moon."

After lunch some of us were unwilling to let the flow of good conversation go, and Peter and a reporter named Ken Whiting and I went into a nearby bar. We were immediately accosted by half a dozen bar girls in pretty *ao dai* with flowing white satin trousers, all intent on our buying them drinks. We finally satisfied them by buying beers for two of them.

As the girls sat perched on their bar stools, not comprehending a single word since the perfectly understood "You can have one beer," Peter observed that these girls were particularly young, because these clip joints used the quiet afternoon period to break in the high school girls who would later develop into the hardened evening regulars. He said that a nearby bar, the Colisee, was particularly sought after as a place to work because no less than sixteen of the hostesses there had married Americans and gone to live in the States.

Suddenly there was a sound as if a large cat had gone mad. One of the older girls, sort of a den mother to these apprentices, was in a furious argument with a middle-aged American in civilian clothes further up the bar.

"You Number Ten!" she screamed. "You bullshit me!" This last was an accusation of bad faith, and the American was backing off a step or two, holding his hands palm outwards, trying to soothe her.

I decided it was a great moment to stare down into my beer as if nothing were happening. These girls, despite their demure appearance, had a violent combination of avarice, jealousy, and the Oriental concept of face. A medic working in a Saigon dispensary had told me that a regular part of his business was treating GIs who had been so rash as to come into the same place two nights running and to pick out a girl other than the one they had favored the night before. This sometimes resulted in knife wounds on the faces of the soldiers. The girls were apparently very good at this quick, superficial slash with a small knife.

The girl up the bar, a pretty creature in a mauve *ao dai,* was brandishing an empty beer bottle at the offending American. The bartender was busily hiding his glasses and bottles behind the bar and trying to shield a big mirror with his body. The girl sprang, chasing the American out the door with a beer bottle flying end-over-end above his fleeing back.

I sighed, thinking of Mary McCarthy's brief trip to South Vietnam and her observation that Saigon night life was tame. To this day I wonder where they took her.

Two mornings later I had breakfast with Jim and Senator Hart at the Caravelle. The Senator had spent two days with the Fourth Division and was even more impressed with the attitude of the draftees than I had told him he was going to be.

"It makes you wonder whose children they are," he said.

We spoke of various aspects of the Vietnam situation, and he added, rhetorically: "What can you say about a situation like this?"

I murmured something about yes, it's difficult, but I did not realize just how rhetorical the question was, since in fact he said nothing at all about Vietnam on his return to the United States.

I stood up, shook hands with them, and went about the business of heading up-country. I wanted to find the Dragoons and hear more of what had happened to Captain Powers, and how things were going for them now.

SEVENTEEN

The Dragoons were always on the move, and this time I tracked down their newest jungle camp by hitching a ride in a chopper from Dragon Mountain to the Special Forces camp at Duc Co, near the Cambodian border. We circled through wet clouds coming into the camp. The American twelve-man team of Green Berets and the *montagnard* strike force they commanded, along with the *montagnard* soldiers' families, lived within a large triangular fortified area. Outside it were other thatch-roofed *montagnard* houses on stilts, in neat rows as always. There was a rainy montage of tin roofs and sandbags and barbed wire, and then we settled onto a runway of metal matting laid on wet red earth.

I was wet by the time a Dragoons helicopter came in. Tom Lynch waved me aboard, pumped my hand, patted me on the back, and went on working with his map and headset as if I did not exist. In a few minutes we landed in a wet grassy clearing in which I saw my friends of B Company, complete with the familiar smile of Sergeant Higa, who regarded me by now as an eccentric good-luck piece that occasionally fell on him from the heavens. Since the radio operators were usually within a few yards of their first sergeant, it took only half a dozen strides to shake hands with John Collins, cheerful and energetic as always. Mo Thomas had now cleaned out the company for sixteen hundred dollars and was getting tired of carrying all that extra weight of military scrip in his pack. Tomlinson, the young volunteer who looked like Jimmy Cagney with moles, told me that they had found ninety-seven dead North Vietnamese in the bushes where they had attacked downhill to link up with C Company in the recent firefight where Captain Powers was killed.

"All those NVA were wearing red berets," Tomlinson said—headgear never seen on the enemy before. There were two theories: either these attackers had been an elite force, or like anybody's GIs they had picked them up as souvenirs, in Cambodia. In any event, Tomlinson said, the blood-stained red berets were now highly prized American souvenirs.

The B Company commander had lost a thumb in the firefight, and now I was shaking hands with his replacement, Captain Neil D. Buie, Jr., who had a shock of black hair, a permanent case of five-o'clock shadow, and glittering blue eyes. With him stood the platoon leader I thought of as the Bush Pilot, now walking away unharmed from jungle battles as he had from crashes in the Arctic, and beside him was Lieutenant Fletcher Bass, who had been a halfback and still looked as if he could hurl himself with devastating effect.

There was an unpretentious confidence about them all. From Sergeant Higa down to Henry Green, the trotting track groom with the panther's-head tattoo from Painless Brenda, they respected the enemy after this last clash, but they also knew that they had killed ninety-seven enemy for ten Americans.

I stood around, listening a lot and talking a little, and then Tom had finished talking with Captain Buie and we were on our way into the fire base, which proved to be a hellhole of red mud and cold fog.

"How's your work going?" Tom asked me as we heated our C rations for lunch, using little cubes of heating material set aflame within tiny makeshift stoves made from C-rations cans. These heating cubes were becoming more plentiful with each visit, and looking at the cold white mists hanging in the surrounding forest, I was glad that they were. It was sunny now on the coast, but in the Central Highlands it was miserable.

I told Tom that as I looked at all my notes, as I added up my own experiences in the past seven months, I was struck with the difficulty of what I had undertaken. Had I joined this very division in England on the eve of D-Day in World War II, I would have, assuming I survived, been able to recount a story of movement—across the Channel in the Invasion, into

Normandy, the Liberation of Paris, the Rhine Crossing, the fighting across Germany, and, eventually, victory. Here it was first one muddy hilltop and then another, one F–100 mission and another and another, all from the same base. Saigon did not move. I simply shuttled back and forth between largely repetitive situations.

"That's what your book *should* be about," Tom said sharply. "Nobody understands that. This *is* a formless situation. That's what your book should be about—the formlessness and frustration."

"All right," I said, "but how do you write a beautifully constructed book about a completely formless situation?"

That night I lay on my cot in Tom's tent, listening to his reedy breathing as he slept, hearing the rain that was sizzling endlessly on the canvas.

Tom's words from earlier in the day came back to me in the clammy rain-hissing dark: "formlessness and frustration." It was enough, sometimes, to drive one mad. The fact was that the most powerful nation in history was unable to accomplish its objectives in Vietnam. Thus a question posed itself as to whether the objectives were unrealistic or whether the methods used were unrealistic.

I was still inclined to feel that it was the methods which were unrealistic, and under the head of methods I felt that totals of manpower could not be excluded. Here we were at the end of the line, listening to rain on a canvas tent in a hilly jungle. There were really just a few hundred of us up here, and right across the Cambodian border, in an area we were forbidden to attack by land or air, the enemy had more men than we did. Any time he chose he could saturate this area with more men than we had here, and the fact that we had men back along the line who worked to cook hot meals, worked to provide good medical attention, worked to bring mail forward—none of that helped the rifleman up here when the first bullet snapped at him.

I turned over on the hard canvas cot, shivering and pulling the thin quilted poncho liner tighter about me. The inescapable fact was that if we were not going to do more to put North Vietnam out of action, then we were allowing ourselves to be confronted by a situation in which the struggle between a mighty and indecisive nation and a small and determined one came down to small groups of armed men hunting each other in the jungle. The least we could do was to put in more hunting parties than the other side had, which it was certainly clear that we could do on a population basis alone; but we were not doing it. When we were not trying to hit a mosquito with a hammer by sending supersonic jets against tiny, scattered targets, we were playing six-man touch against an eleven-man tackle team on the ground.

I found myself wondering what the hell was really in those reports that Lyndon Johnson was reading back in Washington. He and Secretary of Defense MacNamara and Secretary of State Rusk were not men of low intelligence, no matter what their critics said. A war could be lost by faulty reporting procedures. If what they were reading gave them no indication that nine out of ten men over here were supporting our hunters rather than out hunting, if what they were reading disguised the Saigon government's inertia and corruption, then they were proceeding on inaccurate assumptions. If we were feeding false data into a computer, the computer would lie right back to us.

Our cannon began firing at something, and it was this that broke my thoughts and brought me sleep.

II

Largely to get out of this sea of red mud, I set out on a patrol one morning with eleven men from Crumley's Reconnaissance platoon. In some ways I made a mistake.

The first phase of the mistake was that this was no terrain for any person to be walking in unless he was young, in perfect condition, and under orders to do so. The countryside had absorbed so much moisture that it was a huge sponge. Anything—the trunk of a tree, a branch that one grabbed, pine needles on the ground, a root exposed on a trail leading up a bank—was either hideously slippery or ready to crumble. The moss on rocks might as well have been ice and our rubber-cleated combat boots skates. To go up or down a steep muddy trail after six other men had gone ahead of you was to deal with a trough of bright red mud the consistency of grease.

Today, too, the smaller fauna were with us. Red ants moved in horrifying copper rivulets across wet leaves, and at one point I stopped to watch a centipede move over pine needles. This was certainly the forest primeval, never touched, and I wondered where the sentimentality about unspoiled nature had originated. As we moved, thorns tore a score of holes in my fatigues.

The pace was murderous. Crumley's boys were getting better and better as the year progressed. Leafy branches attached as camouflage to their helmets and every part of their web harness, they slipped from tree to tree like bushes moved by the wind. Their feet seemed not to touch the ground; they moved like a pack of silent long-legged hunting dogs. In such a situation it is both unfair and dangerous not to keep up, and I did, but there were moments when I felt that my gasps must be audible to every North Vietnamese between ourselves and Cambodia.

The patrol leader, the same tall Kentucky boy with whom I had been out before, motioned with his hands that we should spread out in diamond formation and sink to the pine-needle floor for a break.

At this moment I saw something sand-colored bobbing just off the trail down which we had come. I had not the slightest doubt that it was the sandy canvas of an NVA uniform, and I pointed with a shaking hand and whispered to the patrol leader what I had seen. Three of our men took off down the trail. A minute later they came back, grinning, and led me to my North Vietnamese, who I had been sure was only one of many who had been following us and were now closing in for a point-blank firefight under the pine trees.

It was a big beige member of the cattail family. The wind blew as I stared at it, and indeed it looked like the running, bobbing shoulder of an NVA as he ducked through high grass.

I let out my breath with a sigh that was nine parts relief and only one part embarrassment, and moved back toward the patrol leader, shrugging my shoulders. I sat down next to him. After a minute, his glance taking in the silent troops sitting on the ground, rifles in their laps, staring at different angles into the misty rain forest, he whispered: "I hear you're writing a book about this shit."

"Yes," I whispered back, and we sat in companionable

silence. He rose and motioned for me to come over to see something. It was a bird snare. Looking at it, I had that eerie feeling that was so easily available in Vietnam, the clutching sense that the enemy was near you somewhere, that he could see you and that you could not see him.

The young sergeant from Kentucky set off the trap, and suddenly it occurred to me that it might be a little unnerving for the NVA, when they in turn came along and found that someone had glided through here, set off their snare, and passed on into the mist.

We came back into camp five hours after setting out. The portions of our fatigues that were not red with mud were soaked black with sweat.

B Company was in camp, and some of the men were test-firing their weapons as we trudged past them inside the perimeter. Sergeant Higa was looking at me and laughing. It was too good to keep, and he came up and threw an arm around my slimy shoulder.

"One of my boys saw you coming along there like a Pfc. in line, and he says, 'Jeez, are they down to drafting guys that old?'" He looked at me with a pleasant smile, and asked, "Want to fire the M–16?"

"Sure." I picked up one of B Company's rifles and looked over the fern-filled ravine beneath this side of the perimeter. There were several tall trees across it, and, as I studied them, thinking where to fire, I saw sudden quick movement in the leaves near the trunk of one.

Oh God, I thought, remembering my false alarm with the cattail, today's your day for seeing things.

"Sarge," I said quietly, "I think there's something *in* that tree."

"Which one?" His voice was suddenly serious. I pointed it out, and we both raised our M–16s and fired a short burst. There was a sudden crashing sound over there, and a baboon dropped out of the tree, hit the ground, bounced, and sped into the jungle.

I walked into Tom's tent after the evening staff meeting. He was sitting on the edge of his cot, holding a big "I Love

You Daddy'' card from one of his five children, and shaking his head with a dazed smile on his face.

''What?'' I asked.

''You know what my kids want to do when I get home?'' He looked around the leaking tent, the muddy grass, the cans of C rations. ''They want us all to go on a camping trip.''

This time I had brought Tom a bottle of Scotch. I tilted the olive five-gallon can of water and poured water into two plastic cups, added a healthy dollop of Scotch, and we sat talking as the Coleman lantern hissed. There had been a quick rumble a few minutes before, a sound I did not know, and Tom said it was a Skyspot, bombs hitting in salvo from one of the radar-controlled F–100 missions in which the planes flew high and level and the enemy knew nothing until the bombs landed.

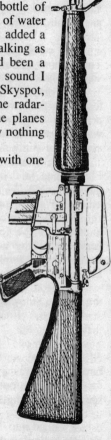

M-16

Tom rubbed the back of his head with one hand, and took a sip of Scotch. For an instant I remembered that first time I saw him, distant, elegant yet tough, at the Taj Mahal Christmas party. Now I knew that he was a man who could brood in the night about his lost troops and get up the next morning and work hard all day trying to find the enemy, doing a job he had sworn to do when he raised his right hand one day in 1945.

He was explaining how in Vietnam one had to become an expert on sounds, to know when it was strange that birds should be chirping, to know when it was strange that they were silent. He spoke of sounds at night.

''You have to know what the sound is, you have to know what hearing it under those conditions means, and you have to know what to do about it.'' He took a swallow of the Scotch and tepid water, and glanced fondly at the card from his children. "If you're going to operate successfully in Vietnam, you have to be prepared to forget everything you ever learned before."

III

Two mornings later I was watching from a slight distance as our mortars fired in a new defensive concentration, the rounds quite visible as they soared from the mortar tubes, arced up, and then plunged crashing into the jungle a few hundred yards away. I followed the quick blurring ascent of one of them, and suddenly, among the wet clouds overhead, it exploded, harming no one but leaving a strange dark smoke ring above us.

I walked over and asked the mortar platoon commander what had happened.

"Well," he told me, "these rounds have very sensitive noses, and that particular one was evidently sensitive enough to be set off by contact with a cloud."

I looked to see if he were kidding me, but he was not. This was Lieutenant Andrew O'Brien, who had been in charge of a foot platoon in Phu Yen until he had been shot through the body in the famous exchange in which just one shot was fired—the enemy bullet, which had gone through him and broken the arm of the man behind, with never a glimpse of an enemy. It was he I had watched with such interest that morning near Ban Me Thuot when the two VC stood four hundred yards away, evidently thinking we could not see them, until they had both been killed by the mortar shell directed by O'Brien.

I had never asked him about himself. He told me he had graduated from Boston College with an ROTC commission. His plan had been to go into the Army for two years, and never go near a uniform again.

"Shortly after I got in," he said, standing in the mud, his jungle jacket open, his helmet off and his hair cut almost to the point of being shaved, "I became interested in it as a career."

He smiled as he saw me glancing at the muddy mortar pits to which this had led him, thinking that if he had followed his original plan he would have been out of the Army by now.

"Yeah." He nodded toward the tilted mortar tubes in their sunken sandbagged holes, the men working under his command. "I like it."

I asked him what there was about it that he liked.

"Basically, I like being outdoors. I don't like being in an office." He went on to say that what he had really liked was leading the riflemen in the bushes, although he saw the wisdom of putting him in a less exhausting slot after he had been wounded and then became sick after returning to duty.

"While I was out there"—he nodded toward the jungle—"I enjoyed it. There's a certain amount of danger out there, and danger for the people you're responsible for, but out there you can see the results of what you're doing—you can't get much closer to it than that."

O'Brien added that he had voluntarily extended his year in Vietnam by another six months, and hoped he would continue to spend it right in the Dragoons. He would take any job up here and be happy to do it, but he didn't want anything back at Brigade or Division.

I nodded. I was getting used to finding these men who had found, early in life, what they really loved—men like Jack Crumley, whom I had met while he was washing his socks on that hillside in Phu Yen, and young men who did not yet shave, like Tomlinson, chewing gum, cleaning his rifle, and talking on the radio. There was no use saying that all sane, reasonable men hated war. These men were not neurotics. There was no use saying that they would come to their senses the first time they were in a really horrible fight, or were wounded, or had a friend killed. They had already experienced all that, had Crumley and Tomlinson and O'Brien, and they were planning to stay in the Army, and in no damned hurry to get out of Vietnam.

I asked O'Brien what he thought of the enemy.

"He's good." The man who had been cut straight through by an enemy bullet stared out at the rainy jungled hills as if he could see the enemy in formation there, silent phalanxes in their sand-colored NVA uniforms. "He's very good. But he's not better."

We talked for a few more minutes. There were dark clouds tumbling toward us from the north. It was not yet noon, but the feeling was that of a rainy dusk.

O'Brien stared at the black hills wrapped in mist across the valley and said: "I don't think this country ever had a beginning or will ever have an end."

IV

Arriving at Pleiku to look for transport back to Tuy Hoa, I found that, at four-thirty in the afternoon, the last plane of the day had gone. Too tired to be angry, I hitched a ride up to a transient barracks, signed a slip for some bedding, made up a cot, and went to sleep.

I woke at seven in the evening, hungry, and made my way to the Officers' Club. Crossing the threshhold, I found myself the object of a dozen disapproving stares. Although I was authorized to use any club in the country, I wore no rank on the collar of my jungle fatigues, and the black lettering above my pocket, indicating that I was a correspondent, was faded and wrinkled and obscured with red mud stains.

I stared right back at all these officers and gentlemen with drinks in their hands. I looked like a bum, knew it, and was ready to fight the whole goddamn lot of them in their clean fatigues if they tried to stop me from getting some food.

A hand touched my shoulder. Here it comes, I thought, taking a deep breath before I turned. This is going to be the goddamned club officer asking me for some identification. I turned, and looked into the warm eyes and broad smile of Captain Rod Rodriguez, the slight swarthy FAC who had the best handlebar mustache in Vietnam and possibly the world. I had known him on the ground and in the air when the first Brigade had its headquarters at Tuy Hoa, and now he told me that he and his colleagues had for some months been working out of Pleiku in support of the Dragoons and other Army units.

"That won't do," Rod said when he heard I was in a stark transient barracks down the street. He took me down there in a jeep, helped me collect my filthy pack and helmet, and installed me in a corner of the FAC barracks that had a desk and a cot with mosquito netting. There was even a hot shower next door, and after twenty minutes under this I got back into my dirty jungle fatigues and rejoined Rod in the club dining room.

It was a good reunion, and even better after I had something to eat. The new boss of the FACs was forty-year-old Major Joe Madden, from Alexandria, Louisiana, who had started his career as a submariner. I could tell by the way the FACs treated him that this father of nine children was establishing his authority not by his rank but by his willingness to press in as low and as hard as the rest of this extremely hard-flying group.

Just at the moment Major Madden was hearing an informal report about a run-in with the Army from "Mad Dog" Cummings, a tall, thin FAC I had known at Tuy Hoa. The evening before, just at dusk, the North Vietnamese had been closing in on a four-man Army LURP team. The four Americans of the Long Range Patrol were on the top of a sharp knob, each facing in a different direction, their feet touching, all firing at North Vietnamese heading up the hill to finish them. They had placed a flashing blue strobe lamp among their intertwined feet to mark their position for Mad Dog, with whom they had contact on their radio. He was preparing to put an air strike on the advancing North Vietnamese when an Army headquarters miles away tuned in and told him to hold it, they had a helicopter on the way to perform an emergency extraction.

"How long will it take?" Mad Dog inquired.

"About two zero."

"These guys don't have five minutes to spare," Mad Dog said, bringing the fighter-bombers in closer.

"We're handling this," the Army declared, and Mad Dog snapped off the radio, brought in the air strike, scattered the advancing NVA, and saved the lives of the four men on the ground, who were still alive to be picked up when the helicopter finally got there. Some FACs had been decorated for doing just what Mad Dog had done, but he was being accused of violating the chain of command and obstructing an emergency extraction.

We walked into the bar and I pulled out my wallet to pay for a drink. It felt strange to be handling money, after being with the Dragoons in the jungle. Up there, whatever they had was free, and they were happy to share it.

EIGHTEEN

I had wanted to observe the activities of Advisory Team 28, the combined American civilian-military group who worked with the Vietnamese in Phu Yen Province. On my return from the Cambodian border I rode up from the air base, crossing the river to Tuy Hoa town, and entered this different sphere.

If one followed the broad boulevard through town toward the beach, the road narrowed and eventually one came to the centers of power. On a bluff just in from the beach there was an imposing two-story yellow house, in front of which flew the red-striped yellow flag of the Republic of Vietnam. This was the home of the Province Chief, Colonel Ba, whom I had met at the Christmas party at the Taj Mahal. Nearby were small compounds in which lived the American civilians and military men attached to the advisory effort. Their offices were interspersed among the many Vietnamese government offices in the yellow stucco buildings spread across the surrounding sandy acres. It was a miniature state-capital complex of governor's mansion, executive offices, armory, and motor pool. From this bluff on the beach one could look inland across Tuy Hoa town, across the heat-misted rice paddies of the valley, to the purple enemy hills in the distance.

The Vietnamese provincial civilian and military bureaucracy were holding their monthly meeting, and I arrived at it with the two senior American officials directly assigned to Phu Yen Province. On my left was the senior military advisor, Lieutenant Colonel Alfred Cade, a trim black officer with a resonant voice and a springy stride. To my right was Dan Leaty, a stocky, red-haired civilian who had been in Vietnam

222

for six years. At the age of twenty-nine, he was the youngest Province Representative in the country.

We took our places on folding chairs in a large room with big French windows letting in the pleasant onshore breeze. A hundred and twenty Vietnamese military officers and civilian officials were present. Colonel Ba presided behind a small table, listening to the functionaries who advanced to make their reports from the front of the room. Just as American officials would have, they frequently used charts, maps, graphs, and columns of comparative statistics to illustrate their verbal reports. The traditions of Chinese calligraphy and French influence seemed neatly combined in the exquisitely drawn columns of figures, which had geometrically perfect bars drawn through each 7.

As each official gave his report, Colonel Cade or Dan Leaty whispered a translation. The people of the northern end of the Province, around that palm-and-beach haven of Song Cau, were complaining of the price of hardwood lumber as compared with other areas. The next speaker reported that ninety animal husbandry classes had been started in the Province. The distribution of boars furnished by the government was discussed at length, but all there was to say about fisheries was that there was no fisheries official available for Phu Yen.

Throughout this Colonel Ba sat behind his table, his hooded eyes alert, listening with an expression that combined mistrust, hope, a conviction of personal superiority, and the threat of punishment for failure. In the manicured hand which emerged from the crisp sleeve of his green fatigues there was a black swagger stick which had the tip of a bullet for its point. This he would occasionally tap on the surface of the table, interrupting the speaker in a shrill, almost womanish complaint. *Tap, tap*. Classroom construction was lagging; it must be improved. *Tap, tap, tap*.

Another report. Twenty-seven midwives had been assigned to serve with the Revolutionary Development Teams, the armed groups of militia trained also as political cadres.

"Allez!" Colonel Ba snapped to a man in telling him to get on with it, French coming to his lips as naturally as Vietnamese.

The Province Public Works Chief was complaining about

his difficulties in building roads. Harassed by Viet Cong snipers and mines, he was trying to widen and straighten some roads, and this meant encroaching on private land. The people whose land was involved wanted not only reimbursement, ·they wanted to work on the roads and be paid for it, and they had no experience and would be useless if they did work.

"This guy gave the same excuses a month ago," Colonel Cade whispered.

The Public Works Chief, sweating in his white short-sleeved shirt and necktie, was not through yet. He was having a problem with contractors who kept giving him the wrong size crushed rock. Also, he desperately needed more trucks.

"*Oui, oui,*" Colonel Ba said, and then told him in Vietnamese that the Public Works Ministry in Saigon had no money on hand for additional trucks. He should put his paperwork through the top public works official in Central Vietnam and see if they had any money for trucks.

The little man nodded. The current cost of roads, he added, was about four thousand dollars per mile of unpaved road. Take it or leave it, his expression seemed to say, and he returned to his seat.

The problems went on. Dan Leaty listened thoughtfully, biting his nails. In some cases there was money for new housing, but no materials, while in other cases there were materials but no money for wages. Out of a population of 390,000, at one time or another 126,000 had been refugees.

Colonel Ba was on his feet, asking where were the taxes from the district markets. Why were they not yet at the Province Tax Office? In Song Cau, he told his officials, the Viet Cong were selling rice on the black market for fourteen piasters a kilo, while the government-subsidized price was seventeen. It was an effort to disrupt the economy. Further efforts must be made to deny the VC the rice in the first place. What were the National Police doing about checking the movement of bags of rice by road?

Next, a complaint about the Popular Forces, the least disciplined of the militia. They had taken a lot of building material away from the side of a blasted railroad track. The material had been for the purpose of rebuilding a segment of the coastal railroad destroyed by the VC, and now the militia were using it for themselves.

Dan Leaty kept biting his nails. My head was swimming. Here I was, finally in the center of the Vietnamese side of the effort, and they had a range of problems of which I had not dreamed.

Colonel Ba was on his feet again, addressing the civil servants of the Ministry for Information. He had received their application for two additional lots of land. They *already* had been given Lots Thirty-Eight and Thirty-Nine to build a new antenna, which was up, and a new radio station, which was not. He was not, he said, going to give them still more land so they could build a house on it and sell it for private gain.

The meeting had been going for two and a half hours without a break. The purely military side would be discussed this afternoon, but for the moment Colonel Ba had some advice for his district chiefs, all of whom were officers in the army.

As they knew, he said, a district chief had been killed a couple of weeks before, driving down a road at dusk with insufficient escort. The VC evidently knew where he was going and when he would be on that road.

"If you don't do your job," Colonel Ba said, "the government might not know about it so that they can execute you, but you may be sure the VC will know about it and be able to kill you."

II

The next morning I was in Song Cau, the paradise where I had seen my first wounded Viet Cong, the first day I had flown with a FAC so many months before. Now I found that my eye was critical, and I saw flaws.

That place had seduced the military advisors. There was brilliant sunlight on the sheltered bay a few yards away, and cool strokes of wind through tall palm trees.

"It's quiet here," the American major said to me. "That's the way we like to see it."

A sergeant poured me another cup of coffee as we sat in a large and comfortable screened dining area. The men had built this porch during the last couple of months, and were proud of its cool comfort. They had not placed a single sandbag anywhere around it, or around the sides of the area where they slept.

The American civilian advisor here in Shangri-La was a slight, earnest young graduate of the University of California at Berkeley. He was wearing black pajamas, evidently on the theory that this would make the Vietnamese think he was one of the boys. The best one could hope for was that the Vietnamese would not think it an elaborate joke at the rice farmers' expense.

A feud existed between the lone American civilian and the half-dozen military men. The civilian was elaborately polite to the Vietnamese and contemptuous of the enlisted men, and they in turn treated him as a joke. The civilian's attitude toward the American major was openly critical of the major's lack of initiative; apart from the fact that the civilian had, perforce, to sleep in the same area with the military team, he stayed away from them as much as possible.

At the moment he was trying to build a separate structure in which he could entertain the Vietnamese.

"They won't go in there," he said, pointing to the military bungalow in which I had been given coffee. His soft hands fumbled with a tarpaper panel of this prefabricated hospitality center he was trying to build by himself. According to the plans that accompanied it, when finished it would look like a tarpaper teepee.

III

By afternoon I was in the next district down the coast, on my slow way back to Tuy Hoa. Here, in Tuy An, the atmosphere in the American team could not have been more different. I was at last meeting the aggressive team of advisors who had been on the ground my first day with the FAC, the day when I had so suddenly become involved in spotting some VC on the ground after these men had popped red smoke beneath shiny purple trees. Even on the ground here on a quiet day, I could remember my hand going to my throat in the back of that plane as we were told there was ground fire in the area above which we were hovering.

The twin driveshafts here, as they had been opponents at

Song Cau, were an American major and an American civilian who worked in friendly coordination. The major, thirty-one-year-old Charles Hanson of Malta, Montana, was one of the first Americans to hear Viet Cong shots fired in 1961. At the time he had been one of three first lieutenants in Vietnam, entering the country in civilian clothes as one of the five-hundred-man advisory team for the entire nation.

I asked him if he had dreamed, then, that American forces would increase from five hundred to five hundred thousand.

There was a smile under his hard blue eyes. "I knew we were going to have to come in with more than we had at that time. We were doing too little, too late."

What did he think of the Vietnamese troops he had been in combat with in 1961?

"I thought the Vietnamese soldier was a real fine fighter, and the only thing he needs is leadership. I've seen their troops do things you could never get an American soldier to do."

Well, I said, here it was six years later. After other Army tours in other parts of the world, he was back again. What did he think of the Vietnamese troops now?

"They still need more leadership, but where you have a good leader, you have a good unit."

I turned to the American civilian, who told me without preamble that he worked for "the Embassy." He had been in Phu Yen for a year, frequently working with refugees. "The refugee camps are our best source of intelligence," he observed, "and it's also our best psychological warfare weapon. We can give them more and better tender loving care than the VC can."

We broadened the discussion. "No matter how you look at it," he said firmly, "the war has to be won at the district level. If we can start building up the administrative capacity in both civilian and military at the district level, then we can work on up—but you could have the best administrators in the world in Saigon, and it wouldn't help at the district level."

Major Hanson mentioned that they had an assistant district chief here, the top Vietnamese civilian in the district, who was unquestionably dishonest, engaging in various forms of graft and misappropriation of supplies. "We're giving him enough rope to hang himself," he said.

The civilian took up again. "As you can see, this country is about as ready for democracy as Lower Slobovia is. Maybe in twenty years it'll be different."

And what else, I asked him; what else should we do?

"A hamlet in one district is quite unaware of a hamlet in another—there's no psychological link. We should take the current generation of elementary school children and teach them history, and a social consciousness of their own country. We have to develop transportation and communication." He went back to the subject of administration. "I think you'll see the military in charge here for a long time—they're the only ones with the actual practical working knowledge of an organization. Also the Army types have a feeling of responsibility for those men under them, which the civil administrators do not."

A sergeant stuck his head in and said there was a chopper coming in, and did Mister Flood want to go back on it?

That had been the plan, but, looking at these men and listening to the candor of their responses to these touchy questions, I said no, if it was all right with them, I'd stay for a couple of days.

They exchanged a look and said in that case, how would I like to come along with them to the offices next door and meet the district chief? This was the good guy, they added, not his corrupt civilian assistant.

Five minutes later we were sitting in low wicker chairs, sipping weak green tea. Behind the desk was a Vietnamese just younger than the American pair, twenty-nine-year-old First Lieutenant Nguyen Van Be.

For a moment, as we all sipped our tea and exchanged pleasantries, there was an atmosphere in the room that eluded me. Then I got it. These three, the two Americans and the one Vietnamese, were absolutely at home with each other. In every other encounter I had had in Vietnam, there had been a feeling of a certain distance between the Americans and Vietnamese involved, no matter how much they were seeing of each other in line of duty. In this room there were only two sides—the Tuy An side, and me.

Lieutenant Be started talking about Tuy An. There were thirty thousand people now in the district. Eighty per cent were farming families, 20 per cent were fishermen.

As he spoke in slow, correct English, I saw through the door the coastal headlands of this area. It was a mean-looking strip of coast, with few trees and a lot of wind and heat. The roads were narrow and rutted, the people were lean.

The Koreans were the major Allied force in the area, Lieutenant Be told me. He pointed through the open doorway at the wall of bushy hills two miles inland, saying how grateful he was that the Koreans were the line of defense out there.

This area, he told me, had spent almost a generation under the control of those who opposed him now. The French had never reasserted themselves in this area after 1945, and the Viet Minh had worked on the people for nine years. When they had to cede control as a result of the 1954 settlement which gave them undisputed sway in the North, many of the strongest local Viet Minh had gone to North Vietnam. They had begun reappearing here as Viet Cong in 1960. Since many of those who had gone North had left their wives behind, they had families of their own with which they could easily pick up their ties.

"When I began in Nineteen Sixty-Five," he said, "there was only one secure hamlet in the entire district. The district population was fifty-five thousand. We had three Regional Force companies and the VC had three battalions. The three VC battalions would attack our companies one at a time. It was very bad."

I nodded. It sounded like a nightmare to me. This was the problem. He was the visible presence of armed might, but he had been outnumbered by men who had been working on it for twenty years.

He spoke of the increasing pace of the war during the time he had been district chief. Twenty-two of the fifty-five thousand had left the district, some herded inland by the Viet Cong, others fleeing south to the more prosperous district of Tuy Hoa and the capital town.

"Now we have control of fourteen villages and about twenty-nine thousand people," he said. "The Viet Cong have absolute control of three thousand. They are beyond our reach, beyond the hills."

When he told me that he had taken over here because the previous district chief was wounded, I suppressed a smile. Before coming here, I had been told that this man's predecessor "shot himself in the leg so he could get the hell out of that place."

Now, Lieutenant Be said, smiling for the first time, did I have any questions?

I did. Trying to grapple with the phenomenon of this enemy so seldom seen in armed form but so potent, I asked him: What is the motivation of the Viet Cong? How do they get men to work so hard for them?

Lieutenant Be was way ahead of me. I had not said what so many Americans did, that one side was braver and more enduring than the other, but he answered as if this had been the question, answered as if he agreed.

"Why VC do best? Good discipline."

Major Hanson interjected: "The VC get more out of their soldiers per mile than the Saigon government does."

All three nodded, and Be went on. The VC, he said, had made great propaganda capital out of the repressive measures, the distance from the people, of the Diem regime. As the VC had increased in power, they had used terror at every turn. In Tuy An their statement was that they would kill the families of anyone who defected in the Chieu Hoi program, and they had frequently carried out their threats. Lieutenant Be looked at me carefully before he said the next thing, as if he had seen Americans doubt what he was about to say, or even accuse him of lying. Criminal elements sometimes escaped to the VC, he said. Of the twelve VC village chiefs out beyond the hills, eleven were wanted on nonpolitical criminal charges. Only one was out there for purely ideological reasons.

He turned the conversation slightly. The Viet Cong, he told me, forced men to assassinate civilians of various types, for the cause. Then, quite truthfully, they would tell the assassins that they were wanted for prosecution by the government authorities. Hence, the VC could at one stroke eliminate teachers, village chiefs, and other influential men, disrupt the workings of society, cow the population, and bind ever closer to them the men who had done the killing.

"Another thing," Major Hanson broke in, gesturing toward Lieutenant Be. "He needs more men. He has responsibility for thirty thousand people. That's more than there are in two Army divisions, and he's a first lieutenant. He has just two officers under him, two second lieutenants, and with this he's supposed to handle three RF companies, fourteen PF platoons, and thirty thousand civilians and their problems. He doesn't even have a single truck that's directly at his disposal."

I sighed, and then we were standing up and shaking hands. I thanked Lieutenant Be, and we left his office.

The next morning Major Hanson, the Man from The Embassy, and I jeeped down the badly potholed road, followed by another jeep carrying the American medic for the district and a load of supplies. We pulled up at a schoolhouse from which the local children were absent during their summer vacation, and waited.

In a few minutes four trucks arrived, driven by Korean soldiers. In the back of each open truck were about thirty refugees, all of them from a hamlet beyond the hills where the Koreans were conducting an operation designed to break up Viet Cong control. These people were being brought to the coast, whether they liked it or not, to be resettled here in an effort to cut off the Viet Cong from their most precious asset—people.

With the trucks came a Korean Civic Action team, complete with bags of rice for the refugees, blankets made of paper, five-gallon cans of water, and kerosene lamps. At the same moment, Lieutenant Be appeared with several militiamen and an electrically powered megaphone. Scores of the local children, living in the thatched houses along the road, gathered to watch.

The tailgates of the trucks were lowered, and those of the refugees who could get down by themselves did. It was a complete cross-section of Vietnamese rural society, including babies, pregnant mothers, and some military-age men who were later to face questioning about their status. The children in the group seemed less tearful and unhappy than I had supposed they would be in the midst of this uprooting from their houses; some of them considered it a lark, and as the group was shepherded across the wide unkempt lawn before the school, some of the local children began edging toward them.

Then, across the lawn, came a couple moving from the trucks toward the schoolhouse, a very old man and woman, stepping with halting fragile grace. Both were tiny and white-haired, and the man was blind. The woman had her hand on his arm, leading him. Among all the refugees no one appeared related to them or concerned for them. The man seemed unaware of what was happening. The woman, carrying not even a single bag of personal possessions, knew exactly what was happening, hated it, and was concerned only for the husband at her side.

NINETEEN

My hoochmate Sully was going home. Because he had
led a squadron on an earlier six-month tour out here within
the past two years, he was getting some time lopped off the
one-year tour the others in the Wing had to serve.

Everyone loved Sully, and everyone at Tuy Hoa liked a
reason to have a party. The going-away parties for Sully were
smash hits, one after another. One evening it was Pres
Flanagan cooking fantastic fried chicken on the outdoor grill,
in a free-floating colonels' party that wandered back and forth
between the Taj Mahal and our hooch. There was lots of time
spent, glasses in hand, standing on the sand between the
hooches under the bright tropic stars, talking of flying and
leave towns and past great fighter pilots, and past wars, and
past war games.

This last, the shoptalk of peacetime deployments and
exercises, was something that never failed to surprise me.
These colonels had been flying in the service of the United
States for twenty and twenty-five years. It was as natural for
them to sit at a base in the Arizona desert and reminisce about
a war as it was for them to stand on the sands of Tuy Hoa,
watching flares rise in the valley, and talk of Operation Desert
Strike or some other Statewide maneuver.

The party happened to have floated back to Sully's room
at half past nine in the evening, and Pres was fiddling with
Sully's portable short-wave radio. Hanoi came on with martial music, and then we heard the unlovely voice of Hanoi
Hannah, their chief English-language propaganda broadcaster.
She was a Vietnamese with a chilly, petulant British accent,
and tonight she was giving the usual exaggerated account of

American losses. This we took in good part, as usual, since she was knocking out our tanks at a faster rate than the Germans had been able to do in the Battle of the Bulge.

Tonight, however, she had something more. An American pilot captured by the North Vietnamese came on the air. The voice was unmistakably American, a voice no different in accent from those of us sitting on the cot and the folding chairs in the narrow room, but it sounded disembodied, groping, speaking like an automaton. Something had been done to the man. He spoke of "American imperialist aggression," a phrase not likely to come from a fighter pilot's lips, and apologized for his crimes against the democratic people of North Vietnam, who wanted only to live in peace with all the other peoples of the world.

I looked around the room. Nobody really cared what he was saying, but there was something shocking in this ghostly voice, something more appalling in what had been done to him than had they broadcast the sound of lashes striking a bleeding back.

We had been laughing and drinking a few minutes before, but we were stony sober now. A silent cold anger was in the room. I looked at Sully, whose eyes were narrowed, and then at Frank Buzze, who had returned to where he had been shot down and had bombed out of existence two of the 37-millimeter cannon that had knocked him from the sky. Freddie Poston, the hard-working commander of the 309th, stared at the radio, nodding his head as if making up his mind to try just twice as hard. Pres Flanagan's big and capable hands twitched, as if they wanted to reach through that radio and pull that pilot back to us.

As a propaganda broadcast, it was a failure.

The pilots of the 308th gave Sully a party, and our return from it in a jeep after many drinks went this way.

Me: Sully, we turn right here.
Sully: Charlie, *you're* driving.

Pres was planning to fly the Gooney Bird down to Cam Ranh Bay, to pick up supplies and to deliver Sully for his flight back to the United States. I came back to the hooch at eleven in the morning to join forces with them for this farewell flight. Sully was in his suntans, trim as ever, and his bags and footlocker were packed.

There was just one thing. Sitting on the edge of his stripped-down cot, red-eyed, was Mama-san. She had slipped one foot out of her open rubber sandals and had it halfway into a worn flying boot that Sully was leaving behind.

"You take me 'merica," she was saying, obviously for the fortieth time.

Sully turned to me with a concerned smile and a shake of his head.

"Vietnam number ten," Mama-san said, " 'merica number one. You take me 'merica."

It was clear that she really thought he could do it. She shook her cloud of black hair as if in pain, and stabbed her foot further into his old flying boot. She saw airplanes going, and she wanted to get on one and go too.

"Mama-san," I asked, "how about your babies?"

"Baby-san *fini*," she said, indicating that she would leave her children.

Sully spoke. "You're a very fine woman, Mrs. Hoa." He picked up his bag. Pres appeared and we wrestled Sully's foot locker out the door.

At Cam Ranh Bay, Sully and I had our last drink together—an uncharacteristic Coke. He and Pres were talking of Sully's new assignment, which would give him a chance to check out in the F–4, the newest of the operational fighter-

McDonnell F-4C "Phantom"

bombers. He had no doubt that he would be back over here within a couple of years.

We shook hands. There he stood, the same short, smiling barrel-chested man I had met months before. He had a few more gray hairs, a hundred and ninety more combat missions, and the affection of every man who had known him at Tuy Hoa. He turned and walked toward a plane in which, for once, he would not be the pilot.

TWENTY

The silence in the hooch after Sully's departure was depressing. I had not realized just how much I would miss his cheerful voice and that conspiratorial smile. His replacement was not due for some time, and in the evenings I would wander over to Pres' hooch. Over a drink we would speculate on just where Sully was now, what he was doing, how he and his family were spending his leave before he reported in to his new assignment.

In the midst of this it occurred to me that Tom Lynch would be going home pretty soon, and that if I wanted to see him and the Dragoons while the original team was still working, I had better get up to the Cambodian border.

The FACs received me with their usual hospitality when I spent the night with them at Pleiku on my way through to the Dragoons. There was one FAC that for a moment I thought was a new man I had yet to meet; then I realized that it was Rod Rodriguez, who had had the most glorious handlebar mustache in Vietnam. His mustache was gone, without so much as a plaque on his upper lip to record the dimensions of what had grown there.

"Rod, what happened?" I asked, awed as by the sight of a fallen redwood. I wondered if the mustache had finally presented a health problem, or proved to be dangerous in an airplane, or even simply too heavy to carry about.

Rod shook his head. "I went on R and R to Hawaii, and my wife met me there and persuaded me to take it off." He smiled the sad smile of a man who knows how clever women

237

are. "She kept saying 'But Rod, it makes you look like an *old man*.'"

I asked him if he was thinking of starting another, but he shook his head.

After dinner Rod and Mad Dog Cummings and I had drinks at the bar. In being introduced to a number of Army men, I noticed a certain tone of respect when the Dragoons were mentioned. Tom's battalion had built for themselves the reputation of being the best infantry battalion in the Fourth Division.

I looked down into my beer, thinking of that long-ago day when Whipcrack sent me to that hilltop in Phu Yen, and how my heart sank when I saw who my tall, cool host was to be. In those days the Dragoons were just getting started in Vietnam, and Tom Lynch had just become their commanding officer. Whipcrack had been gone for months now, but he had known what he was doing the day he sent me to what had appeared to me just another group of muddy Americans in the jungle.

The next morning I was the recipient of one of the services the FACs could render—they could do their job of visual reconnaissance and still be aerial taxi drivers. My pilot was Major Joe Madden, the genial, hard-flying father of nine, and for an hour or so we poked all along the Cambodian border, swooping over trails on the Vietnam side that clearly were well used and could only mean that men were passing along them, coming to and from the low fords in the wide, shallow river that marked the border of the sanctuary we were not allowed to attack.

"I have a Mister Flood with me," Major Madden said over the radio to the Dragoons as we got near their fire base.

The radio hissed back: "Wait one." Then it said; "We'll have a chopper for your passenger waiting at Triple Cross when you get there. Over."

"Roger. Out." Major Madden looked over his shoulder, grinning at me. "Boy," he said, "you get some service around here." The transmission from the ground meant that we should put into the Special Forces Camp at Duc Co, and five minutes later I wrestled my pack out of the back of the FAC plane and headed toward a waiting helicopter.

"Just let us know when you've had enough and want to come back," Major Madden shouted, and I waved at him as he zoomed into the cloudy sky.

The Dragoons were in an abandoned rubber plantation, and the tents around the TOC were nestled under rubber trees with slightly elongated oval leaves and green pods the shape of tomatoes.

Tom greeted me, and I was shocked by his appearance. When I had met him back on that hilltop in Phu Yen, there had been a hundred and eighty-five pounds on his six-foot-one frame, and even then he had been a lean-looking man. Now he was down to a hundred and sixty. He looked tired and pale, but in control of the situation. In a hammock ten yards off lay Paul Titus, the small slender artillery captain. He was sick, throwing up every day, and lay in his hammock at all times except for the many hours he spent with his radios and plotting boards in the TOC.

"We haven't been in to Dragon Mountain since we launched off on that Ban Me Thuot operation," Tom said as we sat on the low wall of gray sandbags outside his small tent that I had come to regard as a home. "We've got only two cases of VD in the battalion. That ought to tell you we've been out in the field."

I walked around, shaking hands with some of the sergeants. Everyone looked sallow and exhausted, but if I had been asked if the Dragoons had one good fight left in them, I would have said that they did. In a few weeks many of these men would be going home and there would be large numbers of replacements, but this was still the machine that had been put together at Fort Lewis two years before. These young men had been drafted together, trained together, shipped to Vietnam together. They had served together so long that each knew what the other man was thinking, what the platoon sergeant wanted, what to do even before he was asked to do it.

One man looked healthy, relaxed, and happy. This was Captain Tony Colburn, The Royal Pineapple, who was back after two months as assistant director of the R and R Center in Japan. He had done so well up there that he had been offered a similar job in the R and R Center due to open in

Sydney, Australia, in September. Toby was thinking the offer over very seriously, he told me, but in the meantime it was late July, and he was glad to be back with the Dragoons.

Chatting with a couple of the young soldiers working in the TOC, they told me that Tom had pulled off one more of his aerial escapades, this time darting into the middle of a firefight, not to get out a couple of wounded men but to be with the engaged company on the ground.

I looked out the tent flap at my tired friend. Tom had gone over to Paul Titus' hammock and was smiling down at him encouragingly.

A hand on my shoulder. It was Chaplain Leland Buckner, a Church of the Nazarene minister from Hillsboro, Tennessee. Of all the chaplains I had met in Vietnam, he stuck his neck out the furthest. Every week he spent at least forty-eight hours with one of the line companies that was moving through the jungle and sleeping away from the fire base. Since he was thirty-six, a year younger than I was, I asked him where he found the energy to hack his way through these mountainous trails beside kids half our age.

"I used to be a farmer," he said in his hill-country accent. "I've followed a mule many a day."

The next afternoon Tom took me along to a meeting at Brigade Headquarters. This was a muddy little place between Dragon Mountain and Duc Co, and Colonel Charles Jackson, who had taken over the Brigade from Whipcrack, had named it Jackson Hole. It was a foggy, rainy Highland day, and the various unit commanders within the Brigade met in a chilly open-sided room of what had been a schoolhouse.

The meeting was to the point. A North Vietnamese radio transmission had been intercepted in our area. Its text had been, *in toto:* "Comrade, begin your infiltration of Duc Co." The possibilities were endless—it could have been addressed to only one spy, telling him to slip into that Special Forces Camp, or it could have been the signal to a regimental commander to start slipping his companies across the border for a full-scale attack. It could have been a decoy, meant to keep our eyes on Duc Co while an attack was launched elsewhere. Nonetheless, the Brigade's senior commanders spent the afternoon working out plans to put the maximum number of men into the Duc Co area in the shortest possible time, with variations if a major action should occur somewhat further out from Duc Co. Nothing immediate was anticipated, since it usually took the North Vietnamese a while to get into gear, but our plan was set.

Life at the fire base was routine for the next couple of days. The misty skies rained. During the spells of fitful sunshine laundry was hung out everywhere, with poncho liners hung in the limbs of rubber trees for airing. There was the whine of power saws cutting down trees to make beams for bunkers, and the troops were always moving deliberately upon one chore or another. Men would move out on patrol past groups that were stringing barbed wire around the perimeter, while young soldiers with their shirts off sat atop bunkers, cleaning their rifles, each man using his handful of rags and an oily toothbrush. Others wrote home.

I had for some time been after Tom to let me spend a night or two with a company while it was away from the fire base. I was hoping that this could be arranged at a time when one of the companies was in place to be resupplied, since I was not at all sure that I could keep up with the troops while carrying a pack on some of the mountain trails I had seen them tackle.

Tom had been reluctant to let me sleep away from the fire base. He was prepared to let me ride with him in helicopters, or to make patrols out from the fire base, but he did not want to cast me out so far that there would be any trouble reeling me in if he chose to do so. He had told me more than once, in a pleasant way, that if anything happened to me it would not really be helpful to his military career. The way that this had worked out in practice was that he did not mind my getting shot at in a helicopter as long as he was in it with me.

Now, however, perhaps because he was going home soon, perhaps because he saw the legitimacy of my argument that I needed more time living with a line company away from the fire base to round out my picture of infantry life, he agreed to let me go out to B Company. They would be in place for a night, and their next move would be an easy one, so I could make that march with them and spend another night with them. Then when he dropped in by chopper to see them we could decide how to work it from there.

I was very pleased, and gathered up my pack. I was issued an M–16 and a canvas bandolier of extra clips to sling around my neck, and off I went to B Company on the next helicopter.

I was greeted with as much hospitality as it is possible to extend when one is at the absolute end of the line. Captain Buie, his remarkably blue eyes glittering above a day's growth of thick black beard, met me at the chopper and led me to his pup tent. I put down my pack, took out my poncho liner, and folded it for my bed on the right-hand side of the tent. Our living space measured about eight feet long, five feet wide, and thirty inches high. I crawled out from under the tent to find Sergeant Higa standing there offering me a beer from a thermal can that had come in on the chopper that brought me.

"Hey, Old Man," he said, "I hear you're going to live with us for a couple of days."

I took the beer, and we shook hands. B Company was being resupplied while they stayed here, and choppers were bringing in food, ammunition, and clothes.

I walked around, being greeted by the Bush Pilot, and Mo Thomas, who had now run his gambling winnings up to seventeen hundred and fifty dollars. B Company had its foxholes dug in a circle at the bottom end of a slanting wild meadow, and the men's pup tents were just one good leap from the perimeter formed by their foxholes. Just beyond us the ground dropped off into ferns and jungle. At the higher end of the meadow, about six hundred yards away, C Company was similarly dug in. We were only a few kilometers from the Cambodian border, on one of the many approach trails from the border toward Duc Co. Both companies were running patrols out of here, C Company off in one direction while we ran patrols off in another, but there was no visiting back and forth between the ends of the meadow. We could not see our neighbors from here, but occasionally a helicopter would drop out of sight behind some thick bushes, into what we knew was their location.

The light drew away into the jungle to our west, and I

ate my C rations sitting among the radio men. John Collins, his cheeks somehow still full and pink amid men who had the jungle pallor, asked me some questions about what it was like, being a writer. Tomlinson, the kid who looked like Jimmy Cagney with moles, laughed and said that he didn't think he'd make out very well in a job where someone wasn't standing over him, making him work. Henry Green, the former trotting-horse groom with the panther's head on his arm from Painless Brenda, listened silently. Mo Thomas chuckled and said that he thought he'd like to be his own boss. I told him that at the rate he was cleaning out B Company, he could probably retire when he got back to the States.

"But, Mister Flood," John Collins said, "you could go home tomorrow, right?"

I said that yes, I could if I wanted to, and this set up a storm of conversation, the gist of it being Why in God's name didn't I? I explained that I was interested in this situation over here, that I was going to try to write a book about it, and that I needed to get the experience if I was really going to know what I was talking about.

"You could write a book about this, all right," one of the boys said thoughtfully, looking at the last light as it threw the trees into a tangled black cutout pattern. "You could call it *How Fucked-up Can You Be?*"

Sergeant Higa was making the rounds of the perimeter, and now he stopped and looked down at me.

"You want some experience, you stick with us. We'll get you some experience."

When troops are in the field, common sense sometimes supersedes Stateside regulations. Whole barracks full of men are awakened at four-thirty in basic training camps, but when they get to what it is they are training for, they may very well sleep to seven-thirty or later if there is no good reason to get up sooner. B Company was not going anywhere until afternoon, a certain number were on guard with their weapons in the foxholes, so the rest of us slumbered until the sounds of jungle birds and earlier-rising comrades slid us into the morning.

As it pulls itself together for the day, an infantry company is like a big family. There are certain things that each one in the family does for himself—rolling up his poncho liner, checking his weapon—but there are other chores done by various groups for the common good. One party takes every canteen in sight and goes to the stream, heavily armed, to refill them, while another starts the cooking fires with brush and branches gathered the day before.

The morning passed slowly and pleasantly. I sat drinking C-ration coffee. On my left was First Lieutenant Fletcher Bass, the rough, smiling former halfback who had been with B Company since the beginning of Royal Pineapple days. He and Captain Buie and the small, wiry Bush Pilot were drinking coffee as they studied a map laid out on the bark-littered earth. The sun was out now, but it was clouding up, and occasionally there was a sharp gust of wind.

I wandered around the perimeter, chatting with some of the troops. At eleven o'clock I dropped back to Captain Buie's pup tent for another cup of the coffee they kept making, and shortly before noon I was talking to Specialist Fourth Class Glander Garcia, who was born in New Mexico but had spent most of his life at Boys Town in Nebraska. Since my knowledge of Boys Town consisted of watching Spencer Tracy play Father Flanagan, I was asking what the place was like when there was a sudden rippling rattle of shots off in the direction where C Company was dug in.

Heads whipped around, weapons were snatched up, and men started heading for their holes. I landed in the chest-high foxhole that Mo Thomas had dug near the open end of Captain Buie's pup tent and went to the end of it that faced over the drop-off into thick ferns and tall vine-netted jungle trees.

The initial rattle of fire was increasing, raging like a lethal windstorm in the middle distance. Mo was in the back end of the hole, digging it deeper, using his entrenching tool alternately like an axe and a shovel, pitching the rich red loam over the side. Neil Buie knelt beside the hole, working the radio that Mo usually carried. Tomlinson came to us in a fast stooping run, helmet on, equipment and weapon set, his radio strapped on his back. Between the two radios, we were linked in to everyone we needed at the moment.

I studied the trees before me, looking for snipers in their

leafy limbs. My M–16 was in my right hand, and my left hand went to the collar of my jungle fatigues, gathering the material together over my throat before I realized what I was doing and that a layer of cloth was not going to protect me now.

The firing hammered right on, the overlapping bursts of automatic fire punctuated by the bang and thud of grenades. An excited metallic voice was yelling something on one of the radios, and Tomlinson, eighteen years old and chewing gum, said "Aw, cool off."

I felt a strange, heightened awareness, as if I could quite consciously react to the situation, on one level, and still reflect upon it, on another. One of these two prongs of thought was concentrating on the situation to my front, the thus-far empty jungle, studying it with whole-hearted attention, and the other prong of thought, listening to the shooting directly to my rear, was thinking They won't come here, well, if they do we're well dug in, but they won't come here. There was a sensation that it was all spreading, engulfing us, and a sense of No, it isn't really happening, don't let it happen, it mustn't happen.

Shots began snapping over our heads from the direction of the firefight.

The radio beside Captain Buie stopped hissing and Tom Lynch's voice said "This is Charger. Leave your packs there and be ready to move to Eight-Three's location."

This meant that we were to be ready to move to C Company's position at the far end of the six-hundred-yard meadow. Neil Buie, now sitting on the edge of our hole, ready to jump in if the bullets overhead started snapping past at a lower height, answered, "Roger. Be advised that we are receiving some small arms fire at this location. Over."

"This is Charger. Be ready to move out."

I thought about that one for a minute, and then I gave Neil Buie a sickly grin and asked: "Does that mean me, too?"

"Everybody," Neil said. I was not keen on the idea of getting out of this nice hole and moving, but I was not keen on the idea of being left alone here, either.

The word was being passed, but everyone was already set to go. I looked for my canteen. Mo had said that he would fill it for me, and then everything had stopped, so I had only the empty canvas canteen cover flapping on my hip.

Tom Lynch's voice on the radio said "Move out."

I clambered out of the hole and started moving among the pup tents. Sergeant Higa was standing in the center of the perimeter, directing traffic with wide, sweeping gestures that looked like every statue I had ever seen of a combat leader pointing the way ahead.

"Move out!" he bellowed. "Don't bunch up! Let's go!"

Just then an enemy rocket hit the trunk of the eucalyptus tree in the perimeter, raking the place with splinters and bark. I had landed on the ground as I heard the rocket whoosh in, and Higa was right beside me. "Old man, you stay right beside me," he said. Just beyond him was John Collins, his radio ready to serve Higa, and we rushed out of the perimeter. I hit the ground once more when I heard something whoosh, but these were the first American artillery shells entering the battle, crashing into the woods to our left.

We moved out through the yellow grass of the meadow, under a gray sky. The hundred and forty men of the company were in a big inner-stitched diamond formation, the top point of the diamond moving straight for the top of the meadow, the rest keeping shape in relation to it.

"Spread out! Don't bunch up!" There were all sorts of noises snapping and whooshing overhead, but the real roaring engine of sound was on the ground ahead of us. I was right in the center of our speeding diamond, between Captain Buie and First Sergeant Higa. Behind us came the radio men; John Collins, Tomlinson, Mo Thomas, Henry Green, the aerials of their radios waving wildly above their backs as they moved in a swift, bent rush.

Even before I saw the C Company perimeter, I saw a gunship helicopter circling above it. As I watched, the sliding chopper released a string of bright red tracers at something near it, the sound of the machine gun a long popping buzz. Another gunship came whirling in behind it, brown against the gray sky, and there was a flash and whoosh as it fired two rockets into the jungle beyond the C Company position.

Some men at the front of our diamond were firing their weapons now as we moved into the clanging anvil. Artillery shells sounded like shaking sheets of wrapping paper as they tore past to crash into the woods two hundred meters to our left. The diamond turned into a triangle as B Company hurried past bushes up the gradual slope, and Captain Buie raced forward, leaving Sergeant Higa, Collins, and me at the base of the triangle. The sound increased with every stride we took toward C Company, but at last we could see the perimeter. There were just three tall trees in the center of their area, and I could see the pup tents and the earthen lips of their foxholes. The first of the B Company men were jumping into those holes, and the rest of us were coming after them in a crouching run.

I was passing a bush, about seven yards beyond it, when the leaves rustled. I kept running, looking over my shoulder, and saw an enemy rifle grenade with a long handle on it fall to the ground without exploding. Then there was a ripping sound of something hurtling out of the sky right at me, and I threw myself headlong onto bare ground. There was a terrific explosion behind me, jolting me forward a yard in place, and my helmet rolled off five feet in front of me.

I looked around. Sergeant Higa was disappearing into a hole ten yards ahead of me and fifteen yards to my right. Collins was in a hole similarly placed to my left. The hole nearest me was fifteen yards ahead, and I was lying on my face, my left hand pressed over my pate, silent in the middle of an ocean of sound. I looked longingly at my helmet, which had rolled well forward of my reach. All sorts of things were cracking and zipping over me. I wanted desperately to be in that hole ahead, but for the moment I thought I had better not raise up an inch. I lay there, feeling vexed and foolish, my face flattened into the earth. It seemed a long time that I lay there, trying to decide when to make my move. Then suddenly I felt, definitely, Now, and rose, stepped forward, grabbed my helmet, and sprinted for that hole, sliding into it feet first from two yards out like a baseball player. As I went in I heard something whisk past me and go *WHAM* and throw dirt all over me. It was a rocket, and it landed exactly where I had been lying.

After a few seconds I peered over what had originally been dug as the back side of this hole, looking across the C Company area, at the wall of bushes and trees beyond the far side of the perimeter. I could not see a single person of any description, and then I heard Sergeant Higa yell: "You stay right there!"

"Don't worry!" I shouted back to my right. A FAC plane was flying low over the woods just beyond the perimeter, right over the area from which the heaviest blast of sound was coming, and I stared at him and wondered why he was not shot down in that instant. He was going in so low, with such disregard for everything in this one continual explosion, that I thought *Rod Rodriguez. I wonder if it's Rod?*

There was a scramble of feet on hard earth, and with a rattle of clods a tall thin boy was crouching beside me. The two of us were in something certainly no longer than a small bathtub, and not much deeper. It was a C Company boy, with UTAH penned onto the front of his helmet. He had his M–16, but whatever had happened up here had come so quickly that he had never gotten to his web gear. I handed him a couple of M–16 clips, and he thanked me.

"Where are you from in Utah?" I asked him.

He shrugged his shoulders and said, "I'm just a dud. You don't want to know about me."

"You don't look like a dud to me."

There was a big explosion and something whicked into the dirt beneath the surface of the hole, into the red earth wall behind my shoulder. This scared me worse than anything had thus far. It sounded as if our artillery might be fusing its shells to explode above the surface of the ground, in which case every hole in here might get steel fragments blasted into it from above. I turned and put my hand into the loose red earth where I had heard, rather than seen, whatever it was, and encountered a hot piece of metal from which I withdrew as if bitten.

I shouted to Sergeant Higa, "I think they're using VT!," but there was no answer. I was looking to the right as I yelled, and I saw Utah's eyes, which were looking past mine, grow huge. There was a *thunk* in the earth two yards to our left.

"What was that?" I asked, kneeling down farther and not looking.

"A dud mortar round," he said in tones of prayer.

It began to rain. A shouted order came around through

the firing for C Company men to move out of the holes, just where I did not know.

"Should I move, too?" I asked him. "I don't have to fight."

"If I were you," he said, "I'd stay right there." He was gone. Neither Sergeant Higa on my right nor Collins on my left had moved from their holes, and I stayed put. Our artillery was smashing down everywhere around this perimeter. I had become convinced that it was exploding only when it hit the ground, but the fragments were doing strange things, zipping all over the place at grasshopper level. The sound was like an endless train pounding across a trestle, every kind of thing rustling through the air and exploding and no end to it.

In the midst of this the Bush Pilot wriggled past my hole, flat on his thin belly, with a cheery smile on his face.

"How's it going?" he inquired.

"Fine," I said, and asked a question I was instantly to regret. "Anything I can do?"

"There're some wounded over by those trees," he said. "You might see if you could get them under cover." He snaked on.

I looked in the direction of the three tall trees in the center of the perimeter. There was a pup tent fifteen yards to my left, in front of the hole in which Collins was, and this blocked my view of the bottom of the trees.

I saw Collins looking over at me, pink cheeks pale and his eyes big, just his helmet and the top half of his face visible above the rainy red earth.

"There are some wounded over by those trees!" I yelled, hoping that somehow the situation would sort itself out without my making another move. "Can you see from there if they're all right?"

He looked and then shook his head. I knew I was stalling. Then the strange duality overtook me again. On one level I was just here, trying to operate in this situation. At the same moment I knew that if I did not do something about those wounded men I would not be the same for the rest of my life. I silently cursed the situation, hated it, stayed in the hole, and then Collins slipped out over the edge of his hole and slid forward on his stomach so that he was lying beside the pup tent. After a minute he yelled back to me over his shoulder, "They're in the roots of the trees! They look okay!"

I stayed in the hole, and Collins continued to lie there beside the pup tent. The volume of fire remained exactly the same. We were so pinned down that I had seen exactly three men move above ground in the entire perimeter—Utah, the Bush Pilot, and Collins—and I had no idea of what was happening. I found myself staring at Collins, thinking that there was no use his lying beside the pup tent, he wasn't going to help the wounded any from there; and then I wondered if he thought somehow that the pup tent was cover. The enemy in the jungle at the edge of the perimeter might not be able to see him behind that thing, but things were flying all over the place, and metal would tear through that pup tent as if it were not there.

I put down my M–16 carefully, took off my web harness, and, lightened as much as I could be, keeping one hand firmly on the brim of my helmet, I bellied over the edge of the hole and slid on my stomach across the wet ground, seeing Collins' boot soles larger and larger before my eyes. Finally I was beside him. I felt that the only way to do this thing was to do it with the appearance of certainty.

"Okay," I said in a dry voice. "Let's go." Together we crawled around the corner of the pup tent, onto center stage, and there twenty yards ahead of us were the wounded, four of them, lying huddled and twisted among the big roots of a eucalyptus tree. They stared at us dully, and then in a hole to my left I saw the gray drawn faces of two other men, one of them a C Company platoon sergeant and the other a medic. Evidently they had been going through the same agonized debate that I had, and now, when they saw us moving, they came out too.

As Collins and I kept coming, I could see that three of the boys in the roots of the tree had been hit elsewhere than in the head. The fourth had taken a slash from something in such a way that his cheek had been sliced into from the top, and he was holding it in place on his face with his hand, the line of cutting marked by a surprisingly thin line of blood.

Collins and I got there first.

"Okay," I said to the nearest two. "Can you move?" They nodded.

"Okay. On the count of three, put your arm around me and we'll go."

The boy nearest me nodded and said "Yes, Sergeant."

I counted to three, put my arm around the boy's waist, and he slipped his arm over my shoulder. We rose and ran crouching and stumbling all the way back to the hole from which I had come, Collins and the other one right behind us. We tumbled into the hole, four of us using the small bathtub now, and Collins got out his canteen and began feeding them water. The boy beside me had trouble moving his arms, and I peeled off his jacket and saw small black needles beneath the gray and flinching skin of his shoulders and back—fragments of the rocket which had wounded all four of them as they had been running, bunched up, toward that tree for cover when the enemy attack struck.

"Here come the fighters," Collins said. I looked. An F–100 was tearing in silently ahead of his sound, terribly close, dropping out of the gray sky so fast that it seemed an optical illusion, the plane doubling in size every second. God, I thought, knowing how easy it was to drop a bomb some distance off at six hundred miles an hour, God, be accurate.

The plane let the bombs go like darts lancing at the jungle. I could see everything about the bombs—fins, yellow stripes painted around them, the nose—and as I buried my head there were two terrific ground-shaking crashes in the jungle.

The next plane was flipped at us almost level. The two long silver napalm canisters dropped off, falling horizontally at first, then slanting. A gold-red sheet of flame raced through the trees, black smoke rising, the bomber gone, and still that FAC plane was putt-putting along off there, miraculously still above the enemy without being shot down.

More fighters. More bombs. The artillery was still firing, and another something whicked into the back of the hole a few inches above my shoulder. After a couple of minutes I dug it out, still warm. It was a jagged piece of metal five inches long and two inches wide, the olive-drab paint cracked but intact on one side, and the rest grainy silver with red earth in its pores. I stuck it in my pocket.

The artillery had been shut off, and now all the noises were slackening.

Silence.

Heads looked over the edges of holes, then men stood upright in holes. Then men were climbing stiffly up out of their holes.

A medical evacuation helicopter whirled overhead and landed, and then another beside it. Moving toward them from every quarter, the earth was giving up the results. Men in the crucified position, arms over their buddies' shoulders, hobbling toward the helicopters. Men walking on their own power, one hand gripping the field dressing on a bloody arm.

We walked our wounded toward a helicopter. Then they were somewhere else and I was feeding a man with a wounded leg water from a canteen I had found on the ground. For some reason I had someone's M–79 grenade launcher, a short weapon looking like a big single-barreled shotgun, slung on my shoulder, in addition to the M–16 in my hand. I had the idea that I had lost my glasses, and found that I was wearing them although I had deliberately buttoned them into a pocket earlier.

I lifted a man aboard a helicopter, and then to my left I saw a scene from Goya. Four men were coming toward us with a dead boy hanging down among them. They were carrying him from his extremities, one man holding each

M-79

wrist and one carrying forward each of his booted feet. For some reason his pants and shorts were gone, and his open fatigue jacket dragged along the ground as they carried him feet first. The long thin naked torso and legs looked like a slaughtered animal, and his head hung back, inches above the ground, his uncut brown hair dusty, his body pale.

Next to me was the one mental casualty. He was sitting on the ground. His weapon was beside him. He was staring at the ground.

I became aware that B Company was forming up. "What's going on?" I asked.

"Now we're going after them."

My heart sank, and at the same instant I had an impulse to laugh. It was too much. I had thought it was all over. Instead, we were going to chase the enemy. I looked around the perimeter, at the C Company men who would stay here to keep it. Then I looked at Captain Buie, Sergeant Higa, the Bush Pilot, Fletcher Bass, Collins, Mo Thomas, all of them checking their equipment, looking each other over, getting ready to move out. Because I knew them better, because I trusted them, because they were the people I was with, I walked over to them.

There was another minute before we moved. Sergeant Higa came over and shook my hand.

"You did fine, Old Man," he said, and walked on. I took stock of myself. I had put the M–79 that had found its way onto my shoulder down in a pile of weapons from the wounded who had been evacuated. I had all the equipment I had started with, and my glasses were back in my pocket. I had not felt any urge toward the natural functions. Now I urinated, and found that there was not much of it, and what there was was an orange color. I still felt very keyed up, as if I had all the strength for anything I would have to do. Since the rain had stopped, a cold wind blew across the yellow grass.

Back in diamond formation again, we walked across the C Company perimeter, some of the men fixing their bayonets, and into that wall of trees where the bullets and rockets and rifle grenades had come from. In the wet leaves and vines were bloody bandages and strange blue-dyed cotton masks, all North Vietnamese, and in a minute we came to an open space in the trees where one of their mortars had been. As we stared at the tubular cartons that had held the shells they had rained down on us there was a ripple of firing ahead, and we dropped to our knees.

A boy next to me, new to the Dragoons, raised his M–79, ready to fire its big bulletlike projectile ahead of us into the jungle.

Sergeant Higa took his arm and pointed to a branch just where the boy was firing.

"Get in a clear space," he said as sweetly as if he were discussing which side of the place mat the fork should go. "If the round hits that branch we're in trouble."

Neil Buie, when he raised his voice, could bellow like a bull. Now his voice echoed through the jungle as he ordered men forward. Fletcher Bass took off directly in front of us, the halfback slamming right through the line of trees with his men right behind him. There was an exchange of shots, and the radio on Mo Thomas' back gave a quick metallic yammer about an enemy they could see moving in the bushes.

Neil grabbed the radio's hand-held transmitter. "If he's armed," he barked, "kill him! If he's not, capture him!" Then all of us were running through a trail in the woods.

"Got one up here, Captain!" a voice ahead of us shouted. We had taken a prisoner and were racing in the direction where he was. Until that moment I had not been aware of the slightest animosity toward the men who had been shooting at me. Now I found myself spitting out particularly foul curses as I ran toward a glimpse of the enemy.

The instant I saw him my anger vanished. A small Vietnamese in his thirties, bareheaded and wearing a sand-colored uniform, was lurchingly limping out of a thicket, wading through brush. He bowed repeatedly as he came, raising both hands in the position of prayer, striking his forehead in the Buddhist sign of mercy. Wine-red blood was congealing on the skin and torn cloth of his left leg. He stared in terror as half a dozen of us surrounded him, looming over him with both hands on our rifles.

"Take him up to the road," Captain Buie said. "If he tries anything, shoot him." The prisoner limped off up the trail, a man ahead of him and a man behind him.

It was news to me that there was a road to our right, but

after a few more minutes of bushwhacking, I too emerged on the road, and a strange scene greeted my eyes. All sorts of American troops were milling around on a wide grassy road. In one direction the road led back out of the jungle to the C Company position and the meadow, and in the other direction it led further downhill into the jungle. These men here were from A Company, which had been brought here by helicopter in the past few minutes as reinforcements. While we had been working through the jungle, they had been making their way down this road. For some reason everything had come to a stop right here, and men were standing around talking, or sitting smoking.

I crossed the road, erect, comforted by the sight of this *kaffeeklatsch,* and suddenly a man spoke to me: "Get down, there's incoming rounds." I flattened out on the spot, but some of the other men moved to cover in leisurely fashion. I ran back across the road to a grassy depression off its shoulder, and found two more North Vietnamese prisoners who had just been herded out of the jungle. One of them, an older man, was silent as he sat down, but the younger one was defiant, sneering at the young GI who was guarding him. The GI flipped off the safety on his M–16 and pointed it at the cocky North Vietnamese, whose smile vanished as he sat down quietly with the older man. A minute later the guard was giving them both a drink of water from his canteen.

Yet another North Vietnamese was brought out of the jungle, a trim erect man in his thirties, and the first two prisoners stiffened. It was apparently an officer. He sat down, saying nothing.

Lying on the other side of me was a dead North Vietnamese I had not noticed until now. He appeared to be about twenty, short, with a big chest and broad shoulders. He lay sprawled on his back, as if he had been advancing up this road to the C Company perimeter and had run straight into something that had flung him backward, unmarked and dead. In other days he had probably had a thick shock of black hair, but now it was in the shortest of crew cuts. His eyelids were open, and his eyeballs had turned up in his head, so that he stared up at the sky with gray orbs.

I crossed the road again, trying to find Captain Buie or some of the men I knew. There was more firing in the jungle, and I landed in yet another depression in the ground, beside a couple of B Company boys who had a somewhat better idea than I did of what had happened. The engagement had started just beyond here, at the widest part of this old logging road, when one of C Company's platoons had been ambushed as they were coming back up this road, nearing the end of a patrol.

"They're over there," one of the boys said, and I looked. About fifty yards on, beside the road, the American bodies were stacked like green logs with white and black arms protruding from them. An effort had been made by the reinforcements to cover them with ponchos, but the ponchos kept slipping off.

I looked back up the road toward the C Company perimeter. I was beginning to see what had happened. Simultaneously with the successful ambush, other parts of the enemy force had sprung at the C Company perimeter from the jungle, and more North Vietnamese forces had been poured into the attack by hurrying them up this road, where they had had the misfortune to run into our gunships, our artillery, and later our bombers.

I lay on my side in the grass. There had been no rounds fired by either side for a few minutes. A helicopter sliced low over our heads and landed on the road beside the American bodies, flinging the last of the ponchos away from them with its propeller blast. A tall man jumped out, and there was a high rattling buzz of enemy automatic fire. Figures moved frantically around the helicopter, the tall figure leaped aboard again, and the chopper took off. Although I did not recognize him, this was Tom Lynch, trying to get in and take charge on the ground. He had to jump aboard again because the chopper was being shot up before Sergeant Major Hannon could toss out the radios Tom needed to keep in touch with everyone.

Silence again, and various squads moved into the jungle.

Another helicopter came in. This one was to take out the prisoners for a rapid interrogation to see if we could find out more about what we were up against. The chopper landed, the North Vietnamese were led toward it, and a hail of shots came from the jungle, aimed at the North Vietnamese by their own men. Everyone up by the pile of American bodies took cover, some of them behind the tiers of American corpses. This chopper got off too, but without the prisoners.

I heard Captain Buie roaring, verbally kicking his company into the jungle, and we moved on down the road past the green woodpile of dead Americans. The road narrowed; we moved bent over.

A murderously personal high-pitched snapping string of enemy machine-gun bullets came after me, and I landed in a leafy depression at the edge of the road, my face down in mud and moss. It was like being on the end of a death ray that is probing right around you. I got my rifle pointed exactly in the direction from which the fire was coming. I felt oddly comforted, because I was still alive and sensed that if that machine gun had not got me a moment before, it could not reach me now. It was good to have the M–16 in my hands, and not just to have to lie here and take it with no possibility of firing back. I felt a strange justification. I was ready to kill now, perfectly willing. I checked the line of fire again and saw that an American had landed three yards into the jungle, right where I would have to fire if I wanted to let go in that direction.

The machine gun let loose another eerie burst, and then there was the sudden clanging sound of an M–16, right in there with it, dueling it. There was a short burst from the machine gun, a longer clip-emptying burst from the American weapon, and silence. I did not know it, but Specialist Fourth Class Stanley W. Dix of B Company had just charged forward by himself, silencing the gun, killed three North Vietnamese, and died, winning a posthumous Silver Star. It was later that I figured out that Dix had laid down his life for his white and black comrades on the same day that there had been race riots in Newark, New Jersey, in which Americans killed other Americans.

Buie was shouting again. By now I was quite content to lie in a place where I was not getting hurt, but his voice was such that it seemed unthinkable not to obey it.

For a change, we were going back up the road. Time of day had meant nothing; now I noticed that the sky had the darkness of very late afternoon. We tramped up the road, looking back over our shoulders every other second, and again came into the milling-around area. This time Buie spread his men out along one side of the road, lying facing into the jungle. He and I sat in a little leafy hollow just off one shoulder of the road, with Tomlinson sitting at right angles to us, his radio still firmly strapped to his back and his jaw still chewing gum.

A helicopter came in. We paid no attention to it, our faces studying the darkening jungle. The wind-blast from the chopper grew as it landed behind us, blowing dust and leaves past our heads. Suddenly I felt something behind me give and shift, and then to my amazement a good-sized tree managed to fall directly between Buie and me, its trunk dropping in such a way that it landed across Tomlinson's legs without touching them. Tomlinson scrambled out from beneath it. I stared behind me. The tree trunk had been so riddled with bullets and shrapnel during the day that it had taken just this one last blast of air to break it off at a point just above my shoulder, where I had been leaning against it.

We three stared at this tree that had landed in our laps and began to laugh. It was so idiotic, it had fallen so considerately in avoiding any damage to us, that it was a sign that we were not going to be hurt, that if we had survived everything else this day we were going to be all right.

Buie's radio told him something, and again we were forming up on the road, spaced out, getting ready to march back to the C Company perimeter. I stood waiting beside the dead North Vietnamese I had seen before. He seemed uncannily suspended as he lay there on his back, his face neither peaceful nor suffering, his body neither comfortable nor twisted in effort or agony.

I had not seen the Bush Pilot since the C Company perimeter, and now he came up, saw me looking down at the dead NVA, and asked if I wanted any souvenirs.

"Sure."

He handed me a red mud-crusted beat-up silvery enemy canteen. "I'll get you some more," he said, and then we were moving up the road. I looked at my watch for the first time. It was six-thirty in the evening, still light. The first shots had been six hours and forty minutes before.

We moved up the road toward the perimeter, and as we walked the intensity of the first phase of the battle became clearer. There were bomb and shell craters all along this road, and, first at every ten yards, then at every five, we were stepping over NVA bodies or walking around them. Some of the bodies were strangely unmarked, men who had apparently been so close to an exploding shell that it had killed them without dismembering them, toppling them backward into the craters where they lay. Others were shredded, like sand-colored bags that have been run through buzz saws. One man lay neatly on his back with the bottom half of his tan-clad leg, shoe downward, lying right beside his thigh.

We walked uphill out of the jungle just at sunset, our faces muddy, tired and quiet, rifles in our hands, past the bodies of our enemies. There was something primeval about this silent procession in the hushed jungle dusk.

At the C Company perimeter things had changed. There were tanks with their cannon pointed toward the jungle, and armored personnel carriers, and all the seriously wounded were gone. As B Company trudged through, on their way downhill across the meadow to where we had started in the morning, I saw Tom standing beside an armored personnel carrier, talking over a radio. I stepped out of line and started toward him. I was ready to go back to the fire base. He looked so busy, and was giving orders to so many men, that I shrugged my shoulders and walked on.

Our perimeter was just as we had left it, except for a few bullet holes and rocket-fragment rips in some of the pup tents. I went to the pup tent I shared with Captain Buie, and there, beside it, was the filled canteen that I had not been able to get to when the shooting first started. I had not eaten since dawn. I sat down, drinking some but not much of the water, and pulled out some C rations. To my surprise, all I felt like eating was two crackers and a small can of pears.

Fires were being lit. Our artillery was crashing down in the surrounding woods, trying to hit pockets where the enemy might be and laying down a defensive concentration to ensure that we would not be attacked again tonight. I still had no idea of the dimensions of what had happened today, but now, with food and the fires, back in our own tents and holes, men became more voluble. There was a strange innocence about the conversations, as if men were describing their roles in a sports event in which we had all participated. Indeed, I found the day singularly free of personalized malice. I had seen far more viciousness displayed among members of a family around a dinner table in the United States than I had witnessed today.

"Did you get off any rounds?" someone asked me in the twilight.

"No," I answered. "I never saw anything to shoot at, so I thought I ought to keep it all in case I did."

"Beautiful," the voice said approvingly.

The Bush Pilot came over to me with a North Vietnamese canvas-covered wicker helmet, and Fletcher Bass gave me the tail fins of one of the first enemy rockets that had landed in this perimeter at the start of the battle.

I listened to an amazing variety of stories, as they were matter-of-factly told in the waving firelight. There had been as many battles today as there were men participating. While I had been at one side of the beleaguered C Company perimeter, Captain Buie had worked his way to the opposite edge, where there had been fighting of an intensity that made my time look like a stay at a resort. The North Vietnamese, at the very moment that I had been looking over the edge of my foxhole and seeing nothing, had made repeated attacks in strength, rushes trying to break into the jungle side of the perimeter. At one point they had turned our battery-operated Claymore mines around at the edge of the jungle, hoping that we would detonate them and shower ourselves with the killing pellets. One of our Claymores that had still been turned the right way had killed nine of them as they charged. At another moment our men had rushed out of their holes and grabbed a North Vietnamese machine gun on wheels, towed it back and opened fire with it on the next wave of attackers. On that side of the perimeter, nobody had any trouble seeing something to shoot at. Buie told me that when he was in a hole with the C Company commander, a sniper in a tree had opened up on them. A young rifleman in their same hole had opened fire on the sniper at just the moment an artillery round had struck the tree, flinging the dead sniper thirty yards through the air.

"I guess that'll fix him," the boy had said, and found something else in his sights.

John Collins was standing by a birch tree, and I went

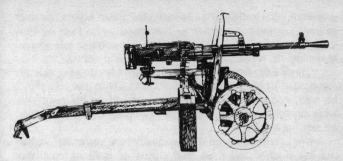

North Vietnam M.G. on wheels

over to him and we talked for a while. What he was really taking about was the hope that he would get through the next months until he went home, not speaking in fear, but in hope. Beyond this, he was thinking about prayer, about the hope that there was some power somewhere that looked after things, that could somehow regulate matters. I told him that I thought there was, and that I thought we had to have faith that there was.

I took off my boots and slid into the pup tent. I felt neither tired nor elated, but at rest. Mo Thomas was lying under a shelter half that he had stretched between two trees, and heavy artillery was crashing into the jungle.

I said, because it was what I was thinking, and because I thought Mo might like the image, "Uncle Sam's big orchestra."

He laughed.

Incredibly, the next morning was just like any other morning in the field. Men who had filled canteens and lit fires yesterday were dead or in hospitals, and yet the canteens were filled, the fires lit, the big family moving about its simple chores.

I was sitting with my radio-men friends, drinking C-ration coffee, when the ground began to shake. We rose and saw, on a distant ridge, a series of close-spaced beige geysers rising from the jungle, as if a huge locomotive were puffing its way past under the trees. It was a B–52 strike, bombs from the eight-engined Strategic Air Command planes raining down unexpectedly in the area where yesterday's North Vietnamese attackers were pulling back toward their bases across the river in their Cambodian sanctuary. The sound swept over us now, a continuous rolling explosion as half our horizon was spotted with leaping fountains of brown smoke and debris.

Tomlinson was still chewing gum as he stood watching, the ground jiggling beneath him. "Sorry about that, Charlie," he said, addressing the enemy, and picked up his pack. We were moving out, breaking camp. I got my own pack settled on my back.

We hiked slowly up the meadow where yesterday we had run and ducked and fired, and closed in, walking erect this time, on the C Company perimeter. B Company was moving on, into the jungle to look for what was left of the enemy, but this time Tom beckoned me out of line. He had spent the night out here, and now he and artilleryman Paul Titus and I took a helicopter back to the fire base in the abandoned rubber plantation. I had been away from it forty hours, and it seemed years.

Until we got to the TOC tent I had not grasped the full extent of yesterday's action. Now I learned that our two companies had been fighting an entire North Vietnamese regimental column which had been on its way to attack and try to overrun the Special Forces camp at Duc Co. Today that shattered regimental column was straggling back to Cambodia in small parties through the jungle. Two hundred enemy bodies had been found around our battlefield and, with the North Vietnamese talent for carrying their dead and wounded away with them, it was entirely possible that we might have put as many as one thousand of them out of action.

It had been a big battle by the standards of the Vietnam War, with twelve prisoners taken, including two officers. On the grass outside the TOC tent were row upon row of captured weapons. Included in the booty were the first two Russian-made B–50 rocket launchers to be captured in Vietnam. One was already being flown back to the United States for study.

Busy as he was, Tom took me aside, and with a piece of paper reconstructed for me what had happened. The first firing I had heard the morning before had been when the North Vietnamese ambushed the platoon of C Company whose bodies I had seen. At the same moment they had launched a terrific attack on the C Company perimeter, evidently expected to overrun it swiftly.

Tom had jumped into a chopper and hovered over the part of the jungle where the trapped and encircled platoon was fighting. He had made contact with the radio man in the suffering platoon below, but the man was wounded and in a state of shock.

"They're all around us," the boy kept saying.

"Can't you give me a smoke grenade and show me where you are?" Tom asked softly from the sky. There was a silence, and then the boy said something about his mother.

Tom looked at me, the paper with the diagram of the battle forgotten in his hand. "I asked him again to pop some smoke, so we could know just where they were and bring in something to support them," he said slowly. "Then the kid said, 'Charger, I'm dying.' That was all." Tom's voice choked, and there were tears in his eyes. He stared at the ground for a moment, and I knew that something had happened to Tom Lynch then that had changed an already strong and capable man into something harder, an even more formidable fighter.

Tom resumed his description of the battle. At that moment he had to write off that platoon; in fact eighteen of them were dead; nine of them were later recovered, wounded, in the bushes. It was then that he brought in everything in support of the C Company perimeter. Even while he had been pleading with the boy on the ground, he had been giving us the orders to be ready to move that we had heard over the radio in our perimeter. Now he threw us in. For some reason the North Vietnamese had been unaware that B Company was at the bottom of the meadow, or perhaps they had been planning to sweep down on B Company after overrunning C Company. Certainly they must have thought the odds were right, for they had at least twelve hundred men closing in on the two hundred and forty we had left. In any case, B Company had arrived just in time, just as the NVA were beginning to get into some of the holes on the jungle side of the besieged C Company perimeter.

"I think the NVA commander may have lost control," Tom said. "They just kept attacking time after time, and we had all that stuff coming in on them by then, and it just kept chewing them up. That guy should have called it off when they didn't get in right away, but he didn't realize what was happening, or maybe his commo went to pieces and he couldn't call them off.''

The rest, he said, I had seen for myself. The enemy had simply run out of gas and fallen back into the jungle, and with B Company I had participated in the beginning of the mopping-up operation which was continuing today, assisted by air strikes at all the likely escape routes to Cambodia.

I wandered around the fire base. Paul Titus was lying in his hammock, looking smaller and sicker than ever, but yesterday he had risen to superb heights in his artilleryman's craft. We talked over the battle, which was becoming known as Three Trees, because of those three tall eucalyptus trees in the center of the C Company perimeter, where I found the wounded. At the height of the action Paul, directing the guns from Tom's helicopter circling to one side, had had thirty cannon supporting our besieged holes. These thirty guns, ranging in size from the 105s in the fire base to the 8-inch howitzers I had seen long ago with Whipcrack, had placed 4688 shells around us and on the North Vietnamese.

8″ Self-Propelled Howitzer

"I never saw a round out of place," Paul added in tribute to the young gunners.

I thought about all those things flying around, and asked him how close in to us he had had those shells landing.

"At one point we had to bring it to within fifteen meters of our own men," Paul said thoughtfully.

I brought out of my pocket the jagged piece of steel that had sizzled into the red loam just behind where I was crouching, the piece I had later dug out. "What is this, Paul?"

He took it. "That's from a One-Fifty-Five. That would have a killing radius of fifty meters, above ground, from where it landed."

I put the thing that had certifiably damned near killed me into my pocket, and walked on around the fire base. The word had gotten out that there had been a hell of a battle up here, and now correspondents were arriving. One of them was a Japanese photographer for UPI, named Mine, who was to die in combat a year later. Chatting, I discovered that he was a graduate of Sophia University, the Jesuit institution in Tokyo where I had taught for two years. We stood in the red mud beside the captured machine guns and rocket launchers, talking of different priests we had known. He had majored in economics, and there we were, an English major from Harvard who was writing about the war and an economics major from Sophia who was photographing it.

I said good-bye to Mine, whom I would see again in bizarre and dangerous circumstances near Tuy Hoa Air Base, and ran into some of the boys in C Company, who had been brought in to pull themselves together and guard the fire base while the two other companies carried on with the mopping-up operation in the jungle. They told me that four of the men in the ambushed platoon had been captured by the North Vietnamese right then. They had tied one man's hands in front of him with rope and had been leading him away when our artillery started crashing in. The boy had landed in some bushes away from his captors. He lay low for a while, chewed through his ropes, and got back to the C Company perimeter. The other three had not been so lucky. They had been found with their hands tied behind them, shot dead through the back of the neck.

I strolled into the TOC, only to find The Royal Pineapple giving me a pat on the back. He didn't know how to express it, but he was glad I was alive, and glad that I had seen his old former command, B Company, do its stuff. As I stood chatting with him, Lieutenant Andrew O'Brien walked past—the mortar platoon commander I had last seen gazing at the Cambodian hills and saying "This country never had a beginning, and it will never have an end." O'Brien flicked my arm with his hand. "Hello, Combat," he said.

A staff officer who had been out in the C Company perimeter last night, working radios after the action, told me something that turned a myth into reality. I had heard tales of a character named McCoy, a soldier attached to Fourth Division Headquarters who modestly referred to himself as the Division Sniper, who would cast off into the jungles by himself for days at a time. Last night, this officer told me, just at dusk, McCoy had appeared in the C Company perimeter. He had been carrying an AK–47, the North Vietnamese automatic rifle, and the last they had seen of him he had been walking into the jungle by himself.

Another helicopter arrived at the fire base. This one was carrying some of the FACs, who were wearing their gray flying suits and looking strangely out of place amid all the helmets and muddy boots.

I walked up to Rod Rodriguez and demanded to know was that he, flying low over the jungle at the height of the action?

He nodded, as if it really did not make any difference.

I was suddenly, irrationally furious. Didn't he realize that it had been suicidal? Did he have any idea of how much stuff had been zipping around while he played Nosey Parker, peeking his plane down every tree trunk?

Rod grinned. "One time there were twenty of them standing up and shooting at me," he said as if it had all happened to someone else. "All I got out of the whole thing was one hole in my rudder."

Later that afternoon I was still walking around the fire base. I think the truth was that I was still wound up, and still terribly glad to be alive, so I just kept walking until I ran into barbed wire and had the sense to stop. Coming back through one of the more populated parts of our fire base, I noticed a flag that was hanging from a limb above a bunker. Clearly the private property of a soldier, it was the flag of the state of Iowa, with the seal in red, white, and blue. On it were the words *Our Liberties We Cherish and Our Freedoms We Will Defend*.

That night Tom had a few words to say in the evening meeting in the TOC tent. It was the first time the entire staff had been in one place since the battle. The atmosphere was a strange mixture of sobriety, satisfaction, confidence, and a thought of lost friends. Twenty Dragoons had died, forty were wounded, and two hundred of the enemy were dead, with each radio transmission reporting more enemy bodies found as the companies continued their sweep.

"Thank you," Tom said to them. "I've always said that we do everything well, that nothing is unimportant, and yesterday it paid off. Whatever you were doing—the man back here loading cans of water onto choppers, the man out there chewing through his ropes—you gave it everything you had. Thank you."

As we left the tent, I noticed that Captain Bill Pratt and a couple of his officers from C Company were walking stiffly, almost hobbling. I found that they had shrapnel splinters in their legs, but they did not want to turn themselves in until the situation had become more relaxed and they could afford a few hours away from their company to have the surgeons pluck the metal out of them.

The next morning was gray and drizzly. I knew that I would be coming back to the Dragoons once more, for Tom's departure and the Change of Command ceremony that would take place then, and I felt ready for the comforts of Tuy Hoa. As I walked past the TOC with my pack, enemy souvenirs dangling from my belt and tied to my pack, a group of forty replacements came shuffling through the wet grass, staring at the rows of captured weapons on the ground.

The chopper that took me out of the fire base left me at the Dragoons' base camp at Dragon Mountain. It was the first time I had been there since the night before we launched off on the operation to the Ban Me Thuot area, and I had an hour to kill before there would be a truck to the air terminal at Pleiku.

I strolled into the wooden administrative building of the battalion and talked with a couple of the clerks who sat shivering at their desks in the clammy concrete-floored orderly room. They were typing up the casualty list, and I looked at it, struck by the ethnic range of names that had just bled. Campbell, Duvall, Erickson, Fischer, Hogg, Kennedy, Mazurkiewicz, Taylor, Tenehara, Valdez, Wurster, Yee.

I wandered down the hallway and found myself in a big unused office. There was only one desk in this room, in the corner, and on it was a small sign, LT. COL. THOMAS P. LYNCH. This was Tom's office. I had not known that he had an office back here, because he never used it.

Beside the desk there was a framed sheet of paper that recounted the history of the Dragoons. I glanced at it curiously. In all the time I had spent with the Dragoons I had thought of them simply as a unit operating today, in these hills, with no thought for their traditions. Now I realized that these low-number outfits, such as the Eighth Infantry, were the oldest American units.

The paper told me that this battalion had come into being 9 July 1838, at Buffalo, New York. Its motto was *Patriae Fidelitas*—loyalty to the nation.

Standing to the other side of Tom's desk were the colors, the battalion's flag, with a forest of battle-honor streamers fixed to the top of its staff. In this cold room on a gray day, the mountains of Indo-China misty through the windows, my hand reached out and began pulling one after another of the colored ribbons away from the others, reading the gold lettering on each that gave the name of a place where the Dragoons had fought. Occasionally I stopped and checked a ribbon against the framed unit history.

The first ribbon read SEMINOLES. That had been against the Indians in Florida, in the 1840s. Then the Mexican War, PALO ALTO; another streamer, MONTEREY, then VERA CRUZ. CHAPULTEPEC. Then the first big campaigns against the Indians, APACHES, NEW MEXICO 1858, NEW MEXICO 1860. Then they were pulled back East as one of the few seasoned Regular regiments ready to fight for the Union. PENINSULA. MANASSAS. ANTIETAM. FREDERICKSBURG. CHANCELLORSVILLE.

I had a whole wad of Civil War battle streamers in my hand, staring at them and thinking My God, what it must have been to be a Dragoon then; they obviously fought all the time. GETTYSBURG. WILDERNESS. ATLANTA. SPOTSYLVANIA. COLD HARBOR. PETERSBURG.

And then the War Between the States was over, and everyone could go home, and maybe tell a few war stories in the evening, except for the Dragoons. They were sent back out to the dusty forts on the plains, the Indians again: MONTANA 1872, ARIZONA 1876.

The war with Spain, and they fought at Santiago. Then PHILIPPINE INSURRECTION. LUZON 1901.

The First World War. The Fourth Division had fought in the campaigns of Aisne-Marne, St. Mihiel, and the Meuse-Argonne.

The World War II streamers. BEACHES OF NORMANDY. They had landed on Utah Beach on D-Day, been first into Paris, fought through the Battle of the Bulge, been first into Germany and fought right across it. Ernest Hemingway had been with the division as a correspondent; he had written about the Hurtgen Forest and what happened there.

I let the battle ribbons slip from my hand and stepped back from the flag. It was a roll call of American military history, and the Dragoons had been there almost every time it got tough, for a hundred and twenty-nine of our years. In their time, each of these wars, too, had its opponents—thoughtful, sensitive men.

I stared again at the streamers. APACHES. GETTYSBURG. ARDENNES-ALSACE. I did not consciously believe in Valhalla, but for an instant I had a vision of all these past Dragoons hovering above the C Company perimeter the other day, protecting the boys in their holes below.

"Hey," a voice said, "the truck's ready."

Out of the Three Trees battle I had learned a few things—the importance of leadership, the fact that a man can be frightened and yet efficient at the same time—but another lesson awaited me at Tuy Hoa.

I came into the hooch with a head-to-toe patina of Cambodian border mud, and my various trophies—the North Vietnamese helmet, two canteens, North Vietnamese belt, tail fins of a rocket that almost killed me—tied onto me or sticking from my pockets.

Mama-san took one look at me and at the enemy equipment with which I was festooned, and her face broke into an admiring smile. She sighed, clapped her hands, and raced out of the hooch, bringing back with her four of the other Vietnamese maids who cared for hooches in the area. They clustered about me, looking at me, fingering the various pieces of enemy gear, helping me empty my pack.

There I stood, a mess, and they gazed at me with warm eyes, chattering, trying in their bad English to find out how many men I had killed. When I tried to explain that I had killed none but that the unit had killed two hundred, they seemed excited merely to be in the same room with me. It was as if the scent and sound of battle were still on me, and they found it aphrodisiac.

I could not have been more surprised. In this instant they were not thinking at all that the dead had been Vietnamese and that I was a foreign devil come from far away—I was a hunter, *their* hunter, back from the biggest hunt of them all.

TWENTY-ONE

The next evening, talking with pilots in front of the old nude in our gleaming new bar, far in spirit from our old Wild West saloon on the beach, I found that this war was a smaller world than I had thought. The FACs had given me the call signs of the flights that were bombing and napalming the NVA while I was crouching in my hole at Three Trees, and now I discovered that my life quite possibly had been saved by that timely arrival of some of my friends here. Carl Miller, who shared a hooch with Pres Flanagan, had been in one of the first two F–100s to arrive on the scene, and shortly after that Freddie Poston, commander of the 309th, had led three planes in to the target. Don Usry, the former West Point end behind whom I had ridden from Hickam to Guam, had been the pilot right behind Freddie, and it interested me to think that the man who had flown me to the war had dropped the bombs that helped me out of the tightest spot I had been in so far.

Freddie and I were standing there comparing notes on what that logging road had looked like from the air and on the ground, when I felt a hand on my shoulder. It was another pilot from the 309th. They were putting tomorrow night's flying schedule together, he said, and would I like a back seat?

I said yes. It was all the old things; wanting to lick my fear of the take-off, and an element of wanting to prove my courage to myself and others. These were my hosts, and I their guest, and one accepted a combat mission, when it was offered, as one accepted a drink. It was undoubtedly a strange reaction, but it was a strange time and place.

*   *   *

The night was a foggy, rainy one. There was a moon behind it somewhere, and when we roared into the sky at midnight, shaking like a javelin, it was as if we entered a vapor lamp turned down to its lowest possible luminosity. We were a flight of two, and the leader's plane was visible only as a dark shadow with a green light flashing on its wingtip. The two of us were locked into thick eerie mist that allowed us no glimpse of lights on the ground and no sense that the moonlight must be coming from above.

The mission was a Skyspot, in which we would be maneuvered to the bomb-release point by radioed instructions from a radar tracking station on the ground. The mission was proceeding in normal fashion and we were a few minutes from the release point when my pilot, a tall young captain named Dave Cronenburg, said over the intercom: "I don't know if I should tell you this, but I've got vertigo so bad I can't believe it."

There it was. I was in the back seat, my fate literally in his hands, and he was in the front seat experiencing that dreaded loss of direction, the inability to distinguish up from down, that had cost us a pilot earlier in the year.

I muttered back "Well, I hope you get over it," and stared out at the lead plane, which was now in fog so thick and dark that his lights were all that was visible of him, despite the fact that he was a few yards away.

Suddenly I had it, too. I felt as if I were in a steep turn to the left. My eyes whipped toward the attitude indicator on the instrument panel, that little representation of the plane in relation to a globe marking the horizon. It showed us flying absolutely straight and level, at just the moment I was fighting an impulse to grab the control stick and bring us out of this steep, diving turn.

Through all this the voice on the ground kept telling us to make very minor corrections in order to arrive at just the right point to release the bombs. Dave was following the instructions: the stick between my legs moved slightly in response to each phrase, moving just a couple of inches at a moment when I felt that pulling it one way about eight inches was required.

We released the bombs, with me feeling that we were

casting them off sideways into the night, whereas they were dropping vertically from our wings. The plane bucked, rising from the loss of weight, and finally I said to Dave "I've got it, too."

"Just hang on," he said. "I've still got it myself."

I stared through the raindrops on the plastic canopy, hoping that it would go away if I looked at the lead plane. It helped not a bit. Since we were closely paralleling the attitudes of the leader, my disoriented senses imputed to him the sensations I was feeling. I was certain that he was leading us down in a swooping left-hand turn, and I began wondering if Dave would be overcome by it, as many a good pilot had been, and lose control of the plane. The idea of ejecting had always bothered me, and the thought of being fired out of this seat into freezing black fog twenty thousand feet up and floating down into the jungle night was revolting.

"Lead," Dave said over the radio, his voice cool, "Two is experiencing a lot of disorientation."

"Roger. Understand," the leader's voice came back without hesitation. "We'll try to break out over the coast here and see if we can shake this fog and pick up some landmarks."

At this point we did go into a turn, a long, descending bank to the right, and now my stomach, and all my balance senses, felt as if we were flying straight and level.

We flew out of the fog as if into a brilliantly lit room. Below to my left was the wide beach at Nha Trang, lights along the shore, and beneath us were the white ripples on the surface of the South China Sea. The feeling receded, leaving me simultaneously tired and keyed-up, my senses totally in agreement with the instruments on the panel and the angle of the planes.

"It's gone," I said.

"Me too," Dave observed, and we drove on back to Tuy Hoa.

II

A couple of days later, I saw more Viet Cong than I had seen in any one place before. They were defectors, or said they were. It was graduation day at the Chieu Hoi Center in Tuy Hoa, and one hundred and sixty Viet Cong men and women were completing the six-week rehabilitation course that followed upon their giving themselves up to the government. After the ceremony which I was attending, they were free to walk through the gate in the barbed-wire fence that had held them until now, free to vote, and also eligible for the draft.

At the end of the long hall, once a warehouse, there were red curtains. A large red-striped yellow Republic of Vietnam flag hung behind a Buddhist altar to household gods, complete with sacrifices of food in dishes on the altar and flowers in vases.

The Center was supervised by two Filipinos, employed by the United States and on loan to the Vietnamese. They stayed outside on the concrete porch that had once been a loading platform, and half a dozen American civilian and military advisors sat with Vietnamese officials in the first two rows of wooden chairs. Sitting on benches behind us were the graduates, all of them neatly and simply dressed. They appeared intent on the proceedings.

The first speaker was a fiery youth, genuinely fiery, with eyes that shone and a voice that was low-keyed but strong. This was the valedictorian, and I wondered if he were not a government plant who had taken the course along with the genuine defectors. I looked over my shoulder at the graduates, who ranged from a woman of sixty to those in their teens, and their expression remained that same intent one. When the youth finished, he led the class in a quick, shouted pro-government slogan. The building rocked, it sounded real, but I had no way of knowing.

Next to speak was the Vietnamese chief of the Province's Chieu Hoi program, the figurehead bureaucrat who did considerably less than the two Filipinos who were watching through a window. I glanced again at the graduates; the faces were resigned, as if they knew exactly what this man was, they had been seeing sleek officials like this all their lives.

Sitting in front of me was Major Heung, Colonel Ba's assistant. His face was displaying a polite, proper sort of interest in the words of the Chieu Hoi chief. I remembered his saying that first evening we met at the Taj Mahal Christmas party that he had been a professor of French Literature at the University of Hue, and that was what he would like to go back to doing. It was almost as far, for him, from those classrooms at Hue to this hall and ceremony as it was from New York, for me. I knew from what the advisors told me that he was a driving worker in his job as Deputy Province Chief for Security. He was always out on the roads in a jeep at night, which was not a prescription for longevity; always, by his example, he was trying to convince Vietnamese civilian and military officials to work hard, to be seen in the countryside, to be forward with the militia. It was clear that he did not view the Viet Cong as the answer for Vietnam. Looking at the neatly barbered back of his head as he tried to look interested in a speech he heard at every Chieu Hoi graduation, I wondered what was his private dream for his country.

The next speaker was another of the graduates, an older man. He spoke hesitantly; while the valedictorian might have been a student who had joined the VC and become disenchanted, this fifty-year-old salutatorian appeared to be a farmer with hard hands, a gentle voice, and a diffident manner. I was sure that no government would be clever enough to plant him in a class. When this man finished, there was no slogan-shouting— just a lot of clapping.

Prizes were awarded. Major Heung gave the first prize, to the youth who had spoken. The Civic Action officer among the American advisors gave a kerosene lantern, with an incongruous red ribbon around it, to the older farmer. Then to my surprise I was on my feet, being handed a canvas rain hat wrapped in pink cellophane and being pointed toward the recipient, another old farmer. I bowed to him, handed him the hat, and our hands found each other for an awkward handshake.

They sang the national anthem with gusto, and it was over. They were free to go, with a small sum of money given to each of them. Most had families in the Province, and some had even defected as little family units and had lived here, children and all, while the adults had taken the course of lectures.

We walked toward the gate. I had my camera with me for a change, and I started to pose Major Heung between two of his friends among the American advisors.

Suddenly the professor of French Literature became very Vietnamese. "Not three in a picture," he said, hastily grabbing another American so that there would be four of them before I clicked the shutter. "If three in a picture, one will die."

That afternoon I stopped in at the office of Dan Leaty, the senior American civilian official in the Province. The stocky red-haired twenty-nine-year-old rose from a pile of paperwork to get us a cup of coffee, and asked what he could do for me. I told him that, through my previous visit up here and my trip up the coast to Song Cau and Tuy An, I was beginning to get some idea of how our side proceeded toward its objectives. On the other hand, the Viet Cong was still, to me, a shadowy presence. At least this morning I had seen the faces of those who previously, in jungles or on crowded streets, had been with the Viet Cong, not all of them armed, but all meshed into the effort that opposed our own. Could Dan help flesh out for me these bones and hints?

He nodded, moved from behind his desk, and pulled open a drawer in the bank of gray metal files along the wall.

"The Chieu Hoi program in this province is the best one in the country," he said in his brusque way. "I made up the questionnaire we use with the defectors we get here, and this questionnaire is now used throughout the whole country."

That was Dan, and the redeeming thing I was to learn about him was that he was as candid and uninflectedly matter-of-fact in recounting his failures as in enumerating his successes. He laid a huge sheaf of interrogations of the *hoi chanh*, the defectors, down on the desk, and asked me to bring them back in a couple of weeks. Their contents had already been passed along to Higher, and Higher Higher, but he would like them back in his files.

I hitched a ride down to the air base with the Army mail clerk who was making the daily run from the advisors' compound. As I thought of the great stack of enemy autobiographies in my bag, I reflected upon the reasons it took an American so long to come to grips with the nature and tactics of this enemy. The concept of the clandestine society was, at most, peripheral to our tradition. There were the secret rites of the Masons and some other fraternities, and at the unpalatable end of the secret spectrum, the Ku Klux Klan and the Mafia. No one in them expected to gain popular political control of the United States, and certainly the population at large did not look to them for whatever popular reforms it desired.

Our jeep passed the little police box at the end of the long bridge spanning the river. The government flag flew above the police box; around it stood policemen with silver-winged crests on their caps, and government militia in uniform. It was to this outward display of strength and authority that an American was attuned. We imputed considerable power to a courthouse, a column of men marching in daylight, a flag flying above an armory. In our experience a post office implied a government which was in fact the single most powerful entity in the nation. In our country these symbols bespoke a political reality, and we assumed that the same reality attached to these symbols when we encountered them elsewhere. I was realizing now, after months in the Republic of Vietnam, that there was an equally or more highly organized governmental structure of which there was not a single outward symbol. I remembered that day at the house of the Tuy Hoa tycoon, when he and the interpreter had dwelt upon the advantages of the challenger. The party of revolution could choose the areas in which it felt it could most successfully compete, and the defender had to meet them on those grounds while still trying to run all the other services of government with which the revolutionaries chose not to encumber themselves.

That night I spread out the imperfectly translated questionnaires in my hooch, stacks on my cot and on my desk, and the Viet Cong government took shape before my eyes. It could be assumed that those who would defect were not the most enthusiastic of the enemy, nor those highest in its local government, so the degree of involvement shown on these pages implied a considerably tighter organization further up the pyramid. Nonetheless, it rapidly became evident that every person in a Viet Cong hamlet, unlike every person in a government-held hamlet, had a specific place in a specific activity. Ho Van Tu, aged seventeen, listed his position as Hamlet Guerrilla. His squad leader was twenty-two years old, and the other members of his squad were thirty-seven, eighteen, eighteen, sixteen, sixteen, fifteen, fifteen.

"My duty," he had told the interrogator, "is to defend

and put spikes on the trail at night; in the day time I always guard the top of the hill, to signal when Allied Forces come and to encourage the people to service work, defense, dig the spike-hole and communication trench, etc.''

A twenty-one-year-old girl, Le Thi Hon, was her village's Youth Executive Committee Commissioner, in charge of teenagers directly under her command, including "Cell leaders of Teenager Cell No. 1 and Cell No. 2."

Regarding "Duties," she gave this description: "To conduct the teenagers in acting, singing, camping. To teach the teenagers in village defense and making spikes. To instruct and explain to the teenagers about VC instructions and policies." Included in her duties was the monthly collection of the Contribution Tax to the Viet Cong, which was in the form of rice set aside by each household in a "saving rice-jar."

The duties and the titles varied somewhat from village to village, and there were certain specialized activities, such as midwife. There was a "district liaison" courier whose job was to carry messages from the leadership of one district to the next and to keep the villages in the hills in touch with the clandestine movement in the coastal towns.

Certain activities served the Province as a whole. Nguyen Thi Bic Lang, twenty, gave her job in the Viet Cong as "actress."

"The show crew of the Phu Yen Province Military Forces included ten men and five women. The mission of my crew was to sing songs for stimulate the people participation in the production-increasing and American opposition campaigns." The chief of her troupe was Nguyen Tam Hung, thirty-five, a man from Phu Yen who had gone to North Vietnam years before and had been infiltrated back in 1964. "We often show in areas at Tuy An, Song Cau, Tuy Hoa and Hieu Xuong districts." These were precisely the districts in which I had been visiting the American advisors, and this air base was in Hieu Xuong District.

I stopped for a moment, thinking this one over. While I sat in this air-conditioned trailer there was an excellent chance that out there in the night, in a forest cave, that show crew was leading an audience in singing a hymn of hate.

*   *   *

By the next day I had worked my way through the hundred and ten questionnaires that Dan had given me, and chosen twenty which provided a cross-section of reasons for joining the Viet Cong and for defecting.

There was a certain candor in the responses. "My village infiltrated by VC in 1962," a thirty-eight-year-old man stated. "Due not to leave a lot of my rice fields, and large houses, I and my family had to follow the VC for our living."

And why had he defected? "I should be brought to People's Court because I am a Well Off Class, stay with VC I might be starved and thirsty, so I turned in to Chieu Hoi, when I hear the government's clemency."

Only once was the Communist Party mentioned. Pham Lui, a thirty-nine-year-old fisherman who used the alias Tien, became a Viet Cong in 1965 and stated that he had joined the Communist Party on June 18, 1966.

"When I was an Inter-families Chief," his deposition read, "the VC often come over my house and spread the revolutionary propaganda that all the people will be liberated and get equal, happy and in the days to come all fishermen will have fishing boat with motor on it. I was very happy to hear that, therefore I participated with them." His task included "Leading fishermen association, providing fish when ever the VC cadre needed. I also propagandized to our members that when the war is end, the fishing association proceed on our present cooperative basis."

This man went on to identify his District Political Commissioner.

"Mr. Van, he went to the North in 1954, now he's back. District Military Commissioner: Mr. Phuoc, he married at An-Ninh village, went to the North in 1954, now he's back."

Q. Why are you turning in yourself?

A. Hungry and sufferings.

Occasionally there was an answer which could not have made cheery reading for Viet Cong officials.

Pham Dong, forty-four. With VC December 1965 to April 1967.

Q. Why did you leave the VC?

A. First I was constrained. Then I was cheated.

When this man got angry at the VC, he dismantled the

entire hamlet guerrilla unit of which he was the leader, and bringing some in with him and giving away the locations of the others. "Under my command, there are four guerrilla cells. Cell No. 1, three men, one leader and two members, all with guns, all became Chieu Hoi. Cell No. 2, five men, four with guns, all Chieu Hoi. Cell No. 3, one leader with gun, four without guns, all captured. Attached to this cell were one intelligence man and one liaison man, both Chieu Hoi."

One of the men, twenty-year-old Nguyen Tong, had been an executioner for the Viet Cong. His story began this way.

"In 1964, VC attacked my hamlet, I escaped toward the sea but I was wounded by their shot and captured, they then constrained me to be with them. Nobody worked under my command. I was only a guard at the detention camp and had to obey their order of murder. My duty is to guard the village detention camp, and to kill people when I got the order of village security leaders. I killed fifteen people with the order of Mr. Ban and Mr. Lun."

Why had he defected?

"I think I was stupid and involved by their propaganda. I obeyed their murder orders, and made many offenses, if I went on to live with them, I will do more and they never gave any right to me, so I returned."

Other answers as to why they had defected brought some poignant phrases.

"They said about the liberation but hungries every day."

"I lived area of VC too unhappy, bomber is violent consequently I come back return with the Nation because I realize free, happiness, eating wear is too enough."

Whatever else had emerged from this admittedly small sample, the picture of an organization was clear. In some villages the Viet Cong required thirty-six full days of work a year from everyone, in addition to their regular organizational duties. This often was in the form of serving as porters carrying supplies supporting main force units, requiring an absence for days at a time. The highest figure given was a requirement of ninety days.

Even knowing that this countryside was loaded with cleverly concealed arms, I was surprised by some of the statistics. A Main Force guerrilla, operating just a few miles from this base, had been part of a unit that had three hundred and forty-five automatic and other rifles, carbines, and pistols, two .30-caliber machine guns, and two mortars. At least this unit was primarily engaged in fighting, but those whose primary duties were other than fighting were also startlingly well-armed. Five men in their questionnaires were able to pinpoint the weapons of their neighbors by name, so there was no possibility that the same gun was being counted twice. They identified by owner thirty-nine rifles, carbines, and pistols. Other neighbors had charge of three hidden machine guns and several caches of hand grenades.

I looked at this last statistic of forty-two weapons, what might be called in-the-neighborhood weapons. If each of the five men who identified these weapons knew that eight of his neighbors carried guns, it must have had a deadening effect upon any desire to oppose or thwart them, or to attempt an escape through such a bristling countryside. Those hills out there were locked in a combination of idealism, fanaticism, coercion, and terror, an iron network. I remembered the Air Force colonel sitting at Pacific Air Force Headquarters in Hawaii who had told me I was coming out here too late, that all significant armed resistance would be over in six months.

III

A message was passed to me at the stand-up briefing, telling me that I was expected at the Dragoons' Change of Command ceremony three days later. It was something I wished very much to attend, so again I trudged up the ramp of a C–130 bound for Pleiku.

Getting off at the Pleiku air terminal, eating dinner that night with the FACs, I gazed at everything with a valedictory air. I felt that this would be the last time I would see the Dragoons, and the FACs, and this part of the country. Tom was going, most of the men I knew would be going in the next few weeks, and this was the end of it. I had a lot more to see in Phu Yen Province, the national elections could be observed there and in Saigon better than in these uninhabited mountain reaches by the Cambodian border, and I felt that I had pressed my luck about as far as it would go with the Dragoons.

*   *   *

I found them dug into the ruins of yet another Special Forces camp that had been abandoned in the Central Highlands. It was a dismal place with a rotting odor, in a muddy valley of ferns with war-blasted gray tree trunks stretching away on all sides toward hostile ridges. A chilly mist over the barbed wire completed the illusion that this was where you woke up just after you had been killed in action.

The only thing warm was the welcome, and that was warm indeed. Over by the crumbling concrete remains of one of the Special Forces buildings, Sergeant Higa was familiarizing some new men with the enemy weapons, in case the day came when enemy weapons were the only things available to fire in some situation. When Higa had a beer in his hand, he would give me a beer, and when he had a can of food in his hand, he would give me that. At the moment he was holding an SKS, a Russian semiautomatic rifle carried by some of the NVA and Viet Cong. He pressed it on me and urged me to try it.

I raised it. The front sight was a simple ring, with the post located in the hooded rear sight, and I drew a bead on a beer can sitting on some cindery earth. To my surprise, the beer can jumped obligingly when I fired at it. I waited for it to come to rest and fired again, and it danced off another yard. I hit it again, and again. It was far and away the most accurate rifle I had ever handled; the sights seemed to draw me in on top of the target, to make it easier to be on target than off. Higa took the rifle back from me with an approving smile.

Tom was in his tent with the man who was replacing him, Lieutenant Colonel Glen Belnap. Glen was a small dark-haired man, forty-three years old, soft-spoken, with a quick, nervous way of moving.

SKS

He was dressed in rumpled fatigues with a minimum of insignia. When they walked to the TOC, it was almost a Mutt-and-Jeff effect, Tom in his tall striding elegance, and Glen stepping along beside him as if content to give him center stage. It would be hard to imagine a greater contrast between two men, and all that this proved, eventually, was that good commanders come in many sizes, shapes, and attitudes.

"I want you to come up here again after Tom leaves," Glen said firmly. "I want you to feel you're welcome up here any time, and I want you to come up again."

I told him I would, not meaning it, little thinking that the next time I saw him would be at the biggest battle of the war.

Tom was the Dragoons' commander until the moment of the ceremony the next day, and that night he held his last staff meeting in the TOC tent. I stood at the back, knowing every man there, remembering the first time I had entered this tent on a hilltop in Phu Yen, and how I had spilled coffee over my then-shiny fatigues when a cannon went off as Tom was briefing me in front of the map. I had seen this tent in a lot of places and these men under a lot of conditions. Standing beside me was Jack Crumley of the Reconnaissance Platoon, whom I had first met washing out his socks in his helmet on that hilltop. Sitting on a metal chair in front of me was Toby Colburn, The Royal Pineapple, and next to him was Paul Titus of the artillery, throwing up every day from stomach trouble and still doing a better job than any other artilleryman in the division. Neil Buie was next to me, and Sergeant Higa beyond him. Standing just inside the open tent flap was Sergeant Major Hannon, still chewing whatever it was that he chewed, and beside him was Mortars, Lieutenant O'Brien, who was still putting out the firepower up here nine months after an enemy bullet had passed through him in Phu Yen.

Tom stood beside the old easel, new maps of a new area on it, and the tent became silent except for the hissing of the radios on their tables and the rain on the canvas.

"There's one individual," Tom began, "who's been following us around for months. He and I have had a couple of close ones together. He's eaten me out of house and home, drunk up all my Scotch, eaten up all my Cs—'' He said a few more things in the same vein, and then said: ''Come on up here.''

I made my way around the men sitting on the gray metal chairs and stood before Tom. Someone handed him something, and he handed it to me.

In the dim light in the tent, the rain coming down on the canvas, I looked at what was in my hands. It was a black wooden plaque, and on it was affixed the Combat Infantryman's Badge. Below it was a small square of brilliant brass, the only thing in the room that twinkled. It said,

CHARLES B. FLOOD
HONORARY DRAGOON

I shook hands with Tom and walked back to my place, and then he said good-bye to his staff.

''Thank you,'' he said. ''You've had to put up with my snapping and yelling and chewing you out, but it all had one purpose—to save lives. I wish you luck and success and I know you'll go on doing a fine job. Thank you.''

The next morning was cold, misty, rainy, but a sartorial miracle occurred. Phoenix from the mud, young Dragoons appeared in fatigues they had somehow made clean, and sergeants produced fatigue jackets they had been hiding somewhere which had chevrons and the division patch.

Everyone stood about self-consciously. There would be no thought of pulling companies out of the jungle for a ceremony, and the perimeter had to remain manned, so a composite group of twenty-one men, including representatives of all the companies, formed in three trim ranks behind the officers and sergeants of the staff. The battalion colors were brought out from Dragon Mountain, and chopper after chopper whirled in and out, bringing the commanders of other battalions and officers from Brigade and Division. There were more spectators for the ceremony than participants.

Two helicopters circled low over this muddy field and landed among the ferns at its edge. The division commander, Major General William Peers, a big man with the kind of weathered broken-nosed face one sees on the skippers of tuna boats, came wading through the ferns.

The troops snapped to attention in their small phalanx behind the flag with its fluttering battle streamers. At the point of the phalanx stood Tom Lynch, saluting the commanding general.

It went quickly. There was Tom, taking the colors from Sergeant Major Hannon and handing them to Glen Belnap, who returned them to the Sergeant Major. At that instant Glen became the battalion commander.

Tom was required to make another speech. He turned and faced his men.

"I'm just passing through," he said. "Men come and go, but the important thing is that the battalion should go on. No man has ever had a better battalion than this one. I'm proud of you." His voice started to break. "Thank you," he choked, did a perfect parade ground about face in the mud, and was once again facing General Peers.

Then the adjutant was reading a citation, mentioning Tom's leadership at Three Trees, flying low in an under-fire helicopter as he turned the initial ambush into a resounding victory, and General Peers was pinning the red-white-and-blue ribbon of the Silver Star on Tom's fatigue jacket. Another citation, this one the Legion of Merit. Then the Bronze Star, for swooping into a firefight and leaping from his helicopter to pull a wounded boy to safety.

Tom's face was a study. The only medal he had known he would receive was the one coming next, the Air Medal with a "V" clasp for valor, given for being the first man out of a helicopter on an Eagle Flight in which he had successfully led an assault on a defended hilltop, but the staff had pushed forward the paperwork on the others without telling him.

Then it was over. The ranks of troops behind Tom dissolved, turning into little knots of men moving toward their respective holes. I walked toward the TOC with Joe Guerra, the tall sergeant from the Recon Platoon who had carried the flag except for the moments when the Sergeant Major handed it to Tom and received it back from Glen. Reverting to my reportorial self, I asked him how he felt about carrying the flag.

"It's a privilege," he said quietly, carefully slipping the forest of battle streamers back into a canvas case.

Inside the TOC the atmosphere was one of a school graduation day. The cooks at Dragon Mountain had baked several huge cakes that had been brought out here by chopper, and we had cakes, coffee, and even paper napkins. Men crowded about Tom to congratulate him and wish him godspeed. Some of the other battalion commanders, talking with Tom, who still had his four new medals on his chest, had an air of envy for his decorations, his record, and his battalion.

I shook hands with Captain Paul Titus, the best officer of his rank I had met in Vietnam, and told him I hoped his stomach would stop troubling him soon. I said good-bye to Sergeant Higa, Neil Buie, Jack Crumley, Toby The Royal Pineapple, Lieutenant O'Brien, and then I was waiting out by the helicopter.

Tom came walking out of his tent for the last time. A couple of young soldiers behind him were carrying his pack, one half-filled barracks bag, and a brief case—everything he had needed for a year in the jungle. The medals were gone from his chest, and he had left his rifle out here, just carrying a .45 for this last trip to Dragon Mountain.

The Sergeant Major appeared from another direction, and stood waiting by the helicopter door. He saluted, Tom returned the salute, and then they were giving each other a bear hug, shaking hands, slapping each other on the back, the Sergeant Major still chewing without missing a beat.

Tom and I were in the helicopter and it all dropped away in mist. The last thing I saw was Chaplain Buckner, who had "followed a mule many a day," moving along the barbedwire perimeter, preaching his sermon with his feet.

Back at Dragon Mountain a hundred and fifty men fell into three ranks outside the battalion orderly room. There was a draft of new replacements, and some wounded men back from the hospital waiting to be sent forward again.

Tom awarded Purple Hearts to the wounded men, and there were several Bronze Stars, decorations just coming through from Three Trees. Then he put the formation at ease and addressed the new men. It was brief, and the last words Tom Lynch said to his Dragoons were these:

"Up here you can forget about all this political bullshit—up here it's you on one end of a rifle and the NVA on the other."

TWENTY-TWO

A hangover was in some ways the appropriate condition in which to ride through the Vietnamese countryside. I was on my way from the air base for a long stay with the advisors, and the ruts and potholes on the road were guaranteed to bounce one into a fine state of misery, as if some ghoul were taking random whacks at the base of the brain with a small mallet. To add to my discomfort, there was the maddening serenity of the surroundings. To what end was I being jolted up and down, choking with dust, while Cheop Chai sat majestic in the distance under a baked blue sky? No one else was in a hurry. In the paddies, scores of men and women in black bent under their conical straw hats, working hard, but doing it in a day-long rhythm that made it seem from a rattling jeep as if they were pasted into the huge, heat-shimmering valley.

Today I got off well before the town of Tuy Hoa. Where the road from the air base fed into Route One, at a point near the river and the long bridge into town, stood a compound of weathered dun buildings surrounded by loops of barbed wire. This was the headquarters complex of Hieu Xuong District, which comprised the southern half of the valley, from the river down through the air base and below. The northern half of the valley, Tuy Hoa town, and Cheop Chai all fell within Tuy Hoa District. After all these months I was getting around to see the American advisors who were responsible for the immediate area in which I lived.

I found them in a tin-roofed, screen-sided wooden structure in a far corner of the compound.

"I was told you were coming. Welcome." This was

Major Katsuji Kobata, a short, energetic Nisei with a friendly but formal manner. He gave me a Coke and we sat talking in the concrete-floored living room that was shared by the six American soldiers and one civilian in this district advisory team. On the walls were various photographs of nudes, interspersed with captured Viet Cong flags and AK-47 automatic rifles. One of the flags was red, with a crude white hammer and sickle in one corner—the first time I had seen this emblem in Vietnam.

Kobata had qualifications beyond what could be assumed from his rank of major of Infantry. His Bachelor of Science at Berkeley had been in psychology. In addition to his Japanese, which he had improved considerably during a two-year tour in Japan, he spoke French and Vietnamese. He had established the language training program at the John F. Kennedy Center for Special Warfare, the home of the Green Berets at Fort Bragg, North Carolina. Like Major Hanson at Tuy An, he had been in Vietnam at the beginning of open hostilities with the Viet Cong, in 1961 and 1962, as one of the ten American soldiers at Hue, which was now loaded with Marines.

Kobata had been the senior American advisor in Hieu Xuong District for ten months, and as he spoke I began to understand the exceptional responsibilities that were his. He not only had the responsibility of coordinating American efforts in helping the Vietnamese maintain security in a district with a population of ninety thousand, but this district, in contrast with the others in Phu Yen, was the site of important Allied installations. In addition to the air base, there was the Army's Ninety-first Evacuation Hospital, farther down the beach, along with an elaborate Army logistics base. The Korean Twenty-eighth Regiment was headquartered on the beach and had outposts in the valley, with its own set of responsibilities for providing security for the district.

It was a tricky spot for a young major. He was constantly dealing with forces of three nations, including his own, and the problems inherent in fighting a war in three different languages. There were also egos to be considered. The nation belonged to the Vietnamese, who resented foreigners even when they were dying beside—or ahead of—them on the field of battle, and the Vietnamese were sensitive about their own shortages and shortcomings. The Americans felt they should have a powerful say because they were making the major aid and financial commitment, as well as a commitment in blood. The proud and tough Koreans were determined to be recognized as autonomous equals, and sincerely believed themselves to be the best troops in Vietnam, with little to learn from anyone. The Koreans were notoriously secretive about their operations even after their attacks had been launched, and it was hard to coordinate with a commander who wouldn't tell you what he was doing.

We went through a screen door and headed toward a jeep. Standing beside it was the most unusual American soldier I had seen in Vietnam. He had the face and build of a huge gorilla.

Major Kobata introduced us in his usual courteous and correct fashion. This was Sergeant First Class Shermaiah Iaea, a Hawaiian. The human mountain with low short-cropped black hairline and widow's peak took my hand gently, as if he had broken hands inadvertently before.

"Hello," he said in a soft, husky voice, and beneath his snub nose his big mouth and tall teeth opened to give me a pleasant smile.

I climbed in the back of the jeep, and with Sergeant Iaea at the wheel and Major Kobata beside him, we turned out of the compound, heading for the district's advanced command post further out in the valley. Just as we got under way on the road, weaving among bicycles and donkey carts, I noticed that the courtyard of the school next to the district headquarters was packed with women.

"What's that all about?"

"Those are the Popular Forces widows getting their pensions," Major Kobata explained. "There are a hundred and sixty-four of them."

I thought about that as we threaded our way through the district headquarters town, moving among open-sided motor-tricycle buses and women carrying jars hanging from each end of poles over their shoulders. If this district had one hundred and sixty-four widows of men who had been killed in the Popular Forces militia, before one even considered the Regional Forces, the Revolutionary Development teams, and the ARVN, it indicated a higher level of violence going on right outside our gates than any of us at the air base supposed.

We left the market-place town, rolled along Route One between rice paddies, and turned off on a road heading out the valley. Another quarter of a mile and we turned into a front yard of pebbly grass and went into what had been a small Catholic church. In a chilly plaster room to one side of it there were a telephone switchboard linking various Vietnamese, Korean, and American posts, and radios over which two Korean soldiers were talking. To American ears, the Korean tongue is filled with hooks, most of them sounding like *ika,* while Vietnamese sounds like an ascending scale of notes climbing out of the throat and saying *Waaang ba eh.* The combination of these two languages being spoken in the background, while Kobata and I spoke to each other, made his description of the difficulties of coordination sound a modest appraisal indeed.

Major Kobata gestured me to a chair placed before a large-scale map of the valley. Standing beside this, he briefed me as thoroughly as if I were to assume direct responsibilities in the area. In this district of ninety thousand there were eleven villages, each with its cluster of hamlets, some of them a considerable distance from the nearest village center. Four of these villages were under government control, six were contested, and one was totally VC.

"The Government exercises some degree of control over eighty-seven thousand people," Kobata said in his precise way. "One thousand five hundred to five thousand are under full Viet Cong control."

Twelve thousand persons in the ninety-thousand population had become homeless as a result of the war. Four thousand of them were living in the one refugee camp in the district, and the others were living with relatives or friends.

I thought about that one for a moment, too. Up in Tuy An, twenty-two thousand of fifty-five thousand had moved right out of the district to escape violence, and at the meeting of Vietnamese officials in Tuy Hoa I had heard a statistic indicating that one out of every three people in this Province had been a refugee at some time in recent years. Here was another hidden bomb, another reason that we could not expect anything but a hard, expensive pull in Vietnam. In relation to South Vietnam, this province was the equivalent of an American state. One had to imagine state after state in the

United States with a third of its population in a refugee status, and then ask if it was likely that the nation would be able to mount much of a war effort.

Pointing to various spots on the map, Major Kobata outlined the composition of the Korean and Vietnamese forces deployed in the valley, pointing out that there were no American ground troops other than the handful of advisors who went along with the Vietnamese. Then he turned to the enemy organization. The enemy's militia consisted of local platoons composed of men who were farmers by day and guerrillas on call for operations at night, having access to hidden weapons. They were backed up by the usual VC infrastructure, everyone having his assigned task, that I had seen laid bare in my study of the Chieu Hoi debriefings. These platoons, and indeed everyone else the Viet Cong could get their hands on, were always available to support the more professional enemy units in the area.

Next up the enemy ladder, striking anywhere in the district, were two full-time companies, Main Force units. One of these was a CK company, a demolition unit that mined roads and bridges. The other and more prestigious was the 377 VC Company, which launched down out of the hills for hard-hitting attacks on Allied installations. This was composed of about one hundred and thirty-five well-armed men, complete with machine guns, mortars, and rocket launchers.

"The commanding officer of the Three-Seventy-Seven is Captain Quy," Major Kobata told me, "and in all fairness I must say, considering what he has done to us, he is an outstanding commander."

Backing up the Viet Cong effort were two battalions of the Fifth North Vietnamese Division, who spent most of their time in the hills. This strength was variously estimated between six and eight hundred. From prisoner interrogations and the identification of bodies on past battlefields, it appeared that there were occasionally North Vietnamese on loan in the ranks of the Viet Cong units, and vice versa. The last time there had been a really mass attack of combined North Vietnamese and Viet Cong, on an ARVN battalion command post north of the river, they had been thrown back with sixty bodies left behind, while the ARVN lost twenty-two. There had not been a major battle in the valley since that one, six weeks before.

The briefing was over. A Vietnamese in black farmer's pajamas and a floppy hat came into the clammy room from the doorway, where he had been waiting to speak with Major Kobata. They shook hands formally. Several minutes of conversation in Vietnamese ensued between them, while I had time to take in the fact that I was the one Caucasian in the room—there were Koreans and Vietnamese working the radios and switchboard, and the other two Americans were a Hawaiian and a Japanese.

Major Kobata and the black-clad Vietnamese, both of a size, were nodding their heads. A snapshot was produced from his pocket by Major Kobata, and the Vietnamese looked at it and smiled and nodded vigorously. The Vietnamese shook hands and left.

"That fellow." Kobata slipped the snapshot back into his pocket. "He used to be one of Captain Quy's platoon leaders in the Three-Seventy-Seven Company."

"Whose side is he on now?" I asked, my head turning toward the empty doorway through which the black-clad figure had disappeared.

"Well, he's sort of in business for himself. I showed him this picture of Captain Quy, and he said that was him. I told him we would pay a reward for Quy, on delivery. Dead or alive. He was quite happy about it. He thinks he can do it."

We walked out into the steamy sunshine.

Neil Ross Miller was a tall, spare man with olive skin, black crew cut, and a face that looked as if he were constantly deciding whether to be a saint or a Jewish comedian. A twenty-six-year-old graduate of UCLA, for eight months he had been the one American civilian advisor in Hieu Xuong, working hard and harmoniously with Major Kobata.

Neil was clearly a man with energy to spare. As he drove me the miles from the Hieu Xuong district compound, across the long bridge, toward the advisory compound on the beach, he kept swiveling his head toward me in swift, birdlike movements, either making a point or asking for my reaction to it.

"We're so critical of the Vietnamese effort," he said. "I'm not critical. What amazes me, after all they've been through, is where they get one more guy to do anything. How would *you* like to be a lieutenant in the ARVN? How would you like to be a little PF sitting out there night after night, wondering when they're going to clobber you with a whole Main Force company?" He smiled a warm smile and shook his head. He described some of the people with whom he was working, praising their spirit, their willingness to be things like hamlet chiefs and village chiefs when they knew that the VC would try to assassinate them if they leaned too much toward the Government.

"Our Revolutionary Development cadres are teaching the people how to read and write, in the hamlets in the evenings," Neil told me. "I asked this one old woman—she must have been seventy—why she was learning to read. 'We are going to have an election,' she said, 'and I want to be able to read my ballot for myself, and I want to be able to mark it in the right place.'"

As we moved past the open-fronted shops along the broad main streets of Tuy Hoa, I thought of the September elections, just a month off. Everyone, American and Vietnamese, was discussing them now. General Thieu, who had outmaneuvered Air Vice-Marshal Ky to become the head of state, bearing the rather Gallic title of Directory Chairman, was the odds-on favorite to become President, with Ky as his vice-presidential running mate. There were ten other presidential candidates on the ballot, appealing to the nearly six million registered voters in a population variously estimated at between fourteen and seventeen million.

I shook my head as I thought of the complexity of this election, and I heard the voice of that man in Tuy An: "This country is about as ready for democracy as Lower Slobovia is . . . I think you'll see the military in charge here for a long time to come." Be that as it might, the preparations were going forward. The electorate was also being asked to choose sixty men for the Senate, and this was going to be absolutely wild, with each voter choosing six ten-man senatorial tickets out of forty-eight ten-man tickets that would be on the ballot.

We passed the post office, and I thought of my earlier discovery that power in Vietnam may have no outward trappings. Behind this plethora of candidates lay the fact that there were at least seventy-four political parties in Vietnam, besides the Viet Cong's National Liberation Front. Most of these operated like secret societies, but all had aspirations to national leadership, to be achieved one way or another. Twenty-four of these seventy-four splinters were recognized as fully legal by the incumbent government, and the assumption was that the other fifty parties had horse-traded at least one senatorial candidate apiece onto one of the forty-eight ten-man senatorial slates. The *Götterdämmerung* was scheduled for September third, when a semi-illiterate electorate would go to sixty-eight hundred polling places throughout the forty-four provinces to cast their ballots without voting machines or computers to tally the results.

Someone had remarked that it was all too complicated for anyone to rig, and I tended to agree.

The next morning after breakfast in the military advisors' mess hall on the beach near the Province Chief's house, I dawdled over several cups of coffee, talking with Captain Jim Dooley, a bulky, animated man from Trenton, New Jersey. He was the detachment commander, responsible for this compound, the men assigned to guard duty, the mess hall, supplies, and all the minutiae of this small complex from which the different districts' advisory outposts were supported.

More or less in passing, I mentioned to him that I was beginning to get a grasp of the way the war was being fought in many of its aspects, but that I had yet to see the advisors working with the Vietnamese troops in a real operation against the Viet Cong.

"What are you doing tonight?" Dooley asked quietly.

"Nothing," I said, with that same impulse to laugh idiotically that I felt every time I was asked if I wanted to go on a bombing mission. Before my eyes, Dooley had changed into a man who was a good deal more interested in fighting than in housekeeping chores.

Dooley would not tell me what was going on, but at five in the afternoon I met him by his jeep, carrying my carbine, with the Browning pistol at my side and my little .25 Colt in the side pocket of my jungle jacket. I had with me my pack and helmet. We got in and rolled off, away from the beach, through the broad lazy streets of Tuy Hoa, and eventually right past the Hieu Xuong district headquarters where I had been the day before. We turned off Route One on the same road that I had traveled the day before out into the valley, but this time we rolled past the abandoned church where Major Kobata had briefed me.

Finally, as we rolled on, the only vehicle on this road running between rice paddies, Dooley told me what was up. We were going to a place called Phu Tu, which was the farthest point out in the valley under government control. We would spend the night there, and, before dawn, jump off with a Regional Force company in a sweep farther out from there. We were to be one jaw of a pincers formed with another RF company, which would jump off from another point before dawn, and between us we would hope to close on a suspected Viet Cong hiding place in a deserted hamlet. Major Kobata would be with this other force, and Dooley would be the American advisor with our force.

Kobata, I thought. He is really a cool cat. There he had been yesterday, map in front of him, giving me statistics, but not a syllable to indicate that he was on the eve of an operation involving three hundred Vietnamese soldiers, a sweep he must have been planning for some time.

When we reached it, Phu Tu was a large and prospering hamlet, divided by the road along which we had come and the irrigation canal that ran alongside the road. We drove right to the far end of the hamlet, where there was a thick barbed-wire roadblock. The road on which we had come continued beyond it, on out the valley, straight as a die, toward the blue hills. If one drove on, the next people encountered were armed Viet Cong.

We got out of the jeep and Dooley briefed me, gesturing with his big arms. On one side of the road was the larger part of the hamlet, inhabited by the Vietnamese farmers who worked the surrounding fields and paddies by day. Their houses were protected by a platoon of Popular Forces militia, and there was a fifty-nine-man Revolutionary Development team, who wore black pajamas and carried weapons, assigned here helping to protect the village while building useful projects and engaging in pro-Government propaganda.

On the other side of the road, reached by a small arched bridge across the irrigation canal, was a short street of deserted shell-blasted houses. A nine-man Korean liaison team had already moved in here for the night. The Regional Forces company, ready for tomorrow's operation, was bivouacked among other deserted, often roofless, houses, and in an abandoned and burned-out Catholic church across a field.

We got back into our jeep and crossed the arched wooden bridge over the irrigation canal, going down this torn-up alley of former residences, and came to a stop behind a jeep with a big radio aerial on its side. Looming beside it, making Captain Dooley look like a sylph, was Sergeant Iaea, who had been sent over here as the liaison man from Major Kobata. He, Dooley, and I were to be the three Americans in our otherwise all-Asian jaw of tomorrow's pincers.

Two Asian lieutenants approached us, saluted Captain Dooley, and we talked. For once the Vietnamese officer, a handsome man who looked as if there could be at least one Frenchman in his background, was larger than his Korean counterpart, the lieutenant in charge of the ROK liaison team.

The sun was setting. We thought there was not much to be done until the hours just before dawn, so Captain Dooley and I put our gear beside a couple of canvas cots in the corner of a two-story deserted house that still had part of its roof. Then he and Iaea and I walked across the road into the populated part of the hamlet. We shook hands with the forty-year-old Vietnamese who was the head of the Revolutionary Development Team, and he showed us some of the things they had built for the people here: a barber shop, much in use; a dispensary, empty at the moment; and a small reading room filled with government propaganda, a room which was dusty and deserted.

In a rough field near the center of the hamlet, some of the RD team and the boys of the Popular Forces were playing volleyball, sensibly stripped down to their undershorts in the summer evening, their slender small bodies leaping far higher than I would have expected they could.

At one corner of the field a Vietnamese woman had an old wheeled vending cart with bottles of Coca-Cola and Vietnamese beer, and Captain Dooley and I split a quart bottle of Tiger Beer in the cool evening. Vietnamese children crowded around us, beautiful faces as they so often have, shouting "Okay!," "Number One!," and "You!"—the three best-known English terms in their vocabulary. The hairiness of Caucasians fascinates many Asians, and small smooth Vietnamese hands reached inquiringly for a tug at the hair on my wrists. It was a pretty, peaceful sunset scene, and I felt charged with a sense of invincibility, as if even three Americans were somehow a guarantee of the safety of this village.

We ate C rations, and Iaea and I strolled up and down the empty street on our unpopulated side of the hamlet. Through blasted-out walls we could see the Vietnamese troops squatting about little fires burning on the concrete floors, cooking their rice.

Iaea told me a bit about himself. In contrast to his massive, frightening exterior, he had a soft, resonant voice, and he told me that before he put on even more weight he had been a running guard for the Berlin Bears, one of the Army's European football teams. He had married over there, a Danish girl.

"My beautiful Danish wife," he said softly, almost reverently in the still evening, as if he still could not believe it. Getting back to his profession, he told me that he was assigned to Hieu Xuong as the medic for the team, but that he was also a radio man of long standing. In his quiet way, he indicated that he knew a little something about fighting, too. In the Korean War he had been in the Hundred and Eighty-Seventh Regimental Combat team, an outfit composed of paratroopers. He had already been trained as a Ranger then, and made patrols behind the Chinese hilltop positions.

"I had a lot of close calls," he said in his husky voice, his incredible shoulders and chest and thick neck and big head a huge shadow beside me in the night. "I learned to be careful. I never stop being careful."

We walked back to our shattered house, and I arranged my equipment carefully beside my cot, knowing just where everything was. Then, despite the routine booming of the Korean artillery batteries farther down the valley and the duller thud of their rounds landing beyond us in the hills, I was asleep.

There was an explosion that was so obviously unfriendly that I came out of sleep and off the cot in the same instant, dropping onto hands and knees on the concrete floor. There was another loud explosion, several snapping strings of shots, and a general cracking of small arms fire. I pulled on my jungle jacket without bothering to get into my pants or boots, buckled on my pistol, grabbed the carbine, and took a few barefoot steps away from my cot, All around me there was excited chattering in Korean. Some of the ROK team had been sleeping on the second floor, and they came tumbling down the wooden ladder and disappeared into the night.

I turned and saw that Captain Dooley was putting on his boots, so I returned to the side of my cot and got fully dressed in a hurry. Then I followed Dooley as he ran down the moonlit street past wrecked silver houses, toward the arched bridge that led into the inhabited part of the village, where the shots were rattling back and forth. He cut to the left just before the arched bridge, and jumped into a trench beside the irrigation canal.

I jumped in beside him. There were a few more shots, and then silence. I slipped a round into the chamber of my carbine and looked around. Time was frozen. There was moonlight on the scarred plaster wall beside me. The houses across the road were dead silent, and the barbed-wire road block beyond the irrigation canal stood black against mists that clung to the paddies. The one sound was the water running through the irrigation canal. I gripped the hard comfort of the carbine in my hands, staring around cautiously, Dooley three yards off kneeling like bulky, moonlit statue. I had no idea of time. It was as if the entire valley was holding its breath. I stared into the moonlit mists suspended just above the paddies. I could see nothing out there. It was all shadows. Nothing

M1 Carbine

was telling me anything, and the water in the canal echoed against the torn moonlit walls.

The statue of Captain Dooley suddenly whirled, scattered pebbles sprinting past me, and raced to Sergeant Iaea's radio jeep. He got on the air, ordering artillery to fire illumination rounds over the paddies beyond the hamlet and to drop high explosive in there as well. He and Iaea were the only men moving, responding, acting; about the time the first artillery parachute flares broke their swaying silver light above us, fired by Korean cannon in response to a request translated to them from all the way back at the American advisory compound on the beach, the Korean liaison lieutenant appeared, asking if there was anything he could do. Then the Vietnamese lieutenant came out of the shadows, composed but evidently with no ideas at all about what to do next, and asked for instructions. Captain Dooley was no advisor now; the Korean and the Vietnamese were looking to the senior officer for instructions, and he became the commander. He told the Vietnamese to get through on his radio to the RD team radio on the other side of the canal and find out what was happening. Quick talk into the radio by the Vietnamese lieutenant; no reply. The Vietnamese nodded. He had finally found something to do, and ordered a squad to follow him as he ran across the arched bridge, their feet a hollow drumming for a moment before they disappeared into the night.

We moved toward the arched bridge ourselves, Iaea carrying a hissing back-pack radio, and stood in the shadowed corner of a moonlit angle of walls, watching the ghostly arched bridge, ready to jump into the trench next to the irrigation ditch. Minutes, silent minutes, the water an oddly cheerful sound. Then figures began shadowing back up the inhabited street across the irrigation canal and the road, the tall Vietnamese lieutenant waving forward the knots of men behind him. In the moonlight I could see why they were going slowly. They were bringing the wounded; a man in a lurching, reeling limp, supported by two others; another knot of men carrying someone. Their feet on the road were now the one sound.

Captain Dooley was on the radio. "We've been hit at this location. Need a dustoff." Having requested the medical evacuation helicopter, Dooley stepped out of the shadows, followed by Iaea and me.

Here were the wounded, four of them, blood glistening black in the moonlight under a furry gray sky. All Popular Forces militiamen, possibly the ones who had been playing volleyball at sunset. Their job was to stay awake at night, so that the Revolutionary Development team could work on their various building projects during the day and sleep at night. It quickly emerged that the militiamen had been asleep right along with the RD team, and the price they paid for it was that the Viet Cong had been able to sneak up near a sleeping bunch of them and hit them with two rounds from a rocket launcher, and several bursts of automatic weapons fire, before slipping back into the mists.

Was it over now? No one knew. In the meantime Dooley had stopped the flares and shells. With what seemed miraculous speed in the midst of the milling around in our darkness, a flashing red light was heading toward us, high in the sky. Sergeant Iaea got this medical evacuation helicopter on the radio, and they asked for our exact position.

"Are you displaying lights now?" the metallic voice from the chopper asked.

"Negative at this time," Iaea replied.

"Well, somebody's flashing lights at us."

I felt a chill. The VC were still out there, and now they were trying to lure this unarmed helicopter with a red cross on its side to a false rendezvous and shoot it down.

Captain Dooley turned to Sergeant Iaea. "Bring the jeep up here and put its lights on." In a minute we were bathed in white light, standing in the crossroads beside the irrigation canal and the arched bridge, the barbed-wire roadblock and the hostile valley at our backs.

"See that?" Dooley asked the chopper.

"Affirmative. Pop smoke just where you want us in there."

Captain Dooley advanced down the road some thirty yards from me, with a smoke grenade. I had seen hand signals given to helicopters before, and since Iaea was now on the jeep radio and Captain Dooley had to put the smoke in place, I decided that I was elected to guide the chopper in. Feeling frightened and foolish, I stood with my arms extended to my sides, the barbed-wire roadblock and the hostile night just behind me. We were all brightly lit targets, but in that moment I found myself admiring the pilots and crew who were coming in here, no machine guns on their craft, in moonlight and fog, in a tricky landing, to pick up four wounded Vietnamese. I had never seen the Vietnamese do anything comparable for Americans.

The smoke grenade poured out a twisting column of yellow smoke, eerie in the jeep headlights, the fog, the moonlight. The helicopter landed, and all of us lifted the wounded Vietnamese aboard. Then the chopper was gone, and no sooner was it again a flashing red light in the sky than more Vietnamese appeared, carrying a man more seriously wounded than the others had been, a militiaman older than the others, his leg twisted and half torn from his body. For some reason they had not received the word to bring him up here until now.

Captain Dooley cursed, strode to the jeep radio, and asked if the medevac chopper would come back and do it all over again. The chopper came back, we put on the jeep lights again. I took my arms-out position, Captain Dooley popped violet smoke this time, and the chopper was off once more. We went to our cots, and for the second time that night I was swiftly asleep.

I awoke in darkness, this time to the sound of men moving around, the clicking of harness and slapping of clips into weapons. Sergeant Iaea had C-ration coffee heated for us three Americans, and with this in my stomach the night seemed less dark. After the events at midnight, I was beginning to take a little personal interest in seeing the Viet Cong lose a round or two in this fight for control of the valley.

The three of us, Iaea with the hissing radio on his back, walked out to the crossroads from which the wounded men had been lifted into the sky four hours before. It was darker now, near dawn, than when the moon had been up. Everywhere there were small dark silhouettes of Vietnamese with long American rifles slung on their shoulders, the muzzles in the air above their heads. Then we were in motion, a long spaced-out file walking down either shoulder of the road, walking back down the valley as if we were going back to Hieu Xuong district headquarters, but in reality preparing for a move off to the right.

As we marched silently, the only sounds the hissing of radios and feet on pebbles, lights began coming on in the farmhouses across the paddies to our left. It was an hour when farmers might rise, but watching the blink-blink-blink flashing of some of the lights, I had the feeling that some of these, at least, were signals to the Viet Cong in the hills across the valley, telling them a force was on the move. I thought of mentioning my suspicions to Dooley or Iaea, then shrugged my shoulders and trudged on in the graying darkness.

We turned off the road and made our way across the narrow strips of earth and sod which served as dikes separating the checkerboard of rice paddies. The Vietnamese troops seemed to glide along these, nimbly jumping small irrigation ditches when they came to them, but the tufts of grass and claylike mud snagged the rubber cleats of my jungle boots; half a dozen times I crashed into an irrigation ditch up to mid-thigh in brown water.

Now we were on grassy trails and ducking through deserted flat orchards, coming up behind abandoned knots of houses, slipping down dusty empty lanes and through openings in thorny hedges. Near me was a Vietnamese who looked almost fifty; he was small and wiry, and carried over his shoulder a 60-millimeter mortar, the heaviest weapon we had with us. He was carrying on him half a dozen mortar shells. With his helmet tilted down before his eyes, he looked like a beast of burden that might or might not know what it was doing. He kept right up in line but seemed utterly removed from the proceedings.

The sun had not risen, but it was clear light now, and with it came the roaring sound of a flight of F–100s taking off from the air base, in a different world behind us. I turned my head and saw the first one lancing off, a tiny sparkling dart hurtling toward a sky of such a glowing blue that for a moment I could believe that the world starts afresh at each dawn. That pilot would be halfway across Vietnam, the other two planes formed up on his wings in a whooshing **V**, before we were out of these deserted houses and halfway up the grassy slope that rose before us.

It was getting to be work now as we moved up the green slope, moving quickly. The place where the Viet Cong were supposed to be was in a knot of houses that would become visible from the top of this hill, an abandoned small hamlet in a rice paddy area tucked between this hill and the really steep valley wall beyond.

Gaining the top of this hill, we moved even faster across the bare crest.

Snap! Snap! I knew the sound only too well from Three Trees, close and personal, and this time one of the Viet Cong bullets hit a rock and set up a chilling *WHIIIING*.

Then the only sound was the thudding of feet and the jingling slap of bodies hitting the dirt all over this bare hilltop. I landed in a grassy depression just at the far edge of the crest, staring down at the valley from which the shots had come. Just to my right lay Captain Dooley and Sergeant Iaea, both of them like chunky green-clad walruses, their feet trailing uphill behind them, their massive backs arched as they supported themselves on their elbows on this downslope, both of them smiling with intense interest at what was going on.

Dooley nodded at something Iaea was saying, and took the black-plastic radio speaker that Iaea was proffering him, attached by a cord to the radio on Iaea's back. Speaking into it in a quick, cheery voice, Dooley grinned at me. I had heard the expression *light of battle,* but this was the first time I had seen it, there in Dooley's pale blue eyes. It is an expression of intense, immediate excitement and pleasure, mixed with determination and barely suppressed laughter. He spoke over the radio to Major Kobata, with the other force, as if he could not wait to give him the marvelous news that we were being shot at.

The nine Koreans of the ROK liaison team had all hit the grass a few yards ahead of me down the forward slope. One of them opened up with a light machine gun, the tracers flicking down into the knot of abandoned houses on the valley floor a quarter of a mile away.

"VC! VC!" the Korean lieutenant was shouting excitedly, pointing toward the houses and then talking in a shrill voice over the radio strapped to the back of the Korean beside him.

I looked hard at the houses, but could see nothing. Judging by our tracers, the Viet Cong were trying to get out of the houses on their far side, and the idea was to keep them in there.

Just then there was a metallic sliding sound behind me, and a big *WHANG-BLAAM-HUSH*. I spun my head around. By himself, the old Vietnamese mortar man had set up his weapon, managed to aim it without the usual positioning of an aiming stake and the elaborate corrections necessary on the leveling mechanism, and had gotten off a round. As I turned my head, it landed perfectly, just beyond the farthest house down there, certainly the perfect discouragement to anyone wanting to sneak out the back way. He dropped in another round, and another, and then he gave me a smile, one that said "I don't know about the others, but I do know what I'm doing."

The enemy fire had stopped, wherever it was coming from. Dooley consulted over the radio with Kobata, whose face was in the treeline below our hill to the left, farther from the houses than we were.

"Roger. Out," Dooley said cheerfully, and, looking over at the Korean lieutenant, pointed his big hand in the direction of the houses. The ROK team rose and gathered up an equal number of these Regional Forces Vietnamese troops. Fanned out in a widespread line, the men moved downhill, the Koreans whipping out bayonets and snapping them into place on the muzzles of their M–16s. The lieutenant and the radio man had to stay behind, in case we needed to talk to the Korean artillery in a hurry, and one of the Koreans waved back at his lieutenant, patting his rifle with a bloodthirsty smile.

They moved in among the houses as we lay quietly watching them. We could check their progress from house to house by the clouds from the tear-gas grenades they were tossing into tunnels and shelters and attics in an effort to smoke out anyone in there.

After twenty minutes they reappeared, empty-handed. I had no idea of how the VC had gotten away, unless they had been shooting at us from somewhere other than these houses to begin with. This was their part of the valley, and they certainly knew how to play hide-and-seek.

We came down this hill and linked up with Major Kobata and his company, who were walking out of the treeline. Kobata looked annoyed and unhappy, but with his usual perfect manners he said "Hello, Mister Flood" and introduced me to a tall, weedy Vietnamese captain beside him. The captain gave a small, awkward bow and said "How you do" in a manner that suggested that he wanted to be liked, was unsure of himself in general, and certainly did not want to be out here where one could get hurt. He was wearing not only a helmet, which the other RF had, but the only armored flak jacket on any of the three hundred men who were now starting the march homeward.

I asked Captain Dooley, when we all started moving, who the Vietnamese captain was. This was Captain Hy, the District Chief of Hieu Xuong, and the man who had to agree to anything Major Kobata wanted done. The way in which Captain Dooley mentioned Hy's name suggested a rather pitying contempt, mixed with frustration.

We trudged back to Phu Tu, the sun up and the farmers working in their fields. They stared at us without curiosity; we were as much a part of the scene as they. I found myself thinking about this morning. This had been a real try. There was no use saying that the government never bestirred itself. Looking at the Vietnamese District Chief, I did not doubt that it was Major Kobata who had conceived this operation, but nonetheless there had been three hundred militiamen up and marching long before dawn, miles and miles from town, miles from our outposts and barbed wire, really out hunting. There had been something there; it had gotten away.

It was getting hot now, and it seemed a lot longer going back in than coming out. I thought about all the hue and cry in the States about using artillery and air strikes against villages. What I had just witnessed might very well have gone differently. Those houses might have been filled with farm families; instead of vanishing, the VC might have chosen to make a stand right there. I knew very well that if the engagement had become a major one, if all of us on that hill had been ordered to move in and take that town, I would have had to move with the company, just as I moved with B Company at Three Trees, because you never knew what else might be prowling around if you stayed behind on a hilltop as a lone spectator. If I were in a stooped run moving toward those houses, I would want my side to be supporting me with everything we possessed, doing everything to knock out the source of that *snap snap snap* that could kill me any second.

My concern for my own health would be greater than my concern for any of the inhabitants of those houses.

As for the Viet Cong, they had no compunction about attacking inhabited villages, as they had shown the night before. They restricted themselves to rockets and mortars because those happened to be the biggest weapons they possessed.

We had come back to the crossroads at Phu Tu, the place by the arched bridge and irrigation canal where the helicopter had landed ten hours before. Now a two-wheeled donkey cart moved across the dust, and a little boy prodded the flanks of a water buffalo. Our march was over.

One of the RF soldiers pointed at my watch, and then pointed at his. I smiled. He wanted to trade, although he never believed that I would. I slipped my watch off my wrist and pointed at it, and then at his. A dozen RF's were standing around now, grinning and giggling.

The soldier nodded his head emphatically; he wanted to trade. Everything like this that the Americans had had to be good.

"Sure?" I asked. Mine was an old Japanese watch that I had bought in Tokyo three years before; recently it had been losing time. I doubted that his watch could be worse.

The RF took off his watch. I looked at it for a moment, holding it up to my ear to make sure there were some kind of works inside it. The thing ticked, and the time it showed was sufficiently far ahead of the time mine said to convince me that it was about right. We traded, and he went off happily.

The next morning I awoke at first light, restless, and prowled off to the mess hall. Apart from a sleepy cook having a cup of coffee at the far end, the only other people were the two young naval officers attached to the advisory team. In close to ten months in Vietnam I had never dealt with the United States Navy, and I went over and had a cup of coffee with them. The two lean young men were wearing "tiger suit" fatigues covered with a camouflage mottling of purples, browns, and blacks, and although they were preoccupied they were polite. I finally asked them if some day I could come along and see what they did.

The senior of the two, a lieutenant junior grade, equivalent to an Army or Air Force first lieutenant, arrested a cup of coffee that was on the way to his mouth.

"What are you doing right now?"

I looked at him. He was small and wiry, with a face like a hatchet and skin baked to a dark cedar. His eyes were unreal; the whites were glazed porcelain, and the gray was as truly that color as if cut from slate.

"I'm not doing anything right now," I answered, thinking, oh God, not everybody can put his foot into it even before the sun is up.

"You have any weapons?"

I nodded.

"Bring everything you've got."

Half an hour later I was following the two officers through a twisting dirt lane formed by fishermen's thatched shacks. We emerged on the wide beach of fine gold-white sand, and a marvelous composition met my eyes. The calm ocean was pale gold, and the rising white sun was tearing a great horizontal gash in the gray clouds piled on the still rim of the South China Sea.

There were three long craft pointed toward us, the first few feet of their keels heaved up on the wet sand. The bows of these gray patrol boats curved up in the wild way of a Chinese temple's eaves. On each side of the upthrusting prow there was painted a large slanted eye with a black rim and lashes, and a red pupil.

Standing aboard these vessels was the jauntiest crowd I had seen in Vietnam. These boats were converted, motorized junks, and these Vietnamese were the men of the Coastal Force, better known as the Junk Fleet, with the sailors being known as "junkies." A few of them wore recognizable Vietnamese Navy uniforms of gray trousers, faded blue work shirts, and white sailor hats, but the majority were in one-of-a-kind costumes for this outing. A young sailor was wearing a bathing suit, a helmet, four hand grenades on a web belt, and a Thompson .45 submachine gun, the old "Tommy Gun," the first I had seen. Another sported a brown wool Ike jacket that must have dated from the French Army's days in Vietnam. Others favored black undershirts, tan fishing caps with long green bills, Bermuda shorts, and footgear ranging from high black basketball sneakers to white rubber *zoris*

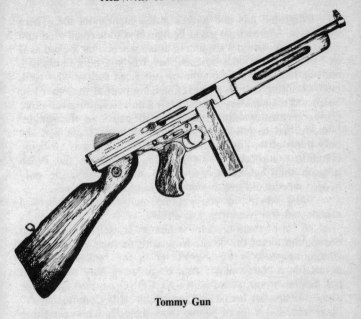

Tommy Gun

with rubber thongs passing between the big toe and the other toes. Weapons ran from a bazooka and a mortar to such accessories as machetes and fishing knives.

We pushed off, thirty-five men aboard each of the three narrow motor launches, and headed down the coast. Now I was told where we were going. Some miles south of the air base was a wild forested headland, the easternmost point in Vietnam, and on its cliffs stood a deserted lighthouse.

I told the lieutenant that I had often seen it. Flying back in to Tuy Hoa, I had been struck with its remote beauty, the combination of gold cliffs, moss-green jungled mountains, and the white tower and barrackslike building attached to it.

There was a report, my host now told me, that the Viet Cong were comfortably bivouacked in there at the moment. It was a place almost impossible to reach by land, fraught with endless possibilities of ambush and booby traps, so his unit of the Coastal Force had been requested to go down there and make an amphibious landing on the narrow beach under the cliffs by the lighthouse and see what happened.

I digested this and looked at the men about me. There was a trim Vietnamese naval lieutenant who seemed alert and eager, a gray-haired Vietnamese at the wheel who looked as if he had been born on a boat and never been ashore in his life, and we had with us a couple of American sailors who were busy checking their weapons. Glancing over at the other two boats and their motley crews, I felt a unit isolation even more profound than walking with a small patrol in the jungle. Nobody had to tell me that this amphibious force was the only thing of its kind within fifty miles, and it was all being committed at once. If we got into trouble on the beach beneath that lighthouse and those jungled cliffs, the only people who could get us out of it would be ourselves.

"Just where do you get the men for this outfit?" I asked, and the American j.g. smiled.

"A lot of them used to be pirates. It used to be quite an occupation along the coast. Now with the war they're either smuggling stuff in for the VC or in the Junk Fleet." He pointed at a young junkie near us, wearing only blue denim bell-bottom trousers and with SAT CONG tattooed above the nipple of his left breast. "That means 'Kill Communists,'" he chuckled. "A lot of people think the guys who have those all got them voluntarily, but it started because a lot of these men were convicts. They let them out of prison, tattooed that on their chest so the VC *would* kill them if they caught them, and sent them into the Junk Fleet."

As we slid through the flat sea, moving south past the broad mouth of the river that split the valley and was the boundary between Tuy Hoa and Hieu Xuong districts, I asked this tough-looking young bantam about himself. He had started out at Harvard, finished up at Stanford, and was one of those men who thought that civilian life was a not very exciting bunch of baloney. The military life was baloney, too, but with more excitement. He had been in the Navy for a while now, and had been aboard one of the destroyers of the force involved in the Gulf of Tonkin incidents in 1964.

"A tissue of lies," he said when I asked him about the veracity of the official explanations concerning the North Vietnamese torpedo-boat attacks on the American ships. He had gone back to the United States and come out here again aboard destroyers, firing in support of some operations in Phu

Yen at a time when the Viet Cong were so strong that there was no possibility of keeping Route One open between any two coastal towns. Since he had come to this job, his third tour in Vietnamese waters, he had been in ten firefights with the Viet Cong.

"I've been shot at a lot by friendly forces, too," he observed. "I have the utmost contempt for the marksmanship on both sides."

We spoke of the over-all conduct of the war, and for the first time I encountered an officer who was prepared to say that he thought the war was a mistake, that we would never achieve our objectives, that we were simply prolonging a mistake, and that we should negotiate as good a settlement as we could, and get out.

"The French lost five general officers in the Vung Ro Mountains." He was pointing at the misty chain of deep green hills toward which we were heading, beyond the bottom of the Tuy Hoa Valley. "You could put a division in those hills and the VC would still hang in there." He shook his head, both of us looking at the silver and green buildings of the air base as we cruised past, and said that the regular military forces of the United States, the officer structure, had now been stretched to its limit. If we wanted to increase the war, we would have to call up the reserve officers and go to a general mobilization. He added that the entire war had been put on a kind of deferred bookkeeping, and that the American taxpayer would not really begin to feel it until 1968 and 1969.

He took off his floppy jungle hat, pursed his lips, and said the first good words I had heard from anyone in the military about Secretary of Defense Robert MacNamara.

"He gave the Navy a good kick in the ass. The Navy needed a good shaking up. He attacked nepotism in the Navy." Then, flipping his camouflaged hat back on his head, he started in on the corruption of the Saigon government and how this had played straight into the hands of the Viet Cong. "All the best people in this province are up in the hills," he said. "Three out of four of the doctors who were practicing in Tuy Hoa are with the VC." Referring to the VC shadow government that had been startlingly visible in my study of the Chieu Hoi papers, he added, "The VC Province Chief used to be the high school principal downtown." He stared out over the sun-shimmering water. "What this country needs is a revolution."

I offered the thought that a revolution was what it was having, all right, but I was not at all sure that the Viet Cong had the popular mandate some people supposed. If what they were going to give the people of South Vietnam bore much resemblance to what had gone on in North Korea, mainland China, and North Vietnam, that was no bargain either. There was undoubtedly more freedom under the corrupt Saigon regime than there would be under an unbribable Viet Cong regime.

My companion shrugged his shoulders.

I said that at the very least a Viet Cong victory would mean a terrific purge in South Vietnam, just as had happened attendant upon the Communist victory in China.

"Yes," he said, shrugging his shoulders again, indicating that it was all too late, there was no good merchandise at the counter, so why even look at it?

I had only one more question. "Do you really think that any other parties could survive in a coalition government with the Viet Cong?"

He gave me a most engaging smile. "Of course not."

The sun was hot now, and the men were quiet as the lighthouse rose out of the heat mists. We cruised along a quarter of a mile offshore as if we were going to pass the lighthouse, moving in single file, and then all three of our craft pivoted and headed for the beach as fast as we could go. Men were crouching or lying on the deck, weapons cocked and safeties off. We had half a dozen machine guns among us, set up pointing toward the forested ravines back in among the chalky beige cliffs. Other men sat along the deck with their weapons trained at the bushes and trees packing the tops of the cliffs and at the lighthouse, which was already to our left as we slid into the wide cove.

I liked it even less than I had thought I would. With the exception of the gray-haired Vietnamese sailor at our wheel and the older of the two American sailors, I was the oldest man of the hundred gliding toward this narrow strip of sand. I felt that it was only the courage of youth, the mixture of youth's trust in this sunlight and water and youth's illusion of immortality that could fuel such a headlong exposure to the silent cliffs.

By now I had to crane my neck almost all the way back to see the tops of the cliffs that were sliding up over me. At any moment we might have an unsung little Anzio that could be even more bloody in relation to the numbers engaged. If there was anybody, any hostile body at all up there at the top of those cliffs, they were now looking straight down into our boats. Even a few well-thrown rocks could brain us.

The machine guns started firing, and then every Vietnamese on all three boats joined in. I kept staring up at the sheer rock walls before me to see what they were shooting at, occasionally glancing down at the water to see if there were spurts of water from anything coming the other way, but I could see nothing. No one was firing at us, but we were laying down a barrage anyway. Men leaped over the side, landing armpit-deep in the swells, and started thrashing their way ashore.

The lieutenant put his hands to his web belt, moving it side to side like a lady tugging at her girdle, and picked up his M–16.

"Coming?" he asked, and vaulted over the side.

Like the old man that Sergeant Higa of the Dragoons had said I was, I sat myself down on the edge of the deck, feet dangling above the water. Far from the splendid image of Marines charging forward as the ramp of the landing barge goes down, I entered the proceedings by kicking my feet against the hull and smashing down into the water in a bent-over stance that promptly drenched my carbine, the pistol at my side, and the tiny Colt in the pocket of my fatigue jacket. With the grace of a frightened cow I floundered ashore. Men were stumbling and falling headlong into the water, but all of them seemed to bob right up again, unhurt.

As I came onto the beach I was alone in a giant shooting gallery. Everyone else was already in the rocks and bushes at the foot of the cliffs, firing copiously. The acoustics were phenomenal in this space between the cliffs and the towering lighthouse, and the echoes sprang back and forth like passing trains. Most of our bullets were striking rocks above us, and this produced a steady shrill *WHEEIIING* of ricochets.

I found myself in a file of men making their way up the steep pebbly trail to the lighthouse. As far as I could see, there were men from all three boats in this party. It seemed that the criterion for who should storm the lighthouse was that if you wanted to, fine, and if you wanted to stay behind a rock on the beach and keep us covered, that was fine too. I kept slipping on the pebbles and dodging behind a rock every time one of the men in front of or behind me let go a burst. The result was that I was soon being passed every five seconds by a lithe and smiling young Vietnamese who glanced amusedly at the funny panting foreigner.

There was no one in the first couple of rooms we entered in the big concrete barracks attached to the lighthouse, but there were coals and ashes of recent cooking fires. I quickly found that there was no plan at all for an orderly search of the labyrinth of rooms. At one moment three Vietnamese would be beside me as we went up an outside stairway to the second floor of the barracks. As we crossed the terrace they would literally vanish with that genius of the race, that talent for invisibility, that I knew so well by now. I would proceed alone into a room, only to have my heart stop a moment later when a carbine muzzle poked its way around the doorway toward which I was stepping. I decided that it would be better to take the apparently slim chance of being shot by a VC than to commit the *faux pas* of letting one of our own men have it through the chest at a distance of seven feet. After a few minutes my heart became used to my turning a corner and finding my carbine pointing straight at the navel of a small young pirate, while his weapon was lined up even lower on my anatomy.

Finally I stopped and studied the graffiti with which all the white-washed cement walls were covered. This building had been at various times either searched or occupied by the Viet Cong, the ARVN, the Koreans, and the American 101st Airborne Division, and none of them had been able to resist these white walls. Some of the words and drawings had been made with charcoal from the fires, others were in pencil, and the American contributions were made with ballpoint pens. What interested me most was that the Vietnamese government forces—I cannot think it was the Viet Cong, unless they were in a fit of pique—had made many crude drawings of Ho Chi Minh in various degrading pornographic poses, the pictures and various sexual sketches being surrounded by Vietnamese words. Since I had been led to believe that everyone in North and South Vietnam had a respect for Uncle Ho as a figure who was somehow beyond reproach, it came as a shock.

Returning to the beach, I found that the gunfire had kept right on. No enemy bullet had come our way, but the junkies were spraying the bushes in the ravines so hard that the branches appeared to be flying apart in a high wind. I began to understand something; these men liked to fire their weapons.

We put out to sea in a final frantic fusillade of our own fire. Just off a sheer rock face that plunged into clear blue water, one of the men aboard my boat suddenly hurled a hand grenade at a shadow darting below. There was a slight shock and a screen of bubbles. A kite-shaped ray, some four feet across, came spinning to the surface. In a moment a junkie in a bathing suit was in the water beside it, the knife in his hand flashing into the blue-gray mottled skin between the two wide-set eyes. The wide tooth-studded mouth opened in astonished, outraged agony, the prehistoric face saying all too clearly No, this shouldn't be happening, this is a mistake, stop it, let go.

The big ray came smacking aboard, pulled by a dozen suntanned hairless arms that somehow managed to stay clear of the lashing spike of a tail. The ray landed on its back, the triangular belly heaving, and proceeded to abort a small pale baby, and then another. Someone hit the mother with a rifle butt between the eyes, and the big convulsions stopped, followed only by a hunching and twisting shake.

I turned away, and after a few minutes fell into conversation with the elder of the two American sailors, a small pot-bellied man with a shaved pink head that looked as if it had been sunburned, rather than tanned, for the past thirty years. He was Boatswains Mate Joseph Sherman, the senior Navy enlisted man in the Province. One day in November 1942 he had been off Savo Island aboard the cruiser *Juneau* when a direct hit from the Japanese exploded her powder magazine. Of the fifteen hundred men aboard, fourteen hundred had been blown to bits along with the ship. One hundred were blasted clear, into the water, and of these ninety later died. He was one of the ten survivors.

"After that," he said, looking over the brilliant blue sea, "I quit worrying about what was going to happen to me."

II

I was planning to return to the air base on Saturday, but now I learned that this weekend would be the time the district advisors came to Tuy Hoa to give their monthly reports.

Saturday morning we assembled in a high-ceilinged room borrowed from the Vietnamese. This was the place where Colonel Ba presided at Vietnamese briefings, which were usually attended by the American advisors. Now it was an all-American show, with Dan Leaty and Lieutenant Colonel Al Cade sitting in the center of the first row of chairs.

It was hard to imagine two men more different in appearance—Cade's black skin, erect posture, graceful gestures, and Dan's red-headed bulk bent forward attentively as he bit his nails—but each in his way was working night and day trying to stay ahead of the situation in Phu Yen Province. For Al Cade, it was a matter of strengthening our defenses, of urging the Vietnamese to push patrols and sweeps out at the hills in Tuy An, the hills beyond the valley in Hieu Xuong, probing, keeping the enemy off balance, spoiling his chance to get set and hit us with the real power we knew he had. For Dan Leaty, the war was fought with paperwork and meetings and excruciatingly faint long-distance calls to Nha Trang and Saigon. The enemy would attack in this "other war" with propaganda and the dumping of black-market rice to disrupt the economy. We would counterattack with a new schoolhouse, a new pump in a village, a new maternity clinic.

One advisor after another mounted the stage at the front, carrying maps of his own district and charts detailing his own problems. Looking, listening, I thought how hard it was to bring these various "nation-building" programs forward in the midst of a war. It would have been hard enough to try this kind of an American aid program here in peacetime.

On the stage, behind an advisor who was using a map on an easel to explain something, there was a huge wall map of this part of the coast, used by the Vietnamese at their briefings. Staring at it and remembering my days way inland with the Dragoons, I realized that by some standards we were a peaceful enclave on the coast. The funny thing about this perfectly correct conclusion was that if this was an enclave, then automatically I had to be against the "enclave theory" that had attracted some pretty good minds in the States. The problem was that the good minds, including that of General Gavin, who had proposed it, had not been inside bodies that had spent time with the day-to-day realities of our effort here.

I looked at Al Cade's back, thinking of a conversation we had one evening. I had been wondering out loud whether the Fourth Division was really best employed by having it up there on the Cambodian border, companies out there cutting trails in the jungle with machetes, often bushwhacking for days on end without finding anything.

"Listen," Al Cade said firmly, "if the Fourth Division wasn't doing what they're doing up there, I'd have a whole NVA division on my neck down here."

That was the flaw in the seductive notion that we could just button up in our little bases on the coast. Even now, when we were out looking hard for the enemy, hitting his supply lines by air, pushing him off balance, he was still getting down here to the coast and giving us plenty of hell. If we really came back in to our bases, just patrolling a few miles out from them, he would be on top of us with his 122-millimeter rockets, human-wave attacks on the perimeter, and a far greater number of saboteurs he could infiltrate inside. There would be nothing but burning fuel tanks and exploding ammunition dumps on the coast of Vietnam.

One officer after another got up on the stage, and the reports were not without their humor. A major who was a senior district advisor spoke of holding a dental sick call in several hamlets.

"The beauty of this," he said, "is that the only people who show up really need what we're offering."

Another major spoke of an intelligence report he had received in his district.

"The VC," he told us, "have measured off an area up in the hills that is just the size of my headquarters compound, and are holding repeated rehearsals on how to attack it. They have five rows of barbed wire around their mock-up and I have six rows around my place, but that's close enough to get my attention."

Each district emerged in these reports as a separate embattled nation. In every district the enemy was mining roads and making converts and attacking when he could, but apart from this each district had a different priority of problems. In one area there were no building materials to be had, in another the rice supply was short, in another there were more refugees than places to put them. I thought again of that American civilian at Tuy An who had made no bones about working for "The Embassy." I could still hear him saying "The war has to be won on the district level."

It was true. Each province could not be greater than the sum of the districts thereof, and if these reports were any indication, the struggle was often bitter, discouraging, and inconclusive. We built schools without really knowing whether this made the population any more loyal to the government. We built roads, and the Viet Cong used them too, until they decided to mine them. Sometimes I felt as if the two competing parties in Vietnam scarcely got in each other's way. Our programs simply bypassed each other.

Listening to all this, I could see that there would be a terrific temptation, at the province level, to ignore the bad news, the behind-schedule projects, the lesser terrorist incidents, and send on to higher headquarters only the good news, the reflections of that "light at the end of the tunnel" which the top American officials in Vietnam constantly professed to see. If we sent on something cheerful to Nha Trang, and Nha Trang took only the most acceptable news from this and the other provinces in II Corps, and forwarded *that* on to Saigon, and Saigon took the most acceptable news from all over the country and forwarded it to Washington, then we were living in a dream world.

A major was up now, our top man in the insecure interior district of Dong Xuan. He reported that some Vietnamese troops there had come across a cache of weapons being used by the Viet Cong. The haul included some recoilless rifle rounds that had been made in China, but instead of painting the instructions on the shells in Chinese characters, which only Chinese people could understand, the Chinese had painted on the instructions in English.

I made a note of that one. It was quite an idea, an all-purpose export item. It would be equally good whether the particular guerrillas receiving them spoke Vietnamese, or Arabic, or Spanish, since it would be far easier for them to translate it from English than to struggle with deciphering the Chinese characters.

As we descended the steps outside the meeting room, Colonel Ba came up and asked Dan Leaty and Al Cade to lunch at his house, including me in the invitation after a second's hesitation.

It was a mansion, by any standards. Major Heung greeted us in the marble-floored entrance hall of this big two-story structure on the bluff above the beach and introduced us to an ARVN colonel from Saigon who was inspecting some construction projects in II Corps. Colonel Ba had not yet appeared, and Major Heung led us to a bamboo-and-glass table in a corner of this breezy hall, where glasses, ice, and all kinds of liquor were arrayed. A drink in hand, we sat on cushioned wicker chairs and spoke of almost everything but the war. In one of our conversations during the past months, quick pleasantries when we ran into each other coming opposite ways in jeeps on unpaved roads, Major Heung had elicited the fact that I had written five novels. He mentioned this now to the colonel from Saigon, who was impressed by this in a way that I do not think any American colonel of engineers could be. He immediately gave me his card and asked me to drop in on him and his family in Saigon when I was down there. Everyone seemed very pleased with that, and I noticed Dan Leaty smiling approvingly. He was a good people-shuffler, and I thought I saw in his mind a position for me, when I was available—unpaid cultural attaché to Advisory Team 28.

Colonel Ba appeared, shook hands with us as if he had not seen us outside the briefing room a few minutes before, and led us in to lunch. A minute later he was talking about having been in New York City in 1965. I stared at him. He seemed such a perfect Oriental warlord, his manicured right hand with its purposely long nail on the little finger now delicately handling a fish knife as we began a course of cold eel with *nuoc mam*, that it was a shock to hear he had ever been out of Asia.

I asked him what sights he had seen in New York.

Well, he answered in his very passable English, he had

just been there a few days, after finishing a course at the Command and Staff School at Leavenworth, Kansas, before reporting in for a conference in Washington. "I went dancing every night," he said with a cheery little chuckle.

And where had he gone dancing?

"Many places. I liked Arthur."

I almost dropped my fork. That had been *the* fashionable discotheque in 1965, and the picture of our Province Chief doing the Watusi amid those flashing lights and blondes with bare midriffs and white sailor pants was almost too glorious to bear. Glancing at him again, I supposed he cut a perfectly graceful figure, probably in a well-cut dark silk suit, and probably turned up with something pretty damned snappy on his arm.

The meal proceeded, one Vietnamese servant in a white jacket serving the food, another one pouring white wine with the fish and then red wine with the meat. We were on our way through six courses, everything delicious, and the table was a beautiful piece of dark polished wood, with lace place mats. Sitting here, it was interesting to contemplate that probably, in the history of this war, many an American civil servant or career officer had first learned about fish knives and finger bowls at the tables of men like these, Asians who ate most of their meals with chopsticks.

Through it all Colonel Ba sat quietly at the head of the table, eating little. He seemed not at all interested in the food, and merely tasted the wine. I knew from Major Heung that he was forty-three years old, and in the past I had seen his wife, a quiet, plump woman, wearing a beautiful subdued *ao dai*. Kids were running around this house all the time, and I understood that three of them were his, the eldest a boy twelve.

The colonel from Saigon was saying something in Vietnamese, and Colonel Ba and Major Heung laughed.

Colonel Ba turned to us three Americans. "We talk about corruption," he said in great good humor. "I think in Vietnam we have it in the blood. You call it genes? We have it in the genes. We cannot get it out."

I ate a piece of cheese while I took that in. The way I had heard it, ARVN pensions were very small. Frequently an officer with good connections could get the job of Province Chief for a few years before he was retired. It was understood that this was his last chance to provide for his old age, and it was accepted practice for him to take a certain percentage of everything that passed through his hands.

The interesting thing was that no one really seemed to have anything on Colonel Ba. Young American officers standing around the bar in the advisors' compound would say that he was crooked, but I had yet to hear a specific instance. Certainly this house and this meal proved nothing—the house belonged to the Government, the cook and servants were soldiers who doubled as body guards, and the food and wine were from the good-sized expense account given province chiefs for entertaining.

Colonel Ba was talking now about the days before he had this job, the days when he had an ARVN regiment. Al Cade had told me that he had been a real fighter, his regiment one of the best. Looking at him now, I could imagine that this cool, distant, definite little man could easily make up his mind to go forward and die if that was his fate, and that this type of determination could communicate itself to those around him.

Looking around the room, I thought it was not a bad cast of characters, and in some ways their day-in, day-out roles made interesting theater. The lead was Colonel Ba, perhaps corrupt and perhaps not, but certainly an agile politician, never losing a post no matter who came to power in Saigon, and pretty good at keeping the Americans favorably disposed. Major Heung, perhaps the idealistic former professor of French Literature he appeared to be, perhaps the colonel's bag man, not Deputy for Security, but Deputy for Collections.

And on our side of the table? Al Cade, a black man who had graduated first in every class he had ever been in. An ambitious man, a man who had to fight his way up and now had what must at times have been the entertaining problem of avoiding any implication that he was rejecting a suggestion because the subordinate making it was a white man. I had seen Al in action a number of times at all-military briefings, just Al and a lot of white staff majors, captains, and lieutenants, and it took only a few minutes to see that he was the most intelligent man in the room. It was a demonstration that every American should have, at least once.

I watched Dan Leaty as we ate a delicate ice for dessert.

There was an Irishman who was a good deal more subtle than he looked, and his holding this job at the age of twenty-nine proved it. He was a combination of pragmatist and idealist, and moved and spoke with a sense of confidence and authority he had developed early in life. On his father's big produce farm in Williamstown, New York, at the age of thirteen he had been in charge of a hundred and fifty migrant workers during the summer harvest. He had been in college just at the time that President Kennedy had announced the Peace Corps, and had been swept into government service on the brief tide of hope and pride that marked those days of Camelot. Like Neil Miller working out at Hieu Xuong, Camelot had left him, but he was hanging in here, doing a job because he said he would do it and because he believed it needed to be done.

We had coffee out in the hall, sitting in the wicker chairs again. It was interesting to speculate on who in this group knew what. I knew that every time Colonel Ba went to Saigon, or Nha Trang, anywhere outside of the Province, it was Dan's duty to report the fact to his superiors in Saigon, so that, by keeping tabs on forty-four province chiefs, we might have a clue when something was brewing. I knew that we had Vietnamese in our employ who were supposed to tell us all sorts of things about both the Viet Cong and the government officials, and I wondered whether they did not pick up the big paychecks from us, and then a smaller sum for telling the government side what they had just told us, and perhaps even a few piasters from the VC for keeping them posted, too.

Just at this moment I felt Colonel Ba looking at me. I kept my eyes down at the coffee. Just as if he were shouting it, I realized that he did not believe for a minute that I was an itinerant author spending a year in Vietnam. Perhaps he had not made up his mind whether I was the senior political officer in the province, or simply a watchdog living at the air base and also checking the officials up here, but he was sure I was something.

Well, Colonel, I thought as I finished the bitter Vietnamese coffee, if that is the only mistake you make this year, you have nothing to worry about.

III

It had been a long week. My skin was still peeling from sunburn acquired from my day on the water with the junk fleet, and somewhere I had picked up a vicious fungus rash in my crotch.

I was in a jeep beside a young advisor, an Army lieutenant who was driving down to the air base. He was pouring out gripes to me as if I were his Congressman. Right now he was telling me that all the Vietnamese truck drivers, ARVN, Regional Forces, Popular Forces, considered it their right to take a bit of what they hauled.

"Let me give you an example," he said, and gave me several, his hands clenching the wheel as he thought about them again. If an American advisor were accompanying a column of trucks headed to resupply an outpost, the advisor sooner or later would find that his jeep had been maneuvered either to the head of the column, or its tail.

"You know why they do that?" he asked me indignantly.

"No." My crotch was itching badly.

He explained. If the advisor had been maneuvered to the head of the line, he could be sure that the trucks at the tail were stopping somewhere in a village and making a quick sale or barter of a bag of rice or cement. In one instance, my companion had been at the tail of the column, and the truck in front of him had faked a breakdown on a narrow bridge, blocking him from catching up to the seven other trucks in front. The drivers raced ahead to the next market place, and each sold one one-hundred-pound bag of rice, complete with the stencil on the side showing a red-white-and-blue shield, a picture of two hands from different nations clasping each other, and black lettering saying that this came as a gift from the American people.

"I actually saw the bags in the market when I got there," the young lieutenant said, "but I couldn't get it back from the Vietnamese civilians. From their point of view, they had paid for it legitimately."

That night I sat at the desk in my hooch at the air base, wearing only a cotton bathrobe and experimenting with the effects of various types of foot powder and even anti-burn ointment on the raging orange rash in my crotch.

My mind was burning a bit, too. It was late in my stay in Vietnam, three-quarters of the way through, and only now was I really beginning to understand the huge gap between the conception of the war as seen from within a conventional unit such as this fighter wing or the Dragoons, and the effort as seen by the advisors.

It seemed so stunningly obvious to say "The Vietnamese are the key to the situation." But they were. It had taken me exactly nine months in Vietnam to discover that the Vietnamese were the key to the Vietnam War.

I thought about what little I knew of the cultural psychology of this country. In Vietnam, considerable merit was attached to any custom or practice that had been in existence for a long time. The Vietnamese were reluctant to change a long-standing method of doing something. They resisted many forms of change, and yet practically every American advisor over here was trying to get them to change something.

I went into the bathroom and washed the anti-burn ointment from my hands. When I considered the polite but definite xenophobia that existed in Asia, when I thought of the scarring memory of Western imperialism and business exploitation throughout the Far East, I was amazed that we were hanging in here as well as we were. I would not have been surprised if the Viet Cong had managed to turn this into an anti-American war in the minds of all the Vietnamese. They had tried, but thus far they had failed.

TWENTY-THREE

The national elections were two weeks off, and my plan was to go down to Saigon, talk to the pundits, get a glimpse of the electioneering on the higher plane, and then come back to Phu Yen to see the farmers casting their ballots.

By the usual happy chance, Room 22 had an unused bed, and after checking in I walked over to the Associated Press office. To my delighted surprise I found myself shaking hands with an old friend, Peter Braestrup, who was the correspondent for *The New York Times* in Bangkok. He had come over here to beef up their Saigon bureau until the elections were over, and he told me that almost every journalist who had ever been connected with this war was in town right now, and the reunions were coming on fast and furious.

I beamed at him as we talked of present-day things. In our early twenties, Peter just out of Yale and I out of Harvard, we had downed many a gin-and-tonic together on evening lawns at cocktail parties on both sides of Long Island Sound. To both of us, this meeting triggered memories of those innocent days when we knew that all things were possible, that we would stride as undisputed champions in our careers, and that the world was an entirely perfectible place.

At just this moment, reminiscing with Peter, the door of an inner office opened and I caught a glimpse of a gorgeous golden-tanned back and shoulders in an orange print sun dress, surmounted by a sweep of yellow hair and supported by long, smooth, elegant legs. I had not seen anything like this in the eight and a half months since New Year's Eve, when I had met and talked with Horst's beautiful wife Ursula, and I assumed that she had come down to the office for some reason.

The girl turned. She was of equal beauty, but she was not Ursula.

"Charlie," someone said, "have you met Kelly Smith?"

We shook hands, and my eyes drank in her perfect features, perfect teeth, and friendly smile. So this was Kelly Smith, the AP's secret weapon. She had made a reputation covering the White House and the Washington congressional and social scene. Now, still based in Washington, she was being loaned out to foreign bureaus for short periods. In addition to her general reporting and feature stories, she was expected to come up with the woman's angle on everything from coronations to mine disasters, and did. Kelly had arrived in Saigon two weeks before, the first woman the AP had sent into a war zone since World War II, and was to remain until the elections. She was a simply gorgeous blonde. I had forgotten that there were American girls that looked like this, although there had never been many.

I stood there gawking and muttering a few pleasantries until Peter Braestrup took me by the arm. Accompanied by Barry Cramer, a young political writer who had recently been assigned to the AP bureau here, we headed for lunch at the Atterbe.

After Tuy Hoa, the menu in this Saigon restaurant was calculated to delight. We ordered *bouillabaisse*, and when it came I fell upon it eagerly, only to stop at the first taste. My eye met Peter's, and then Barry's, and we all looked down at the elaborate fish soup and tried again, and looked at each other again. It was terrible.

We called the manager, a Frenchman who clearly had contempt for the culinary taste of Americans, and told him there was something wrong with the *bouillabaisse*.

He shook his head and doubted it. We nodded our heads and affirmed. He asked us if we had ever had *bouillabaisse* before, if we knew what it tasted like.

I told him that I had. In Marseilles.

He sniffed, and ordered one of the Vietnamese waiters to remove our dishes. He followed the waiter out to the kitchen, his back rigidly indignant, intent on trying the soup. A minute later he emerged, sagging, his face ashen, and politely asked us what we would like instead. He looked as if he were about to faint.

I never did learn what was in that *bouillabaisse*.

After lunch we took a taxi to a large government building known as Dien-Hong Palace. In this handsome structure, facing the river, almost all the candidates except the Thieu–Ky ticket were having a press conference.

We sat in wooden lecture-room seats in an impressive hall and watched the various candidates, most of them in tropical suits, white shirts, and dark ties, settle into their places around a horseshoe-shaped table. Flashbulbs popped all over the place, and floodlights were being rigged to help the line of television cameras set on tripods against the wall. The microphones sitting in front of each of the Presidential–Vice-presidential teams were plugged in for a live broadcast on the Vietnamese national radio, and a large percentage of the nation's five and a half million registered voters would be able to hear the candidates' statements and answers to questions.

The foreign press was here almost without exception, TV cameras and all, because of the importance being attached to whether this was truly a representative and free election. Thus far, judging by the fact that serious antiadministration speeches had been quoted throughout the press in Vietnam and that the candidates had been able to tour the country freely, it seemed at least that the candidates were not being muzzled.

The first speaker was Presidential candidate Truong Dinh Dzu, a lawyer who wore a navy-blue silk necktie with a small Rotary International emblem embroidered on it. Some months after the election he was to be imprisoned for urging, as he did now, that there be negotiations with the Viet Cong.

Dzu teed right off on the administration. He charged Premier Ky with having told a meeting of National Police in Dalat to rig the elections "by whatever means at your disposal." He went on to charge Ky with bribery of voters in a recent trip to An Gian Province. Speaking calmly, as if he had the evidence right in his pocket, the chunky little lawyer said that Ky had distributed envelopes to townspeople on his electioneering tour in An Gian, envelopes which, when opened, contained three thousand piasters and a photograph of Ky.

This was meaty stuff, true or not, and the foreign press was bobbing up and down in its seats. There was no official English translation, and our information was reaching us through whispered running commentaries from Vietnamese reporters and cameramen.

I stayed a while, getting the drift of the gripes against the Government, gripes which were undoubtedly reaching millions of Vietnamese ears as they were spoken, and then walked back to the Continental-Palace.

Question: After nine months in Vietnam, was it possible to be much more tired than one realized?

Answer: I walked into Room 22 at four in the afternoon, the sun still shining at the tired white-net curtains by the tall French windows, and lay down on the cream bedspread. Sixteen hours later I awoke to the sun of the next day.

Lunch was a kick. I sat across from Kelly Smith, and Peter Arnett was informally briefing a journalist who had come out here for an unusual reason. The man's wife was a major in the Air Force, and she had been assigned for a year's tour in Saigon, so he had quit his job on a newspaper and come out here as a free-lancer. They were looking for an apartment in Saigon.

"Were you on the international news desk?" Peter asked him, referring to his previous job.

"Hell, no," the man said. "I was a sports writer. Now I'm an instant war correspondent."

While Peter considerately gave him advice on military air transportation and leased wires and the time difference between Saigon and Washington, I seized the chance to talk to Kelly Smith. For a beautiful girl who constantly rubbed elbows with Jackie Kennedy and President Johnson's daughters Luci and Lynda, for a girl who had just that morning interviewed the striking young Madame Ky, Kelly Smith was a singularly unspoiled lady, not averse to telling stories on herself.

The evening before, she told me, she had been at a diplomatic garden party and had noticed a handsome tall man in a blue tropical suit. She kept thinking she had seen this American someplace before, and finally she introduced herself and asked him who he was.

"I'm Bill Westmoreland," the four-star general in command of the half-million troops hereabouts had said. I was glad to learn that he occasionally wore something other than a uniform, and the conversation moved on. Since both Kelly and I were professional askers of questions, we found out a fair amount about each other while Peter was explaining to his companion the procedures for a reporter getting permission to enter Laos.

Kelly's rise in the journalistic world had a certain Cinderella quality about it. After graduating from the University of Kansas, in no particular hurry to take life seriously, she had mailed out a few applications for employment and gone off to a mountain resort in Colorado to work as a waitress. The Associated Press had offered her a job in their bureau in Miami, and she had arrived there in the sweltering, newsless off-season, starting as a girl-of-all-work, being given the most routine and unexciting assignments.

She had an eye for stories. Having no prominent people to interview, no important events to cover, she looked for and found the man-bites-dog angle in the daily life about her. Her lively prose managed to win the approval of the men on the New York desks who decide what is to go out to the rest of the world, and soon the AP realized that it had a girl in Miami who was somehow managing to produce a great deal out of almost nothing. She was transferred to Washington, and the byline stories of Kelly Smith started appearing all over the world.

So here she sat, having been shot at a few days before when she and Peter were driving back from a trip to the Delta. Here we were, and what momentous thing were the glamorous lady correspondent and the well-traveled novelist discussing? We were trying to figure out what kind of cheese the people at the next table were eating.

Late that afternoon I was sitting in a wicker chair on the terrace of the Continental-Palace, having a drink with Doctor Tom Durant, who was the American advisor to the Vietnamese government on the subject of public health in the Saigon area. He had often been along on our noisy AP lunches, but in big groups he preferred listening to talking. Now for the first time he opened up, and the impression was of intelligently harnessed anger. This small, neat, intense man was incisive and informed, and he was seeing things that infuriated him. He told me that the United States government was sending huge quantities of medicinal drugs to the Saigon government. Having received all this free, the Saigon government then sold it to wholesalers, with individual government officials pocketing the proceeds. The wholesalers then sold to everyone, including the Viet Cong, and gave the Viet Cong some free, as protection.

He had harsh words for American self-deception. He pointed out that Americans were constantly excusing our failures in Vietnam in terms of the fact that this was Asia, and that we could not be expected to fathom the Asian mind.

"We keep thinking there's something so different and mysterious here because they're Asians." He smiled for the first time. "We wouldn't like it ourselves if these same programs were applied to us in the same fashion. Some of our programs wouldn't work in Bridgeport, Connecticut."

The next day's lunch was wild. Peter Arnett's wife Nina had given birth to a baby girl, and Peter was celebrating. The baby had been born at home, and in the middle of the night Peter had seen Nina's sister Miriam, the one who so charmed me, coming in from the garden with fresh dirt on her *ao dai*. Peter asked her what she had been doing, and she replied that she had been burying the placenta beneath a tree. Miriam added that she had done this when his son was born three years before, but she had not told him then, "because you wouldn't understand."

"She's right," Peter said, shaking his head, a grin on his wonderful broken-nosed, rolling-brown-eyes face. "I don't."

With all the grace of a cowpuncher cutting someone out of the herd, I had managed to get Kelly Smith down at my end of the raucous table. This afternoon she was going over to Cholon, the Chinese area of Saigon, to cover chief of state Thieu's electioneering visit to the Chinese Chamber of Commerce.

I could not think of anything better calculated to further my study of both the elections and Kelly, and we set off under a bright blue sky and an unaccustomed fresh breeze. As we rode in the back of a tiny Renault taxi she told me she thought

I had a good disposition. I resisted the impulse to tell her that nothing in ten months had sweetened my disposition so much as sitting beside her. Although I thought Asian women were marvelous, she was batting a mighty inning for the home team.

The Chinese shall inherit the world. There is a greatness about them, a style at once massive and subtle, crass and delicate, devious and loyal, and it was all present in the scene at the Chinese Chamber of Commerce.

There were fifteen hundred young white-shirted Chinese boys and girls massed in columns on the boulevard before the building. They had been arranged in such a way that there appeared to be many thousands of them. From where I stood on a side balcony of the wide-verandaed gold-plaster building with its green lawns and high-staked metal fences, I could see that some columns were Boy Scouts, Girl Scouts, and various schools. The leaders of each column, nearest the imposing metal bars of the fence, bore large white placards with red Chinese characters proclaiming what not one of them believed, that Chinese and Vietnamese were all the same people and the same culture.

Kelly was interviewing various officials, and I stood leaning on the plaster ledge above the courtyard. Chauffeur-driven cars pulled up outside. The best-dressed men I had seen in Vietnam descended from them, passed through the big wrought-iron gates, crossed the lawn, and entered the marble-floored reception rooms. These men in their silk suits, some of them holding the passports of Taiwan and Hong Kong, others Chinese whose families had lived in Vietnam for generations, controlled many billions of piasters in this wretched, tricky economy.

The Chinese. It was interesting to gaze down at them as they awaited the arrival of the Chief of State. Stockier and taller than Vietnamese, they moved with less grace, more definitely. They seemed to be using every passing sunlit second for the process of thinking. Each seemed more physically isolated from his fellow Chinese than would have been the case in a gathering of Vietnamese. On the streets of Saigon or Tuy Hoa it was common to see two young militiamen walking along innocently holding hands, drifting through the day, but the sharp-eyed Chinese youths in the columns outside this fence stood each to himself, eyes taking it all in, mind learning what it could.

The Chinese merchants and bankers were coming out on the lawn, forming a double line which would applaud when Thieu arrived. I had been told that three-fourths of the invited businessmen had declined, because they did not wish to offend the other candidates or the Viet Cong. If that was crass, it had to be remembered that the Chinese were a guest people in Vietnam, that they had seen a spectacular range of rulers in the past decades, and that the cardinal rule of their lives was to survive. Their loyalty was not to a flag, but to families, clans, business partners, and a Chinese community that was being taxed heavily by the government and milked where possible by the Viet Cong. The men milling around below me on the grass, all of whom had ostentatiously signed the guest book to be presented to General Thieu, were gambling that their presence here would be forgotten by others and remembered by Thieu. There was even the possibility that a few of them felt, with Chinese pragmatism, that the Thieu–Ky ticket was really the only hope for a situation in which they looked not for progress but for an avoidance of breakdown and anarchy.

Thieu arrived, wearing a white linen suit and a prissy smile. He looked like the little man on the wedding cake. The weakness of his appearance was offset in my mind by the fact that he had managed to rise past Ky, who had been the nation's champion political in-fighter.

Standing on the balcony of the Chamber building, addressing the two hundred merchants on the lawn and the fifteen hundred youths on the avenue, Thieu gave a speech that was loaded for the Chinese community's consumption and was promptly denied, modified, and explained away when the Vietnamese press got hold of it the next day. He told the Chinese traders that he was ready to sit down and talk with the Viet Cong about anything they wanted to discuss. Since this was exactly the type of statement that was to send candidate Truong Dinh Dzu to prison a few months later, it could safely be said to be far from the government line at that time.

After the speech there was a reception in a high-ceilinged

hall just inside the balcony from which he had spoken. Thieu shook hands with one after another of the merchants, his shiny black hair parted as if with a scalpel and his head jerking in nervous polite bows. He seemed miscast in the twentieth century. Those delicate hands should have been clasped and hidden within a broad-sleeved brocade robe of the mandarinate. Instead of making himself agreeable he should have been saying, in a small testy voice, "Cut that one's head off, and castrate the others." One saw him cross-legged on a lacquer throne in a royal gondola decorated with dragons, reading a report from the governor of a distant province while a poet recited a tale of archers and portents in the sky.

Behind him stood his wife, looking on with the air of a mother at the school play. What his bland face lacked in strength was more than made up for by the determined features of Madame Thieu. It was said that she, like many a Vietnamese wife, was a singularly good businesswoman, and it was easy to believe. Looking at her prideful, composed face, one had the feeling that she would find any theory of democracy to be pure misinformation.

I had to return to Tuy Hoa the next morning, but that evening I had a date with Kelly Smith. She arrived on the terrace of the Continental-Palace wearing a low-cut white dress with big black polka dots, her beauty stunning group after group of Americans into silence as she walked among the tables to where I was standing with an idiotically pleased grin upon my face. The elections were pulling into Vietnam all sorts of writers who had been connected with the American effort to date, and we had drinks in a large group that included Bob Elegant of the Los Angeles *Times*, one of the foremost "China Watchers," who was usually stationed in Hong Kong, and Dean Brelis, a correspondent for NBC television. Next to me was David Halberstam, now a contributing editor of *Harper's* magazine, who had as a reporter for *The New York Times* covered the downfall of Diem, and had in some quarters been accused of helping to bring about that downfall through his articles at that time. Men such as Robert Shaplen of *The New Yorker* were in town, and the only really significant figure who had not come back for this election was Malcolm Browne, another Associated Press reporter who had won a Pulitzer Prize in Vietnam. Malcolm was already at work scouting out our next Vietnam as a roving reporter in Latin America for *The New York Times*.

All sorts of reminiscences and observations floated through the evening air on this terrace, but I was busy looking at Kelly. Eventually I took her off to dinner at La Pagode, a restaurant a block away. We talked about simple things, the details of past lives, things that would be unlikely to be divulged in large-group lunches in the middle of an election race. After dinner she was scheduled to go to the airport to cover the arrival of Miss America, who was on a tour to entertain the troops. She asked me if I wanted to come along, but I had already spent the evening with my vote for Miss America.

Kelly took my arm as we walked back to the Associated Press office, and this simple touch from a vital, worthwhile American girl put me in a state bordering on exaltation. I walked back to the Continental-Palace and fell asleep, a child who has discovered that the ugly rumors are not true, and that Santa Claus does indeed exist.

TWENTY-FOUR

I arrived back at Tuy Hoa with a sense of moving against the clock. The elections were a few days off, and I decided to throw in my lot with Major Kobata, Sergeant Iaea, and the rest of the small American advisory team responsible for the district in which I lived. In this way I would go on learning about the advisory effort, and be privy to their efforts to aid the elections and the Viet Cong efforts to disrupt them.

It was an airless, silent day in the Hieu Xuong district compound. Sergeant Iaea was working under the hood of a jeep, and he gave me a warm smile and a grunt, and with a huge greasy hand motioned me toward the screen-sided living room. Major Kobata rose, smiled politely and shook my hand, but there was a strained expression on his face. He sat me down and began, in his formal way, to explain the situation.

"It's very insecure," he told me. Two VC battalions, "which have held repeated rehearsals in the hills," were known to be planning to attack something soon. Whether the blow would fall here, or upon the air base, or north of the river, was a matter for conjecture. "We expect a mortar attack at the very least," he concluded, "but you're most welcome to stay."

The atmosphere in the compound was oppressive. There were only five American soldiers assigned here at the moment, and the civilian, Neil Miller. They had been spending their nights either on guard in the bunkers or out with the militia on probes to keep the Viet Cong off balance, but this threat was a hard one to counter on the district level. The Vietnamese Regional Forces and Popular Forces that could be mustered from this district were too few and of too low a caliber to attempt a spoiling attack far into the hills where the two VC battalions were, somewhere, biding their time. There was no indication that the Koreans or the ARVN were going to take the initiative, either. Thus the Allied forces in the Province remained stationary in various small units, almost any position of which would be at a great initial disadvantage if the full strength of two VC battalions fell upon them by night.

Most of the Americans were asleep, having been up all night and knowing that they must be up again tonight, but Neil Miller and I went for a ride with Captain Hy, the District Chief I had met on that operation out in the valley.

"A very funny thing happened today," Neil said to the tall Vietnamese. A jeep driver had hit a PF militiaman on a bicycle. When the PF arrived at the hospital, papers had been found on him proving that he was a VC.

Captain Hy shrugged his shoulders and tried unsuccessfully to smile. He was a thin, awkward man with a kind face, and I could not imagine why he had ended up in anybody's army. He had no military bearing, no confidence. When he raised his voice and gestured to the troops to do something, he sounded like an old woman, and the soldiers responded with insulting slowness, smiling at each other when his back was turned. At the moment he was driving us along a road that was probably safer than the District Headquarters was, and he acted as if he would like to keep driving away from his headquarters forever and was only bound to return because his wife and two baby daughters lived there with him. As he drove along, wearing a helmet and a flak jacket, his long neck twisting as he glanced nervously at everything on both sides of the road, I had the feeling that here was a gentle, decent, stupid man who should be in an office putting pins in maps.

We returned from our pointless drive along the safest roads, and I joined the military men of the American advisory team, who were awake now that it was near sunset. They were shaving, eating, shrugging into fatigues and checking their weapons. The air base now had a small television station, and a television set in this bare living room was carrying a sports round-up. If you turned in one direction you could see a home run in Cleveland, if you turned in another

Claymore Mine

you could see Iaea slapping a clip into a carbine, and if you looked outside you could see the black-clad farmers walking along the dikes between the paddies, coming in from the fields.

After sitting around with the men in the dimming evening, I wrote on my clipboard notes: "It is now 8:30 P.M. here. The atmosphere is one of being able to function, talk, eat, read letters from home, read (distractedly), and watch TV (better) while an air of watchfulness, apprehension, and some discouragement fills the air."

At nine o'clock we assumed the state of high alert that would last until dawn. Weapons, helmets, and flashlights were gathered up and we left the darkened living quarters and fanned out to the sandbagged bunkers just inside the barbed wire. Neil Miller showed me where the triggering devices for the Claymore mines were located. We stood with our elbows on a chest-high sandbagged embrasure that masked the bunker entrance, two American civilians wearing helmets and flak jackets, with a supply of hand grenades nestled like big eggs in the depressions where the sandbags met.

The temperature of the night, its quality, was velvet, but this blackness gave up no secrets to our straining eyes. The silence outside the barbed wire, the darkness over the rice paddies, was complete. Elsewhere in Vietnam there were antipersonnel radar machines that showed unusual activity approaching, and many an American outpost had a fluorescent "Starlight Scope" that made the night thirty times brighter when seen through its lens, but there were no such luxuries at Hieu Xuong. There we stood, two men to a bunker, Neil Miller and I in one, two black sergeants, Hebron and Bradley, in another, and Sergeant Iaea and a Mexican-American Pfc. named Muñoz in a third. Major Kobata was in the command bunker, beside a hissing radio that was now the only warning of attack we could get, other than from our own eyes and ears.

It was not a pleasant feeling, standing amid the possibilities of the night. As my eyes became accustomed to the darkness I would see yet another nearby oil drum or post or bush I had not seen before, and in the first instant it would seem as if the object had just now moved into sight, was moving now, was moving toward me. A dozen Birnam Woods slid toward me, stopped, faded, countermarched, vanished. I felt helpless and impotent, standing silent, alternately bored, frustrated, and worried. This compound was a well-known, easily identified target, just the kind of thing the Viet Cong loved to tear apart both for the military confusion it produced and the propaganda effect of showing they could blast the local seat of government. We waited, wondering whether the blow would fall tonight and, if it did, how bad it would be.

Neil and I were still standing together near midnight, peering silently into the dark, when we heard men going in and out of Major Kobata's command bunker. A minute later there was Captain Hy, arguing shrilly like an old spinster.

I do not know just how facts get around so quickly under such circumstances. No one told Neil and me a thing, and yet within two minutes we were aware of a report just in, that a company of VC were at an abandoned Catholic church in a village several miles south of us along Route One. Major

Kobata wanted to form an immediate reaction force and go after them, and Captain Hy, who had been asleep when Major Kobata awoke him with the report, thought it was the worst idea he had heard in his life.

Looking toward the command bunker I could see the two of them facing each other, Captain Hy's taller, lanky frame dancing about as he waved his hands to punctuate his objections, and Major Kobata, stocky, short, undemonstrative, quietly telling Captain Hy that the people in the valley needed to know that we would come out there and chase away the VC whenever they appeared.

I knew that I was witnessing the central problem in our advisory setup. The troops involved here would be Vietnamese, and Captain Hy was their commander. Major Kobata could request, he could urge, but he could not command Captain Hy to do anything. To get this decision made in his favor required a combination of browbeating and persuasion.

Captain Hy's voice faltered; his protestations became less frequent. Finally with a sigh audible over the whole compound he turned to a Vietnamese lieutenant and told him to round up a company-strength force.

A few minutes later the American contribution to this task force arrived, a big flat-bed truck known as a Duster. This had twin 40-millimeter cannon mounted on it, capable of putting out a machine-gun-like rate of fire with projectiles capable of ripping through walls and fortifications. It packed a terrific punch, and the spirits of the Vietnamese troops rose as they saw the big fluted cannon barrels waiting to accompany them.

Three Vietnamese trucks arrived, their drivers maneuvering them skillfully without lights, and jeep engines started kicking over. I walked over to Major Kobata and asked him whether I should stay here with the men left guarding the compound or go on the operation.

"You're most welcome to come along," he said. In a moment I was sitting in the front of a jeep, the only other occupant being Sergeant Iaea. He backed the jeep past the Duster and some Vietnamese troops crowding aboard a truck, and then we rolled forward out the gate. With a chill at the base of my spine I realized that Sergeant Iaea and I, and our two carbines, were the spearhead of the Allied advance into

the night. Our lights were off, the road was unlit and
deserted, and it took no imagination to picture what a land
mine could do to us at any point in the next few miles.

This really clammy fear passed swiftly. After another
two hundred yards of moving along slowly, Iaea looking back
to see that the other vehicles in the column were following, a
sense of relief swept over me, turning into exhilaration.
Instead of huddling behind sandbags, waiting for the enemy
to choose the instant and manner of his attack, we were
driving toward him in the night, weapons in our hands and a
fresh intelligence report telling us where he was.

Iaea was impressive. His huge frame filling the entire
space between the seat and the wheel, he radiated alertness
and competence. I had the feeling that if anyone were in
ambush for us, they would have to take us on the first shot,
because Iaea would either have driven over them, past them,
or be killing them effectively within a second after the first
muzzle flash.

We moved out of the populated area, Route One now a
causeway moving through rice paddies. Off to our left were
the lights of the air base, the noise of generators quivering
across the water-filled paddies. Two miles ahead lay the first
houses of the village in whose abandoned church the VC had
been seen. If the report was accurate and not a ruse to lead us
into an ambush, it seemed that for once we had the element
of surprise. The operation had been conceived and put into
execution so quickly that there was no chance of the VC
being tipped off. Forty-five minutes before we had not known
of it ourselves.

A few more minutes of cruising along this causeway
with our lights off, and a jeep appeared behind and to one
side of us in the gloom. It was Major Kobata, accompanied
by the two black sergeants, Bradley and Hebron, who were
armed to the teeth. Kobata said that we would walk the
remaining three-quarters of a mile, so that the engines did not
give us away. The Duster could follow as the one vehicle
behind the last men in the column.

Major Kobata led off, a Vietnamese beside him with a
radio on his back, and the hissing of that radio was the one
sound in the night. Iaea and I followed twenty yards behind,
and after us the Vietnamese came on silently, a long file on

either shoulder of the causeway road. Captain Hy was well back in the column.

Ahead of us was a bridge over a stream. It had no walls or railings. Just as Major Kobata stepped onto it, there was a terrific ripping sound in the air above us. In that instant several things happened. Major Kobata calmly stepped off the bridge, dropping seven feet and landing chest-deep in water. Sergeant Iaea dove down the bank in one gigantic spring. I was in the air right beside him, my carbine in my left hand, and my right hand stuck out to break my fall. I landed with all my weight and the thrust of my dive on my right hand and broke my wrist, although I did not notice this for some time.

There was at the end of this sliding instant a huge splash in the water thirty yards off, and I pressed my helmeted head even further into the earth where I sprawled, crossing my arms over the brim of my helmet. Simultaneously there was a weird pop-hiss, followed by a silver brilliance that engulfed everything. Slowly I removed my arms and peered up from beneath my helmet like a skeptical turtle deep in his shell. A big parachute flare was sinking with the usual dribble of molten magnesium and sparks. As I watched there was another rush-crash in the air, another splash, and another flare, and the performance was repeated. What was happening was that some Koreans further out the valley wanted to know who was strolling down Route One behind them in such force and had called in some artillery-fired parachute flares. The flare was inside a regular shell casing, and it was the incoming shell casing that made this wings-of-death rush in the sky, and then, after releasing the flare, smashed on into the paddy waters.

We clambered back up on the road, relieved that we were being shot at by nothing worse than flares, but the question now was what the VC were making of all this. Major Kobata got onto the radio and had the flares shut off, and the Vietnamese troops fanned out into the paddies, an equal number extending from either side of the road in a long line abreast. Then the long line started wading with surprising swiftness toward the darkened houses a quarter of a mile away. Our small knot of Americans was left moving down the road, followed at some distance by the creeping bulk of the Duster.

Shots snapped at us from trees at the end of the paddies, and we hit the dirt. A pale green flare stood for a moment above the edge of the village, its color different from any of our flares. I expected our Vietnamese force to open up with everything they had, *à la* the junkies, but there was silence, followed by another string of snapping VC shots.

The express train rolled in the sky again, and the Korean flares were right above us. This time the Koreans wanted to know what the shooting was, but they were managing to illuminate us and not the enemy. We were naked in a huge cone of silver light. Now some whistles started, the RF and PF commanders blowing shrilly up and down the skirmish line that stretched off across the paddies to either side of me. All the men started yelling and moving faster.

The spectacle at this point was fantastic. The night was clear, and the Korean flares were reflected in a hundred rice paddies on both sides of the road. The silver-bathed Vietnamese soldiers were advancing, each shouting man sharply outlined as he splashed forward. The whistles were blowing wildly, and the air was crashing. I had the feeling that things were not going to be any more dangerous than they were now, that the VC had fired and run. It was a splendid battle panorama, with the usual excellent chance that our efforts were in vain.

We got to the church, slipping among houses that were inhabited, a whole village holding its breath. Nobody in the church, but plenty of VC propaganda leaflets. As we walked back along the causeway to our vehicles, flares started breaking above an area further to the south. There was a terrific rattle of machine-gun fire, and the thud of grenades. We kept walking back along the causeway in the darkness. That firing in the distance was somebody else's war.

The next thirty hours passed in a haze. I slept for a few hours in a cot in the living room at Hieu Xuong, vaguely aware that my right forearm was sore and swollen, and the hot afternoon was passed in a jeep with Major Kobata, inspecting positions in the valley. We ate early, and went into bunkers, on guard for the night.

By this next dawn I was tired enough to drop, but we moved straight from the bunkers into another of Major Kobata's operations. Captain Hy appeared, whining like a sleepless ghost, but Major Kobata had him beaten down. A full company of RF, a full company of PF, and the American advisors, all of us on foot, started a hike at sunrise down a long road that almost immediately passed into a contested area of the valley. There were reports from here, reports that the VC had been in among the people and that the people had been sheltering them and helping them.

As we moved toward a village at the foot of the steep valley wall, I saw a Korean infantry company crossing a grassy slope, sweeping down on the village from behind. From the professional point of view they were admirable, spaced out like a huge diamond and moving swiftly, but there was an inhuman look about the scene. They were a pack of hunting dogs loping down upon their quarry.

There was no shooting from the village. Then white smoke curled from beneath the eaves of a thatched house, one and then another. The smoke became black, with red billowing balls of flame against the black clouds.

We kept walking toward the village down the long road. Soon we saw figures coming the other way, women in pastel-shaded blouses and black trousers, people on bicycles, little donkey carts, an entire fleeing population. Some carried household goods hanging from poles across their shoulders, some had only a sleeping mat and a wicker basket, others had found time to throw a chest of drawers into a donkey cart. They came down the road in a shocked shuffling run. The first of the women, their faces weeping and contorted beneath their conical straw hats, came up to the Americans, not the Vietnamese militia, and began bitter wailing, pointing at their burning houses. We nodded, having neither knowledge nor control of Korean operations, and walked on up the road. Only half a dozen houses in the village were afire; evidently the ROKs were burning just a few, as a selective warning and punishment to the population.

Major Kobata's face was a study in disgust and frustration. He had no control over the ROKs, and he was not in such a close relationship with them that he could bring his force of character and will to bear. The only recourse was to get Captain Hy to protest that the ROKs were burning in Hieu Xuong District, and that procedure was not going to save the half-dozen houses that were ablaze.

We moved up the road, fanned out, searched another village that had been abandoned some months before, and came back out to the road. Just as we were reassembling after searching every house and finding nothing there, the ROK hunting pack swept in where we had been. Saying not a syllable to us, they set afire every house that had a thatched roof, leaving the ones with clay-slate or iron roofs alone.

Major Kobata turned away, almost in tears. I shared his unspoken view, that this might deny the VC a few roofs over their heads during the torrential valley rains, but the hatred we were breeding offset this by miles.

We started back the way we had come, down the long miles under what was now a hot, bright sun. I was near the head of the column as we walked back through the first, occupied, village, in which the ROKs had burned half a dozen houses to start their day. As we came out the other side I saw that the Vietnamese militia of this column were now carrying pots, baskets, anything they could dart into a house and steal on their way through this momentarily deserted village. Some had picked up poles and hastily tied chairs and chests onto them, carrying them out of the village on a pole between two men. Captain Hy was doing nothing to stop it, and Major Kobata was up ahead, not seeing it.

The people who had been living in this village were, some of them, coming back up the road. They stood in silence, watching the militia that was supposed to protect them walk past with clocks and chests that belonged to them. The morning was a victory for the Viet Cong without their firing a shot.

That night was a reprise of my first night there—into the bunkers, a threat report, and then a launching into the darkness for a sweep of many hours through villages and across paddies. We returned at first light, and I slept for three hours. Then I went with Neil to the schoolyard seventy yards up the road, the place where I had seen the militia widows receiving their pensions my first day with the advisors here.

The elections were to be held the next day, also the anniversary of Ho Chi Minh's 1945 proclamation of a Vietnamese Republic, kicking off the war with the French. Thus the prestige of both the Saigon government and the Viet

Cong were on a collision course during the next forty-eight hours, and we were in a state of alert that was limited only by the need for an occasional three hours' sleep between turns on the bunkers and probes in the valley.

Nonetheless, the scene in the nearby schoolyard was cheerful. Two hundred adults and any number of children were listening to speakers representing the various slates that would be voted upon tomorrow, and the ballot boxes were in the schoolrooms which loomed cool beside this sunny dirt playground.

The senatorial candidates who came from Phu Yen Province were in Saigon, making speeches to larger crowds to get their share of the big-city vote, so the speeches here were being made by younger men. One fiery youthful speaker gave an impassioned oration on behalf of one party's candidate, paused for a minute, and then gave an equally impassioned and evidently sincere plea for an opposing candidate. Neil gave me a running translation of the speeches, and the interesting thing was that none of them mentioned the war that was flickering all around us in this valley. They were campaign promises that would have been good in Shreveport—a higher rice subsidy for the farmer and a lower rice price for the housewife, better education for the children, and cheaper building materials for houses. The war was evidently something like the weather; no one would have believed them if they had said they could do anything about the next monsoon season.

The mood of the gathering was cheerful. The adults seemed pleased at the prospect of the election, and the children crowded around Neil and me, touching the hair on our forearms. They would look up and say "You!" and "Okay!," using the terms indiscriminately, knowing only that they were from the language that Neil and I spoke. I lit a cigar and gave the cigar band to a boy, slipping it on his finger as a ring. He was pleased, and went about showing it to his friends.

Neil and I strolled back to the compound, noticing that all the American military men were gone. It was payday at the compound on the beach at Tuy Hoa, and they had driven up there during these quiet morning hours. We thought little about this and were sitting in the living room at eleven in the morning, having another in our series of discussions about the problems of Vietnam, when the command-post radio came to life. Since there were no American military men in the compound, we moved toward it. A VC battalion was attacking a militia company in a hamlet in Tuy Hoa District, out in the valley north of the river. At almost the same moment the sounds of gunfire came to us on a fresh breeze, and Neil and I climbed atop the command-post bunker, listening to the guns, which were perhaps half a mile off. The VC never struck with large forces like this in daylight; this was clearly to celebrate their anniversary and to disrupt tomorrow's election.

The bloody script across the river unfolded. Helicopter gunships began circling, darting in to fire their rockets, and then the F–100s started their towering roller-coaster dives. To attack this near the air base in daylight was like pulling a pistol in a police station.

"The fighters are already beyond the target when they take off," Neil said as we watched, and it was so. The planes soared off, joined up in their bomb-loaded formations over the mountain edges of the valley, and then headed back in the direction of the base, picking up the FAC plane north of the river on the way back.

We heard the FAC talking to someone on the ground as he counted the swarm of F–100s that were being made available to him by my friends at the base. "I'll just keep the fighters coming until you turn them off," he said. It sounded as if the man to whom he was talking had a lot of moving targets coming his way. Neil and I watched the bombs hit the trees, the gray-brown war-dust rising across the river.

A new American voice on the radio. "I have someone here who has turned somewhat chicken. Can you send me a man to escort him to your location?" It turned out to be a Vietnamese interpreter. This was a bad time to lose the services of a man who could explain to the Americans what the Vietnamese wanted, and vice versa.

Standing atop the bunker, I began to worry a bit about the absence of the military men on the team. This was a war developing around here, and I supposed that now it might be hard for them to get back from the Tuy Hoa compound by road, and the helicopters would be held for the action that was under way.

The radio kept going, and now we heard our call sign instead of merely listening in on someone else's war. Neil knew how to work the radio, and he used it while sitting on a crate before a map. It was a second FAC. He had just spotted a sampan in a canal on our side of the river, flying five or six VC flags. The FAC wanted the District Chief's permission to attack.

"Wait one," Neil said professionally to the radio, and leaped jubilantly to his feet. "Five or six VC flags, and they want *permission* to attack!" His long legs were all over the place as he raced toward Captain Hy's quarters. The captain was asleep, but Neil awoke him, got permission, and was back on the radio two minutes later, telling them affirmative on that sampan with the VC flags.

Captain Hy had asked Neil to come back and brief him on what was going on while he was getting dressed. Thus I was alone when the radio came on next. A Korean force across the river was reporting that they were being fired at from our side, an American voice told me. Did we have a VC force in contact here?

"Look," I said, pressing the button on the speaker and establishing contact to answer, "this is a civilian correspondent. If you'll wait—"

"What? Who is this? Over."

"A civilian reporter. Over."

"Jesus Christ. Well, you must know if you're in contact there."

"Negative," I said, reverting to my Dragoon self, "Negative contact here at this time."

Just then Neil came in, listened to the coordinates the radio was giving now, and deduced from the map that the Korean company on our side of the river was shooting at the Koreans on the other side. The radio turned into a rapid exchange of *ikas* and *nikas*, and the Koreans stopped shooting at each other, with the company on our side being sent to the battle across the wide, shallow river bed.

In the midst of all this I wandered out to the screened plywood shed where our cooking and eating was done. The Vietnamese cooks, an old man and a younger woman, were working away, oblivious to the *krum-krump* and a rattle of fire half a mile away. I sat down and the woman served me a hamburger without a bun and some corn on the cob, and I poured myself some coffee. After eating I felt terribly sleepy. Nothing was going on right here, so I went in to my cot in the team's concrete-floored living room and lay down. For a moment I felt as if my legs were moving, feeling a muscle-memory of marching through the valley on a sweep the night before, and then I was in a deep, satisfying sleep.

I awoke to the noise of Neil coming through the screen door, and looked at my watch. It was one-thirty in the afternoon. Neil was pale as he came toward me, the jubilant mood of two hours before extinguished.

"Charlie," he said in a composed, almost formal tone, "we have a report that there is an NVA regiment on our side of the river and coming this way."

"Where's the guys?"

"Still being paid."

I sat up, blinking. There were only a few militiamen in the compound, and a North Vietnamese regiment was coming down the road.

I laughed. The whole thing was preposterous. Two American civilians sitting here and a North Vietnamese *regiment*—I stood up. We both got on helmets, flak jackets, all our weapons, and worked out our plan of defense. Neil would stay in the command bunker with the radio and the map, and I would get atop the bunker outside the metal trailer that Neil and Major Kobata shared. That bunker had an extra parapet of sandbags on top of it, so I could crouch behind that while waiting for the North Vietnamese regiment. When I saw it I would tell him.

That was about as far as either of us was able to think, paralyzed by the idea that there were twelve hundred men coming down the road. It did not occur to me that Neil should use his radio to yell for help. It seemed to both of us that the first thing to do was for me to spot them, and then whatever happened happened.

I climbed up on the bunker with my carbine and two pistols. I had been frightened in a lot of different ways in the past year, but this was a heavy fear, mortal fear. The firing raged across the river, and now they were outflanking it with a regiment trotting down the tree-lined road on this side. I had no doubt that I was going to die soon in this hazy sunlight, and this sad, resentful feeling made my arms heavy and seemed even to dim my eyesight. Kneeling behind the sandbag parapet on the roof of this bunker, there was even a desire to see the first one coming under the trees, coming around the edge of a house, and to start firing and get this last thing under way and go out hitting back just as much as I could.

Perched on one sandbag at the corner of the bunker was a wooden Buddha that Neil had found lying in the grass beside a burned-out temple in the valley. The farmers had told Neil that the temple had burned from an accidental fire having nothing to do with the war, and that if he liked this Buddha, he could take it—they had no plans for it.

I looked up at the Buddha from where I knelt. He was about thirty inches high, scorched at the base and on his folded elbows, and was quite a striking piece of gray weathered wood, a thin erect young Buddha. He stared right down the line of barbed wire surrounding the compound, favoring with his eyes neither the contested territory without nor the Allied compound within.

I was suspended in time, helmet on my head, chin up over the sandbags, waiting. There was a terrific amount of firing going on across the river, real waves of it, clumps of it, initial quick exchanges and then more men opening up on each side until it was a continual clanging. The breeze turned cool. Nothing stirred.

As the afternoon went on, I was able to think about little things again. Occasionally Neil came out and checked to see that I was still there, and we chatted and joked for a minute. The reports were still exactly the same, we had every reason to think that we were in as great danger as two hours before, but one quickly gets used to living on a life raft in shark-infested seas.

A jeep turned into the compound, and Major Kobata and Sergeant Iaea got out. The greatest tribute I can pay the two of them is that, now that they were here, I knew we could handle the North Vietnamese regiment.

Night fell, and no North Vietnamese. Across the river there was a genuine, set-piece battle going on. As it dwindled into the darkness, reports began to come in. Thus far we had advanced across sixty-four enemy bodies and captured a number of rocket launchers and machine guns. The militia and the ARVN had lost twenty-five killed.

We went out to spend the night in the bunkers. Still no North Vietnamese. Perhaps they had recrossed the river and were in the battle over there. Perhaps, intelligence reports being what they were, there never had been any regiment on our side of the river. I spent the night atop the bunker, beside the buddha, swatting at mosquitoes. Part of the time I felt the threat of the enemy like a dark suffocating curtain upon us, and part of the time I felt an ignoble relief that when the attack had come, it had been on the other side of the river and not on us.

At first light of Election Day I climbed groggily down from my post beside the Buddha and fell onto the canvas cot I had been using in the living room. I awoke around nine, feeling attuned to the cheerful relieved conversations in English and Vietnamese going on throughout the compound. The big pre-election attack had not materialized on our side of the river, and reports from across the river indicated that the enemy had taken a beating and gone back to the hills.

As I shaved and pulled myself together, there was another piece of news. I had known that President Johnson was sending a high-ranking delegation of Americans to Vietnam to observe the elections, but now it turned out that part of the delegation was at Colonel Ba's house. They were scheduled to arrive here some time before ten o'clock. They would be briefed in an office opening on the next-door schoolyard where the speeches were made yesterday, and observe the first ballots being cast at ten o'clock.

As an observer myself, I knew that I should hustle over to the schoolyard right now, but I was still sleepy and hungry, so I went into the dining shed and had a fine breakfast. Even then I dawdled, drinking another cup of coffee, and then another, feeling guilty that I was not up the road mixing in with the crowd of farmers who were milling about and lining up to cast their votes. Major Kobata and Neil Miller were on the radio, using code words, asking for details on these incoming American VIPs. They had been identified only as congressmen.

I was just starting a fourth cup of coffee, an excessive amount even for me, when there was a heavy thud nearby. I had never heard a sound quite like it before, and for some reason it did not sound menacing. I rose and walked to the screened side of the shed. In a moment many people appeared on the road, running away from the polling place, women with their conical hats banging on their backs, men with only one rubber sandal, a donkey cart with the donkey galloping frantically out of control, a youth bent over the handlebars of his bicycle.

I had my camera on the table; I scooped it up and walked to the gate of the compound. Major Kobata was standing beside the concrete gate post, his head out to one side of it, looking up the road. I looked too. There were people literally walking around in circles on the road, finally collapsing on the roadside. Others were being helped limping from the schoolyard gate, while other people were still fleeing the scene. The Viet Cong had set off a bomb in the middle of the crowd of farm people waiting to vote.

I raced back to my quarters, slapped on my helmet and pistol belt, and then reappeared at the gate, heading for the scene with my camera.

"Chuck," Major Kobata said in a soft, commanding voice, "don't go up there. You might get shot. It may not be over." It was the first time he had called me anything other than "Mister Flood."

I stood beside him, my face working in a combination of excitement and outrage at what the Viet Cong had done.

"A terrific defeat," Major Kobata said softly to no one.

Some of the militia were going into the schoolyard with stretchers now, and after a minute people were again running into hiding. A second bomb had been spotted at the edge of a culvert beside the road. It was about seventy yards from me, and I crouched beside the concrete post, my helmeted head just out far enough to watch what happened next.

A stocky Vietnamese soldier with the rank of *aspirante*, equivalent to a warrant officer, walked across the road, bent over the homemade bomb, which appeared from this distance a shiny object, and deftly plucked something from it. Then he nodded, called something over his shoulder, and people rose from the ground and began moving again. It was the bravest thing I had seen in ten months in Vietnam.

A few minutes more and we went up the road. By the schoolyard gate a dozen wounded were lying on stretchers, with members of their families crowded about them. The women were keening in a ritual wail, high-pitched, formalized, chanting their protest against the heavens, their kneeling bodies bending and twisting in grief and shock.

Two people were dead. Another twenty-five, not on stretchers, were collapsed in various positions along the shoulder of the road.

I went into the schoolyard. No one was left here, but the testimony was grim. There were bloodspots drying, turning brown on the yellow earth. Coolie hats were everywhere, and rubber sandals were scattered in the dust. The doorway to the ballot boxes stood empty.

My reportorial instinct took over. I started taking pictures of the scattered conical hats and bloodstains lying before the doorway which had above it the Vietnamese slogans urging the people to vote. Then I walked back out to the gate. An old farmer lay on a stretcher. The cloth of the left leg of his black pajamas had been blown away by the explosion. His leg was so mangled that it looked like a red bleeding snake, a twisted crimson spiral in the space between thigh and ankle. His wife knelt beside him. The palms of her hands were joined in prayer, repeatedly rising to her forehead in the Buddhist sign of asking for mercy. She was wailing in the high chanting Vietnamese tones, repeating one long sentence.

I stared at the man's leg. The interior was revealed, in all angles of glistening red valleys, and yet there was no great spurting bleeding anywhere. He was still alive, but I was not sure his wife knew it.

I felt someone beside me and saw Neil. Two militia men picked up the old man on the stretcher and carried him swiftly toward a warehouse down the road, where there was a yard big enough for a medical-evacuation helicopter to land. The man's wife ran along beside the stretcher, her hand reaching out to her husband.

"What was she saying?" I asked Neil.

"She was saying," Neil answered as if stones were dropping from his lips, " 'Why? Why? We have an election, so my family dies.' "

A boy of fourteen was standing nearby, his hands on his bicycle. He was outwardly unmarked. Suddenly he began to cry, making no effort to turn his head or wipe his eyes. He stood there, not moving, sobbing.

Neil and I walked to the yard where the medical-evacuation helicopter would land. Some shooting had begun across the river, and this yard was not far from the riverbank. Once again I did not envy the American helicopter crews who flew these unarmed missions.

"What was the bomb made of?" I asked.

"It was a big bottle with a lot of metal fragments pasted on the outside of it," Neil told me. "It had plastic explosive inside."

A helicopter appeared, racing toward us with no evasive action whatsoever. It circled once, the pilot nodding, and lowered in. I alternated between taking pictures of the Vietnamese militiamen bringing the stretchers up to the chopper and letting my camera swing on its strap from my neck while I helped shove the stretchers aboard.

I helped lift one stretcher into the chopper and found myself staring at the slender ivory body we were putting aboard. The black pajamas were ripped, the face was bloody, and I was staring at a woman's breast. I still had in my mind, because I had seen so many of them, that wounded persons were males.

The helicopter, a red cross on a white background prominently displayed on its nose, both sides, and underside, rose into the air. Immediately the Viet Cong began firing at it, but it sped away from the firing snapping past above our heads.

An hour later I arrived at the advisors' compound on the beach at Tuy Hoa. The reportorial urge really had me now. I probably had the best election-day story in Vietnam. A bomb at a polling place, two dead and thirty-nine wounded, and to top it off some congressmen had narrowly missed being there. I had pictures, and the thing to do was to telephone the story to the Associated Press in Saigon and then take the film down

Dust Off Helicopter

there. I was getting my chance to pay back the AP for all those free nights in Room 22.

There were problems. I only had half the story. No one was going to give me the names of the congressmen over the radio, and, given the current insecure state of the area, I was not sure anyone was going to give me any information at all. My only way of trying to round out this story was to go straight to the top advisors I could find, and this meant driving in exactly the opposite direction from the telephones to Saigon at the air base and the air terminal that might be able to get me on a flight for Saigon.

I finally found one of the top advisors. He looked tired after the battle the day before, but he greeted me in friendly fashion and asked what he could do for me.

I told him that I had occasionally worked for the Associated Press in the past, and that right now he should regard me as an AP reporter. Then I asked him who the congressmen were.

The advisor sighed. He saw the point right away, that it was a hell of a story, high-ranking Americans who had been scheduled to be right where that bomb had gone off. He also saw that his superiors in Saigon were going to be yelling their heads off five minutes after this story broke.

"You have a right to know who's visiting Tuy Hoa," he said, to his eternal credit. "It's not classified." He smiled bleakly, because he knew what he was telling me now made it even more of a story. President Johnson's observers, here right now, were Senator George Murphy of California and Governor William Guy of North Dakota. A prominent United States Senator and a Governor, and one could not even be sure that the bomb had not been a deliberate attempt to assassinate them.

I hitched a ride back to the air base in stages, glancing at my watch nervously in the wire-service reporter's unending race against the clock, any clock, every clock. The bomb had gone off at five minutes to ten. It was now one in the afternoon. As this jeep bumped down the potholed road, a transport plane rose and headed south, and I found myself wondering if that was the last plane of the day for Saigon. Even more to the point, I wondered whether the telephones to Saigon were working today, whether there would be the usual delays. I needed a crystal ball to tell me whether it would be faster to take a plane to Saigon and then tell them the story in the office, while handing them the film, or risk missing additional planes to Saigon while fooling around with the telephones at the air base.

I arrived at the Public Information Office at the air base and asked the sergeant on duty to let me at the telephone. There was an expression of skepticism on both our faces as I started placing a call that we both knew could take hours. Even if one reached Saigon on this military network, the connection might easily be lost while being patched into the civilian exchange.

"Tiger," a tiny Vietnamese female voice said from Saigon, identifying the exchange.

"Tiger," I said gently, "this call is urgent." I gave her the AP number, and in one minute and fifteen seconds I had George Esper of the Associated Press on the line.

"Sounds like you're in the next room, Charlie," he said as he put paper in a typewriter. "Go ahead."

Half an hour later I was at the air terminal, with no baggage except the roll of film in my pocket.

"The last plane to Saigon has gone for the day," a bored

clerk told me, and then I spotted a young black airman who had been booking me around the country all year. I told him exactly the situation.

"We've got a C–123 out there taking four dead ROKs to Nha Trang," he told me. "We're not supposed to manifest anybody on those kind of flights. Bad for morale. Why don't you go out there and talk to the aircraft commander?"

I went out and talked to the aircraft commander.

"Come on," the pilot said. I climbed aboard the transport plane. There in the center of the bare metal floor were four olive-drab rubber bags, each the length and breadth of a man, lashed down as if they were logs. Sitting on a red canvas bench was a blonde American woman. I stepped out of the plane during the remaining minutes before take-off and asked the sergeant crew chief who she was. She was a stripper who had been in a show at an officers' club at Danang. I got back on the plane and rode to Nha Trang with the blonde stripper and the four dead Koreans.

The next morning I awoke with the strangest feeling that I was sleeping on a marble floor. I sat up and found that this was the case.

Slowly I reconstructed the past eighteen hours. I had finally arrived in Saigon during the evening, and handed my roll of film to the photo boys. They had wasted no time on it. Within a few minutes they were transmitting to New York one of my pictures, a scene of Vietnamese militiamen running toward the medical-evacuation helicopter with a man on a stretcher.

It was just after this, standing there punchy in the office, that I learned that Room 22 was no more. The AP had decided to give it up. George Esper loaned me the key to his apartment around the corner, but the problem here had been that there were two beds and a couch, and a large American already asleep on each of them. At that point I had accepted the situation, stretched out on the marble floor of the apartment with a doubled-over bath towel for a pillow, and here I was.

At the AP office I ran straight into John Wheeler, looking sunburned after one of his real submersion acts in a Marine Corps unit in I Corps. "Why did you take so long phoning in that story yesterday?'' he said. ''It was the best story we had.''

Why did I take so long——? I thought about my frantic racing all over Phu Yen Province to put that story together, grabbing reluctant officials, hitching jeep rides, and then I answered. ''Well, there was a long line at the telephone booth in the schoolyard where it happened.''

I decided that nothing was making any sense, and I walked toward the Continental-Palace, ready to have a cup of coffee.

There was a group of about sixty people crowding around someone outside the National Assembly building. For the first time since the bomb had gone off it occurred to me that the elections had in fact taken place, elsewhere, and that I had seen the Saigon papers this morning that proclaimed Thieu and Ky the winning ticket, the elected rulers.

I worked my way into the knot of people. In the center stood a Vietnamese in a gray silk suit. I recognized the portly little figure of Truong Dinh Dzu, the Presidential candidate who had lambasted the Thieu–Ky ticket at that meeting I had attended at the Dien Hong Palace on my pre-election trip to Saigon. Yesterday Dzu and his running mate had polled three hundred and forty-three thousand votes, second only to the Thieu–Ky total of seven hundred and six thousand, and this morning Dzu had plenty to say.

I looked around to see if anyone was here from the Associated Press. No one. I pulled out a pen and the blank back of a copy of my travel orders and went to work for the AP again.

The little lawyer was again wearing his navy-blue tie with the Rotary International emblem on it, and he was not mincing words. He said that the election had been fraudulent. His English was excellent, and he used words like *mockery* and *travesty*. The reporters were bouncing with delight, since they had spent the entire election day looking for irregularities and finding very few. Microphones were waved under Dzu's pudgy little throat as he said that he did not accept the legitimacy of this government.

''I consider this government illegal and incompetent,'' he said, warming to his topic, ''and I do not accept the results of the election, because it is a fraud.'' He went on to say that the government radio had exaggerated early returns from the provinces in an effort to create an impression among Saigon voters, before they went to the polls, that the Thieu–Ky ticket was winning in a landslide. He said that at some Saigon voting places, trucks of ARVN soldiers had arrived early during the voting hours, using up all the ballots and voting for Thieu and Ky, and said that some other polling places did not have enough senatorial ballots to cover the senatorial slates.

I felt that if this was all he could come up with he was on weak ground, but I took it down. There was undoubtedly a world-wide market for the comments of the defeated candidates the morning after the elections, and particularly for such charges. Looking at the little man, who was antagonizing the regime and laying himself open for the arrest that eventually took place, it surprised me that such an ordinary-looking little man should have so much courage. Between Dzu and that *aspirante* defusing the second bomb the day before, I had seen two acts of bravery in two days.

"A nationwide fraud," Dzu was saying. He added that he was in touch with two other defeated candidates, former Premier Huong and Phan Khac Suu, asking them to join in making a formal protest to the National Assembly, to request that the results of the election be disallowed and another election held.

Even the mention of invalidating the election was of course rare roast beef for the press. A few were already taking off for their offices, but I waited, and was not wrong in doing so.

"We must talk to Hanoi," Dzu said on this day eighteen months before the beginning of the Paris peace talks. Speaking of the Viet Cong, he wanted talks with them, too. "Most of them are sincere nationalists," he argued, "and I think they would like to see peace, too."

Sincere nationalists. No one had said this many good words about the VC and gotten away with it, and I think a few of the reporters were looking over their shoulders as their pens flew, wondering just when the police were going to come and take Mr. Dzu away for a long time.

I jogged back to the office and began typing the story. Peter Arnett came in and said "Hey, Charlie, that was a good story yesterday. Why did you wait so long to phone it in?"

I just nodded, and kept typing.

TWENTY-FIVE

Arriving back at the air base the next morning, I decided to have lunch there before rejoining the team at Hieu Xuong to follow up on the bomb incident and their efforts in general. I picked up a pen to write my name on the sheet of men signing in as they paid for lunch and pain shot through my wrist like a flaming string. The swelling of a few days before had ceased, forgotten in this frantic life of bunkers at night, hiking the valley, bumpy jeeps, planes to Saigon, but I decided that a writer who could not sign his name was a writer who had better get over to the dispensary. That afternoon I found myself in the X-ray room at the Army hospital down the beach, even farther from the district headquarters at Hieu Xuong. Now a graying, businesslike orthopedic surgeon with the rank of lieutenant colonel was telling me that I had a fracture of the navicular.

"It's the worst wrist fracture you can have," he said cheerfully, and drew me a diagram. "You'll be in a cast."

"For how long?"

"A minimum of three months."

Three months. My writing hand was going to be immobilized for three months. In a trance I went to the cast room and watched a technician wrap cement-soaked watery tape around my arm from the elbow down to the second joints of my fingers. It was early September, I was supposed to go home in December, and I had a score of things I still needed to see and make notes about. Now my writing hand was immobilized, and I was in none too effective condition to use a weapon if it became necessary.

I dropped in at the Wing command post and found

Colonel Frank Buzze at his desk, down from a mission and working on papers concerning bombing tactics.

"What have you gotten into now?" he asked in a friendly way as he saw the gleaming white cast.

I told him, and asked how this affected my going on missions. He shook his head. I was grounded until the cast came off. I could never operate all the equipment for ejection, the parachute, the survival gear.

I went back to the hooch and sat down at my desk. About me lay manila folders with ten months of work, all of it predicated on being able to make notes on another three months of poking around Vietnam.

After a while I pulled my typewriter toward me. I managed to get a piece of paper into the typewriter, and began poking at it laboriously with one finger of my left, castless, hand.

the quick brown correspondent jumped over the lazy war.

I tried it again. If I avoided making capital letters it was by no means impossible.

That night at supper in the mess hall I discovered that I could manipulate the plastic tray, that I could join the thumb and forefinger of my right hand despite the cement now separating them.

I discovered something else, a piece of poetic justice rich beyond the Wing's deserts. While I had been having the cast put on my arm, Misfitte Glare, sitting in an F–100 ready to taxi out for a mission, made a boo-boo. After ten months of acting a part, of criticizing the hooch maids, of denying me use of a panel truck and making life hell for his subordinates, Misfitte managed to do something that surpassed the wildest dreams of his most fervent enemies. In one quick, inaccurate motion of the hand in the cockpit, he dropped his bombs right on the flight line, three thousand pounds of high explosive dropping from the underside of the wings to the metal slabs beneath where his plane was warming up. The bombs had not gone off, but it had been quite a mess, since he also dropped his auxiliary tanks, which broke open, with hundreds of gallons of gasoline running all over the place.

"Is it an easy mistake to make?" I asked the major who was ecstatically telling me this.

"What he had to pull to do that——" the major said, still savoring it. "The switches are about one foot away from anything he should have been touching at that time." He shook his head. "It's about as smart as driving a car straight through the back end of a garage, except you've had more training so as to avoid making mistakes."

Another officer chimed in, happily bobbing in his seat. "When I got the word what had happened, I drove out there to inspect the situation, make sure the fire engines were there, everything. All I was thinking about was: Now where can we send this guy? I never dreamed it would be a guy who outranks me."

Well, I asked them, was Misfitte really such a bad pilot?

"In the air he's okay," one of my friends said thoughtfully. "It's just on landings and take-offs he should have someone else do it for him."

Back at the hooch, thoughts of the past few days revolved through my mind, the nights and days at Hieu Xuong before the bomb went off. With one finger I typed some of my reactions:

i have been rather profoundly struck by my few days sleeping, when i could, at hieu xuong district hq. i have been interested to learn, first hand, the psychological difference between sitting penned in, waiting to be hit, and launching out into the night, looking for the enemy. i have been depressed to see koreans burning houses, and pf strolling aimlessly, just walking through the motions of an operation, taking their pants off before going through paddies so they would not become dirty, and strolling homeward with loot, sometimes so much it hung between them on a pole. the pf were by and large well-equipped and uniformed, but lackadaisical. one could in the last resort fall back on neil miller's thesis that it is miraculous that any of them will come forward, that any of them will do anything, but this seems to me to be falling back pretty far.

In one rush, in my notes, I was telling myself the truth, forcing myself to be more honest than was usually convenient, or even bearable, when I was talking to other Americans or simply living the experience.

> however, my overriding impression from these past few days is one of being appalled that, in the midst of all my other past experiences and impressions over here, i have at last seen a situation in which six americans, day after day, and more particularly night after night, face the very real possibility of attack by a greatly superior force. it may be that i have been naive in not grasping this before, but it seemed to me that americans were always committed, except in the bombing of the north, on fairly equitable terms. here were guys living with what seemed to me to be very unfair odds. it seems to me to be unjust to them, a bad practice in general, and it begins to make me question how much we are really accomplishing anywhere, if it is not all the same quicksand that hieu xuong proved to be. and mind you, hieu xuong is an area with a big american complex, a rok regiment, a nearby arvn battalion, and is far from the dmz or the cambodian border. it seems to me that it is like putting six u.s. cavalrymen in an indian town and telling them that the friendly indians will fight beside them when they are attacked by the hostile indians. i am not sure that we have ever stuck people's necks out so far before, as part of a regular practice.

Having written this, I brushed my teeth and fell asleep to the sound of the air conditioner. At one o'clock in the morning there was a thud in the distance and a terrific chipping sound of automatic fire, followed by more thuds and a rising volume of fire. I swung out of bed, the unfamiliar cast on my arm almost tipping me onto my face, and opened the door of the hooch. A flare was hanging in the distance, just above where I knew the Hieu Xuong compound to be. Another flare broke above it, and the rattle of gunfire rose, ebbed, rose again. I went back into the hooch, struggled into a flying suit and slippers, and came out again. Now there were three flares at once above Hieu Xuong.

Two red cigarette tips were glowing atop a nearby sandbag bunker. Colonel Lewis and Frank Buzze were watching, while beside them on the sandbags lay their small walkie-talkie radios that would inform them if the focus of the attack shifted to the base.

I climbed up on the bunker and sat down beside them. There was a *krump, krump* from the compound at Hieu Xuong, and then a new sound—*pup pup pup*. This last noise cheered me, because it meant that Major Kobata had, at least for tonight, succeeded in borrowing a quad-fifty, a truck with four .50-caliber machine guns mounted on it. Now that it was firing, the other shooting seemed to wither, rising in brief whirlwinds and fading back. Gunships were up now, darting among the flares the compound was putting up to illuminate the paddies from which the attack was coming.

Frank Buzze had disappeared for a minute, and handed up three cans of cold Coke before he climbed back atop the bunker. I fumbled in the pocket of my flying suit and brought out a cigar. Experimenting, I found that I could light it despite my cast. Thus, smoking a cigar and drinking a Coke, I watched the tracers fly back and forth across the paddies behind the compound where I had slept just three nights before. If I had not discovered this broken wrist today, I would have been there now. The tracers flew through the night like angry red chains, a string of red baseballs flicking to a darkened destination.

Now a new sound. A Gooney Bird was circling above Hieu Xuong, dropping flares. As it banked, an avenue of red sparks slashed down from the sky, and then the sparks solidified and became one long straight red line like a death ray. A few moments later a sound like a buzz-saw reached us, and then both the red ray and the sound ceased, only to repeat a few seconds later, red ray striking from the sky like an arrow-straight bolt of lightning. This Gooney Bird was one of the planes known as a "Spooky," which dropped its own flares, enabling it to make the area around an under-attack outpost bright as day. Then with the four special machine guns it had aboard, the plane could put down that murderous curtain of fire upon the attackers. Since it carried almost unlimited amounts of fuel, flares, and ammunition, a Spooky could protect an outpost from the air, all night long. The VC hated them.

The radio beside Colonel Lewis informed him that some automatic-weapons fire was flicking across the air-base fence and impacting on the flight line. No damage thus far. Apparently the VC were giving us a few squirts for good measure, as long as they were in the neighborhood.

I finished my cigar. There were still occasional exchanges of fire over there. Spooky kept circling, kept dropping flares, but saw nothing to shoot at any more.

I looked at my watch. It was a quarter past two. For an hour and fifteen minutes I had been watching my friends at Hieu Xuong fight for their lives, if indeed they were still alive to fight. I was tired and sleepy, and there was nothing I could do for them. I said good night to Colonel Lewis, thanked Frank for the Coke, and went back to bed, a distant tap of rifle fire accompanying me into sleep.

At the stand-up briefing the next morning there was a report of sorts. The advisory compound on the beach at Tuy Hoa had called in by telephone to confirm that the Hieu Xuong compound had indeed been hit, and that three Americans were wounded. My heart sank, wondering which three they were. Our own report from last night showed one Air Policeman killed on the perimeter.

The Wing's senior Intelligence officer, Lieutenant Colonel Mark Fountain, was going down to Hieu Xuong in a jeep, and I hitched a ride with him. I had my Browning pistol with me in its holster on my belt. Just how I was going to cock it, if necessary, with one hand in a cast, was not clear to me, but I supposed one painful grab could do it.

As we moved from the smooth air-base road onto the potholes that marked the rest of the way, Mark told me that one of the hooch maids had said that the attack last night was to "get the two American majors at Hieu Xuong."

"There's only one American major down there," I told him. "Major Kobata."

"We'll see," Mark replied.

We turned a corner. There stood a Vietnamese in green fatigues, carrying an M-1 rifle. Any other morning he would have been just another militiaman, another part of the landscape, but this morning I reached for my pistol. The Vietnamese stuck up his hand, asking us for a ride. Any other morning we would have given him one, but this morning we sped past him, and I turned and watched him until he shrank into a green dot beside the dusty road.

As we neared the compound we began to see Vietnamese along the road, fewer than usual. Among the adults there were hostile glances, averted faces, or a simple blank stare. The children who usually ran to the side of the road, shouting "You!" and waving, stared at us without moving.

We turned into the compound. The steel trailer shared by Major Kobata and Neil Miller was pocked with a hundred holes, some of them long gashes, others little black circles. The tears in the shiny metal skin curled inward with ragged metal lips, incongruous in the silent morning sun.

Major Kobata came limping toward us, his face composed but ashen, a bandage on his arm. Standing between the metal trailer and the bullet-riddled wooden main living quarters, he told us that there had indeed been two majors here last night. Just yesterday afternoon the man who was to have been his replacement at the end of his year's tour, a Major Underwood, had arrived fresh from the States. Underwood had gone to sleep in the main living quarters on his first night in his new assignment and been hit as he slept by the first round of the attack. He was gone by medical-evacuation helicopter before dawn.

Kobata led us through the screen door of the team's concrete-floored living room, and I stopped, stunned. It was a shambles. He began to reconstruct the attack for us. At ten minutes before one in the morning, unbeknown to any of the American team, the PF squad on guard by the schoolhouse next door, where the bomb had gone off election morning, disappeared without orders, explanation, or any word to the Americans. Then a perfectly aimed

M1 Rifle

B–40 rocket screamed into the wooden living quarters and exploded on the top of the door frame between one bedroom and the living room. Its metal fragments, combined with wooden splinters, had struck the new major and a young lieutenant who had also just been assigned here to round out the team. The worst wounds, however, had been suffered by Muñoz, the young Pfc. who was asleep on the cot I had occupied just three nights before. He was hit badly in the stomach.

I stared at the cot I would have been on last night. There were dark bloodstains all over the brown canvas and on the concrete floor beneath.

An instant after this opening shot the VC let go with automatic weapons, stitching holes through the wall of the other bedroom at the far end of the quarters. I walked in there. Of the three sergeants who normally slept in there, the two black sergeants, Bradley and Hebron, had been in the bunkers on guard. Iaea was having diarrhea, and was in the latrine, which happened to be shielded from the bullets by sandbags and sand-filled oil drums. Thus he was sitting on the toilet when every other man in the building was wounded. I walked over to his cot. There was a horizontal row of splintered bullet holes running just six inches above his mattress. With his huge torso he would have been perforated right down the center from the side.

We walked back out into the sunlight, and here came Neil Miller, unshaven, pale and smiling. He was asleep naked on his bed in the trailer when he heard the rocket hit. He grabbed his helmet and a carbine, diving out of the trailer and into a bunker just seconds before the hail of bullets riddled his trailer. In those same seconds, Major Kobata leaped from the trailer, wrenching his knee and taking shrapnel in his arm as he sprinted for the command bunker and the radio which was to call in all the help they received. In the meantime the PF militiamen on guard in and around the bunkers in the Chinese corner of the compound ran away to the other corners of the compound, where they hid until the action was over.

"They were just after the advisors," Kobata said in his precise voice. "Everything was concentrated on our section of the compound."

The next phase came instantly. Firing their AK–47 automatic rifles, the VC rushed the barbed wire, some men throwing explosive charges ahead to breach it. It was at this point that they ran into the truck-mounted four .50-caliber machine guns, a weapon and crew that Kobata had borrowed from the defenses of the American logistical complex down the beach.

"The quad-fifty cut them down as they were trying to blast their way in through the wire," Kobata said calmly. "They got in so close that they were able to turn our Claymore mines around against us."

The initial attack was beaten off, the Americans seeing the VC carrying away bodies under the light of the flares they were putting up. Then the VC settled into the treelines and earth dikes among the rice paddies and began trying to destroy the defenders and buildings from there. They had a 57-millimeter recoilless cannon that they fired at point-blank range, and kept up a barrage with at least one mortar, machine guns, and the AK–47s and carbines.

At this point the arithmetic was not in favor of the

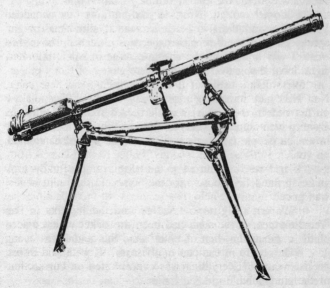

57 mm Recoilless

Americans. Since the PF and Captain Hy were hiding, declining to participate, and with three Americans wounded, the only defense consisted of the quad-fifty truck and its crew, the two black sergeants in one bunker, Iaea in another, Neil Miller in another, and Kobata in the command bunker on the radio. Thus were there eight Americans inside, and the Viet Cong Three-Seventy-Seven Company outside under the skillful command of Captain Quy, a force of at least a hundred.

I asked Neil Miller what it had been like, kneeling naked inside the bunker.

"I never saw anything," the American civilian said. "I just kept firing in the direction where I thought they had to be."

Now the gunships were in, and the Spooky plane. Major Kobata repeatedly asked a Korean company down the road to move to his assistance, but they stayed in their positions and did not come to the compound's defense.

With the air cover overhead, the enemy captain Quy decided against another rush. Three hours after the first rocket was fired, the enemy diffused in the night.

I looked around. Now, in mid-morning, the wounded gone, Iaea and the two black sergeants, slim Bradley and stocky Hebron, were repairing the gaps blasted in the barbed wire. I was witnessing the absolute spine of soldiering. Last night's battle was over, and they were matter-of-factly preparing for tonight's battle, if it should come.

Neil had something else to say to me. "You left too early on election day. I wish you'd been here later. You would have gotten another kind of photograph. A lot of those wounded people got themselves bandaged up and came back to vote."

It had never occurred to me that voting actually took place in the schoolhouse after the bomb. I asked him how it had gone.

"We got a big turnout," Neil said, adding that in Phu Yen Province the winners had been the ticket which placed third in the nation, that of Phan Khac Suu and Phan Quang Da, both men from this part of Vietnam. "I wish you'd seen them limping back up the road to vote," Neil said again, and went into his bullet-riddled trailer to clean up the mess.

*   *   *

That night I and my plaster cast were back at my typewriter. Inevitably I was thinking about my luck, the day at Three Trees when I moved just seconds before a rocket struck where I had been lying, and the chain of circumstances that had saved me a couple of times at Hieu Xuong. The first had been that unnoticed fracture in my wrist, acquired well before the election and apparently biding its time to save me. The other factor was my love for coffee. It was my drinking a third, a fourth cup of coffee that had saved me from being in that schoolyard when the bomb went off. Then, when I returned from Saigon, ready to resume the routine at Hieu Xuong, it had been the discovery of the broken wrist that changed my schedule sufficiently to keep me from Hieu Xuong last night. I was grateful for being spared, but my mood was blue. I put a sheet of paper in the typewriter.

"It may be external things like this cast, or being lonesome and tired, or having been personally frightened by this whole impending Hieu Xuong nightmare and its consummation, but it would take a lot right now to convince me that we are winning the war. God knows we are not ahead of where we were a year ago, in Hieu Xuong District."

TWENTY-SIX

While the Hieu Xuong compound was being repaired, I set up shop with the American civilian advisors who lived behind the Province Chief's house. The evening before I was to launch off on a day of following the Agricultural Advisor around, I did some homework in a screen-sided office. Every time the subject of land reform had arisen there had been a tendency on the part of some of the advisors to say "We don't have a land reform problem in this part of Vietnam." Now I had in front of me some of the documents upon which they quite sincerely based that belief.

Every bug in Vietnam was trying to get through the screen of this deserted after-hours office. I was discovering that, awkward as it was, I could make notes with my plaster-cased right hand, although the words looked like fourth-grade handwriting.

There was not much to take notes on. Exhibit A was a 1962 U.S. Army handbook for Vietnam, which stated that in parts of this area of Vietnam, three-fourths of the farmers owned their own land. Exhibit B was an American-government-financed study of the refugee situation in Phu Yen Province, the research for this having been done in 1966. It cited the 1962 Army handbook, and, from a breakdown of forty-six nonrefugee families undertaken as part of the 1966 research, concluded that 51 per cent of them owned all the land they worked, and that another 28 per cent owned some and rented some, the remainder being wholly dependent on rental land or not involved with agriculture as an occupation.

After three hours of reading, taking notes, and rereading my notes, I came to the conclusion that I had before me about

370

as shaky a set of figures as I had ever seen. The direct quote from the 1962 Army handbook said: "In parts of the area [the Central Lowlands] three-fourths of the farmers owned their own land. . . ." Thus the handbook, by stating that its figures held only for parts of the area, was invalidating any generalizations based upon it. Even assuming that the figure had been valid in 1962, five years of turmoil and relocation had ensued.

So much for Exhibit A. As for Exhibit B, the refugee study, there were four hundred thousand people in Phu Yen Province, and they were basing their figures on exactly forty-six nonrefugee families. Based on this spectacularly thin sampling concerning a vital issue, they went on in the next paragraph to call the results of this forty-six-household study "the land tenure patterns in Phu Yen."

I could not believe that they would not hedge this statement somewhere, and finally, in a footnote, I found them coming clean: "Reliable demographic data for a non-refugee population in Central Vietnam is unavailable."

For a minute I felt like banging my head on the desk. In sum, there was not a single statistic on land tenure in our part of the country which could stand even superficial inspection. Both documents cited a 1958 study undertaken in the Delta which showed that there indeed had been a lot of absentee landlordism in the Delta at that time, but to conclude from that study that we had no land-reform problem here was a *non sequitur*. There probably *were* a lot of absentee landlords in the Delta, quite probably more than there were here, but as far as the situation in Phu Yen was concerned, we were flying blind. Anyone wanting to study land reform in Phu Yen had better start from scratch.

I brought the subject up gingerly the next morning. I was sitting in the front of an International Scout beside the Agricultural Advisor, Willie Bullock, a handsome black man who had been working for the United States Department of Agriculture in Mississippi when he volunteered to come out here.

He turned toward me now, his hands on the wheel as we moved out of town, and agreed without hesitation that we might still have a serious land-reform problem in Phu Yen.

His voice so soft that I could scarcely hear it, he took up the subject as we rolled across the long bridge over the river. His first point was that to a sharecropping farmer who does not own his land, who has to rent the land he works, it makes no difference whether his landlord is a large landowner or a small one, so the absence of the stereotyped large absentee landlord in Central Vietnam did not mean much.

Next he said that he wondered how anybody around here could be sure, anyway, of who owned what. In Phu Yen all records of land titles had been destroyed when the Viet Minh took over in 1945 and held the Province until 1954. Only now, *now*, was the Saigon government establishing land records for Tuy Hoa and Hieu Xuong districts, and the other districts were to be recorded later.

"I think," Willie said softly, "that many men own a lot of land in other districts and do not report it."

Finally, he turned to the facts of life for farmers in the valley. For the farmer who had very little or no land, the law prevented him from renting more than three hectares, just over seven acres, and he usually had to pay a steep 40 per cent of his crop as rent. The farmers were not willing to complain about this exorbitant crop-rent because of a fear that even that land would not be offered to them the following year.

"They do have a fairly effective means of redress through the RD team or the village grievance committee," Willie told me, "if they'd only use it, but they do not, on this kind of a thing."

We were passing by a field, and he pointed. There were two plantings of corn in it, one section tall and luxurious, and the other small and scrubby.

"I asked them if I could plant a strain of my American corn next to theirs," he said. "You see the difference, and so do they. They got the message." He smiled. "Then we had another problem. They planted beans in among the American corn when they started growing it around here, and our corn grew so high it choked off the sunlight and killed off the beans. Now we're straight."

As we rolled along, I stared out the window, thinking that there must be a moral in there somewhere about the

American corn choking out the Vietnamese beans. I asked Willie how the war affected his work.

"If there weren't a war," he said almost silently, "I could do about five times as much for these people."

We rolled out into the valley as I thought about what I was learning about land reform, coupling it with what I already knew about the Far East. If there was one thing ingrained in Asians, it was a devotion to the land, a regard for its importance and an often-mystical feeling about being buried among one's ancestors, in family land.

I looked out at the paddies and fields. Well, here was land, Vietnamese land, and Vietnamese farmers. Here was one thing the United States did not have to send to Vietnam, and it was something that meant more to the Vietnamese than anything else. It was right in front of my eyes, and the gravest problem was that men were working from dawn to dusk in the murderous stooped hours of rice farming, often without the assurance of any future at all on this land, or any idea of how much of this year's crop they could keep, or whether they would be allowed the same house and land the following year.

I shook my head. Here, in a culture which was tradition-oriented, in which luxuries could be foregone but a sense of place was vital, here was where it all broke apart. A man could farm some paddies for years and look up to see a man in a white shirt, accompanied by a National Policeman, waving a piece of paper. The farmer could not read it, but the National Policeman would tell him that it proved that this man in the white shirt had owned the land for years. Result: injustice, and an instant recruit for the Viet Cong.

That was the problem, and almost nothing was being done to solve it. Here was something that would cost only the amount required to administer a real program of registering titles, settling claims, and redistributing the land where it was equitable to do so.

I thought of Doctor Tom Durant in Saigon, saying that some American programs we were trying here would not work in Bridgeport, Connecticut. Well, here was a situation where the Saigon government was as out of touch with the farmers as if Saigon were Reykjavik. What they should do, for their own bureaucratic survival, was to give the land to their farmers in absolute fee simple, giving the farmer confidence in the fact that he had a certain stake in a society which would protect his ownership of land against all comers. If you could instill that in him, then at last you would have the spirit of Lexington and Concord smoldering on the side of Saigon, but of course it was not being done. Who could profit by the foot-dragging? Not the farmer. The men who wanted the cloudy *status quo* were the Establishment boys. It was a lesson so old that it seemed amazing that there was always a new generation coming along who were deaf to it: If the big house will not share with the little houses, the men from the little houses will burn the big house.

Willie and I drove on in silence, out into an area where I had never before gone without a gun. I stared at the land, the land that could be more productive if there were no war, the land that could unify Saigon and its people if only Saigon would see what there was to be seen, and act.

We left the car beside the road and visited families and their animals, a sow here, a goat there, a sick water buffalo lying in the shade. At one house there was a boy with a broken arm, the result of falling from a tree while playing; we promised to pick him up on the way back to the car, and take him to the province hospital.

Willie led the way along a path beside a plowed field. We had heard that a VC mortar round had landed near here last night, a short round that had been aimed to land on an ARVN post a mile farther on. We turned the corner of a thatch-roofed farmhouse. In its mud walls were new, jagged holes. A family group sat about on the ledge of a cement threshing terrace, and one or two of the men rose and greeted Willie as an old friend. The family women were making solicitous noises, solicitous of one woman, when they spoke. The woman, thick-waisted and sturdy, was sitting silently, nursing a baby from a handsome breast that protruded through a plum-colored blouse. Her other child had been killed the night before by the shell that had torn the holes in the mud wall.

On our way back to the road we stopped at the house where there was the boy with the broken arm. He stared at us with grave brown eyes, silent in his pain. A toothless great-grandfather with a bandana on his head had been assigned to accompany the child to the hospital.

"They always have somebody from the family go along," Willie said as we put them in the Scout. "This old man will sleep on a bench in the hospital." We were talking to those in the family who had come down to the road to see the boy and his great-grandfather off to the hospital when a farmer came through a hedge, recognized Willie, and took him aside, speaking quickly.

Willie nodded and trotted back to the Scout, his eyes telling me to get in fast and not ask questions. We were out of there in one second, the family waving as we left.

"That guy says all hell's going to break loose out here," Willie told me in his low, hollow voice, and we drove swiftly toward town.

The man who told Willie to get out of there knew what he was talking about. Not long after we left the child and his great-grandfather off at the hospital the valley exploded with action.

I spent the afternoon standing on the knoll behind the Province Chief's house, looking inland across Tuy Hoa town. The valley was soaked in a sunny silver mist, but within this bright suspension one could see flashes, gray-brown smoke blooms, helicopters, and at last the F–100s, circling above the mist, orbiting leisurely and then slicing down on the long pendulum, the flash, the plane rocketing upward.

I walked over to the military advisors' office. There were rumors, there were reports. Two ARVN battalions were fighting north of the river, engaged by an unknown number of North Vietnamese and Viet Cong. The enemy was again pulling the unusual tactic of attacking in daylight and keeping the contact going, rather than striking at night in one quick hit-and-run.

Another report. Both ARVN battalion commanders were wounded. Jeeps pulled in and out near me, men I knew headed out to the valley, but I walked back to the knoll overlooking the scene. For the moment I was content to be on this ridge far from the fighting, a man in a sports shirt, slacks, and a cast.

This day in Vietnam was the day of the autumn festival. There was a school just down the slope, across the road from where I stood, and in the late afternoon the children gathered in their best clothes to play in the yard. Each little boy and girl was given a paper-and-tinsel star, and they stood about, little children holding each other's hands, silent and awed by the pretty stars they held, admiring the strings of similar decorations festooning the schoolhouse and hung overhead in the schoolyard. Their faces reflected the hope of children, the willingness, the ability to believe in all that is best. It was the same expression seen on children's faces on Christmas morning, the same open expression one sees in the little audience at a puppet show.

Suddenly, between the children and me, an ambulance came racing, an ambulance made of a jeep with stretchers sticking out its back. Two wounded men lay in it, one man's white-bound foot with blood soaking through the bandages. The ambulance had a weird siren that gave a bleating, moaning sound.

The children stood holding each other's hands, looking after it, and the sun went down.

II

We still did not realize what had happened, that with those daylight attacks the day before election day the enemy had begun an all-out offensive in Phu Yen Province. In our these-are-isolated-incidents ignorance, I started off for the valley the next morning in another Scout, this time with Vic Hostetter, the red-haired refugee advisor who looked like a younger brother to Dan Leaty. The fighting yesterday had been in Tuy Hoa District north of the river, so we headed south of the river and into the valley on the Hieu Xuong side, to check a village where some refugees had recently settled in with friends and family.

Our drive came to an abrupt halt when we saw, just off the road ahead of us, long before our destination, an assortment of jeeps, Scouts, and soldiers. We turned in where they were gathered. For the first time we heard shooting, coming from beyond a village that was just across a meadow and partly concealed by a tree-lined road.

I looked around. Here there was an empty tin-sided warehouse and a yellow-walled cement schoolhouse. Halfway between the two buildings, under the corrugated iron roof of an unfinished shed, the whole Hieu Xuong gang was assembled: Major Kobata, Neil Miller, Sergeant Iaea, Captain Hy, and various Koreans. People were yelling in three languages over back-pack radios.

Major Kobata took me aside and gave me the usual flawless quick briefing. Two enemy companies had grabbed two hamlets along the road that ran past the far side of the rough-mown meadow. The Koreans were assuming primary responsibility for this contact, bringing men in from all over the valley.

In a minute things became surrealistic. A helicopter swept in. From it emerged a Korean major general, two silver stars twinkling from his helmet, a baton in his hand, and a carefully studied manner of bluff confidence. He received salutes, shook hands all around, looked at some maps and flew away.

Then I turned and found myself facing Mine, the Japanese photographer for UPI whom I had last seen taking pictures of the Dragoons' booty at Three Trees. He demanded to know why, when we had the best war going in the whole country for over a week now, no one had said anything about it in Saigon. Somehow he made me feel responsible for the whole thing.

I sat down and opened a can of C rations, falling back, as I easily did, on the theory that one had better eat while there was time and food available. I looked at a bag of rice lying on the ground. It said

CONNEL'S RICE
Connel Rice & Sugar Co., Inc.
San Francisco, Calif.

I stared from this to the miles of rice paddies behind me. Here was the rice bowl of Southeast Asia, with the Tuy Hoa Valley the best rice-producing area in this part of the coast, and we were importing rice. It was necessary; that was how badly the war was disrupting Vietnam.

I finished eating my C rations just as the Koreans started

moving their jeeps, radios, and maps from this exposed, open-sided shed to a point behind the yellow concrete schoolhouse. The rest of us followed suit. Soon our miniature version of an Allied General Staff, complete with an American correspondent and a Japanese photographer, was settled down in the brilliant sunshine beyond the yellow wall.

No sooner had we reached cover behind the wall of this schoolhouse than shots started snapping past its corner. Several rounds banged through the corrugated iron wall of the warehouse some forty yards away, and a squad of Korean infantry came tearing out from where they had been resting in there, moving at top speed, but lighthearted, almost laughing. They ran toward holes they had already dug, and leaped in, their M–16s at the ready.

Sergeant Hebron, the stocky black sergeant, wriggled to the corner of the schoolhouse, an M–79 grenade launcher in his hands, its cannonlike barrel waving before him like a finger admonishing the naughty enemy. He stretched out on the scrubby grass at the corner of the building, his face intent, his body wiggling as he took up his firing position like a man arranging his desk at the office. Exposing only his head and half a shoulder around the corner, he fired the projectile. It arced up in a blurred parabola. Seconds later it landed with a flash and a bang, stirring up a gray cloud two hundred yards away, a perfect shot at the hedge across the grazed field.

Captain Hy's radio came alive, and the District Chief broke into his old complaining whine to Major Kobata.

"Say, Sergeant Hebron," Kobata said as if suggesting where to plant roses in the garden, "the Vietnamese say they have some PFs along that road. Better hold it."

"Well, they've got some VC along that road too," Hebron called over his shoulder, but he held it. Some more shots cracked past. I felt a hand on my shoulder. In one of the advisors' jeeps someone had brought out a thermos can loaded with ice, and now I was offered a cold beer.

I took it, grinning. This was the elusive quality of the war in Vietnam. Bullets could be whicking past, one could have an arm in a cast, recurring jungle rot in the crotch, and be acquiring a vicious sunburn, and still have a cold beer and a fairly safe box seat at a battle.

A plane slightly larger than a FAC plane circled over us

now, and Major Kobata motioned to my red-headed companion the Refugee Advisor. The plane was a Psychological Warfare plane from Nha Trang, with an American at the controls and a Vietnamese beside him with a microphone hooked to a huge loudspeaker in the side of the plane. A column of refugees was milling about on a road off the one at which Sergeant Hebron had just fired. It was clear that the people, fleeing from a hamlet just ahead of VC, did not know in which direction to move to gain safety.

Vic and Major Kobata looked at a map, and then Vic radioed the American pilot of the circling plane to have the refugees move behind our position and then down a road which would eventually bring them to the Province's largest refugee center, near the beach. A minute later the Vietnamese in the plane, his voice magnified two hundred times, was telling the refugees to move in the direction in which the plane was flying as he spoke. The plane buzzed low over the road to make it doubly clear, and the refugees hurried along in the misty sunlight. When they came to the one intersection at which they could go wrong, the plane slipped down again, indicating the right direction as the Vietnamese voice urged them to keep moving.

"We call these 'Sheepdog Flights,'" Vic told me. I asked him a bit more about them, and it developed that he had been one of the originators of the concept.

The refugees on the road taken care of, the plane went back, somewhat higher, over the hamlets in which the enemy were, urging the people to get out if they possibly could.

Neil Miller was sitting beside me against this concrete wall, and he told me that they had recently captured documents in which the enemy command urged units to "Clutch the people to the breast." This, he said, was what we were witnessing now. The enemy troops moved into a village, allowed no one to leave, and then in effect asked us what we were going to do about it. If the Allied forces ignored it, we were admitting that the enemy could occupy any village with impunity, quite possibly murdering or kidnaping officials, and certainly taking any men of military age with them on the way out. If we attacked, there were bound to be some civilian casualties. This was just what the enemy wanted. Their theory was that the villagers would be more angry at the

attacking Allies than at them for having started the thing in
the first place.

All across the area to our front there was now a growing
ripple of small arms fire, and occasional long popping bursts
from machine guns. The Koreans had two infantry companies
trying to get into the hamlets held by the VC, and these ROK
foot soldiers were supported by armored personnel carriers,
the light topless tanks that were furnishing the machine-gun
support. The Koreans were trying to drive out the enemy
without bringing in artillery or bombers which would wreck
the houses and raise the chances of killing more civilians who
had been "clutched to the breast."

In the sunny haze a low fog of gray weapons smoke rose
from hedgerows and garden plots. The Korean battalion
commander, sitting with his staff on the ground next to us,
kept looking at a map spread on the grass, and periodically
rose to peer around the corner of the schoolhouse. His
operations officer asked questions over a radio and relayed the
answers to the Korean lieutenant colonel, who was composed
but tense.

A Korean armored personnel carrier came grinding along
the road, moving away from the battle, and turned in and
stopped thirty yards away. It lowered its back metal door and
we could see there were wounded inside. Major Kobata
grabbed his radio and asked for a medical-evacuation helicopter. Then he turned to me because I was the nearest person.

"How many are there?"

I ran toward the Korean vehicle, shouting "How many?"

A chunky Korean soldier turned toward me, uncompre-
hending, and we stared at each other across the language
barrier. I stuck up my hand, an inquiring look on my face,
and flipped up one finger, two, then three, shouting, "How
many?"

He caught on and raised five fingers. I ran back and told
Major Kobata, who told the radio that one medical evacuation
helicopter would be enough for now.

The Korean wounded were being hustled toward us.
Four did not look too bad, but the fifth they brought in a
poncho and put down two yards from me. He was shot
through the left forearm, which was blood-stained in crimson
branches, but that was not his bad wound. A bullet had gone

in the front of his stomach and come out of his back. He lay in a pool of dark arterial blood that had collected in the brown folds of the poncho, sloshing about like red wine. He was handsome, and he was crying silently, his eyes shut and his lips rigidly back from his gums. His trousers had been pulled down around his knees to permit the dark-soaked bandage to be put around his middle, and his stomach glistened with a cold sweat. Seeing the spiky tuft of pubic hair, more wiry than that of Caucasians, I found myself experiencing a strange stab of memory for a Japanese girl I once knew. The helicopter came in, we lifted the wounded aboard, and then again it was the hot sun and the clanging shots among the hedges beyond the meadow.

"I cannot wait much longer," the Korean lieutenant colonel said in English to Major Kobata. "I have lost seven men already." He was referring to making a decision to call in artillery and air strikes. Helicopter gunships were already over the hamlets, lashing in tracers and rockets.

Kobata turned toward me, the memory of the wounded Koreans fresh in our minds, and said, "I don't blame him."

I nodded. There was the problem, again. It was undoubtedly, certainly true that there were some noncombatant civilians inside these hamlets a few hundred yards away. It was equally obvious that the hail of bullets coming from those hamlets was being produced by determined, skilled fighters. The Koreans advancing upon them were tough, well-trained troops, many of them professionals. The problem was that a bullet could puncture a professional just as easily as it could cut through anyone else. It seemed to me that when any soldier was asked to advance under fire, he was entitled to the full support of whatever non-nuclear weapons his side possessed.

Another Korean armored personnel carrier came clattering up. A young Korean captain jumped out and rushed over to his battalion commander, dropping on his knees beside the map the Korean lieutenant colonel had spread out on the hot grass. The battalion commander had asked this captain of one of the two attacking companies to come back here and explain what was going on.

One needed only to look at the young Korean captain to know that plenty was going on. He was breathing hard, his face was covered with sweat and stains. Holding both palms out toward his commander, he pushed them forward and toward each other, then pulled them back as if in pain, repeating the process as he spoke in a quick, agitated voice. It was clear that he was describing rushes forward at the hedgerows surrounding the hamlet, and being repeatedly repulsed.

The lieutenant colonel smiled at his excitement and spoke to him in a soothing voice. The captain calmed down, they spoke for another two minutes, and the captain left, looking far cooler than when he came.

The next actor upon the scene was a Vietnamese FAC plane, painted a shiny brown. The pilot whizzed into the picture with remarkable *élan*, passing about sixty feet above us, leaning well out of the window of the fragile craft. He was wearing huge sunglasses, a flowing Red Baron scarf, and fatigues, and he thrust his arm toward us with a thumbs-up sign. Then this Vietnamese pilot flew right across the Viet Cong positions at treetop height and began radioing back the best information on precise enemy locations we had received all afternoon. He swung over a nearby Vietnamese Regional Forces company that was being held off to one side of the Koreans, waving them forward, and they began closing in on the hamlets from the flank. He turned, swept back over us with a reassuring smile, and asked if we didn't want some nice bombers.

No, the Korean commander decided, not yet. The Vietnamese FAC went back over the Korean troops, and then whizzed over the Viet Cong, dropping a purple smoke grenade right into one of their machine-gun positions, marking it for the ROKs to fire at. He climbed, dove at the hamlet, and fired a white phosphorus rocket at another position.

For those of us who were connoisseurs of FACing, it was a stunning, giddy performance. I forgot the cast on my arm, the rash in my crotch, the blazing sunburn on my face, as I watched this seventy-mile-an-hour crate attacking the enemy with smoke rockets whose real purpose was only to create a white cloud to mark a position. With a lot of luck this FAC might get one VC with each rocket. That he had not yet been shot down indicated that this FAC had all the luck available in Southeast Asia this afternoon. He was out in that area of experience where brave men sometimes get, where the prospect of death has been fully accepted and it will either find you doing something remarkable—or not find you.

The sun sank behind the blue hills that were pouring out more men than we had supposed they possessed. Korean reinforcements arrived to help seal the enemy in these villages, under siege for the night. We drove back toward Hieu Xuong. These days I was carrying sufficient gear with me to spend the night anywhere, so I decided to stay at Hieu Xuong.

We ate, and went toward the bunkers. I had my carbine but little ammunition, so Sergeant Iaea gave me some extra empty clips and a box of ammunition. I sat in the bunker, clumsily trying to fill a clip, painfully holding the clip with the fingers peeking out from the cast on my right arm. Several PF crowded into the bunker because a light rain was falling, and two of them began filling my clips for me.

That's decent of these fellows, I thought. The clips filled, there was still half a box of bullets left, and the PF started to walk off with them. I stopped them, and they gestured indignantly. They had helped me, now I should give them what was left over.

"Number Ten," I said. "No."

They shrugged, smiled the sweet Vietnamese smile, and started talking to me. "Tuy Hoa mama-san boom boom," one of them said with a leer, and the others laughed.

I was suddenly angry. For very good reasons they assumed that all Americans were constantly interested in fornicating, and so their idea of a pleasant exchange was to refer to Tuy Hoa women and boom boom, which was a simple enough reference to the act.

"You guys aren't so funny," I snapped. Fresh kids, I thought. "Can't you talk about anything except that?"

Even as they heard my voice, they looked bewildered and contrite. They were farm boys, part-time soldiers just trying to be friendly. "American Number One," a young PF offered. "Vietnam Number Ten."

I stared at them in the shadows cast by a flashlight among the sandbagged walls. The sad part was that these boys meant it. What they saw of American equipment, training, spirit, luxuries made them believe that American soldiers were better. And the Americans they admired would go home at the end of their year's tour and these men would still be on guard here, badly trained, pitifully paid, with a joke like Captain Hy for a commanding officer. I thought of Neil's contention that it was surprising that any of them would do anything, and muttered something conciliatory, I don't know what, and walked out of the bunker.

III

The enemy was forcing our hand. The next morning they seized a large village farther south in the valley. The Koreans moved against this one, too, but now they were getting spread thin. They needed to wind up the action around the two hamlets that had been fought around yesterday and besieged last night, in order to free the troops to meet new attacks.

So the F–100s were brought in. The ROKs had moved their command post to a point along Route One, and from this knot of wooden structures I watched as the planes whipped in and took those hamlets apart, gray-brown dust rising from behind the trees, the fires from thatched roofs rising in sad straight columns.

A jeep rolled into this yard. In its back, hands clasped behind his bare head, was an erect man in a dirty sand-colored uniform. I had not seen the North Vietnamese uniform since Three Trees, and I watched with interest as he was led into a back room that had a blanket stretched across its doorway. I had heard that the Koreans were cruel in their interrogation of prisoners, and had no reason to doubt it. I waited for unpleasant sounds. After a while I peeked through the back window. They were all talking, two Koreans telling a Korean interpreter what questions to ask in Vietnamese and the North Vietnamese answering. There was certainly no torture going on, and plenty of talking. The North Vietnamese was singing like a canary.

In the midst of all this, I caught glimpses of some of the American civilians driving along Route One in their Scouts, unarmed men more or less ducking between embattled areas,

trying to carry forward such programs as classroom construction and preventive medicine while the valley was going up in
flames.

Neil Miller pulled over to the side of the road in a
pick-up truck and asked me if I wanted to go with him to the
province warehouses. Since all I was seeing from where I
stood at the ROK command post were dismal funeral pyres of
hamlets to the north of me and a village to the south, I went
along.

At first glance, the two pale-yellow province warehouses
looked pretty good. Their loading platforms were just a few
yards off Route One on the northern edge of Tuy Hoa town,
and the buildings were solid and well-kept.

The trouble began when we tried to accomplish something. Neil wanted to load this pick-up truck with some
emergency supplies, mainly food, for the people in the two
hamlets that had been bombed this morning. The hamlets
were still besieged, but he wanted to get these supplies in to
the people as soon as the action stopped.

The Vietnamese civilian who ran the warehouse was
polite but noncommittal. He stood with us in the dusty
sunshine just inside the warehouse door, staring at a sheaf of
tissue-thin papers in his hand, describing some technicality in
paperwork that made it impossible for him to release these
goods at the moment.

I stared at the dim mountains of crates and boxes in the
cool interior. Everything in here had come from the United
States, some of it as direct government aid paid for by the
taxpayers and some of it through charities, the donations of
Americans. Whether in favor of prosecuting the war, or
dead-set against it, the one thing every American would want
to have happen would be for these goods to be used, right
now, to alleviate the suffering of some people whose hamlets
were being fought over and through.

Neil said he would wait, and sat down in such a way that
it was clear that he would wait indefinitely, wait all day, wait
all night, wait until his presence became odd and a source of
embarrassment and possible loss of face for the warehouse
manager. This presented a new problem to the warehouse
manager, one that he obviously took more seriously than the

plight of some farm families in a hamlet out the valley. He said he would see what he could do. Neil said that would be fine.

I wandered out in the sunshine. A pale-blue van from Saigon was being unloaded, and a bright-looking boy about nineteen years old was standing by its front fender, taking no part in the work. He looked bored. A fresh breeze was blowing from the valley, and distant ripples of gunfire could be heard. There were now three separate battles going at once.

"Hello," the boy said, and that one word, rather than "Number One" or "Give me ten P," indicated that the boy really knew some English. He did indeed. He was a medical student at the University of Saigon, and his brother, a big man wearing sunglasses and a plastic-composition fedora, was the driver of this truck. This boy was on vacation, and he was spending his time driving about the country with his brother, seeing parts of Vietnam he had never seen. On this trip, he told me, they had been stopped five times by the Viet Cong, in daylight, and were forced to give a "toll tax" contribution of money before being allowed to proceed on their way. He and his brother always reached a town by nightfall, and drove only during the daylight hours.

I thought about that, being stopped five times in daylight between Saigon and here. Total Allied forces in Vietnam, when one included all the militia, came to more than a million troops, and we still could not secure the two hundred and forty miles of Route One from here to Saigon. Despite FAC planes, helicopters, armored personnel carriers sweeping the road, the VC had stopped this truck five times on the way here, in broad daylight, stopping traffic just like a toll station. I looked at the boy with interest. To him the VC were something more than a shadowy reality. He had seen their faces, the weapons in their hands, five times in the past few days.

Neil came over, still waiting, and talked with the student in Vietnamese. When Neil walked off the boy gazed at him with admiration and said, "I never heard an American speak such good Vietnamese." We talked some more, and I asked him what his own views were on the situation in Vietnam.

"Students do not like the VC, of course," he said. "But

we also do not like the Government." He added that the election had been unfair, not citing any examples, and said that Ky "is not serious." He added that farmers did not like the Americans "acting like their father in the villages."

All this time he was speaking against a background of rolling gunfire, and I thought of the nonintellectual Vietnamese troops out there in the valley, fighting. I told the student that I thought he was indulging in a rather expensive luxury, debating the pros and cons of the two sides, since I thought he would really dislike what would happen if the Viet Cong and North Vietnamese won.

He nodded, as if this were about what he expected me to say. He acted as if the gunfire were a distant thunderstorm, an act of nature unrelated to him or his life. He said that as a student he was deferred from the draft, and that in two or three years more he would be a doctor.

I asked him what he would do when he became a doctor. About this he seemed unclear. He did not mention going to Paris, as so many Vietnamese doctors did, but he said nothing about working to bind up the wounds of his people.

He spoke briefly of his father, who had died years before. "He fought against the French all his life," he said. His mother was dead, and he lived with his forty-year-old unmarried sister, who was a schoolteacher in Saigon.

"She has sacrificed her life for me," he said with some feeling.

Neil emerged from the warehouse, smiling, a slip of paper in his hand. I said good-bye to the student, and, with a couple of Vietnamese warehouse employees, Neil and I began loading the panel truck. My cast rendered me somewhat useless, but with my left hand I was able to move some cartons around in the truck, once they were lifted over its low sides. This was Neil's ammunition in his side of the war, and we loaded on twenty bags of corn meal, twenty cases of powdered milk, two boxes of paper blankets, two bales of mosquito netting, and a case of candles. The *pièce de résistance* was a bale of old American clothes from CARE, faded but clean, including women's dresses. In the sunshine, under the palm trees, I blinked as I saw a woman's heavy cloth coat with a fur collar. That would be something new in women's styles in Phu Yen.

*   *   *

We took the loaded panel truck out to Hieu Xuong. Since the truck did not belong to the Hieu Xuong team, and since the fighting was continuing in the hamlets for which these supplies were intended, we had to unload the truck and deposit the supplies overnight at the district warehouse, opposite the advisors' compound.

Neil backed up the truck, uncoiled from behind the wheel, and went up to the Vietnamese militiaman in charge of the warehouse. He explained in Vietnamese what the goods were for, and that we would have to leave them here until the fighting was over. Could he please help us unload the stuff?

The man shook his head. He slid open the warehouse door, indicating that the interior was ours to whatever extent we wished to fill it, and sat again on a crate against the wall, his face blank. Neil asked him again, in Vietnamese, politely, if he would help us, and again the man shook his head.

"This is for your own people!" Neil said loudly in English, and repeated it in Vietnamese. The man turned away. Some farmers out in the valley were not his people. His village was here.

The next morning the siege of the two bombed hamlets ended. It was Captain Hy who told me of it. Speaking his nervous, stilted English, he said that by last night the Koreans had encircled the two hamlets with a total of seven companies, determined to kill or capture what was left of the two enemy companies. When they went into the hamlets this morning, they found that the enemy had slipped out during the night.

As he told me this, Captain Hy's expression was an odd one. On the one hand, he disliked the enemy's escaping, because it meant that they would be giving him trouble in the future. On the other hand, it demonstrated that the Koreans were not supermen, and he rather enjoyed pointing this out to me through this example. Beneath it all, I had the feeling that even those Vietnamese who stood the most to gain from an Allied victory could not resist a feeling of admiration when they saw their guerrilla countrymen surviving the attacks of these powerful foreign armies. It reminded me of the un-

doubtedly loyal American citizens, third-generation Chinese
in San Francisco, who at the time of the Korean War could
not help but be proud that China was able to fight the United
States to a standstill.

Vic Hostetter rolled into the Hieu Xuong compound, and
after an hour he and Neil and I had the goods from the
warehouse loaded into two International Scouts. Then we
drove out the valley road to the nearer of the two hamlets that
had been bombed the day before. We got out of our vehicles
and walked into what had been a hamlet.

It was not a good scene. The first house I saw consisted
of a concrete floor and part of a charred doorframe. Further
along, women were sweeping ashes from their concrete
living-room floors as if oblivious of the fact that there were
no walls and no ceiling. People squatted in the cinders of
their homes, eating rice and drinking tea under the sky.

A large group of villagers was clustered about one
house, helping to dig possessions out of the rubble. As we
approached, three unarmed American civilians, I had a tight
feeling in my stomach, wondering if they were going to tear
our eyes out. I would not have blamed them.

They were quiet, dull, undemonstrative. Their clothes
appeared cleaner than I would have thought possible, considering what they had been through. Neil and Vic greeted them
in Vietnamese, and the farmers replied politely. Neil explained
what we had brought, and they nodded, agreeing that this was
the kind of thing they needed now. It was as if we were all
discussing an act of nature that had occurred, rather than
deliberate human violence and counterviolence. After a few
more minutes I found myself convinced that this really was
the way these farmers thought of it. It was simply that their
experience of acts of nature had been forcibly expanded, and
that in addition to lightning, fire in the dry season and floods
in the monsoon season, now violence was heaped on them by
men in black pajamas and men in brown helicopters.

Neil drew them out a bit on what had happened, trying
to see if they understood the sequence of events. They
understood. The North Vietnamese and Viet Cong had entered
the village and started shooting out of it. Just as they had
expected, people outside the village started shooting back at

the North Vietnamese and Viet Cong. They seemed to bear us no ill-will, and what feelings they had left were bent upon the reconstruction of these shattered houses.

A group of them came with us to the road to help unload the supplies. Passing a brick-rimmed well at a corner of a cement threshing terrace, I noticed what they were using as a bucket. Dangling from a rope at the end of the long balanced pole used to lower it was the silver nose cone of a napalm bomb. It made a good bucket, and must have been picked up from earlier actions in the valley. I shook my head, feeling the whole world of sometime reality lurching about me, and walked on.

That evening at Hieu Xuong all the threats were present again. Captain Hy was waving his hands at Major Kobata, telling him of a just-received intelligence report that "many, many VC" were in the area.

It was late to get help. The sun was down, the light was fading from the sky. Tonight there would be no Duster with its twin 40-millimeter cannon, no quad-fifties. I had drunk a couple of beers from the refrigerator in the team's living room, and now I had another. After the day in the sun, the general pace of sleepless nights and upsetting sights, I felt light-headed and sick. I climbed up on the bunker that had the Buddha sitting on the parapet, a helmet on my head, a white towel around my neck. All year I had been meticulous about turning out in either totally civilian or totally military dress, but now I was military at top and bottom, helmet and jungle boots, with a dirty sports shirt and slacks in between, carrying my carbine and wearing a web belt with my big Browning and little Colt.

A hand touched my shoulder. A PF beside me was pointing insistently at the white towel around my neck, gesturing eloquently that it could be seen at a distance and made a perfect target for a sniper. He was right, of course, but I muttered ungraciously as I removed it. I had no idea what I was doing with a white towel around my neck in the first place.

Darkness came, with a few glittering stars. I left my pistol belt and climbed down from the bunker to use the latrine, and when I struggled back up, my arm itching in its cast, I saw that the PF had my little Colt in his hand. He was pointing it out into the night, fascinated by such a small weapon, and was gesturing with it as if firing, saying in a low voice, "bang, bang."

I was angry at the sight of someone with my pistol, but I took it back from him with a weak smile and then began looking for the holster from which he must have drawn it. It was not on my folded-up pistol belt. I held up the bigger holster for the Browning, pointed at it, and asked, "Same same?" This pidgin phrase was universally understood in Vietnam, meaning "Where is something like this?" The man looked blank and I gestured again, pointing at the big holster, then at the small pistol, gesturing with the small pistol as if slipping into a holster. He shrugged his shoulders and looked at me as if I were not quite bright.

It was one too many shrugs from a Vietnamese. Suddenly I was cuffing him about the shoulders with my good hand, saying "Same same, goddammit, where is it?"

He recoiled and leaped off the bunker. A moment later three of them were looking up at me as if I were a strange beast outlined against the sky. I cursed again and crawled about the sand-bagged bunker roof in the dark, my good hand feeling everywhere for the holster. Finally I found it lying in a fold where a sandbag met the front parapet, and placed my little pistol in it, as close to tears as I had been in Vietnam. I was breathing hard, and I had no idea of whether I had placed the holster there myself and left the little gun on the parapet apart from it, or what.

After a few minutes the same PF climbed back up on the bunker and took a position as far away from me as he could, doing his job, looking out at the night with his carbine at the ready. I was ashamed by now, and held the holster up to him, showing him what I had been looking for.

"Same same," he said in a low, wondering voice. It was clear now that he had not known what "same same" meant, that he had had no idea of what had been troubling me. "Same same," he repeated, soft in the night, as if memorizing the words.

I choked. *"Sinh loi,"* I said. "Sorry."

On and off that night I slept, lying on the bunker, the Buddha sitting atop the parapet a couple of feet above me.

Someone put a helmet on the Buddha's head. There were mosquitoes, and my arm itched in the cast. From time to time I heard the PF moving about, whispering a few words, and then it was first light in the sky above where I lay flat on my back, the stars receding through a few racing grey clouds as a rainy day began. Later I was told that at midnight a long burst of automatic fire had passed just over the Buddha's head, tracer bullets searching out what they must have thought was the helmeted head of a soldier. None of it had awakened me.

IV

I took my shameful performance with the PF as a warning sign, the closest thing I had yet shown to anything approaching combat fatigue, or nerves, or loss of control. I decided to leave Hieu Xuong for a while and set up shop with the advisors behind Colonel Ba's house, and the next evening found me drinking beer at the officers' bar in the military compound along the beach.

There was some pretty candid talk going on in the bar. The enemy offensive was not gaining its objective, which was to hand the government a really sweeping defeat, but the VC was raising hell all over the province in every conceivable way, mining roads, shooting from ambush, terrorist grenades, and this damned "clutch the people to the breast." We had never supposed that he could mount an offensive and keep it going at such a pitch, day after day, lacking nothing in the way of men and ammunition and supplies. It was in a sense the Vietnam War in microcosm—his Sunday punch was not enough to knock us out, but our steady heavy punching was not putting him away either. He was failing to topple the government, and we were failing to get at his roots.

"When I came out here," a young major confided to me this night at the bar, "I was determined to win the war in my district during the year it was my district. Now I'd be the first to say that I haven't won the war in my district." He paused, looking down at his drink. "The VC have kept every promise they've made. Every time they've threatened to destroy something, eventually they've done it."

I looked out the screen window. Flares hung everywhere

in the night sky, and all of us were wondering how long the enemy could keep up this offensive.

"You're going to see something around here you haven't seen for a while," another officer said to me. I thought that one over, and realized what it had to mean. American units were being brought back into Phu Yen to stem the offensive.

At the briefing the next morning, Colonel Ba was a worried man. The big wall map of the Province was covered with a transparent overlay showing all sorts of flags for enemy units that were in the vicinity.

"We must ask for more help," Colonel Ba said, turning to Al Cade and Dan Leaty. His querulous voice made it clear that he meant American units.

Dan and Al nodded sympathetically but noncommittally, and I suppressed a smile. For a year I had been exposed to Vietnamese poker faces, and now Al and Dan, both knowing that American units were already on the way, were looking sympathetically at Colonel Ba and murmuring that they'd look into the matter and see if anything could be done.

I walked out of the briefing with Vic Hostetter. We picked up an interpreter and headed down the road to town in Vic's Scout. The first thing we saw was a line of vehicles from the 173rd Airborne Brigade, American paratroopers who had been unloading from transports at the air base since dawn.

Vic and I rolled up the coastal road, leaving thoughts of paratroops and reinforcements behind, and went on through the town of Tuy An. As we drove, Vic explained that we were going to a refugee center that had been established a few months before. He was worried about it. The American advisors I had met up here were good, and the Vietnamese first lieutenant who was the District Chief was exemplary, but there was another factor, the Vietnamese civilian who was the Assistant District Chief.

"Mister Tau." Vic spoke the man's name thoughtfully as we bumped across a temporary bridge. Mr. Tau, Vic told me, had been caught transporting two hundred bags of bulgar wheat from Tuy An to Tuy Hoa with the intention of selling this American aid shipment for his own profit. The case had been reported to Colonel Ba but nothing had yet happened.

The trouble, Vic explained, was that it was Mr. Tau who was responsible for making this refugee reception center livable. He had been given the funds and authority that should make it possible, and Vic wanted to go to the camp now, before checking in with Mr. Tau, and see how it was coming along.

We hit another bump, and the young interpreter muttered from where he was slumped in the back seat. He was a Saigon University graduate, and, although I was sure that he understood everything that we were saying, he appeared drowsy and not much interested.

The camp was located on one of the bare headlands characteristic of the coast at Tuy An. A fresh sea breeze reached us as we got out of the Scout, but this healthy salt-smelling air was balanced by a broiling sun and the lack of shade trees. We began walking among the cinder-block houses, tin-roofed, which comprised the camp. It was a dismal scene, children playing in rubble and old people squatting before whichever walls cast a shadow at this hour.

As we moved along, Vic not needing the interpreter as he asked simple questions of the people, his voice took on a quiet controlled anger as he pointed out the things he had been told were done and which were clearly nowhere near completion. Cement floors were supposed to have been poured in all these low one-story houses, and few had been. Some had not yet been roofed, and there was not a window or a door installed in the entire place. Seventeen hundred people were living here. The plan called for twenty-four latrines, and not one latrine had been built. The camp population defecated in the bushes down the slope from the camp or while they were foraging for sticks of wood in the neighboring scrubby ravines. Refugee camp sites inevitably received the land which was not being used for residence or farming by the farmers who had been here before the population upheavals, and the nearest natural spring was one and a fifth miles away. Wells were supposed to have been dug, admittedly a hard task on a hilltop, but no efforts had been made to sink a shaft. The water for seventeen hundred people was brought back from the spring by the refugees, some of whom we saw toiling up the hill carrying water in old kerosene cans balanced from each end of wooden poles.

"Not one thing has been done here in the last month," Vic said in a low tone. He went on to say that security here was minimal, and that the VC had come in a week before, pulled two old women out of a house, and made them kneel down. They had shot them through the back of the neck, leaving their bodies for sunrise as an advertisement to the population of the VC wish that they leave government territory and join them in the hills.

As we came out of this brilliantly sunlit and breezy nightmare village, we saw our first signs of government activity. Two big ARVN trucks had pulled up and were unloading sand to be used in making concrete for more houses. Vic and the interpreter went up to the driver of one of the trucks and began talking with him.

The driver, who might be hauling sand today and ammunition tomorrow, did not at all mind answering Vic's questions. He said that he had brought this load from Tuy Hoa. He was not being paid anything extra to do this, he said, looking a bit wistful, as if he certainly could have made a little profit somewhere if it had only been bags of rice or something which he could have sold a bit of on the way. For sand, however, there was no market.

Who *did* get paid, Vic wanted to know. The driver replied cheerfully that the ARVN was getting seven hundred piastres a load from Mr. Tau.

And how, Vic asked, was Mr. Tau getting the seven hundred piastres to pay for this? That was easy. Tau sold the ARVN four bags of bulgar wheat, which were not his to sell, at two hundred and fifty piastres a bag. Then, with the thousand profit, he paid the ARVN seven hundred, and pocketed the three hundred piastres difference on each load of sand.

We got into the Scout. I glanced at the interpreter, wondering how he was reacting to the absolutely marginal living conditions we had just seen, and the explanation of graft. As on the ride up, he appeared sleepy and indifferent, as if all this had no relation to him, and I supposed that this was just the way he felt.

We rolled down into the town of Tuy An, past the district warehouse, and went into Mr. Tau's office. He was a pleasant-looking little man in his thirties, who rose, offered us a seat, and produced cups of lukewarm green tea. It was clear that he thought we had just driven straight up from Tuy Hoa.

We chatted in English about a variety of inconsequential subjects, and then Vic asked innocently: "How is the refugee reception center coming?"

"It's finished," Tau said promptly. He added that it had cost more than the budget for it, because he had to pay civilian trucking contractors in Tuy Hoa to haul loads of sand for concrete.

Vic received this lie with a straight face, looking like the red-haired All-American boy while he led Tau into other lies concerning the camp. I felt my face go crimson. We had just seen the ARVN trucks carrying sand, and learned that Tau was making three hundred piastres personal profit on each load. Now he was evidently going to put in for additional sums for hauling by Vietnamese civilian trucks, hauling that had never been done, and pocket that, too. In the meantime the people out there were defecating in the bushes, sleeping on dirt floors, and making a two-and-a-half-mile round trip for water.

"We have just been there, Mister Tau," Vic said in the same smooth voice.

Tau started, turned to our Vietnamese interpreter, and began berating him for not letting him know this.

Vic went through the catechism again. Now about the wells. Annoyed explanation in Vietnamese, duly translated by the interpreter. About the latrines. More of the same high-pitched, irritable tone.

Suddenly the interpreter started saying something quickly to Tau, in a tone of contempt. Tau switched back into English and told Vic that it had all been difficult, very, very difficult.

Vic asked when we could expect some improvement.

It would all be done next month. All of it.

"That's what you said last month," Vic replied, his voice still thoroughly self-possessed. He rose and we walked out to the Scout. As we drove out of the compound I told Vic that the man should be put in jail.

The interpreter said from the back seat, "Not in jail." For the first time today he was wide awake. Not in jail. Jail would be too much. I gave the interpreter a lecture about the duty of public officials to do something for the public. He nodded and said that things were a little different in Vietnam. This man was bad, yes, but jail—his face, his tone suggested that gentlemen really did not discuss such ideas, nor even think them.

I turned my face forward. Slowly, his voice like iron, Vic explained to me that this was the problem of being an advisor. He would report this, in detail, but it was up to the Vietnamese to reprimand, to punish, to transfer their own officials. He had no direct power. The only thing that he could do was to withhold commodities, and who would that hurt? It would only hurt those people on that hill.

TWENTY-SEVEN

The ARVN was having an awards ceremony at the soccer field near the center of town, and I rode down there with Joel Fischman, who was the United States Information Service officer for the province, having responsibilities ranging from psychological warfare leaflets to the giving of prizes for English essay contests in high schools.

It was a cool, brilliantly sunlit September morning, and Joel and I were the only non-Vietnamese in the throng around the edges of the burnt grassy expanse. The mood was festive. Since the arrival of the 173rd Airborne Brigade the North Vietnamese and Viet Cong had slipped away, and their month-long offensive seemed to be over.

This was an all-Vietnamese ceremony this morning, and with good reason. The 47th ARVN had killed more of the enemy the past month than the Koreans had. They had two of their three battalion commanders in the hospital with wounds, and today they were presenting forty-one officers and men with the Vietnamese Cross of Gallantry.

All the province officials, civilian and military, were sitting on chairs in a raised covered platform at one side of the field. Joel and I, both dressed in sports shirts and slacks, were planning to stand in the crowd near this platform, but Colonel Ba saw us, came out of the stand, shook hands, asked me how my wrist was coming in its cast, and invited us to sit near him. We settled down among the Vietnamese officials, who were awaiting the ceremony with a boyish pride and anticipation.

At ten on the dot two companies of ARVN marched onto the field. In my entire year at the war I had never seen so much as two men of any nationality marching in step, and I had seen more of the ragged-moving militia than the ARVN. I enjoyed this picture of two parallel columns, each of a hundred and forty men, all wearing exactly the same combat uniform with camouflage nets over their helmets, not a man out of step.

A ripple of applause came from the crowd. The troops halted as one man, and I looked at their World War II weapons which had repelled the North Vietnamese with their AK–47s and rocket launchers, and again I had that strange sometime feeling: maybe they can do it, maybe we can pull it off somehow after all.

A dozen trumpeters appeared, wearing helmets, with crimson scarves at their throats and bright embroidered banners hanging from their golden horns. They tipped up their trumpets, banners flapping in the cool wind, and played a quick, stirring flourish that had come down to them from the French. From behind the grandstand a double file of soldiers appeared, marching smartly. These were the men to be decorated, and they came to a halt twenty yards before us. I stared at the tough faces under the helmets, noting how many of them were sergeants. Half a dozen among the others were just boys, their M–1 rifles almost as tall as they.

The regimental colonel appeared, moving with the willow walk of a man who had never bent in a rice paddy. The adjutant, standing beside him, raised his soft hands and read the citation for gallantry, naming the dates and places where the fighting had occurred. The colonel moved down the line of men, followed by an officer

AK-47

carrying a scarlet velvet pillow on which the medals lay. Pivoting sharply before each man, the colonel stood before him as they exchanged salutes and the man snapped out his name and rank. The colonel spoke a few words to each man as he pinned on the medal. He paused longest before a squat old sergeant, then smiled and talked for a few seconds to a boy who was standing tiptoe in rigid eagerness as he nodded and answered.

The medals were distributed, and the colonel returned to the stand. I thought that this was the end, but now a double file of high school girls from Tuy Hoa appeared. They were all dressed in white *ao dai*, and each carried a hoop of flowers. As they advanced upon the double line of helmeted green-clad men there was a tide of murmuring and giggling from the younger high school girls around the edge of the field. The two lines of long-skirted girls, moving gracefully and blushing, came to a halt before the soldiers, a girl before each man. A few moments passed, the girls smiling while the soldiers, their faces a bit pink, maintained their military bearing.

In the center of the line there was a tall, broad-shouldered young lieutenant. The girl opposite him was a beauty, tall too, her hair a long black waterfall down her white-clad, slim-waisted back. They stared at each other, quite taken. On a signal, the girls advanced and placed the hoops of flowers over the soldiers' helmeted heads. Then the girls retreated quickly, gliding across the grass, leaving the soldiers standing there in the sunshine, flowers around their necks and their medals on their chests.

That afternoon the soccer field was put to its normal use. The team representing the National Police played a team from the Korean Army. The very fact that such a game could be held indicated at least a slight improvement in relations between the Koreans and the Vietnamese. I had seen documents that convinced me that the Koreans had killed a total of four hundred unarmed Vietnamese civilians while moving through four hamlets in Hieu Xuong District on an operation in February 1966. These documents had also convinced me that men of the original Korean contingents had frequently raped Vietnamese women. The Koreans had reversed this

rend of rape by executing some of the soldiers guilty of these
offenses and by an indoctrination of the men who arrived to
replace those rotating out of Vietnam and back to Korea at
the end of the first year.

Now the bigger, stocky Koreans raced up and down the
cool sunlit field, their red jerseys accentuating their size in
contrast to the white-clad Vietnamese, who were slender,
fast, and clever.

Standing in the big crowd of Vietnamese, perhaps twice
the number that had turned out to see the award of medals this
morning, staring at these healthy, happy Korean soccer players,
I found myself seeing through these red jerseys and sunburned
grass to the valley, the Korean troops sweeping into a village
like hunting dogs and the thatched roofs blazing. I sometimes
wondered if it were not because they came from a land with
so pitifully few trees, so little wood, that the Koreans became
pyromaniacs here.

The game ended, fortunately, in a tie. As the crowd
broke up, I saw a little Vietnamese girl, lost and crying. I
stood beside her for a few minutes as people walked past,
people who spoke her own language and were heedless of the
situation. Eventually I walked away, the sound of her weeping
still in my ears. I realized that I had reached a point where I
was unmoved by seeing corpses, but upset about a lost child
who would certainly be found by her family as the crowd
thinned.

It was a day involving children. Darkness came, and
with it a beating rain. Half a dozen of us were sitting drinking
beer in one of the civilian advisors' rooms when Neil Miller
opened the door. His hooded black rain jacket streamed water
on the floor as his long face, so quick to flash a smile when
there was reason, now seemed numb as he spoke.

In a hollow voice he said that the daughter of his PF jeep
driver at Hieu Xuong had become sick the night before, had
been taken to the Province Hospital, and now there was word
that she had died. The problem was that no one could
produce the child's body. There was a possibility that she had
been taken to the Army hospital down the beach, but he and
the distraught father had just been down there, and there was
no record of her there. Did any of us know anything about it?

None of us did. Neil closed the door and went back out in the rain to where the driver was sitting in a jeep.

II

I came out of the advisors' mess hall after the next day's lunch and saw up the coast the biggest column of black smoke I had seen in Vietnam. It was boiling into the sky, soaring past the white clouds, and I climbed atop a nearby bunker and saw gold-based, red-topped flames thrusting the thick-ribbed smoke away from the earth. As I watched, a dive bomber, at this distance just a hurtling speck, slid down the sky and was lost in the smoke. More planes appeared in zipping circles like bees over honey.

I went on about my errands around the compound, but every time I looked up I saw smoke spreading out like a huge black tree filling the sky. At last I had seen something that dwarfed Cheop Chai.

Two days later I managed to get in there. Vic Hostetter took me on one of his endless runs of bringing supplies to refugees. The village was called Wah Dah, and was classified as an Ap Doi Moi, meaning that it was considered as thoroughly pacified, stable, and progressive. At the same time that I was watching the ARVN receive their medals, at the same time the Koreans and Vietnamese were playing soccer, at a time when all of us thought the enemy were evaporating to avoid the American paratroop reinforcements, two companies of North Vietnamese were slipping into this village north of Tuy Hoa.

It had been the same sad story I had witnessed in the valley. The enemy was playing "clutch the people to the breast." The Koreans tried to get in with ground troops only, finally asked for our F–100s, and bombs fell in abundance. When it was over there were one hundred and seventy bodies in the ashes. One hundred and ten were said to be North Vietnamese, sixty of them villagers, but how they could really be sure about that was beyond me.

The scene was one of greater devastation than anything I had witnessed in Vietnam. Slowly Vic and I drove for a half-mile among knots of house foundations barely visible among the ashes. There were trees everywhere, but for one half-mile I did not see a green leaf. Everything was black.

The miracle was the people. Somehow the great majority of them had lived through it, some escaping from the village at the outset and others cowering in improvised bomb shelters. They were coming back in now, visiting back and forth among the ruins of their houses, cooking in what was left of their kitchens.

Vic asked me if I had seen enough. More than enough, I said.

III

The following night I was back at the air base, back in my own hooch with its good shower, catching up with my mail and letting the war take care of itself for a while.

It seemed as if the advisory effort dogged my steps now. No sooner had I gone into the bar with the nude in her place on the mirror, intending to catch up with my pilot friends, than I turned and saw Al Cade and Major Kobata. They seldom took hours off from their respective posts as senior military advisor in the province and senior man at Hieu Xuong, but tonight the air-base club was serving good steaks secured from Navy supplies at Danang, and they wanted a well-deserved break from their usual food.

Kobata was a man always under control, but tonight he was excited. Just this morning he had been on an operation in the valley. There had been a firefight across a rocky streambed, and the Viet Cong had broken off the contact and pulled back. He and a militia force had been scrambling after them across the stream bed when a man in black pajamas had risen from the bushes. The man held up one hand as if surrendering. He was bleeding, but his other hand produced a pistol and started to lift it at the men closing in on him. The militia had opened up and killed him.

The man had turned out to be Captain Quy, the commander of Viet Cong Company 377. This was the man whose picture I had seen Kobata showing to the free-lance warrior who wanted to try to kill him and get the reward. Instead, the man of whom Kobata had said "and in all fairness, considering what he has done to us, he is an outstanding command-

er" had met his end on one of Vietnam's ten thousand tiny
battlefields, pulling a ruse to see if he could kill one more
government soldier before he died.

Kobata's expression was sober as he told me what had
happened next. The body had been carried back by the
militia, and the Americans had not further concerned themselves with what would happen to the remains of Captain
Quy. I am certain that Kobata would have been present and
ready to salute if his year-long enemy had been given a
military funeral but the Vietnamese had other plans. They tied
Quy's body to a post beside Route One near the district
headquarters, and spread the word that it was there. The
widows of slain militiamen began appearing. They tore the
black pajamas from his body, they cursed him, they stubbed
out cigarettes on his skin. The crowd grew larger, and
someone tried with only partial success to char his body with
flaming gasoline.

It was a horrid story, but true. It deserved, I felt, to be
balanced against the notion that the Viet Cong leaders were
invariably popular heroes. All afternoon, I was told, hundreds
of people had passed by, not a few of them going out of their
way to spit on the remains. The Americans were asking
Captain Hy to stop it, to cut it down and bury it, but the body
had still been there at sunset.

"He used to be a Robin Hood," Al Cade said softly, his
black face thoughtful, "but not any more."

I sat on a stool beside Al and spoke about the Viet Cong,
remarking that I had yet to see that they had received from
the people any genuine mandate to take power and to rule. I
spoke of their exploitation of people, and I saw a sad smile on
Al's face.

"You know what I'm thinking," he said in a way that
hovered between a question and a statement.

Exploitation. His mind was back in the country from
which we both had come.

"Of course," I answered.

"You know," he said, "the reason I'm willing to fight
for the United States is not for what it is now, but for what it
will be, for what I see it becoming. That's where my family
is. I'll fight for what it'll be for my kids, and their kids."

That was all he had to say, after my knowing him for months, and I had the sense to nod and shut up.

I was standing on a hilltop, wearing a sports shirt and slacks. I had none of my weapons with me. It was a bare hilltop, and over its crest rose a hundred Viet Cong, some dressed in gray, some with floppy black hats and some in black pajamas and some in khaki shirts, all of them armed and coming for me and I had not a chance in the world.

I was rigid upright in bed. Sweat covered me. I was in my bed at the air base, and the air conditioner high on the wall of the hooch hummed soothingly. In the distance artillery thudded in the valley.

TWENTY-EIGHT

I hit Saigon moving at full recreational tilt. For about seven minutes, the first evening looked as if it might be quiet unless I did something definite about it. Then I felt a hand on my shoulder as I sat on the terrace of the Continental-Palace. It was an advisor who was heading back to Tuy Hoa the next morning. Wearing civilian clothes, this major was on the last night of a brief leave, and we went to work on several bottles of beer just to loosen up. An American civilian contractor he knew joined us, a big man with a soft voice and a great thirst.

Giving too little attention to food, we began moving through the bars in the area. All year I had avoided most of these clip joints, remembering from Japan, where they did these things better, that one could spend a lot of money for very little female companionship. But it was a cool October night, Kelly Smith was gone from Vietnam, and the three of us American men were in one of those moods—each of us thought the other a prince of a fellow, each of us had important things to say and to hear; life might be short and there were things to be remembered and forgotten.

All this led to a bar called Eve, in which I had last set foot in January 1965, on my first trip to Vietnam. At that time an average evening found no more than twenty American officers there, dancing decorously with the fifteen young and pretty bar girls. I had fancied a demure young Chinese girl named Helen, and a beer had cost about sixty cents.

Helen was gone. No one remembered her. The dance floor was gone, too, to make way for an additional score of tables at which sergeants and sailors and pilots sat talking to the hundred harder girls of the Class of 1967. I stood at the bar, buying drinks for a little tigress wearing a gauzy blue *ao dai*. She perched on a bar stool, delighted by the speed with which I consumed the bottles of beer which now cost a dollar and a quarter. Each time I wanted another beer she broke off her sweet-toned broken English and screamed the order in a snarling tone to a bartender who would at the same time produce for her a more expensive glass of tinted water known to the Americans as Saigon Tea. She was given a small plastic chip with each glass, which at the end of the evening she would redeem for cash.

I was being taken, knew it, and did not care. I had forty dollars in my pocket, some of it in piasters and some in military scrip, and it became a race to see whether she could relieve me of it faster than I intended to spend it. She found me a model patron. When sweat broke on my face in the hot and smoky bar she lifted the gauzy front panel of her long blue skirt and used it to wipe the drops from my brow. It was a quarter to ten, then ten-fifteen, then a quarter to eleven, and the bar was frantic with last-minute drinking and arrangements before Saigon's eleven-o'clock curfew. Girls were propositioned; people were leaving. My major friend from Tuy Hoa wanted to get moving.

"Nobody's going to check your papers if you're walking on the streets a few minutes past eleven," I told him in my best man-of-the-world foreign correspondent tone. "They never check."

He muttered something about how he could just get back to his hotel before eleven o'clock if he started now, but he stayed.

The witching hour struck, the little tigress vanished in a whirl of blue skirts and long black hair, and the three of us walked out of the door at two minutes past eleven, right into the arms of two MPs. The American civilian and I produced credentials showing that we were not under their jurisdiction, and my major friend, his face a mixture of anger and amusement, was reconciled to the fact that a report on his sin would be sent to his superior in Tuy Hoa, who would tear it up.

We parted under a chestnut tree and I started walking along the sidewalk, back to my hotel. The night was cool, my walk was a bit unsteady, and I thought the world a fine place.

Something made a swipe at my left arm, and a finger caught at the expandable metal wrist band of my watch. The finger slipped away, having just missed pulling off the watch, and what had been coasting up behind me with its motor off, a motor scooter with two teen-aged Vietnamese sitting one behind the other, now roared to life and bounced off the sidewalk onto the street, speeding into darkness. With the cast hampering my right arm and an expandable band on my left, I must have looked the perfect target. I thought of what a decrepit watch it was—traded to an RF for a worse one, that day out in the valley, and through all sorts of beatings since. It was hardly worth their while. But the incident sent me walking on swiftly, glad that they had been after my watch and not my life.

II

Columns of Buddhist monks had been marching through Saigon in the past few days. One afternoon I caught a glimpse of them—shaved-headed men in dull orange robes, tramping up dust in cool sunshine as they marched back to their pagodas. No one knew exactly what the Buddhists wanted, but they were marching, gathering, listening to speeches by other monks wearing saffron or light gray. They were protesting the election, protesting the government, nonviolently agitating for a greater voice in national affairs.

Now, on a gray rainy morning, martial law was declared. The streets were silent and riot police gathered in platoons near the National Assembly, carrying wicker shields to ward off stones that might be thrown at them. In a devious society, the Buddhists were the most devious, the least predictable force. No one took them lightly.

I had breakfast and arrived at the Associated Press office to find a small task force setting off for the Presidential Palace. Tri Quang, the most powerful monk in Vietnam, had been sitting on the lawn before the Palace since last night, beginning a fast. His objectives were not clear, but Buddhist monks had been international news for four years, ever since some of them died by setting themselves afire in the turmoil and rioting that led to the downfall of the Diem government in the autumn of 1963.

* * *

The AP photographers trotted on ahead of us, and John Wheeler and I showed our credentials and were passed through barbed-wire roadblocks to enter the parklike area leading up to the Presidential Palace. Normally there was a roar of traffic on the streets bordering the chestnut-flanked parade ground, but today all was silent. We strolled across the wet grass toward the modern white-concrete and plate-glass building, its outlines dim in the fog.

At the end of the lawn, by the street running past the elaborate iron gates of the Palace, there was a small knot of figures between two huge dripping chestnut trees. There were correspondents and photographers standing about, and in the center were three monks, reclining on the wet grass.

Tri Quang, in his gray robes, had a white-lined blue raincoat over his head. The effect was of an Arab burnoose, and he looked to me like a fuller-faced, Vietnamese Lawrence of Arabia. He had large luminous brown eyes, a strong jaw, and a sweet smile. After his night in the rain, he had a growth of whiskers far heavier than that of the average Vietnamese. He was in complete repose and seemed like a wild animal. It would have been easy to imagine him as an armed guerrilla leader. He radiated vitality, and his innocent face was in contrast to the extreme cleverness of the scene he had created. Here he sat, alone except for his two attendants, unarmed, smiling, challenging the authority represented by that huge white building in the mist. On one side of the street stood the white-clad sentries before the Presidential Palace, red sashes about their waists and rifles with fixed bayonets at their sides. On the other side of the street, Tri Quang.

I stared at the Presidential Palace, thinking of how its very name indicated the difficulty of fusing the traditions of a mandarinate, the experience of colonialism, and the present version of a democracy that called itself the Republic of Vietnam.

Tri Quang seemed to be enjoying it all. His was a tough face. With the exception of some of the old farm men and women, it was the most interesting face I had seen in Vietnam. To one who had seen both this unforgettable face and the prissy little puss on President Thieu, there was no comparison possible.

A Vietnamese reporter was standing near Tri Quang, who asked him a question. This was eventually relayed to us.

"Where is downtown?" Tri Quang had wanted to know. John Wheeler and I smiled. We were almost as downtown as one could be, a couple of blocks from the very heart of the city. It was hard to believe that Tri Quang was quite so unworldly, quite so cloistered and quite so unaware of the geography of the city in which he was chief abbot of a principal pagoda, but perhaps he really did not bother his head about such matters. It made good copy, the Tri Quang and the Buddhists were always approachable when the press was concerned. Photographers circled about him, and one could decide for oneself whether he was a genuine innocent or assiduously projecting an image. He would not pose, he kept the raincoat over his head, and yet always he had his face to the cameras, those wide eyes showing the world that here was a simple man of God, driven by his concern for the people to go without food sitting in the rain.

"One time," John whispered to me, "they found a VC battalion headquarters in his pagoda. Do you think he wasn't aware of *that*?"

That evening Tri Quang was still sitting in what had now become a blinding tropical storm, and I was sitting in a room at the Vietnamese American Association, listening to a talk by Robert Scalapino, a professor of political science at the University of California and one of the leading American experts on Asian affairs.

The beauty of Scalapino's talk was that it offered a perspective on present-day Asia that escaped those like me who had lived there but had made only a limited study of its history. He began by saying something that I *had* realized, that many of the American troubles in Asia stemmed from the power vacuum left by the disappearance of colonialism after World War II, but then he went on to offer something I had never understood. He pointed out that Nehru and other Asian nationalist leaders had been bitter about the American Marshal Plan support of Europe because this strengthened, for a few years at least, the ability of the European colonial powers to hold onto their Asian possessions. I had been in college at the time Marshall announced his plan, and it had seemed to me an altogether admirable program for rebuilding the European economy and the Western European ability to resist what was quite clearly the Communist policy of establishing Communist regimes in as many European nations as possible. This other aspect had not occurred to me once in the intervening twenty years.

Scalapino turned to the conception of nation-building, a phrase that made me wince a bit since I had seen how hard it was to do even a little province-building in Phu Yen. His point, accurate at least in regard to the Communist nations, was that the first postwar generation had been idealists, thinking in political terms, and that the second generation were turning out to be the technicians, engineers, and organizers. I had my doubts about the idealism of the first postwar generation leading South Vietnam, but I certainly agreed that one thing needed now in Vietnam was the development of a body of experts in the technical and management fields. As I listened, my peripheral reaction was that I hoped this second generation, in China, North Korea, and North Vietnam, would mellow as the Russians had relatively mellowed. I believed that the Dragoons, the 31st Tactical Fighter Wing, and those PFs in Phu Yen were buying the time in which this mellowing could occur. The opposing argument to this was that our resistance here would keep the other side more militant and slow that mellowing process, but my own thought was that the mellowing would occur in any case. The question was, to me, how much of Asia had to go behind Communist-state boundaries during the years of transition.

After an interesting excursion into the subject of China, which was then convulsed with the Red Guards and the Cultural Revolution, Scalapino closed on the subject of the American public's support of the war in Vietnam. On this October evening in 1967 he categorized the opponents to the war as isolationists, and said: "I don't think the isolationists are going to win. In both the Republican and Democratic parties the majority of people understand the necessity for a commitment in Southeast Asia. If Hanoi expects us to throw in the towel, I feel they are going to be disappointed. It is not going to happen."

The rain had let up and I walked home in the light of thick-misted street lamps. I was thinking of something that

Scalapino had no reason to touch on in his talk, but one of the possibilities that sometimes crossed the minds of those who thought about Asia. If Russia and China should fight each other, that would be the day that we needed maximum military strength, not now. Just to protect our crowd in the grandstand we would need all the power we could generate, and if that day came, I had the feeling that suddenly all this criticism of the military as an immoral profession would stop. Suddenly it would be perfectly all right for a man to be trained in shooting down an enemy plane. We would be damned glad we had him, and wish that we had more.

III

For many months I had been engaging in friendly talks with a Miss Cuc, one of the waitresses on the roof at the Rex officers' billet across the street from the Associated Press, and now I asked her to lunch.

It was her day off, and she met me on a sunny street corner, a lavender-flowered parasol above her head, wearing a burnt-orange *ao dai* with long flowing black trousers.

We walked toward the river. She was not really Miss. She was thirty-five, and her husband had died of an illness some years before, leaving her with the three children whose snapshots she had often shown me at quieter moments in the Rex. She was a broad-bodied woman, originally from one of the Delta towns, with a pretty, square face, her thick black hair cut just at the top of the high tunic collar of her dress. She walked with me through the crowds of Vietnamese, her bearing regal and somehow beyond reproach, exempting both of us from the usual quick conclusions the Vietnamese reached about any American man and Vietnamese woman seen together.

I took her to lunch at the My Khanh, a floating restaurant tied to a jetty on the river. This had been the scene of a bloody and internationally reported terrorist bombing incident some years before, but today it was serene and cool.

My companion was enjoying herself. Her English was limited, but she managed to get her thoughts across successfully and with candor. She seldom went out, she said. One of her friends had lived with an American for a year, but she did not see the point of having an American boyfriend who would just go home at the end of a year. She devoted all her efforts to her children. She made seven thousand piasters a month, about sixty dollars at the official rate, and of this she needed to spend three thousand piasters a month on tuition for her children. Her mother lived with them, which was helpful in the baby-sitting department.

We looked at the menu, which consisted of Chinese food with a Vietnamese accent. I asked her to order. When the dishes came, she served me, lifting all the choicest bits from the serving platters to the top of the mound of rice in the bowl before me, and was delighted that I liked *nuoc mam*. I ordered a big bottle of beer, and she poured it for me each time my glass got low, drinking orange soda herself.

She made it clear that she did not for a minute believe that I was not married. For some reason I was carrying my passport with me, and showed it to her, half-convincing her on the point. She ate delicately and asked me if I thought that a lot of American troops would be leaving Vietnam in the next couple of years. She was worried, she said, because if too many left she would lose her job, and then she might have to go to work as a bar girl. She did not want to do that, even though it paid much more, but she had no skills other than being a waitress and her little knowledge of English, and no connections that would help her become a saleslady in a store.

I told her that I saw no prospect of large numbers of Americans being withdrawn. I thought we would need even more men before we were through.

A plane flew overhead, and she pointed after it, clearly referring to the whole phenomenon of airplanes, asking me a question. Finally I understood what it was. She had seen airplanes in the sky over Saigon, but she had never seen an airplane take off or land. She wanted to know how they got off the ground and back onto it. I began making gestures, and she nodded, interested and grateful, and ladled some hot melon soup out of a serving bowl into the small bowl before me.

We sat for quite a while after we had finished eating, looking at the gray Vietnamese Navy launches and the sampans moving on the dirty river. I found her a most admirable person, with great dignity, sincerity, and the unexpected smile and tilt of the head that added the charming feminine dimension.

"When is yo' birsday?" she asked me suddenly.

I told her that my birthday was November fourteenth.

She thought about that carefully, about the astrological signs that I was under, and then regarded me, all in all.

"You very good man," she said matter-of-factly.

I don't know what I said in return, but I thought it the best compliment I had received in 1967.

We walked down the gangplank of the creaky white-painted restaurant barge, she ahead of me. An urchin approached and said "Give me ten P."

Just at the moment I wasn't in the mood. I shook my head and passed by him. His hand grabbed the wristwatch from my left arm before I knew what was happening. I turned just in time to see the little boy vaulting out of sight beyond the pilings of the pier. I walked to the edge, but he had disappeared. I stood in the sunshine, Miss Cuc under her parasol muttering against the boy. I remembered that day in the valley, when I had traded an even-worse watch for the one just taken from my hand, the one the boys on a motor scooter had tried to grab a few nights before. Vietnam had finally gotten back its watch.

IV

I was enjoying my vacation in Saigon, but I felt that the time had come to return to Tuy Hoa. My last evening in the city it was raining in great lashing sheets, with cracks of lightning turning every plaster wall to flickering silver. Thunder shook the rooftops.

Peter Arnett was driving home after finishing work in the early evening, and he gave me a lift to the German Cultural Center, attached to the West German embassy, where they were to have a recital of the Vietnamese national epic, the *Kim Van Kieu*. On the way over there, the car feeling more like a speedboat than an automobile in these torrents, Peter told me of a trip from which he had just returned. The Viet Cong had warned a *montagnard* village that they should move away from government protection, and the villagers had ignored them and gone about their business. As part of an over-all offensive in their area, a Viet Cong company had systematically destroyed this village, using flamethrowers.

"The Cong were brutal on this one," Peter said, shaking his head as the rain poured from the windshield wipers. He had just written and filed the story. The people had hidden in improvised bomb shelters, and the Viet Cong had poked their flamethrowers down the earthen entrances, roasting them all. Two hundred and ten men, women, and children had been roasted to death. "It was the worst thing I've seen yet," Peter said quietly as the rain washed over the windshield. His voice sounded sick.

I entered the high-ceilinged room at the German Cultural Center. Intent-looking Vietnamese youths in white shirts and dark slacks, student girls in white *ao dai* talked as they waited for the performance to begin.

I had read *Kim Van Kieu* and heard one of our hooch maids sing a few verses of it for me when I showed her the book. It is a tale of three thousand, two hundred and fifty lines, alternating between six and eight syllables in a type of Vietnamese prosody, the whole broken into twenty-seven chapters and an epilogue. It tells the story of Kim, a beautiful girl who forsakes her fiancé and sells herself into concubinage to save her father. Like so much in Vietnam, it is derivative of Chinese culture, is set in China, and was adapted from a literarily less distinguished Chinese novel by the nineteenth-century diplomat Nguyen-Du. In the manner of Asian classics, it promises no justice in this world, but says only that a man can keep his word and that loyalty, particularly family loyalty, is the greatest of virtues.

Tonight we were to hear excerpts sung by men and women, and a small orchestra took its place, carrying Vietnamese flutes and string instruments.

I supposed that shortly we were to hear the music, but this was not so. A young German official of the Cultural Center arose from his place among the strong, dowdy German wives of the embassy. Teutonically condescending and pleased with himself, he welcomed us all at some length, speaking in German. Then he produced a young Vietnamese man who, also speaking in German, told us about the *Kim Van Kieu* for forty minutes. On my program I jotted down "Only the Germans would put on a program where a Vietnamese speaks German for forty minutes of explanation, to a Vietnamese audience, about their national classic."

At last the young Vietnamese sat down, presumably having furthered the Center's goal of encouraging young Vietnamese to study German, and the recital began. I found the twanging music and quavering voices pleasant and sweet, and thought again of the virtues of a classic which could be enjoyed as a tale, as poetry, and as music.

When it was over, the storm had stopped. I walked to my hotel down misty streets.

TWENTY-NINE

Major Kobata was on his way home. He was good enough to invite me to his going-away party at Hieu Xuong, and I was glad to be there.

It was all a little strange because, in addition to the usual feelings of regret at the close of a long and successful association, Kobata's team knew that they had survived under his command, and the question was, what next? I could see them—Sergeant Iaea, slender black sergeant Bradley, stocky black sergeant Hebron—looking at Kobata's replacement, a cheerful, bald major. They had nothing against him, but could he cut the mustard?

Captain Hy was on hand, and one would have thought that Major Kobata and Captain Hy had never disagreed on a thing all year long. They were exquisitely courteous to each other, as if there had never been midnight wavings of arms while Kobata wanted to launch forth and Hy was pointing into the darkness and screeching "Many, *MANY* VC!" Seemingly forgotten was the night of the attack on this compound, when Hy and his men had hidden as far from the bullets as they could get, leaving an American civilian, Neil Miller, defending one bunker by himself.

Beers were consumed as we stood beneath the captured VC flags on the wall, the captured weapons, and there was a big cake from the mess hall on the beach. Gifts were presented, and finally there came a time for Major Kobata to speak.

I was interested by what he did not say. Never did he refer to Captain Hy or to the Saigon government. He spoke of helping the people, how we must go on trying to help the people. That was all he said, and he said it well. I had not the slightest doubt that I was saying good-bye to the best man with the rank of major that I had met in either the Army or Air Force.

II

It was drizzling early the next morning when I walked behind the Province Chief's house and knocked on the door of our public health advisor for the Province.

"Come on in. How 'bout some coffee?" This was Cliff Rench, from Belton, Texas, who had retired as a major in the Medical Service after twenty-one years in the Army, twenty-one years that had involved coming up through the ranks and being a combat medic during the Korean War. Now he was in the midst of another war as a civilian, taking care of Vietnamese civilians.

We sat and talked over that cup of coffee. Cliff's hooch was particularly neat, and he seemed a totally efficient man, moving effortlessly in a one-piece beige coverall.

He was not fond of some of the visiting firemen he had been receiving from higher headquarters. He said that earlier in the year everything had been going along effectively, with U.S. Army hospitals in Vietnam taking care of many Vietnamese civilian casualties, and also doing some fine surgical work on non-war-related conditions such as harelips.

Then a United States Senator had come through Vietnam. Learning that this treatment of Vietnamese civilians was done on an unofficial basis, he had gone back to the United States and announced "We have no Vietnamese civilian war casualty program." The result was that all treatment of Vietnamese civilians at Army hospitals had slowed or stopped, pending implementation of an official program.

"Now," Cliff said bitterly, "instead of seven minutes to fly a chopper up here from the Ninety-first Evac, it takes me seven forms on each patient—to be approved in Saigon—and weeks."

We launched off in his Scout in the rain, and he took me to the province hospital, which I had passed a hundred times but never entered.

The place shocked me. I do not know why I had

expected the hospital in Phu Yen to resemble an American hospital, but the first thing I saw was two adult male patients sharing the same bed. This overcrowding was standard throughout the hospital, and in the children's wards there were sometimes three to a bed. For a population of three hundred and ninety thousand in Phu Yen, there were one hundred and forty beds in this hospital. There were three Vietnamese doctors on the staff, only one working full time, and the place was saved from complete chaos by the presence of a Korean civilian medical team.

The entire complex was wretched. The floors and walls were grimy, and everything, from needles to pans, looked ten-thousand-times used. As Cliff and I walked from the main building to a secondary two-floored ward building, I noticed human feces all about the low-cropped field next to us. Cliff told me that people who came to visit the patients did that, and sometimes the ambulatory patients themselves. Only recently, through Cliff's efforts, had the hospital finally received electricity and running water.

The next wards were even dirtier. There was a cheeselike stench that sent me reeling. It was worse than anything I had smelled in refugee camps, Saigon slums, or battlefields. I leaned against a dingy wall, waiting to see if I would vomit, did not, and managed to finish Cliff's conducted tour. As we crossed back through the hospital yard, Cliff told me of Senator Edward Kennedy's visit here. Kennedy had looked at some of the worse patients and said: "These people should be taken to a hospital." It was then that an aide told him that this *was* a hospital.

Cliff and I drove up Route One to a refugee camp called Ninh Tinh. As we arrived, bumping over a sandy, cactus-flanked road, the usual crowd of children materialized. We got out. As always, I was struck with the beauty of Vietnamese children and their extraordinary vitality, considering the lives they led. It seemed an appalling contradiction to see these lively faces, bodies still growing normally for their ages, faces as eager and intelligent as any in the world, and then to look above their heads and see these temporary shacks, built on land that no one else wanted, rotten infertile land, no school here for the kids to go to, no future for them to go to.

A helicopter from the 91st Evacuation Hospital arrived to join us here, bringing in an Army doctor, two nurses, and a couple of male medical technicians. Soon they had their equipment laid out in a mud-walled room in the center of the camp, and a long line had formed outside the door.

It interested me to see how many in this line of patients were children. They were wearing their Buddhist amulets, all right, but those who knew they had something wrong with them were right here, more adventurous than many of their elders, willing to give the foreigners' medicine a try. At the very front of the line there was a child who could only crawl on misshapen limbs, a boy of eight who had tuberculosis of the bone. He was not going to give up, he was going to ask every time we came if we could not someday make him walk.

"I'm going to try to do something for him," Cliff said. "It's going to take a lot, and all he may do is improve somewhat."

The people came in, mothers with children, dirty, dusty, the babies with sores—the whole sorrowful pageant I had seen repeatedly this year. The children were very good about pain, and only the small babies cried. Mothers were given soap, urged to use it on their babies.

Cliff had been walking around the houses and had discovered that there were a good many older heart and tuberculosis patients who were just staying on their beds. Some had been told by the Viet Cong that they had to pay the Americans for medicine, others had been told that we would poison them, and others just wanted to be left alone.

The Army doctor joined Cliff, and we headed toward these sick people's houses along a sandy trail through the cactus, passing an occasional small vegetable garden that somehow existed in the gray sand. Since we were the big event of this day, children were following us everywhere, and a little girl was walking beside me. She wore clean faded pajamas and a faded cloth hat with flowers on it. She was a grave child, but she gave me one friendly smile and seemed content to walk beside me. On her right wrist were five rubber bands, her toys. As we walked along I pulled her aside protectively when a couple of older boys ran past, and from that moment she put her hand in mine. The two of us walked along holding hands as if it were the most natural thing in the world, the child with no future and the foreigner, with a cast on his arm, from a country halfway around the world. If I had a moment of guilt in Vietnam, a moment of feeling that, although both the government and the Viet Cong were shooting up the farmers' villages, the Unites States should have no part of it, this was that moment, with that child's hand trustingly in mine.

By afternoon it was clear to me that Cliff put in a stupendous day. After a visit to a maternity clinic, he had driven down to the American Ninety-first Evacuation Hospital on what he called a "blood run," to get whole blood for the province hospital. I took the opportunity to have a fresh cast put on my arm while Cliff did some other errands and consulted with medical officers, and now, with my new cast on, I was watching something less than pleasant. The 173rd Airborne was still operating out in the hills beyond the Tuy Hoa Valley, and a medical-evacuation helicopter had just brought into the hospital's emergency room four Viet Cong who had been smoked out of a hole by tear gas.

I had never seen anybody really thoroughly tear-gassed. The four men lay with their skins green, their bodies twitching, moaning. One had been wounded with grenade fragments in such a way that there were small red holes all down his right side. Finally one of the Viet Cong regained consciousness and began spitting at the American orderly who was bending over him, taking care of him.

"I will fight you to my last breath!" the Viet Cong choked in Vietnamese, and began spitting again. The American orderly shrugged, applied a big square of tape to the prisoner's mouth, and continued working on him.

I wandered through the wards, looking for Cliff. I found it easy to stop for a second by the side of any wounded GI's bed. Most of them were friendly, and they reminded me of the boys in the Dragoons. These wounded paratroopers were feeling pretty good, because the general in command of the 173rd had just come through the wards, giving them candy bars and cigarettes. It was not the gifts that mattered, it was that the man had come to see them, to talk to each one of them.

There was a boy with a sheepdog head of blond hair lying in bed, chatting with a buddy who had managed to get in from the hills to visit him. The buddy had his helmet and M–16 with him, the shoulder harness, the grenades. I glanced at the face of the boy in bed, wondering what was wrong with him, and then I noticed that, under the sheet, there was a place where one foot stuck up, and the place where the other foot would be was just flat.

A kid smiled at me. He was from Special Forces, and on his bedside table was the leather-bound citation for the Purple Heart, with the medal itself in a small leather box. He had walked on a mine, he told me. It had hit his spine. He was waiting to see if he would walk again. The boy was from a farm in North Dakota, and had been in the Army for six years.

"I was planning to make a career of it," he said quietly. "Now I expect I won't."

In the next ward, to my surprise, I found Neil Miller sitting on the edge of a bed, dressed in the same blue bathrobe worn by the wounded soldiers. A FAC plane had gone down near the river, and Neil had waded across a paddy to the flaming plane and pulled out the pilot, wrenching his knee so badly in the process that it might require an operation. He was cheerful, but preoccupied about how things were going at Hieu Xuong, anxious to get right back there and work on everything. We shook hands, two civilians who would much rather laugh than cry.

Finally, in the next ward, I caught up to Cliff Rench. This was a ward for Vietnamese children, and he was bending over each bed in turn, talking and joking with each child until the child laughed or at least smiled.

I looked down at one boy who had bandages all over the lower half of his stomach. He was about ten or eleven, brown-faced, with a warm, friendly smile. He looked happy and healthy. I took a couple of steps down the aisle and asked Cliff: "What's wrong with that kid?"

"His parents wouldn't cooperate with the VC," Cliff said, "so the VC shot off this boy's penis and testicles. He doesn't have any idea what's wrong with him."

III

A few mornings later at the stand-up briefing there was word that Hieu Xuong had been attacked again. Just as we had the first time, the Wing's senior Intelligence officer and I piled into a vehicle and made our way off the base, down the pot-holed road to the compound. Just as we had the first time, we stood in the living room where I had said good-bye to Major Kobata a few nights before and looked at the same scene of bloodstains and splinters. The attack had been an exact repetition of the first, even starting with a rocket round

Starlight Scope

that came through the patched-over hole that had been made by the opening round of the earlier attack.

There had, however, been one stunning difference in our response. Sergeant Bradley had been atop a bunker with a Starlight Scope, the fantastic toy that enabled one to see the ground, at night, illuminated as if there were daylight. After the first enemy round hit, Bradley began traversing this scope until he saw the enemy coming. He cut them down with the M–16 on which this scope was mounted, and directed everyone where to fire with what they had and where to fire with the support the radio called in. The attack had never gotten to the wire, and only one American had been wounded. Ironically, just as in the first attack, a man had been wounded on his first night at Hieu Xuong. This time the casualty was a sergeant from Saigon who had come up the day before with a brief case to investigate a civilian claim of damage to property by American forces. He had been scheduled to fly back to Saigon this morning, but instead he was in the Ninety-first Evac.

The VC had left a dead man behind as they disappeared across the paddies, and Captain Hy had ordered him put in the field across Route One, lying where the VC Captain Quy had been the last display. I went over and took a look at the man. He appeared to be close to fifty, and had gray hair. I wondered if he had been a porter, a carrier of ammunition, forced to serve and then flung forward with the younger men. In death, it was certainly not the face of a man who would willingly die for anything. Like most people in the world, he looked like a family man—in this rural society he was probably a grandfather, at his age—a man who just wanted to mind his own business. There were flies circling above his nose as his dead face pointed at the sky.

Back at the air base, I saw men of the 173rd Airborne standing beside the flight line, waiting to be loaded onto C–130 transports. I had an idea where they might be going. At our stand-up briefings the last couple of mornings there had been word that something was brewing around Dak To, a small Special Forces camp and village well to the northwest of us, close to the point where the borders of Laos, Cambodia, and South Vietnam meet. The 173rd was used as a fire engine, running to crises all over the country, and looking now at the laughing, healthy paratroopers, I felt a chill, wondering what they were to be thrown into.

IV

My birthday came, and with it some pleasant cards from friends. Sitting in my hooch, I opened the one package I had received, a package from Saigon. In it was a perfectly beautiful Vietnamese lacquer box, dull red with figures of fish seeming to swim in the lacquer depths. Beside it was a narrow plaque with a black lacquer background and a painting of a slender, tall Vietnamese girl in a silvery *ao dai*. It was from Miss Cuc, the waitress at the Rex whom I had taken to lunch at the floating restaurant. I could not help thinking that the waist in the picture was thinner than hers, but the classically pretty, vacuous face in the picture bespoke a heart less than one tenth as great. I hate to think what these had cost her.

V

By November seventeenth it was clear that there was a hell of a battle on at Dak To. We were sending half of our missions up there, and the pilots invariably came back talking of bombing in very close support of our troops, and frequently receiving enemy machine gun fire.

After about three mornings of this I asked our Army liaison officer if he could identify any of our units involved. I had a hunch that the Dragoons were in there, and when he said "Well, the first outfit in there was the First Brigade of the Fourth Division," I felt a strange pang. I went back to my hooch, I busied myself with notes and correspondence, but every couple of hours I stopped and stared out the window at Cheop Chai looming in the distance. I remembered that day at Tom Lynch's Change of Command Ceremony, when his successor, Glen Belnap, short, soft-spoken, looking more like a rumpled old sergeant that a lieutenant colonel, had asked me to make a point of visiting the Dragoons again. I had told him I would, but I had not meant it. For me the Dragoons had been Tom Lynch, some of his men, and the Battle of Three Trees, and enough was enough.

Now, as I worked all afternoon and the sun dropped toward the enemy's blue hills, I felt the stirrings of something I tried to fight down. They were still my Dragoons, and they were in the middle of what was the biggest battle thus far in the war. I tried to tell myself that most of the men I had known were gone, The Royal Pineapple and Sergeant Higa and Jack Crumley, but other, younger faces floated before me. Tomlinson would still be up there, the kid with the Jimmy Cagney face who had been beside me at the end of Three Trees when the helicopter winds had blown the riddled tree down across our laps. John Collins, the thoughtful boy who had been the closest of my friends in B Company, the boy with whom I had crawled out at Three Trees to get the wounded to shelter—he would still be there.

I went to sleep, and the next day at stand-up it was even clearer: Dak To had already exceeded in casualties any battle of the war, and was blazing higher every day. It was a matter of history now. I had come to Vietnam to write about things, I had followed the Dragoons about, I had a standing invitation to rejoin them. I had a chance for a ringside seat.

That was the trouble. It sometimes turned into something more than a ringside seat, as I knew pretty well by now. I was tired. It was November twentieth. In just three weeks, possibly less, I was planning to go home at the end of my self-imposed year. I had made it this far, I had nothing more to prove to myself, and I did not want to go wandering up there with a cast on my arm and become a more severe casualty.

I had big aerial maps of Vietnam in my hooch, and I pulled out the one that included Dak To. It was a real Dien Bien Phu situation, with our base in a valley surrounded by mountains on all sides. I had a vision of the little Special Forces camp there, the enemy pouring in for the kill from Laos and Cambodia, gaining control of the surrounding hills, and closing the small runway there with mortar fire and rockets. There I would be, in there when they played out their Dien Bien Phu and overran the Americans who were cut off from receiving the air-delivered supplies on which they depended. I did not like the look of it at all.

I stared out the window toward Cheop Chai. A big gray flying suit was walking toward me, the black-clad legs of a little hooch maid just visible beneath it as she carried it, and the picture made me laugh, a welcome laugh, because I was afraid. I felt that I had played out my string, that if I went up there I would be pushing a fortune that had already been more than kind.

The next day I had decided two things. I had decided to go, and I had accepted the fact that I would probably be badly hurt up there, or killed. I stared out the window, wanting to stay among these silver hooches with their air conditioning and refrigerators. Life seemed something terribly sweet and precious, life just as it was right here. Just to breathe the air, to look down and see life in my fingers.

THIRTY

I got under way for Dak To early the morning of November twenty-third, Thanksgiving Day. Two hours later I had gotten as far as Qui Nhon, up the coast, and was having a ridiculous argument with an Air Force major as to whether I could get permission to fly into Dak To aboard a C–130 loaded with ammunition. A couple of C–130s had been blown to bits on the runway up there in the past few days, but on the other hand there was an ammunition plane ready to leave for Dak To right now. The thought of getting up there like a salmon swimming upstream, hitching one ride after another all over the country, seemed to me even worse than the risks of the ammunition plane.

Permission refused. I walked through the waiting room of the terminal at Qui Nhon, and lined up at a van behind it that was selling hamburgers, soda, and ice cream.

It was here that I saw the first man who had unmistakably been at Dak To. A young 173rd Airborne trooper, unshaven, moving as if in a trance, was standing beside the van, drinking a milkshake. Then he started walking into the terminal in a groggy, wavering step.

"How was it?" one of his traveling companions asked him, about the milkshake.

He stared at them as if coming back from a great distance. "Delicious," he said in a sleepy small child's voice, and walked on in a daze.

At Pleiku my transportation luck changed. A C–123 had suddenly been ordered to carry an Air Force Forward Combat Controller team into Dak To, and I hopped aboard. These Air

Force men wore black berets and paratrooper jump wings and were trained to parachute into a place, if necessary, to guide in parachute drops of supplies. Today, however, the plan was to roll off this plane with their jeeps. I stared at the jeeps, never having seen quite such a display of radios and signaling equipment. I asked one of the team how much such a jeep cost.

"Twenty-five thousand dollars," he replied. "About twenty-two thousand five hundred of it is in radios."

We did not fool around going into Dak To. The pilot came up a road and stream running north into the horseshoe of hills, made a straight-in swift approach, and we bounced and were taxiing along beside mountains of supplies, sandbag bunkers, rows of vehicles. As I watched us pass acres of crates and cartons, little unit signs and guidons everywhere, I got over my idea that I was going into a beleaguered Special Forces camp. It might have been that a few days before, but airlift had changed that overnight. From what I could see, damned near the entire Fourth Division was here.

I got out of the plane, wearing my old full outfit complete with helmet and the ARVN pack, and trudged off the airstrip, looking for my FAC friends. The first tent I went into was a mistake. It was a big tent, filled with 173rd Airborne boys who had just been pulled out of the fighting. They lay sprawled on their bunks, out cold. I approached one young trooper who was sitting silently on his cot, and asked him where the First Brigade of the Fourth Division had its headquarters. He just shook his head. I backed out and moved on down among the tents, suddenly hearing the noise of a party. I came to the doorway of a smaller square tent. Inside it were the sergeants of the men I had just seen. Their faces were tired, but already they had shaved and changed, and now they had a bottle out and were laughing and talking. I asked them, and they told me exactly the route to take through these tents.

I walked into the FAC tent. It was just like coming home. Rod Rodriguez and Mad Dog Cummings had been rotated to the States, but I knew a few of the more recent arrivals, and there was Major Joe Madden shaking my hand, telling me to put my things down. It was getting late in the afternoon, he said, and I should stay with them tonight and head off for the Dragoons tomorrow. There was a cot I could use, and he was planning a little flight just at dusk. Would I like to come along?

"Sure." I slumped down among them. They asked me about my cast, and then Joe Madden went off somewhere, and they told me about some of the things Joe had been doing. My friends the Dragoons had been the first unit in here when the North Vietnamese came pouring through the hills to the west, and at the beginning everyone had to fight with just anything they had. Repeatedly, Joe had turned his FAC plane into a seventy-mile-an-hour fighter plane, circling over attacking North Vietnamese with his M–16 out the window, t' is forty-year-old father of nine popping away at the advancing NVA, dropping grenades on them, calling in F–100 strikes every moment he could get them.

I sat on a crate, listening, nodding, suddenly aware that I had not eaten for many hours. Even in this camp at Dak To, on this Thanksgiving Day, the Army had managed to have hot turkey, but it was all gone by now. I decided that I should have turkey nonetheless, so I ate an unheated C ration of turkey loaf, and drank some water with it. I had no way of knowing it, but as I sat here the battle was reaching its climax. A 173rd Airborne unit was at last taking Hill 875, from which they had been repeatedly pushed, but in these hills a battle did not cease at once, but trailed off in crackling smaller actions.

I got into the air just at sunset, sitting behind Joe Madden, who was humming away in the earphones. Looking past his shoulder I saw that the terrain up here was massive and wild, with huge steep-curving slopes, green forests, mists, and very high winds. This had clearly entered into the NVA calculations, to engage us in these mountain valleys at a time of year when winds tossed helicopters about and fog could make resupply most difficult.

We rose above the evening ground mists, and the runway and base camp were soon parts of a shadowy little rectangle in the valley below. We crossed a ridge, and suddenly a unit was on the air saying they were "receiving incoming mortar at this time." Joe banked and we swooped down this slope, out beyond our fire bases. I saw a telltale blue flash from an enemy mortar beneath some trees, and then another. I pointed it out to Joe, who nodded and began talking to the artillery. Soon big brown clumps of smoke were sprouting all through the area in which I had spotted the muzzle flashes. The American unit reported that the fire on them had lifted. Joe turned in the front seat, lifting his thumb and giving me a big smile. We toured the peaks a bit more as the red sunset drew back into Laos and Cambodia, and landed just at dark.

When it came time to go out to the Dragoons the next morning, I walked down to their sandbagged Supply bunker, one of many dug-in office-warehouse combinations on the side of the airstrip where choppers were landing and taking off. I introduced myself to a new young supply lieutenant, thinking of that first day at Tuy Hoa when I had stumbled up the steps of the Dragoons' van with the WE TRY HARDER sign on it, dropping equipment all over the place on my first trip out to Tom on his Phu Yen hilltop.

The supply lieutenant said he had heard of me, and asked me to sit down. He radioed the TOC at the fire support base, telling them that I had appeared. Thirty seconds later Lieutenant Colonel Glen Belnap's voice came on the air. He had taken the call sign Sabre when he succeeded Tom Lynch's Charger.

"This is Sabre," he said to his supply lieutenant. "Tell that individual at your location that we're waiting for him with open arms."

A few minutes passed before the right chopper appeared, and in those minutes I discovered that the Dragoons were still the proud, aggressive, competitive unit I had known. The supply lieutenant and one of his sergeants were explaining to me that there had been a shortage of everything, the first few days up here. When this thing started, they were just told to load up everything they could at Dragon Mountain and put their trucks on the road moving north. They raced up here, set up shop and got ready to receive further supplies, and then found that the Division's truck convoys coming in behind them were arriving only sporadically, some of them with things the Dragoons needed desperately.

"Of course," the lieutenant said, "once a convoy actually got in here, then everybody and his brother was fighting to get what they had."

"Well," I asked him, "how did you get around it?"

The answer bespoke some ingenuity. The lieutenant had sent some of his lighter trucks well down the road south of Dak To, plenty of men on each one, equipping them with a shopping list of the items the battalion needed. When a convoy came barreling north from Kontum toward Dak To, the Dragoon vehicles fell in beside them, traveling in the left hand lane and shouting their needs across to each driver. When a driver nodded that he had the right items on board, grenades or sandbags or C–4 blasting powder, then the Dragoons' truck would swing in tight against the bigger truck, the Dragoons' boarding party would leap across, and they would toss over the needed items until the entire shopping list was checked off.

"Hell," the lieutenant told me, "the drivers in the convoy were glad to do it. Saved them the time and trouble of unloading some of it when they got up here."

The chopper from the Dragoons came in and we whirled out in winds that buffeted us from the moment we were off the ground. We moved toward a hilltop to our northwest. The big hill's northern face dropped sharply; on its south, it slipped down into a ridge that formed the wall guarding Dak To from the enemy's most direct line of approach. This hilltop was 1001, and from maps the FACs had shown me and reconstructions of the battle to date, it was clear that the NVA had planned to go right over this hilltop and down into Dak To, in overwhelming strength. The only thing that had stood between them and success on their first try was the American unit that set up its fire base on this hilltop in the first days of the action—the Dragoons.

It was a gritty, battered hill, and as we lowered into it I could see all the things to which I had thought I had said good-bye; fires burning up crates and cartons, a GI sitting on an open-air box latrine, ponchos flapping in the doorways of sandbagged bunkers, and a patrol heading out downslope through a break in the barbed wire.

As I toiled up the steep slope from the precarious

hacked-out landing place, Glen Belnap came hurtling down through loose earth in short, sliding steps. He looked more rumpled than ever, but alert, cheerful, vital, and very much in command. He slapped me on the back, asked solicitously about my cast, took half the stuff I was carrying, and, six years older than I, led the way back uphill with steps far springier than mine. Glen deposited my things in a cot-choked room deep in a command bunker, and proceeded to introduce me to the new officers of the staff: "This is Charlie Flood, a good friend of this battalion. He's one of the family."

I looked around the command-post area on this peak. Glen had broken the TOC into separate rooms, each department—Intelligence, Operations, Supply, Artillery—having its maps and radios in a separate sandbag-covered metal compartment.

In one of these small metal offices, just coming off duty after a shift working a radio, I found Tomlinson, still chewing gum and looking more than ever like Jimmy Cagney.

"Why aren't you out with B Company?" I asked him cheerfully.

He shrugged. "They stuck me in headquarters before this thing ever started." He looked at me, turned me aside from the other men, and walked me out onto the muddy earth overlooking an extraordinary panorama of wild lavender hills stretching away to the west.

"Collins was killed," he said gently.

I swore.

"He was helping the wounded. He dragged in four of them, and then he was crawling up by Captain Falcone to help him when a mortar round killed both of them. They've got him in for the Bronze Star."

I swore again. He began telling me of how B Company had been the first rifle company into Dak To after reports of a suspicious NVA buildup in the area. A few days had followed during which Tomlinson and the other headquarters men had set up shop on this hilltop, while the rifle companies had patrolled the avenues of approach down which the NVA had been planning to come.

"When we got the contacts, they were big ones, right away," Tomlinson told me. "I heard them all on the radio out there in B Company, yelling for help. It was the most frustrating experience of my life. I wanted to pack my stuff and get right out there.'' He left me for a moment, and came back with the casualty lists. Thirty-seven Dragoons had been killed so far, including Captain John Taylor, the A Company commander I had known, Captain John Falcone, whom I had known when he was the Intelligence Officer before taking B Company over from Neil Buie, and Lieutenant Larry Wade, who had been with B Company as a platoon leader at Three Trees.

The casualty list in my hand was an unreal thing. I was not at all convinced that I would not see Collins smiling at me as he climbed up this slope at sunset, cheerful, helpful, apple-cheeked.

''Hey, Mister Flood,'' he would say.

''Hi there, John. How's it going?''

I stared down at the black letters on the casualty list, and saw the date that John Collins had died. It had been November 11, Armistice Day.

Tomlinson came back with the log book, the TOC's typewritten record of those first frantic outnumbered days of action. I sat turning its pages on a bunker cut into the steep slope, overlooking this tangled landscape of volcanolike hills where these fierce clashes had occurred.

In the waning hours of the afternoon, studying this record and making notes on my battered clipboard, I began isolating some extraordinary records of heroism. I had been told there was a Lieutenant Perkins, whom I had never met, being put in for the Congressional Medal of Honor. From the chronology of the action I began to see what he had done. A newly commissioned second lieutenant, the first enemy bullets he heard were right in these dense forests before me. Twice in four days he assumed command of his company when all the senior officers were killed or wounded, and on the second occasion he saved the company by skillfully directing a hilltop defense against human wave attacks of North Vietnamese coming at them from three sides. All this he had done on his fourth day of combat, with enemy grenade fragments immobilizing one shoulder, in pain and with darkness closing upon them.

The transcript of radio transmissions had about it the

dramatic brevity of men who do not have one syllable to
waste on heroics. By five thirty-four on the afternoon of his
final crisis, Perkins had A Company inside some bunkers on a
hilltop that had changed hands several times. Under a beefed-
up organization which put four rifle companies into the field
from a battalion, instead of the three I had known, D
Company was around the other side of this massive hilltop,
also under attack and not directly linked up to A Company.
The worst of the enemy charges were coming at A Company,
and in this darkening late afternoon they were reduced to a
desperate situation.

"Get us something in here," Perkins radioed the TOC.
"We are under a heavy mortar attack from three sides."

His words produced action. Sixty seconds later Glen
Belnap, in a helicopter over the hill, was saying "Get all
available artillery in here," and sixty seconds after that the
Brigade commander was calling back to say that every artillery piece in the brigade was starting to fire in support of
them. Joe Madden in his FAC plane was radioing for fighter-
bombers: "We have called for everything we can get."

People were responding, but the North Vietnamese were
surging up the hill.

1745—Perkins to Belnap: "Get gunships—I need them
now—receiving heavy ground attack."

1747—Perkins to Belnap: "We need help—I have a lot
of wounded."

1755—Perkins to Belnap: "We are receiving mortar,
rocket, and a heavy ground attack."

At this point Joe Madden delivered his first flight of
F-100s.

Perkins to Madden: "I want napalm twenty-five meters
from my position. (Pause. First bombs are dropped.) Bring it
in closer. (Pause.) Adjust the air strike closer."

For me it made almost unbearable reading, knowing how
desperate one had to be to call for napalm twenty-five yards
away, the terrible life-and-death demand for accuracy being
placed on the F-100 pilots, the horrible rocking, shaking
hilltop scene.

The bombs had stopped the NVA only for a few minutes.
They came swarming back up, and now Perkins had to appeal

to the almost equally beleaguered D Company for extra men.

1840—To Company D: "Give me at least a squad here—I need it now."

1847—To Company D: "I need help. We are tore up pretty bad."

1852—To Company D: "Have your men watch out coming in here. Some NVA are in my bunkers. You have only two men that got here."

There it was. They were fighting hand to hand.

1905—"NVA are in my third and fourth platoon bunkers."

It was as bad as things could be. Now Perkins had to try to control one kind of fighting, yard-apart duels in the holes on the hilltop, and still fight off the NVA who had not yet gotten into the perimeter. Joe Madden was zooming overhead with some helicopter gunships he had called for, and now Perkins gave him a transmission I could scarcely believe.

1905—To FAC: "When I toss a trip flare—have the gunships fire five meters out—south to north."

There it was, helicopters being ordered to fire fifteen feet in front of the American holes, at the North Vietnamese who were still coming.

I put the record down, shaken. Somehow he had gotten them through it, through this North Vietnamese version of a *banzai* attack, with hundreds of men rushing the American hilltop position from three sides.

I rose and stretched. It was late afternoon, and the sky was powder-blue above the swampy, prehistoric mist in these hills. Glen Belnap was walking toward me with a freckle-faced, stocky young soldier at his side. He introduced us, and I discovered with a shock that this innocent young face, soft voice, and gentle manner belonged to the Perkins of whom I had just been reading.

This was the first man I had met in Vietnam who had been recommended for the Congressional Medal of Honor: a serious recommendation, not just a battalion prejudice in favor of one of its officers, since Division had endorsed it and sent it on. I did not want to plunge straight into a "How did it feel, son? How did you really feel? How did you do it?" sort of conversation, so we sat on the sandbagged top of the bunker where I had been reading about him, both of us facing toward the seam of smoky turquoise that had opened in the sunset sky.

He spoke softly in answer to my questions, and I made notes in the failing light. He was Charles Wayne Perkins, twenty-one, of Rohwer, Arkansas.

"How big a town is Rohwer?"

"It has ninety-two people."

"What's the nearest big town?"

"Well, McGehee's got five thousand."

He had been born and raised in Rohwer. "My Daddy's a logger."

Had he gone out hunting with his father?

For the first time Perkins smiled. "Anything you could get a crack at. I had a twenty-two and a four-ten and a twenty-gauge. We went after deer, rabbit, squirrel, doves." He had worked on and off on some farms, and gone fishing when he had a chance.

Sports? He had played basketball at Desha Central High, the county high school. "I was on the baseball team, too. We was too small to have a football team."

Perkins had quit Arkansas A & M after a couple of years, joined the Army, and here he was.

We talked about the afternoon and evening of which I had read.

"About four P.M. we were in the perimeter. Then we had walking trees coming down the hill in front of us. We called in air strikes and some of those trees started dee-deeing back up the hill." He smiled.

A somewhat taller, black-haired young man had joined us, and Perkins introduced him. This was Lieutenant David Watson of Miami, an artillery forward observer who had been with Perkins right through the fight.

At five that afternoon, Perkins told me, "All hell broke loose." By six o'clock he was asking the FAC to put napalm bombs twenty-five meters in front of him. One of the napalm bombs landed right in a group of NVA who were lying in the bushes just down the slope, firing up at Perkins.

"About thirty of them jumped up and came toward me. Some of them were on fire. I guess they had decided that their only hope to escape the bombs was to get inside our perimeter. One got into a bunker where there were two

Americans, and he killed one and wounded one. Then we got him with a grenade."

Lieutenant Watson chimed in. "I was standing right next to him," he said, nodding toward Perkins. "About then I had an M–16 in one hand, an M–79 in the other, and my telephone tucked to my neck, and I was using all three. I saw three NVA fall from my own fire." He paused. "It's surprising how hard it is to kill a man—even at five yards."

I thought the typed report had managed to indicate an ultimately hazardous situation, but I had not realized that things were as bad as what the two men described next.

"We were running out of everything," Perkins told me. He ordered Watson to bring in artillery fire right on their own positions, in the hope that they would survive because they were in bunkers, while the NVA for the most part were still swarming about in the open.

Watson shook his head as he told me the next thing, his smile indicating that all he could do about such a close call was laugh, now that it was over. "One of the first rounds I called in hit the bunker from which we were fighting. I thought I'd killed us."

By this time Perkins was wounded, his shoulder numb from shrapnel from a grenade thrown at him by a North Vietnamese. "I was saying my prayers just then—I was afraid we weren't going to be able to hold."

For the next few minutes it had been a point-blank shoot-out in the dusk. Watson spoke in a flat voice. "The last grenade we had killed the last NVA in the perimeter."

Perkins held the company together during the night, firing back at movement all around their front, and supervised the med-evac the next morning. By ten-thirty in the morning the wounded had been taken out, and at noon Charles Wayne Perkins was the last man to leave the hill. Of one hundred and forty-two men who had been fully fit three days before, seventeen were dead, fifty-eight were pretty badly wounded, and half the remainder had minor shrapnel wounds.

I asked him if his company had been in any fighting in the few days since then.

"No contact," he answered, "and we ain't looking for any."

I asked him if he had realized at the time that he was doing a remarkable job.

"I was surprised at myself. I never thought I could do what I did. But I had a lot of help—from Sabre, and from the man upstairs." He stopped, and then went on, his voice soft in what had now become a purple twilight. "I was scared the whole time, but there was one squad leader I thought a lot of, and he got killed. He lay there the whole night, and I got mad at the enemy. Then Lieutenant Watson, he was scared but he was like me, he wouldn't let on, so we got through." He looked out over the darkening valley. "After I'd been over here and hadn't seen Charlie I began to doubt he was here, but when he did show up he gave a heck of a show."

I asked him what he thought of the war.

"It's a job that has to be done," he said, and thought for a minute. "I don't like some of the things they say about this war back in the States, but if we're fighting for anything now, it's for those who have been killed, so they can rest in peace."

I thanked him, and sat alone on the bunker, watching the stars come out. I remembered those summers in Maine in the late thirties, the nights coming on cool like this one, a time when I was a child. I would miss seeing the first star come out, looking up to find there were three or four already there. Then I would pick one and whisper "First star I've seen tonight." I wish I may, I wish I might, have the wish I wish tonight. I wish John Collins was still alive. I saw his round, cheerful face, saw him helping everyone around him. He would arrive at the gates of heaven carrying a wounded man.

II

I awoke to the sound of our cannon banging away into the dawn. It was chilly, and I huddled under the blanket on this cot against the sandbag wall. Glen Belnap was already up and shaved, and now a young soldier appeared with two paper plates. Glen took one and motioned to the boy to bring the other to me. I sat up, still keeping the blanket around me, and gratefully took the plate of scrambled eggs, sausages, and toast. The young soldier returned in a minute with two plastic cups filled with coffee, and I put mine down on the dirt floor beneath the cot.

Then the full humor of the situation struck me. I was having breakfast in bed at the Battle of Dak To.

At eight in the morning I was standing outside one of the sandbagged TOC compartments when a radio came to life, with my old outfit B Company announcing that a machine gun had just opened up on them. They had been moving up a slope toward a landing zone, and now they were pinned down.

Glen Belnap pulled on his web harness. "Want to come?" he asked me. I said yes, but as I got my helmet and pistol and went swinging down the damp slope toward the helicopter, there was a terrible this-is-where-I-came-in feeling. This is how it had all begun, back in January on a hilltop in Phu Yen, following Tom Lynch into a helicopter that had been shot at from a grassy slope near Cheop Chai, but that had been January and now it was the end of November and I ought to be careful. The helicopter's blades were beginning to turn as I climbed aboard, and I was thinking that with the winds I had felt up here, it was not safe to fly around these hills, even without enemy machine guns.

We rose over the misty ravines, and in a few minutes we were directing artillery fire into the area where the enemy machine gun had opened up on B Company. When the shells stopped, the B Company commander reported that the enemy machine gun was not being heard from any more, and that he would press on up the slope to the landing zone to be resupplied. Glen said that would be fine, and what did he need first when he got there? Ammunition, the voice from beneath the high trees said, grenades, and a lot of blasting powder to blow down additional trees and improve the landing zone.

Glen nodded, and we headed through racing clouds over the ridge, and angled down to the Dragoons' supply point beside the airstrip at Dak To. When we got there, we released this helicopter so it could return to our hilltop fire base, and walked over to another chopper. The crew of this new one were anxiously looking up at the vertical driveshaft that turned the overhead blades. They had just gotten out of a fire base that was under mortar attack, and they pointed out to us several nicks from fragments on both the driveshaft and the blades.

The boxes of supplies were already being brought out to us, and the helicopter pilot finally shrugged his shoulders, said he hoped the mortar fragments hadn't thrown anything out of kilter, and indicated that he was ready to load up and take us.

I shook my head as I watched what was going aboard. Metal cases filled with linked machine-gun bullets, crates of grenades, box upon box of blasting powder. It took up so much space that the metal-and-canvas seats were folded against the rear wall of the cabin, and I rose into the turbulent Dak To sky sitting cross-legged atop four crates of grenades.

As we crossed over the ridge the winds tossed us all over the place. We moved slowly down the ridge at treetop level, while I kept wishing that the pilot would move faster, whatever he did. We had just had abundant evidence that the enemy was around here, equipped with machine guns that certainly could knock down a hovering helicopter. I wanted to see a swift delivery of this cargo of explosives, and an immediate departure from this hillside.

Instead, we moved slower. I saw the landing zone open beneath us, a small square that had been hacked out of these hundred-foot-high trees some time before. It was like an elevator shaft walled with vines. Mists were whipping all around us, and the wind was throwing us from one side of the elevator shaft to the other. We started down the shaft and then hung there, our blades beating the air as the wind shook us.

It occurred to me that we might crash without any help from the enemy. The vines and treetops were just level with us now, hemming us in, and all we had to do was be buffeted to one side, catch our blades in those eucalyptus branches, and we would go on down the next ninety feet without any help from the pilot.

I peered over the edge of the grenade crates on which I was sitting. The B Company men on the ground were standing well back under the trees, hands to the brims of their helmets, staring up at us with skeptical expressions.

"I'm pulling fifty," the pilot said in an unhappy voice. I didn't know what it meant, but I was sure that nothing good could happen to us here. This was it, I thought, this was what my premonition of death had been. It was happening right now and I was going to go out in the biggest bang of the whole battle of Dak To.

The pilot shook his head and we rose out of the jungle shaft and flew away without further efforts at getting in. I looked over at Glen, who seemed unshaken. A month later he was to die in a similar situation.

Late that afternoon I was sitting in the sandbagged room where our cots were. A relay speaker from the TOC radio was on in here while Glen sat on his cot looking over some papers, and the North Vietnamese were jamming our frequency. They had a recording of two Russian women's voices. The moment one of our companies tried to get in touch with us, a Russian woman's voice cut in, counting from one to ten in Russian, followed by a maddening feminine giggle. Then the other woman would start in and do the same.

"You think that's bad," Glen said to me without looking up from the papers he was studying. "They have a guy on their side who sometimes gets on the air to our companies and says he's Sabre, and the worst part is he sounds just like me."

I wandered outside and found myself talking to John Mirus, the D Company commander who had been on the other side of the hill from Perkins during their critical hours. In my conversations I was beginning to realize that every man up here considered himself a survivor, lucky to be alive. The battalion had had a traumatic experience, and most of them were only too happy to talk some of it out of their systems. Mirus spoke calmly, even comically when he referred to "an *unbelievable* rocket and mortar attack" in tones that suggested that something so out of proportion to normal experience had to be laughed off, but he, like Perkins, had been fighting for his life. At one point he had been pinned down in a slight depression under a fallen tree trunk.

"That tree saved my life four times," he said.

The worst horror for him had come one night after they beat off an attack and he was trying to cut a landing zone so that some of his wounded could be gotten out. In the darkness some of the men cutting down trees in that tight perimeter had stepped on wounded men they had not known were lying there. One man had stepped on the hanging-out entrails of a boy with a ripped-open stomach, causing him to die instantly of shock.

"Every one of my medics is in for a decoration," he told me, and spoke of how hard all this had been on the medics. One medic in another company had done a marvelous job night after night, pulling in men and keeping them alive until they could be gotten out at dawn. After several days and nights of seeing his friends killed and wounded, of bandaging them and putting their bodies, alive or dead, into helicopters, this medic had been taken by a sergeant to a point on the perimeter where a wounded enemy soldier had been discovered at dawn. The medic had bent down and shot the wounded prisoner through the head.

Another medic had been marvelous for days. One night his company lost several men, and at dawn the corpses were piled at the edge of a landing zone, with ponchos spread over them. When Glen Belnap arrived in a helicopter, the wind from its blades blew away the ponchos, revealing the twisted pile of bodies of this medic's friends. The medic fell on his knees before Glen, crying, "Save us, Sabre! Save us! Get us out of here before we're all killed!" A full-scale breakdown was rare in Vietnam, but this medic was still in a psychiatric ward.

I left Mirus, and found Glen sitting on a bench outside the bunkered TOC complex, speaking with some of the radio operators. Tomlinson and I began to talk of Three Trees, and Tomlinson turned to Glen and tried to explain about the tree being blown down across our laps, how funny it had been at the end of that day of fighting. Glen nodded, but I could see that he could not feel about it as Tomlinson and I did. One had to have lived it, had to have felt that idiot urge to laugh, the wave of relief of knowing that even a tree could fall on you and not hurt you today.

Glen stood up, looking over the hills in the distance, all these hills where his men had climbed and dug and fought and died. He began talking about the United States, about whether a superpower really could afford to lose the limited wars in which it engaged.

"I think history will show that we started to decline as a great power in the early nineteen fifties," Glen said, looking out over the evening mists on the ridges. "That was when we accepted the idea of just coming out even in Korea. You can't just come out even in a war."

Darkness covered our hill, all the hills, and suddenly there were orange flashes on a hill lower than ours, off to the north. Flashes, the several-seconds-later thudding sound of shells landing over there, and then half a dozen fires were burning on that hill.

It was an American fire base under a mortar attack, and the enemy had scored direct hits on some artillery powder and supplies. We began looking frantically for the enemy's blue muzzle flashes in the great black carpet of jungle stretching away beneath us. Finally we spotted some, on a hill due west, and used the cannon on our hill to blast away in that direction. The enemy's firing ceased, and we turned off our cannon and stood outside the TOC, watching the huge golden blazes in the stricken American base, tossing off big red sparks in the windy night.

III

General Peers came to our hilltop late one afternoon. The Fourth Division commander was here to present what are known as "impact awards." Since the paperwork for the Congressional Medal or the Distinguished Service Cross takes a lot of time, men who have been recommended for these are given a lower-ranking award, on the theory that they deserve at least that. If the higher medal is approved, then the lower decoration is canceled, and in the meantime some immediate appreciation has been shown for an act of valor by a man who may be killed any day.

The wind was blowing the remnants of rain clouds across a pale-blue sky. Five men lined up in front of General Peers on the most level spot of muddy ground available on the crest. On the right-hand side stood Lieutenant Perkins, and the big major general pinned the red-white-and-blue ribbon of the Silver Star on Perkins' wrinkled jungle fatigues. The other four men, two of them fair-skinned, one black, and one a Puerto Rican, received the Bronze Star.

Peers talked to them in a hoarse outdoorsman's voice. "It is fitting that you should receive these medals here, in sight of the hills where you won them." He went on to say, in effect, that the Dragoons were the best battalion in the Fourth Division and that everybody knew it, but please not to rub it in with the other battalions, because they were fighting hard, too.

It was my last night with the Dragoons. I would be going home soon, and I sat on the bench outside the TOC, my back against the sandbagged wall and my head tilted toward the stars that appeared between speeding gray clouds.

Two boys had come to visit a kid who was sitting on top of a bunker a few yards away. They chatted, talking about a letter he had received from his girl, talking about another boy's car at home. Finally the two boys said good night to their friend.

"Thanks for coming over," he said as they walked into the night, their rifles in their hands.

THIRTY-ONE

It was December, and everyone I had known at Tuy Hoa Air Base was going home. Many had left already, and in the mess hall half the faces were new. Those of us who had made the original deployment here sought each other out, and when we were introduced to a new face we were polite but not interested.

Even the Wing Commander was going home. All the officers gave Colonel Lewis a smashing farewell dinner, complete with myriad bottles of California wine. I was sitting across the table from the Korean battalion commander I had seen in action during the enemy's September offensive in the valley. He and his operations officer were just beginning to get in the spirit of the thing, their square faces beginning to take on the quick Asian alcoholic flush, when one of their junior officers came in and handed the Korean lieutenant colonel a message.

"We have contact in the valley right now," he said to me. "Sorry." He and his operations officer stood, shook hands with the fingers protruding from my cast, and were gone into the night.

II

The advisors were having their monthly meeting, and they asked me to appear as part of the regular program of province-level specialists and district advisors, speaking for half an hour on my conclusions at the end of this year.

I stood up in the Vietnamese briefing hall where I had so often been a listener, and told them the truth. I told them that they, military and civilian advisors, had the most difficult and most interesting job in Vietnam. I told them that if all correspondents in Vietnam were treated with the hospitality and candor they had shown me, the press would have to do less guesswork, would be more prone to believe the military, and would be more likely to give a balanced picture of the effort in Vietnam.

Turning to my experience with the Air Force, I said that I was convinced that we were not indiscriminately laying waste the countryside. My many rides with FACs across a year had impressed me with their care in selection of targets, and their reluctance to bomb in areas where there were innocent civilians. In the twenty-three missions I had flown in the F–100, only one had involved a village, and there had been intense fire coming from that village at our troops.

On the Army effort by big units, I reiterated my belief that the jungle ate up our battalions, and that we needed two million men if we were really to control the terrain in Vietnam. During the year I had repeatedly said that we needed two million men and five to ten years, starting from 1967, to gain our objective of a pacified countryside and the hope of political stability. I observed that I had not met one American officer or civilian worker who disagreed with my estimate that that was what it would take, although many thought the American public would not underwrite it.

Regarding the advisory effort, I stepped on almost every toe in the room. I told the CIA men to stop saying that they were from the Embassy; I told the senior advisors to reopen the question of whether Phu Yen did not have a serious land-reform problem; and I had unkind words for Revolutionary Development teams, the Popular Forces militia, and the Koreans, citing examples. I told the Army men who worked at this headquarters that they were better qualified, even for advisory jobs, than the American civilians. The Army men in the room looked pleased with that, but their smiles faded when I told them that they should emulate the Dragoons, stop taking most of the weekend off, stop working just from nine to five, stop taking the same after-lunch hour's nap that the Vietnamese did.

"I have come, this year, to mistrust both idealists and ambitious men." Finally, I told them, "I wish I could say that

I leave with a feeling of confidence. I do not. My test of the security of the Tuy Hoa Valley is simple: How far out the valley can you drive? The answer is, no farther than you could a year ago at this time. I wish I could say that we are making progress, but I do not think we will get near our goals if we go on with only the present inputs of men and effort.''

I sat down, and to my surprise they applauded hard. We had an Army officer visiting us that day who was of a higher rank than we usually saw at Tuy Hoa. At lunch I was told that after my talk he leaned over and observed, ''That's what I wish I could say.''

That evening the advisors, civilian and military, had a steak cookout, using the grill outside Dan Leaty's bungalow behind the province chief's house. There was one major whom I had never really talked to, and now, with three days left until I got on a plane for Saigon and thence home, I found myself terribly curious about him. I remembered, in my sophomore year at Harvard, seeing a piece in the *Crimson* about a fourteen-year-old prodigy who had just entered with the Class of 1952. This genius had grown up to be the crew-cut major in the corner who was drinking a can of Budweiser, and I got out my clipboard, almost for the last time, and asked him to tell me about himself. He was Alexander M. S. McColl, of Kalamazoo, Michigan. He had first enlisted in the Army just before his nineteenth birthday, the only difference between him and other eighteen-year-olds being that he had a Harvard degree and a year of graduate study under his belt.

''I enlisted on July twenty-second, nineteen fifty-three,'' he told me. ''Five days later the Chinese got the word and called off the Korean War.''

He had tried the Army for four years, rather enjoying it since they had commissioned him and made him a plainclothes counterintelligence man in Paris. Then he had gone to the Harvard Law School, graduating *cum laude*. He was quietly practicing law in Kalamazoo, doing very well, enjoying himself and not trying to be anybody's genius any more, when he heard something he felt he should think about.

''In the summer of nineteen sixty-two the Army put out the word that they would be very glad if any reserve officers

not on active duty would come back on active duty, so I did."
Since then he had volunteered for two tours of duty in Vietnam,
the first in 1962 in the highest military intelligence headquarters
in Saigon, and this year as the senior American advisor in
Phu Yen's insecure interior district of Dong Xuan, where he
had a North Vietnamese regimental headquarters a few miles
from his own tiny compound.

I asked him why he had come back in the Army, why he
had volunteered twice for tours of duty in Vietnam.

He nodded, and gave it to me without descending to the
vernacular.

"The survival of our civilization is ultimately a function
of the military power of the United States."

I interrupted him to ask how he defined civilization.

"What used to be known as Christendom," he answered.
"The survival of our civilization depends on that American
military power." Explaining why he had volunteered, he said:
"The basic feeling was that there was nothing more important
to do, nothing more worthwhile doing, than what we are
doing in Vietnam. In view of the apathy of most people, it
becomes incumbent upon those who do care to do something
about it." He raised the beer can to his lips. "I've got the
very old-fashioned sense of allegiance that means that when
the country goes to war, *you* go to war."

It was an unusual Harvard reunion, the only two Harvard
men in Phu Yen, and neither of us feeling those doveish
things that many of our fellow alumni felt in such abundance.
I asked McColl what he thought of the mounting criticism of
the war.

"My theory is that Fulbright and a lot of other intellectu-
als refuse to recognize the existence of evil. I also have the
feeling that the slogans the Communists have put out have
confused these people so that they think that communism is
basically a radical form of their own type of liberalism."

III

I was packing to go back to the air base when Dan Leaty
asked me if I would like a quick chopper trip up to Song Cau
and back. We flew past Cheop Chai and half an hour later
settled into the tropical paradise where I had landed that first

day with the FAC, a year ago, the day that I had seen that first wounded VC boy in the dispensary.

Nothing had changed for the better in the advisory compound in which the American team lived, bemused by their palm trees and splendid beach. The wood bungalow in which they lived still had not a single sandbag around it, but they had added a screened lounging area to their elaborate dining porch.

Dan had come to see the American civilian advisor. We found him wearing his black pajamas, standing amid the wreckage of the prefabricated tarpaper shelter he had fixed up so that he could have a place to entertain the Vietnamese. It was not yet the monsoon season, but a recent harsh December wind had shredded his intercultural dream palace, the place where he and the Vietnamese were going to really talk it out and really come to understand and respect each other. It was clear that he and the American military advisors were still not speaking, and he stood amid the torn collapsed remains of his tepee-shaped shelter, his face stubborn but his voice whining and beaten as he complained of everything—the advisors, the Vietnamese, the beginning monsoon storms.

Dan nodded and said all the right things. It was clear to me that he had made up his mind to relieve this man, get rid of him, and I thought of how far Dan had come from that first Peace Corps volunteering time in Camelot. He was still an idealist, but now he was an idealist who could hire and fire other idealists without flinching, and we would always need men like that, results men.

As we flew back down to Tuy Hoa, Dan told me an interesting thing. Colonel Ba's twelve-year-old son had broken his leg falling off the back of a motor scooter. Dan had alerted the Ninety-first Evac that the Province Chief's son would be coming in for surgery, and the American Army hospital had sent a helicopter to the landing pad in front of Colonel Ba's house.

"He refused," Dan told me. He was yelling in my ear over the noise of the chopper engine, but even so, there were awed tones in his voice. "He said his son would go to the province hospital like any other citizen of Phu Yen." Dan looked at me. "That hospital."

I was impressed, and once again I felt that strange siren song of optimism, the ghost of so many American hopes that had died in this distant land. Maybe, maybe, maybe....

I left the advisors' compound for the last time at the wheel of Dan Leaty's Scout. Dan was coming down to the air base that night with some men in another vehicle, so he had loaned me this one and told me to leave it in front of the officers' club.

There was a blinding rain, and I drove slowly through Tuy Hoa, the only vehicle moving. I passed the soccer field where the medals had been given to the ARVN soldiers, passed the market place where bunches of bananas hung brilliant in the rain, passed the street leading to the house of the tycoon with the laundry contract. Occasionally a woman in a pastel American-length raincoat, down to her ankles, would run across the street, or an old black-clad farmer would trudge past, shoulders bent under his conical coolie hat, impassive in the storm.

I stopped, looking to my right and left before I turned onto Route One, which would take me back to the air base. Cheop Chai was a massive shadow behind the rain. To my right was the Catholic church. Its square bell tower was a misty orange plaster shadow, and there were Roman numerals on the four square clock faces that looked out toward the sea to the east, Tuy An and Song Cau to the north, the Tuy Hoa Valley to the west, and the air base to the south. Absolutely the only problem with looking at those clock faces to check the time was that those clocks had no hands.

I drove the Scout at a creeping pace across the long bridge over the swollen December river, yellow water thundering beneath me. The thatched roofs on the far bank were a shiny orange-brown, and a boy came along that riverside road, dressed only in a dirty gray shirt and dirtier khaki shorts, prodding a cow.

At Hieu Xuong I stopped. I had given Neil Miller everything I was not taking home with me—my weapons, most of my field uniforms, and my pack and web belt and poncho—and he had asked me if he had anything I wanted. I had told him that this was a gift, not a trade, but if he really did not want that wooden Buddha beside which I had kept guard so many nights, I would like to ship it home in a foot locker.

"Take it," he had said.

Neil was not at the compound, nor Sergeant Iaea, nor the two black sergeants I had come to know. I climbed up on the bunker and took the wet Buddha in my arms.

That night, my packing almost finished, I went over to one of the new officers' dormitory buildings to say good-bye to my pilot friend Special Stud. I found his room, one of a score along this corridor paneled in Air Force Oak, and knocked.

"Hi, Charlie," he said, his alert face smiling, impish as ever, and pointed to his desk. On it was scattered a collection of Princess rings from Thailand, little cones of semi-precious stones mounted on something that looked like gold.

"I'm taking twelve of them back with me," he said, gazing fondly at the snapshots of the half-dozen American girls with whom he had been corresponding all year. "That ought to keep me going for a while."

On my way down the corridor, having said good-bye to Special Stud, I heard a voice through an open door.

"Well, our A. T. and T. is just where it was, but our General Motors is——"

I stared as I passed. It was some of the new administrative officers, men without wings. They had formed an investment club. I thought of the first days at Tuy Hoa, the pilots wearing pistols in the old bar by the beach, that maniac in the gray flying suit roaring through the bar on his motorcycle, Sully and Pres Flanagan and Frank Buzze, the tape deck playing the Tijuana Brass, and nothing but storms and tents and soup and sandwiches.

IV

My plane came in at ten in the morning, and I walked out to it, carrying my typewriter in the hand from which my cast had just been removed. The doctors said that it had healed perfectly, and it felt weak but fine. In my other hand was a gray parachute bag, holding the few sports shirts I thought might be salvaged for wear in the States. There were some souvenirs in there, my helmet and one set of jungle fatigues and one flying suit, and there was a stack of manila envelopes containing the notes of my year in Vietnam.

The plane's ramp came down, and men started climbing aboard. I put down my bag, waiting, and looked around at all these silver buildings where there had been only cactus and tents and sand. In the distance Cheop Chai stood against a sky that was clear this morning and might have seventy-mile-an-hour rain by noon. Then I picked up my bag and put down what was left of my youth, and got on the plane.

ABOUT THE AUTHOR

After graduation from Harvard and service in the United States Army, CHARLES BRACELEN FLOOD was launched into a literary career with the publication in 1953 of his first novel, *Love Is a Bridge*. Widely praised by critics, it was on the *New York Times* bestseller list for six months and was a recipient of the Houghton Mifflin Literary Fellowship. Four novels—*A Distant Drum; Tell Me, Stranger; Monmouth; and More Lives than One*—followed, and his short stories and articles have appeared in the *New Yorker, Atlantic, Esquire,* and other periodicals. Mr. Flood's articles for the Associated Press have ranged from political and war reportage in South Vietnam to coverage of the past four Olympic Games. He is the current president of the American Center of P.E.N., the international writers' organization, and is a member of The Authors Guild Council, the governing body of The Authors Guild.

The history of man in flight....

THE BANTAM AIR AND SPACE SERIES

The Bantam Air and Space Series is dedicated to the men and women who brought about this, the era of flight -- the century in which mankind not only learned to soar the skies, but has journeyed out into the blank void of space.

☐ 1: THE LAST OF THE BUSH PILOTS
     by Harmon Helmericks   28556-4 $4.95
☐ 2: FORK TAILED DEVIL: THE P-38
      by Martin Caidin   28557-2 $4.95
☐ 3: THE FASTEST MAN ALIVE
     by Frank Everest and John Guenther 28771-0 $4.95
☐ 4: DIARY OF A COSMONAUT: 211 DAYS IN
     SPACE by Valentin Lebedev   28778-8 $4.95
☐ 5: FLYING FORTS by Martin Caidin 28780-X $4.95
☐ 6: ISLAND IN THE SKY
      by Ernest K. Gann   28857-1 $4.95
☐ 7: PILOT
     by Tony Le Vier with John Guenther 28785-0 $4.95
☐ 8: BARNSTORMING
     by Martin Caidin   28818-0 $4.95
☐ 9: THE ELECTRA STORY: AVIATION'S
     GREATEST MYSTERY by Robert J. Serling
                                    28845-8 $4.95

Available now wherever Bantam Falcon Books are sold, or use this page for ordering:

Join the Allies on the Road to Victory
BANTAM WAR BOOKS

William L. Shirer

A Memoir of a Life and the Times Vol. 1 & 2

- ☐ 34204   TWENTIETH CENTURY JOURNEY,
  The Start 1904-1930 $12.95

- ☐ 34179   THE NIGHTMARE YEARS,
  1930-1940 $14.95

In Volume 1, Shirer recounts American/European history as seen through his eyes. In Volume 2, he provides an intensely personal vision of the crucible out of which the Nazi monster appeared.

Charles B. MacDonald

- ☐ 34226   A TIME FOR TRUMPETS $12.95
The untold story of the Battle of the Bulge.